A PHOTOGRAPHIC HISTORY OF
BRITISH FOOTBALL

A PHOTOGRAPHIC HISTORY OF
BRITISH FOOTBALL
FACTS, FIGURES, STATS AND LEGENDS

Bath • New York • Cologne • Melbourne • Delhi
Hong Kong • Shenzhen • Singapore • Amsterdam

This edition published by Parragon Books Ltd in 2014

Parragon Books Ltd
Chartist House
15–17 Trim Street
Bath BA1 1HA, UK
www.parragon.com

A catalogue record for this book is
available from the British Library.

ISBN: 978-1-4723-6426-5

Printed in China

Contents

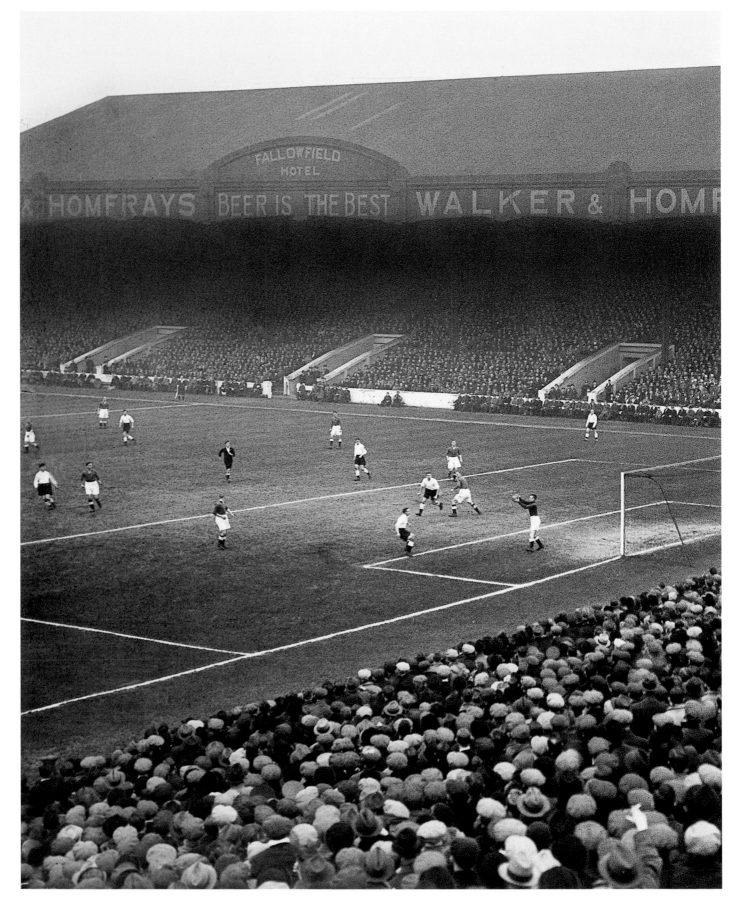

Introduction

The People's Game

Britain is "the motherland of football". Two centuries before FIFA president Sepp Blatter coined that phrase, Sir Walter Scott – an early celebrity fan – said "life is but a game of football". Scott was writing when the game was in a state of flux, but once the split from rugby was effected in the mid–19th century, Association Football flourished throughout the land. England and Scotland contested the world's first international in 1872, and founded the two oldest cup competitions. By 1880 all the home nations had established football associations – the first four countries to do so – and soon launched an annual round-robin tournament. All would enjoy bragging rights at various times during the next century.

League football was no less hotly contested, and all around Britain there were local rivalries to stir the blood: Manchester-Liverpool, Glasgow's Old Firm, London, Tyne and Wear, the Midlands. Add in the South Coast, South Wales and East Anglian derbies and a picture emerges: victory over the neighbours is almost akin to silverware.

Expatriates spread the footballing gospel to all corners of the globe with missionary zeal. The People's Game in Britain became the world's most popular sporting pursuit, and the students eventually became a match for the masters. Even so, Britain still leads the way in terms of European trophies won, and the unique blend of power, pace and passion is a magnet to TV audiences worldwide.

This lavishly illustrated book charts the key events in the history of British football, from the time when players wore knickerbockers and tasselled caps, balls had laces and the first £1,000 transfer raised a storm, to the game we know today. It covers shocks and controversies, tactical developments and rule changes, with a wealth of statistics to settle most arguments. There is ecstasy, but plenty of agony, too. It is the story of a great unending soap opera, set in the nation that gave the Beautiful Game to the world.

The Origins
of the Game

The beginnings of football cannot be dated exactly. A rudimentary form of the game was played in China as early as 200 BC, and the ancient Greeks and Romans also had their own versions. Suffice to say that throughout history inflated animals' bladders, indeed any spherical objects that would serve the purpose, have been kicked, thrown and headed, in the name of sporting endeavour.

Britain was just one of many countries that absorbed football into its cultural fabric. It is said that after the Anglo-Saxons repelled an attack by the Danes in the early Middle Ages, a celebratory game of football was played, using the head of one of the vanquished as a ball. Entire villages would participate in long attritional sporting battles with their neighbours, often on Shrove Tuesday or other public holidays. One such took place between the Derbyshire villages of All Saints and St Peter's and gave rise to the expression "local derby". Several monarchs, including Edward III and Richard II, attempted to ban football, fearing that their subjects were spending too much time honing their ball skills at the expense of their dexterity with the longbow. The Puritans were equally concerned, regarding football as a form of revelling that the country could well do without. Needless to say, all these efforts came to nought.

RIGHT: A recent re-enactment of the famous occasion in 1823 when William Webb Ellis decided to pick up the ball and run with it. In 1839 Queen Adelaide, widow of William IV, visited Rugby School and watched a game on the famous sporting field. The boys had been given a tasselled cap to commemorate the visit, and some of them wore the headgear on the field of play. That didn't catch on, but the idea of presenting caps as a way of honouring international appearances did.

1848 Cambridge Rules drawn up at Cambridge University and form a basis for the rules later adopted by the FA

1855 Sheffield FC founded by members of Sheffield Cricket Club and becomes the oldest football club in the world

1856 Sheffield FC publish the "Sheffield Rules"

1862 The world's oldest league club, Nottingham (Notts) County is founded

1863 26 October, the Football Association formed at a meeting at Freemasons' Tavern in London

1867 The Wednesday founded. The team would later become Sheffield Wednesday in 1929. Wednesday refers to the day of the week in Sheffield, which was set aside for workers' recreation.

1867 Queen's Park, Scotland's oldest club, is formed

1870 Eleven players become the standard size for a football team

1872 First FA Cup Final between Wanderers and the Royal Engineers at the Kennington Oval sees Wanderers winning 1-0

1872 England's first international fixture is a game against Scotland resulting in a 0-0 draw

1873 Scottish FA established Rangers founded

1874 Cricketers at the Villa Cross Wesleyan Chapel in Aston, Birmingham found Aston Villa FC

1874 First mention of umpires in the game's laws

1874 Shin-guards first introduced by England and Nottingham Forest player Sam Widdowson

1874 Queen's Park beat Clydesdale in the inaugural Scottish Cup

1875 A crossbar replaces the previous method of using tape strung between the goalposts

1875 Blackburn Rovers formed by ex-public school boys – it turned professional in 1880

1875 Birmingham City founded by cricketers of the Trinity Church, Bordesley

1876 Welsh FA established Wales' first international match, a 4-0 defeat by Scotland in Glasgow

1878 Referee uses a whistle for first time during a game at Nottingham Forest

1878 Everton founded as Domingo FC, which later changed its name to Everton after the region of Liverpool in which it was based

1878 Floodlights first used in a game at Bramall Lane, the home of Sheffield United

1878 Newton Heath LYR founded, the club that would re-form as Manchester United in 1902

1879 Preston North End Cricket Club forms a football team of the same name

1880 Irish FA established

1881 Referees given power to order players off the field

1881 Newcastle United founded as Stanley FC in the Byker district of Newcastle; the club went on to be known as Newcastle East End

Public schools and universities lead the way

It wasn't until the 19th century that a number of games, which could all be loosely united under the umbrella of "football", finally spread their wings and stood alone. Diversification was the new zeitgeist, and it was not achieved without a degree of acrimony.

The game of football in the 18th and early 19th centuries was championed by the elite educational institutions. Thomas Arnold, the headmaster of Rugby School in the 1830s, took the progressive view that football ought to be positively encouraged, not suppressed. He felt that exercising both mind and body were equally important,

ABOVE: An illustration dating from the 1860s shows a group of boys playing "football". Public schools, such as Eton and Winchester, had taken up the game but each team played according to its own set of rules making competition almost impossible.

and football was far preferable to drinking and gambling as a leisure pursuit. Many other public schools and universities took the same view, and it was here that the game flourished, although each institution developed its own version of the game.

before finally settling on the current name in 1893

1882 Ireland's first international match, a 13-0 defeat by England in Belfast. It remains Ireland's heaviest defeat and England's biggest win

1883 New rules require throw-ins to be two-handed

1884 Preston North End use professionals in the FA Cup and is expelled as a result

1884 Blackburn win the FA Cup at the start of a run in which it would win the trophy five times over the following decade

1884 Scotland win the inaugural home international championship

1885 The Football Association legalises professionalism

1886 Arsenal Football Club founded by workers of the Royal Arsenal in Woolwich, London

1888 William McGregor, a director of Aston Villa suggests a football league, which is established with twelve teams

1888 Celtic founded

1889 Preston North End win the first League Championship

1890 Scottish League founded, the world's second oldest. 10 clubs contest the first championship, Dumbarton and Rangers finishing joint-champions

1891 The old system of using referees and umpires to monitor games is replaced with referees and linesmen

1891 Introduction of a goal net

1891 The penalty kick was introduced at the request of William McCrum of the Irish FA, as it was considered that a free kick was not adequate enough for fouls, which prevented almost certain goals

1892 A second division of the Football League is formed

1892 Liverpool founded

1893 Scottish League expanded with the creation of a Second Division

1894 Manchester City are formed following financial difficulties of Ardwick, the club which had preceded it

1894 The FA Amateur Cup is played for the first time

1895 Crystal Palace Stadium is first used to host the FA Cup Final between Aston Villa and West

Bromwich Albion; the stadium would go on to hold the event twenty times

1895 The FA Cup is stolen from a Birmingham shop window where it was on display after being won by Aston Villa

1897 A Players' Trade Union formed

1897 Aston Villa secure the "Double" by winning the FA Cup and the League

1898 Teams can now be promoted and relegated between the football leagues

1899 Rangers set a record by completing its 18-match league programme without dropping a point. Its sole defeat is in the Cup Final, 2-0 to Celtic. Ibrox Park becomes Rangers' new home

William Webb Ellis "disregards the rules"

Ironically, a fictitious event at Rugby School a decade before Arnold took up his post remains a key date in the annals of sport. In 1823 William Webb Ellis is supposed to have shown "a fine disregard for the rules of football" by picking up the ball and running with it. This landmark event is almost certainly nothing more than an apocryphal tale, but it did usher in a period in which a number of distinct sports emerged from a plethora of broadly similar ball games.

Contrary to the view expressed in the William Webb Ellis commemorative plaque, which speaks of his celebrated exploit "originating the distinctive feature of the rugby game", it was those who wanted to play only a dribbling, kicking game who were the real innovators. All the other football-derived sports – including Australian Rules, American football and hurling, as well as rugby itself – embraced handling as a key element. It was these sports that represented a link with the past. In the mid-19th century, it was Association football that was the brand new package on offer, although the term itself had not yet been coined.

Hacking becomes the key issue

It wasn't simply a case of a handling game versus a dribbling game, however. Proponents of the latter, including those at Eton and Charterhouse, wanted to do away with hacking – kicking an opponent's shins. This was the issue of greatest concern. The hacking that went on at that time made the on-field misdemeanours of the modern era seem tame by comparison. Broken limbs were commonplace, and fatalities not unknown. Etonians and Carthusians were in the vanguard of those who wanted a game in which the ball – and only the ball – was kicked. There were many who harrumphed at the idea; the aggression that was central to the game of rugby football was the stuff on which Great Britain had built her empire. A more "civilised" game, so the argument ran, risked the country's pre-eminence as a military power.

BELOW: Richmond rugby team pictured in the 1890s. In 1863 eleven southern clubs formed the Football Association. Blackheath refused to accept the majority decision and left the FA to form the Rugby Football Union.

OPPOSITE LEFT: An early advertisement for boots mentions both rugby and "association", but a clear distinction between the two games was not properly made until the second half of the 19th century.

OPPOSITE BELOW: Not every match was played according to the regulations but the rules of the game gradually expanded from the 14 agreed upon by the FA in 1863. In 1865 the height of the tape which formed the crossbar of the goal was set at 8 feet although nets were not compulsory until 1891. Goalkeepers were first mentioned in the rules in 1871 and the penalty kick was introduced in 1891.

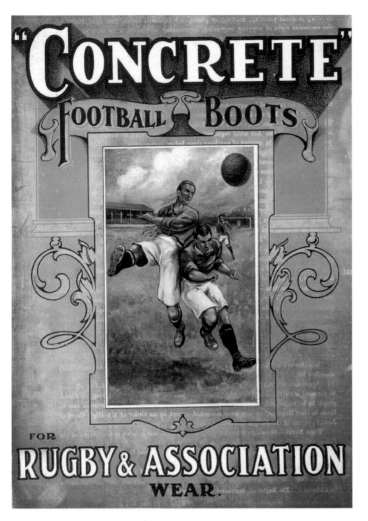

Football Association formed

When Old Etonians of the 1840s moved on to Cambridge University, they continued to express their opposition to the version of football as played at Rugby School. The battle lines were drawn, and the battle itself would be fought over the rules. In 1848 some of the proponents of the dribbling game drew up the Cambridge Rules, which were forerunners of those of Association Football. This was a key event, despite the fact that these rules were not widely taken up. Even within the walls of Rugby School itself there had been no standard set of rules. There were no inter-collegiate fixtures, and so the students themselves could make up and amend rules on a whim. A revised version of the Cambridge Rules was drafted in 1862. The time was fast approaching when the rival camps would have to face each other and thrash the issue out once and for all.

Historic decision

On 26 October 1863 representatives from eleven leading football clubs met at the Freemasons' Tavern, Great Queen Street, London. Of the dribbling game's champions in academia, only Charterhouse School was represented. The decision to form a new body, the Football Association, was uncontroversial. Some six weeks later, at the fifth meeting, the laws of the game were up for discussion and the temperature rose. The majority view favoured outlawing handling the ball and hacking. A vocal minority, led by Blackheath FC, would not countenance what they perceived as a bastardisation of their beloved game. Once again, the objectors were more concerned over the abandonment of hacking than they were at the prospect of seeing running with the ball in hand outlawed. Having lost the vote 13-4, Blackheath's representatives resigned and withdrew, hardly realising the historic significance of their decision.

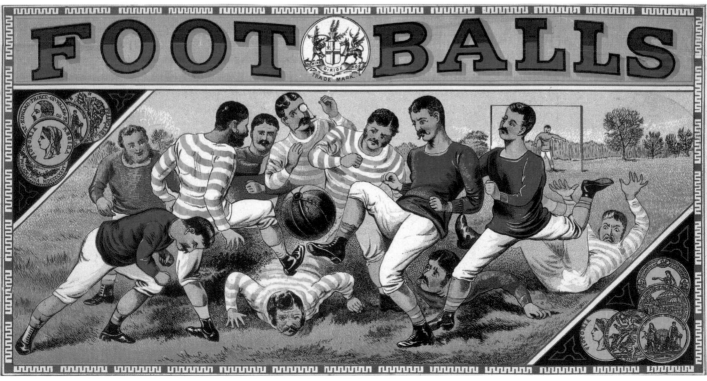

The "new" dribbling game

There were many clubs who chose to follow Blackheath and stick with the traditional handling game. But these were far outnumbered by those who subscribed to the "new" kicking and dribbling sport. And so, ironically, the traditional roughhouse working man's game of rugby lost out in the popularity stakes to a perceived less manly code whose champions had been public schoolboys! Association football quickly established itself as the sport of the masses, while rugby became something of an elitist pursuit. In a remarkably short space of time, orthodoxy had been stood on its head.

Hybrid games still common

Football in 1863 still retained many of the elements of rugby. Hacking had gone, but handling the ball was still permissible, and a kick at goal could be won by touching down over the opposition's goal-line. Nor did the formation of the FA have an immediate unifying effect on the game that was played up and down the country. Many clubs played "soccer" – a word coined from Association football – others played rugby, while it was common to see games that were a hybrid of the two codes. When the FA was formed, Sheffield FC had already been in existence for at least five years. But this club had devised its own

rules and when it sought FA membership, the Association did not even deign to reply. Notts County, established in 1862, thus became the oldest club among the founding members of the Football League. That was still a long way off, however. During the 1860s and 1870s the FA's priorities were consolidation and standardisation, amending the laws and, in 1871, establishing a cup competition.

Rule changes

Rule changes that made the game far more recognisable as the one we know today included the introduction of goal kicks (1869) and corner kicks (1872). Offside was integrated into the laws, with three defenders required between the attacking player and the goal. In the mid-1860s tape was stretched between the posts at a height of 8 feet; a decade later it was replaced by a crossbar. In 1871 the term "goalkeeper" made its first appearance in the game's legislative framework, and sealed the end of handling the ball for the outfield players. 11-a-side games became the norm and the rules were enforced by an umpire. Thus, by the time the Rugby Football Union was formed in 1871, the two codes had diverged dramatically.

ABOVE: Cambridge University football team in 1894. Until the 1880s football was dominated by the gentlemen-amateur teams coming mainly from the public schools and universities of the south. In 1881 Old Etonians played Old Carthusians for the Cup, the last time two amateur sides appeared in the final.

The birth of the FA Cup

One of the key events in this period was not a change in the way the game was played but an administrative appointment. Charles Alcock was an Old Harrovian who, along with his elder brother James, had helped to found the Forest club. Forest was among those clubs represented at the historic meeting at the Freemasons' Tavern, although Alcock himself was not present. James Alcock became an FA Committee member when it was first constituted, but within three years Charles had replaced him and it was he who became one of the most influential figures of the day. Alcock was a driving force in the effort to establish a unified game throughout the land. In 1870 he was appointed Secretary to the FA, a position he held for 25 years. His greatest contribution came just one year into that appointment, when he was the prime mover in the birth of the FA Cup.

> *"It is desirable that a Challenge Cup should be established in connection with the Association, for which all clubs belonging to the Association should be invited to compete".*

15 clubs enter inaugural FA Cup

It was at an FA Committee meeting on 20 July 1871 that Alcock proposed the following motion: "That it is desirable that a Challenge Cup should be established in connection with the Association, for which all clubs belonging to the Association should be invited to compete". The idea was probably based on the inter-house competitions he had participated in during his time at Harrow.

As there were no league matches at this time, fixtures were an ad hoc mishmash cobbled together between club secretaries with varying degrees of success. A Cup competition suddenly gave football a focal point, and it quickly caught the imagination of the clubs. By this time some fifty of them were affiliated to the FA, yet logistical problems meant that only 15 entered the inaugural competition, held in the 1871–72 season. There was an overwhelming southern bias, 13 of the entrants coming from that region, including eight from the environs of the capital. Donington Grammar School in Lincolnshire was England's most northerly participant, while Queen's Park ignored a daunting travel schedule and flew the flag for Scotland. With the aid of two byes and a walkover – after Donington scratched – Queen's Park found themselves in the semi-finals without having kicked a ball! They funded their trip to London to play the Wanderers from public subscription. The game ended in a goalless draw, and as the Scottish club's resources wouldn't stretch to a replay, it was the Wanderers who went on to contest the Final.

BELOW: By the 1880s the game was more structured. Rules were recognised nationally and the FA Cup was a well-established competition. In 1888 William McGregor, a director of Aston Villa, took the initiative and invited 11 teams to join his club in the formation of a league.

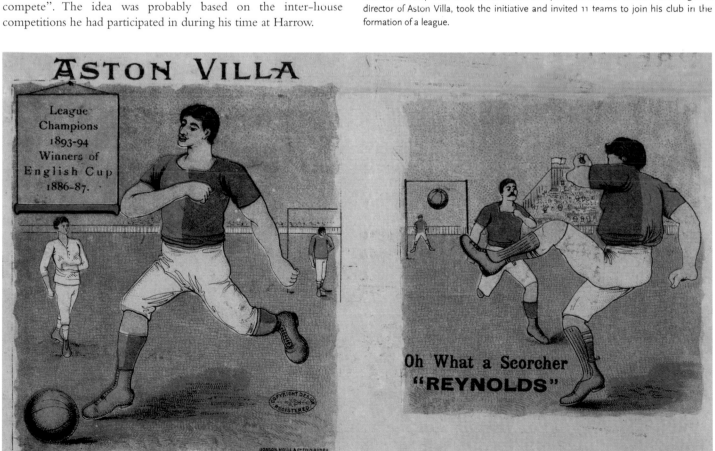

Wanderers win the first Cup Final

The captain of the Wanderers was none other than Charles Alcock himself. Alcock had founded the club, which had no ground of its own and played its home matches at Battersea Park. That meant early kick-offs in winter, as the park closed its gates at 4.00 p.m.!

The Wanderers' opponents in the inaugural Cup Final were the Royal Engineers, the latter being installed as warm favourites. The match took place at Kennington Oval on 16 March 1872 in front of a 2000-strong crowd who had paid a shilling each for the privilege. The Wanderers upset the odds and ran out 1-0 winners. The goal was scored by Matthew Betts, who had been a registered member of the Harrovian Chequer Club, which had scratched earlier in the competition. He turned out for the Wanderers under an assumed name, a clear breach of the regulations. The first FA Cup Final thus saw the deciding goal scored by a player who really shouldn't have been on the pitch. If that wasn't bad enough, the Royal Engineers had been handicapped by the fact that one of their players, Lieutenant Cresswell,

BELOW: In the late 19th century football teams sprang up all over the country. Some of these, such as Bolton, Southampton, Wolves and Everton, originally called St Domingo's, were established by churches. Others, like Spurs and the two Sheffield sides, were offshoots from cricket clubs. Newton Heath, later re-named Manchester United, began life as a works team started by employees of the Lancashire and Yorkshire Railway Company.

was nursing a broken collarbone for most of the match. Nearly a hundred years before the era of substitutes, players had to be made of stern stuff.

Clash with the Boat Race

Wanderers went on to win the Cup four more times in the 1870s, although this was not a feat that could be compared to the modern era. In 1873, for example, the club was given a bye to the Final as cup holders. That match, in which Wanderers beat Oxford University 2-0, took place at 11.00 a.m. to avoid a clash with the Boat Race. For all the strides football had made, the latter remained a much more prestigious event in the sporting calendar.

Of more significance was the fact that gentlemen-amateurs, the leisured classes, dominated the competition in the early years. The Wanderers had the cream of the players from the public school and university systems. Old Etonians appeared in five Finals in that first decade, finally winning the trophy in 1879. Oxford University beat Royal Engineers to lift the Cup in 1874 and were also beaten finalists in 1873 and 1877. Clearly football in the elite educational institutions was still strong enough to get the better of the teams from the industrial Midlands and North. One of the stars of the day was Arthur Kinnaird, who was said to have been a dynamic, skilful performer in any position on the field. He appeared in nine FA Cup Finals, picking up winners' medals with Old Etonians in 1879 and 1882, and adding three more victories to his tally with Wanderers in 1873, 1877 and 1878.

The rise of professionalism

In 1879 Lancashire side Darwen almost produced an upset of seismic proportions. In their 4th-round match against Old Etonians at Kennington Oval they came back from 5-1 down to force a draw. Darwen were in the ascendancy at the end of the match, and the Old Etonians' captain hastily declined the offer to play extra time. There was no question of the Old Etonians heading north for a replay, so Darwen had to make another trip to the capital. That game finished level, too, and although Old Etonians prevailed in the third clash, it was clear that dominance of the gentlemen-amateurs was under threat.

End of the road for the gentleman-amateur

The pendulum swung after 1881, when Old Carthusians beat Old Etonians in the last all-amateur Final. By then, many future illustrious clubs had been formed. Some had their roots in church schools, including Aston Villa, Wolverhampton Wanderers and Everton. Others, such as Newton Heath and Stoke City, sprang up as works teams. Sheffield Wednesday and Preston North End were among those formed as offshoots of existing sports clubs, often ones for which cricket was the chief pursuit. But it was the town of Blackburn which ushered in the new era. Rovers reached the Cup Final in 1882, with Old Etonians providing the opposition. Blackburn boasted several classy Scottish players and, like many other clubs, was covertly organised along professional lines. One of the players' fathers was so confident of the result that he bet a row of houses on a Blackburn victory. It was an expensive gamble, for Old Etonians won the match 1-0. But the writing was on the wall. This would be the last time that an amateur club would lift the trophy.

> *Some had their roots in church schools, including Aston Villa, Wolverhampton Wanderers and Everton. Others, such as Newton Heath and Stoke City, sprang up as works teams.*

The Cup goes north

The following year, Blackburn Olympic took the Cup north for the first time. The backbone of the team was made up of weavers and spinners, plumbers and sheet-metal workers. It also included players who appeared to earn their living purely from football, professionals in all but name. Olympic had a player-manager, Jack Hunter, who used advanced methods to prepare the team, including taking the players away to Blackpool to get them into peak physical and mental condition for the Final, in which they were up against the holders. Blackburn won the match 2-1 after extra time. For Old Etonians, a sixth Final appearance in twelve years was to be their last. They, together with the other clubs spawned from academia and the military, represented the old guard. And the shift in footballing power was not just away from the gentleman-amateur to artisans and professionals; it was also from the Home Counties to the industrial heartlands of the Midlands and the North. In the next 37 years the Cup would return to the south-east just once.

PLAYER'S CIGARETTES

NICHOLSON   READER   McCULLOCH

REYNOLDS   GROVES

PERRY

BASSETT   GEDDES

McLEOD   NICHOLLS   PEARSON

ASSOCIATION CUP WINNERS
WEST BROMWICH ALBION, 1892

ABOVE: West Bromwich Albion appeared in the Cup Final on five occasions between 1886 and 1895, winning once against Preston in 1888 and later defeating Aston Villa in 1892.

"Shamateurism"

By the 1870s it was clear that what would later be dubbed "shamateurism" was rife. Teams were vying for the best players, and it was inevitable that inducements would be offered. There was a game of cat-and-mouse between the clubs and the Football Association. The clubs found all manner of means to reward their players. These included giving nominal jobs which required little, if any, work to be done; putting money into players' boots on match days; and having phoney sets of accounts, which would suggest to any enquiring eyes that everything was above board.

> *Manual workers at that time might have earned one or two pounds a week. For many Saturday was still just another working day.*

For a time the FA stood firm. In 1882 the Association reaffirmed its commitment to an amateur game, with payments strictly limited to out-of-pocket expenses. While the clubs made it difficult for the authorities to prove any underhand dealings, they did sometimes slip up. One of the victims was Accrington, who were thrown out of the FA after being found guilty of paying one of their players. Another was Preston, who were disqualified from the FA Cup after brazenly admitting to a misdemeanour that virtually every club was guilty of. The same issue was affecting rugby, and along the same geographical lines. In the case of the handling code, the rival camps became so entrenched that many northern clubs eventually broke away and established a new professional game; Rugby League was born.

FA relents

Football came close to suffering the same kind of split which divided rugby down the middle. Manual workers at that time might have earned one or two pounds a week, and although more liberal employment laws had been introduced, for many Saturday was still just another working day. Matters came to a head in October 1884, when a number of northern clubs banded together with a view to setting up a professional football league. In July the following year the FA relented. The administrators initially tried to impose caveats and restrictions, imposing a two-year residence rule to prevent clubs from importing star players for Cup matches. But the door was now ajar and it was soon fully opened. The age of the professional footballer had officially begun.

England's first international

The 1870s also saw international football take off. Five England-Scotland matches were staged between 1870 and 1872, but these took the form of London-based players from north and south of the border taking part in representative fixtures. Once again it was Charles Alcock who was the driving force behind these encounters. The first international proper between the two countries took place on 30 November 1872. Alcock initially set a midweek date for the match, rearranging it for a Saturday when he realised that Scottish players and spectators might not have the same independent means that he and his team enjoyed.

The match took place at the West of Scotland cricket ground, Partick. At that time cricket enjoyed a higher profile than football in Scotland and the formation of the SFA was still a year away. One of the country's leading clubs, Queen's Park, thus took responsibility for organising the team to take on England. A crowd of just over 2,000 paid a shilling apiece to watch the match, which ended in a goalless draw. The embryonic state of Scottish football was illustrated by the fact that the photographer who was due to record the event wanted a guarantee that he would be able to sell his prints. No guarantee was forthcoming and the photographer thus withdrew, seeing little market for such pictures. Nevertheless, the game created a lot of interest in Scotland. It wasn't long before football, which could be played on almost any patch of ground, supplanted cricket as both a participation and spectator sport.

Scots influence English game

The Scots came to the Oval for a return match on 8 March 1873. Alexander Bonsor, who played for Old Etonians and the Wanderers, wrote his name into the history books as the scorer of England's first international goal. England won the game 4-2, and it became a fixture on the sporting calendar thereafter.

As well as promoting the game in their own country, the top Scottish players of the day influenced the development of English football, too. Dribbling was a feature of the English game, a legacy of the public schools and universities, which concentrated on individual skills rather than teamwork. It was the Scots who saw the advantage of playing a passing game. Many were recruited by clubs in the north of England, a practice that had gone on long before the FA embraced professionalism. They were usually the star players. Fergus Suter and James Love, the leading lights in the Darwen team that had given Old Etonians such a scare, were prime examples of this trend. It was the influence of Suter, Love and their ilk, which made English clubs realise that packing a team with dribblers was not the way forward.

12 teams that founded the Football League in 1888

Accrington Stanley	Everton
Aston Villa	Notts County
Blackburn Rovers	Preston North End
Bolton Wanderers	Stoke City
Burnley	West Bromwich Albion
Derby County	Wolverhampton Wanderers

Villa man proposes league football

By the late 1880s professional footballers were playing international matches and clubs were competing for the FA Cup. Rule changes had given the game all its distinctive features. The last big piece of the jigsaw was league competition.

At the time fixtures were often anything but "fixed". Shambolic was a more apposite description. Postponements or cancellations were commonplace, and the game was crying out for organised fixture lists, not least because spectators who turned up to find there was no game were bound to feel aggrieved. Regular matches were also vital to meet a club's overheads, which now included players' wages. The establishment of a competitive league was the brainchild of William McGregor, a Scot who had relocated from Perthshire to Birmingham and ran a draper's shop. McGregor had no track record as a player, but his decision to join the board of his local club, Aston Villa, was to have a profound effect on the game.

12 teams contest new league competition

On 2 March 1888 McGregor wrote to Blackburn, Bolton, Preston and West Bromwich Albion about the prospect of forming a league, and naturally he also sounded out his own club on the idea. Throughout the spring of 1888 a series of meetings took place to thrash out the details and agree a name for the new body: the Football League. 12 teams were incorporated as founder members. These were the original five clubs that McGregor contacted, together with Accrington, Burnley, Everton, Derby County, Notts County, Wolverhampton Wanderers and Stoke. Other clubs, including Nottingham Forest, had also been keen to join, but the dates set aside for the matches, which were to be held on a home and away basis, meant that only 12 teams could be accommodated. Teams would be awarded two points for a win and one for a draw, a system which was to endure for almost a hundred years. McGregor became the Football League's first president, and the opening matches were played on 8 September 1888.

At the time fixtures were often anything but "fixed". Shambolic was a more apposite description.

BELOW. This West Bromwich Albion team of 1888 were founder members of the Football League. "The Baggies" have been champions of England once, in 1919–20, but have had more success in the FA Cup, with five wins.

OPPOSITE: The original FA trophy.

"Invincibles" of Preston set the standards

Preston set the standards in the early years, winning the League in the first two seasons and finishing runners-up in the following three campaigns. The inaugural season, 1888–89, was the most remarkable, Preston remaining unbeaten on their way to the championship, and not conceding a goal in the FA Cup, which they won by defeating Wolves 3-0 in the Final. Quite justifiably they were dubbed the "Invincibles". The team's star striker was a Scot, John Goodall. Goodall had previously shone for Great Lever, and representatives from Deepdale all but kidnapped him to acquire his services. Apart from his goalscoring feats, Goodall was also noteworthy for the fact that despite his roots he played international football for England by dint of residence. Goodall left to join Derby after Preston's Double-winning campaign.

Rise of Sunderland

Supremacy passed from Preston to Sunderland. The Wearside club had replaced founder-members Stoke in the 1890–91 season and finished in mid-table in their first campaign. They would have finished fifth but had two points deducted for fielding 'keeper Ned Doig before his move from Arbroath was sanctioned. In the next four years Sunderland lifted the title three times and were runners-up once. Of the 116 games played during those four campaigns the "team-of-all-talents" won 81, drew 13 and were beaten just 22 times. Their success was based on a phenomenal home record; the team lost just once in six years on their own ground.

The first of Sunderland's championships came in 1891–92, when the league was also extended to 14 clubs. Stoke were back, and Darwen were admitted. These clubs occupied the bottom two places, and Darwen had the dubious honour of becoming the first-ever team to suffer relegation to the newly-formed Second Division. The following year saw the League expanded again, to 16 clubs. Nottingham Forest were finally admitted, and ended their debut season in mid-table. The other debutants didn't fare quite so well. Newton Heath, the team that would eventually be reconstituted as Manchester United, propped up the table five points adrift of their nearest rivals.

ABOVE: 1895 works team Woolwich Arsenal was founded in 1886 as Dial Square FC and played their home matches on Plumstead Common. In 1893 it was admitted to the newly-formed Second Division, becoming the first southern club to be admitted to the League.

Promotion and relegation

Promotion and relegation were not automatic, however; a series of "test matches" was held between the bottom three clubs of Division One and the top three in the new Second Division to decide the issue. Newton Heath survived that year but weren't so lucky the next. After finishing bottom in 1893–94, too, Newton Heath went down 2-0 to Division Two champions Liverpool, and the two teams swapped places. For Liverpool it meant promotion to the top flight at the first time of asking. Having had considerable success in the Lancashire League, the club had applied for a place in the Second Division after hearing that Accrington Stanley had resigned. Another club which achieved league status in the same year was Woolwich Arsenal. The Gunners had been formed in 1886, turned professional in 1891 and had already undergone three name changes. The team didn't quite have the same impact as the men from Anfield, but they had the honour of becoming the first southern club to be elected to the Football League.

Villa win the Cup – and lose it

In 1893–94 Aston Villa prevented Sunderland from making it a hat-trick of league titles, finishing six points ahead of the Wearside club Villa went on to win the championship four more times in the next six seasons. They added the FA Cup to their trophy cabinet in 1895 and 1897, and were also runners-up in 1892. By completing the Double in 1896–97, Villa matched Preston's feat of eight years earlier. The Midlanders did lose four league games that season, yet still equalled Preston's achievement of finishing 11 points clear of the field. A thrilling 3 2 win over Everton completed the Double, an achievement that would prove elusive for the next 64 years.

Villa were also involved in a major off-field drama. Following the club's 1-0 FA Cup win over West Bromwich Albion in 1895, the trophy was put on display at a Birmingham bootmaker's shop belonging to William Shillcock. It was stolen on 11 September and never recovered. As a result, the FA fined Villa £25 and put the money towards a replacement trophy.

Townley the hat-trick hero

Following their three successive FA Cup wins in the mid-1880s, Blackburn Rovers notched two more successes at the start of the next decade. In 1890 Blackburn thumped Sheffield Wednesday 6-1, the biggest margin of the 19 finals that had taken place thus far. Blackburn had finished third in the championship and were hot favourites to beat Wednesday, despite the fact that the Yorkshire club had taken three league scalps in previous rounds. Blackburn winger William Townley hit three of the goals, becoming the first player to score a hat-trick in the final.

The Gunners had been formed in 1886, turned professional in 1891 and had already undergone three name changes.

The following year Notts County thought they had a better chance of beating Blackburn, having just thrashed them 7-1 on their own ground in the League. But three first-half goals at the Oval meant that the Lancashire club lifted the trophy for the fifth time in eight years.

BELOW: In 1895 Aston Villa won the FA Cup for the second time. While on display in Birmingham the trophy was stolen and is believed by some to have been melted down to be made into counterfeit coins. Three more trophies have been used since this time, the most recent being introduced in the early 1990s.

Cup Final moves north to Goodison

West Bromwich Albion put Rovers out in 1892 and went on to beat their much-fancied neighbours Aston Villa in the Final. There was another upset in 1893, when Wolves beat Everton 1-0. This match took place at Fallowfield, Manchester, after Surrey County Cricket Club expressed concerns that the Oval might not be able to cope with the huge numbers that the Cup Final now regularly attracted. Wolves' first victory prompted the club to award miniature replicas of the trophy to the players. This proved very handy two years later after the Cup was stolen; it meant that an identical replacement could be made.

Manchester City and Glossop were the first beneficiaries of the new two-up, two-down system.

1893–94 was a bitter-sweet year for Notts County. Having been relegated the previous year, the team won through to face Division One side Bolton in the final, which was staged at Goodison Park. County were unhappy about the choice of venue, feeling that it favoured their opponents. They needn't have worried as they ran out 4-1 winners, with Jimmy Logan grabbing a hat-trick to equal William Townley's feat of four years earlier. Notts County failed to make it a Cup-promotion double, though. Having finished third in Division Two, they were beaten 4-0 by Preston in the play-off.

Glory for Sheffield clubs

The Cup Final returned to the capital in 1895, Crystal Palace hosting the clash between Aston Villa and WBA. It was the third time in nine years that these two clubs had met in the Final, both having registered a win each. There was no upset this year. Form side Villa won 1-0, the goal scored by the captain John Devey after just 40 seconds. This remained the fastest goal ever scored in an FA Cup Final until Louis Saha scored after just 25 seconds to put Everton ahead against Chelsea in the 2009 Final.

The city of Sheffield briefly enjoyed a spell in the limelight in the late 1890s. Wednesday beat Wolves by the odd goal in the 1896 Cup Final, neither club having set the League alight. The following year United finished as championship runners-up to Villa in the latter's Double-winning season. The Blades went one better in 1897–98, becoming only the fifth club to win the title. Their league form slumped dramatically in the next campaign, and they narrowly avoided relegation. But they made it to the Cup Final, where they faced Derby County, whose side boasted goal ace Steve Bloomer. United managed to shackle him, although they did find themselves a goal down at half-time. A storming second half saw the Blades hit four goals without reply for a famous victory. Full-back Harry Thickett was the hero of the hour, having played the game out with two broken ribs.

Automatic promotion and relegation

The "test match" system was scrapped at the end of the 1897–98 season. A suspicious play-off prompted the Football League to adopt automatic promotion and relegation. Stoke and Burnley, who had finished bottom of Division One and top of Division Two, respectively, played out a tame goalless draw, which saw both teams secure top-flight status the following season. At the end of the 1898–99 season, Manchester City and Glossop were the first beneficiaries of the new two-up, two-down system, with Bolton and Sheffield Wednesday becoming the first clubs to suffer the drop without the lifeline of a play-off.

BELOW: This victorious Aston Villa team won both the League Championship and the FA Cup in 1897, thus becoming the second team to achieve "The Double".

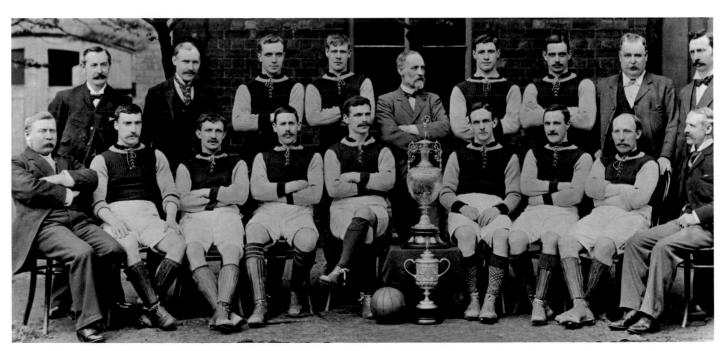

A new century dawns

As the new century dawned, the interest in football continued to grow exponentially. An aggregate of seven million people turned out to watch two 18-strong leagues battle it out for supremacy. And in less than thirty years the FA Cup had grown into one of the pre-eminent events of the sporting calendar. A record 73,833 crowd watched Sheffield United's win over Derby in 1899; attendances would soon comfortably exceed the six-figure mark. It was the showpiece event of the people's game, and had come a long way since the day it was moved to accommodate the Boat Race.

Football League 1888–1899
Top 10 League Positions

1888–89

1	Preston	40
2	Aston Villa	29
3	Wolverhampton W.	28
4	Blackburn Rovers	26
5	Bolton Wanderers	22
6	West Bromwich Albion	22
7	Accrington	20
8	Everton	20
9	Burnley	17
10	Derby County	16

1889–90

1	Preston	33
2	Everton	31
3	Blackburn Rovers	27
4	Wolverhampton W.	25
5	West Bromwich Albion	25
6	Accrington	24
7	Derby County	21
8	Aston Villa	19
9	Bolton Wanderers	19
10	Notts County	17

1890–91

1	Everton	29
2	Preston	27
3	Notts County	26
4	Wolverhampton W.	26
5	Bolton Wanderers	25
6	Blackburn Rovers	24
7	Sunderland	23
8	Burnley	21
9	Aston Villa	18
10	Accrington	16

1891–92

1	Sunderland	42
2	Preston	37
3	Bolton Wanderers	36
4	Aston Villa	30
5	Everton	28
6	Wolverhampton W.	26
7	Burnley	26
8	Notts County	26
9	Blackburn Rovers	26
10	Derby County	24

1892–93

1	Sunderland	48
2	Preston	37
3	Everton	36
4	Aston Villa	35
5	Bolton Wanderers	32
6	Burnley	30
7	Stoke	29
8	West Bromwich Albion	29
9	Blackburn Rovers	29
10	Nottingham Forest	28

1893–94

1	Aston Villa	44
2	Sunderland	38
3	Derby County	36
4	Blackburn Rovers	34
5	Burnley	34
6	Everton	33
7	Nottingham Forest	32
8	West Bromwich Albion	32
9	Wolverhampton W.	31
10	Sheffield United	31

1894–95

1	Sunderland	47
2	Everton	42
3	Aston Villa	39
4	Preston	35
5	Blackburn Rovers	32
6	Sheffield United	32
7	Nottingham Forest	31
8	The Wednesday	28
9	Burnley	26
10	Bolton Wanderers	25

1895–96

1	Aston Villa	45
2	Derby County	41
3	Everton	39
4	Bolton Wanderers	37
5	Sunderland	37
6	Stoke	30
7	The Wednesday	29
8	Blackburn Rovers	29
9	Preston	28
10	Burnley	27

1896–97

1	Aston Villa	47
2	Sheffield United	36
3	Derby County	36
4	Preston	34
5	Liverpool	33
6	The Wednesday	31
7	Everton	31
8	Bolton Wanderers	30
9	Bury	30
10	Wolverhampton W.	28

1897–98

1	Sheffield United	42
2	Sunderland	37
3	Wolverhampton W.	35
4	Everton	35
5	The Wednesday	33
6	Aston Villa	33
7	West Bromwich Albion	32
8	Nottingham Forest	31
9	Liverpool	28
10	Derby County	28

1898–99

1	Aston Villa	45
2	Liverpool	43
3	Burnley	39
4	Everton	38
5	Notts County	37
6	Blackburn Rovers	36
7	Sunderland	36
8	Wolverhampton W.	35
9	Derby County	35
10	Bury	35

English FA Cup Winners 1872–1899

1872	Wanderers
1873	Wanderers
1874	Oxford University
1875	Royal Engineers
1876	Wanderers
1877	Wanderers
1878	Wanderers
1879	Old Etonians
1880	Clapham Rovers
1881	Old Carthusians
1882	Old Etonians
1883	Blackburn Olympic
1884	Blackburn Rovers
1885	Blackburn Rovers
1886	Blackburn Rovers
1887	Aston Villa
1888	West Bromwich Albion
1889	Preston North End
1890	Blackburn Rovers
1891	Blackburn Rovers
1892	West Bromwich Albion
1893	Wolves
1894	Notts County
1895	Aston Villa
1896	Sheffield Wednesday
1897	Aston Villa
1898	Nottingham Forest
1899	Sheffield United

Scotland's industrial heartlands

While football in 19th-century England was being championed by the public schools, in Scotland the game flourished in the industrial heartlands. Queen's Park put the country on the footballing map in 1867, the year in which the game's most famous amateur diehards first took to the field. Scotland's oldest club was also its most successful until the advent of professionalism a quarter of a century later. It was five years before Queen's Park conceded a goal, let alone experienced defeat. The Glaswegian side reached the semi-final of the inaugural English FA Cup in 1872, and might have gone further had they been able to fund a return trip to London after drawing with Wanderers in the first match. Twice in the 1880s Queen's were beaten finalists.

By then Scotland had its own cup competition, established in 1873–74 with 16 teams taking part. Queen's Park breezed past Dumbreck, Eastern and Renton before beating Clydesdale in the final.

After notching a hat-trick of wins, the team finally tasted defeat at the hands of Vale of Leven in a fifth round tie in 1876–77. The latter went on to lift the trophy by beating Rangers, who reached their first showpiece four years after being founded as an offshoot of a rowing club. Rangers met Vale of Leven again in the 1878–79 Cup Final, a controversial affair that saw Gers incensed at having what they deemed a perfectly good goal chalked off. It ended 1-1, and Vale of Leven collected the trophy after Rangers refused to entertain a replay.

Queen's clash with Dumbarton

Along with Queen's Park, Dumbarton was the powerhouse side of the era. The two met in successive Cup Finals, 1881 and 1882, both incendiary affairs. The first ended 2-1 to Queen's, but Dumbarton protested that fans had spilled onto the pitch. It was upheld and a replay ordered, which Queen's won 3-1. A year later, there was another disputed goal in a 2-2 draw, and Queen's again prevailed in the replay. Dumbarton got their revenge in 1883, beating Queen's in the quarters before overcoming Vale of Leven in the final.

That would remain Dumbarton's sole success in the premier cup competition, but the club did enjoy early success when league football finally arrived, in 1890–91. Dumbarton shared the inaugural title with Rangers, the two having identical records and a play-off ending in a 2-2 draw. Third place in the 10-strong division was taken by Celtic, founded three years earlier by Brother Walfrid, of the Roman Catholic order of Marist Brothers. The club's primary aim was to raise money to help the impoverished children of the Irish immigrant community. That went hand-in-hand with success on the pitch, Celtic finishing runners-up to Dumbarton the following season, then claiming their first championship in 1893, pipping Rangers by a single point. This was the year professionalism was finally accepted – eight years after England had bowed to the inevitable – and it marked the beginning of a new order. Queen's Park, who cleaved to their amateur principles, enjoyed their tenth and last Cup victory in 1893, and refused to embrace league football for a decade. Celtic, by contrast, had four championship titles in the bag before the turn of the century, and Rangers joined the party in imperious style in 1898–99, taking their first title without dropping a point in the 18-match programme. Gers' sole defeat came at Celtic's hands in the Cup Final. It was a sign of things to come in the new century.

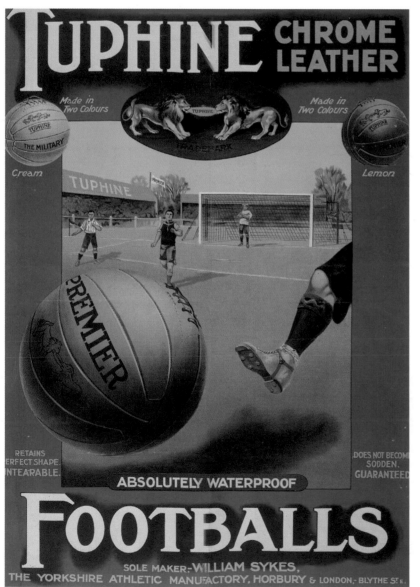

LEFT: The popularity of football among the masses had grown rapidly. By the turn of the century an estimated seven million spectators watched league matches each year and in the 1890s the first newspaper devoted to sport was published. At the same time manufacturers saw the opportunity to make money by producing football equipment and began to advertise their products.

First international

Scotland made its mark on the international stage with a series of games against England in 1870 and 1871. As the players were recruited from the environs of England's capital, it was more of a "London Scottish" side, thus the match at West of Scotland Cricket Ground, Partick, on 30 November 1872 is regarded as the first official international between the two countries. There was no Scottish FA – that wasn't formed until the following year – so Queen's Park assumed organisational control as well as packing the team with its own star players. The Scottish side turned out in the dark blue shirts that were then Queen' colours. The game ended in a goalless draw, but Scotland comfortably had the upper hand in those early years. Between 1876–1884 England were beaten eight times out of nine, including a 7-2 mauling at Hampden Park in 1878. It was a mere 1-0 victory over the Auld Enemy in 1884, but allied to a 4-1 win over Wales and a 5-0 demolition of Ireland, it gave Scotland the inaugural home international championship. The team would win four of the first seven tournaments outright, and share top spot twice.

If the results were impressive, Scotland's style of play was of greater significance. For while their opponents focused on individual dribbling skills, Scotland made a virtue of the slick passing game. The shift didn't go unnoticed by observers. Lancastrian sides peppered with Scottish talent had been in large measure responsible for the FA Cup power base moving northwards. And after Scotland thumped Wales 9-0 in Glasgow in March 1878, *The Times* reported: "The Welshmen played a very plucky game, but were deficient in the passing and dodging tactics observed by the Scotchmen."

Scottish League 1892–1899

1891–92

1	Dumbarton	37
2	Celtic	35
3	Hearts	34
4	Leith Athletic	25
5	Rangers	24
6	Third Lanark	21
7	Renton	21
8	Clyde	20
9	Abercorn	17
10	St Mirren	15
11	Cambuslang	10
12	Vale of Leven	5

1892–93

1	Celtic	29
2	Rangers	28
3	St Mirren	20
4	Third Lanark	19
5	Hearts	18
6	Leith Athletic	17
7	Dumbarton	17
8	Renton	15
9	Abercorn	11
10	Clyde	6

1893–94

1	Celtic	29
2	Hearts	26
3	St Bernard's	23
4	Rangers	20
5	Dumbarton	19
6	St Mirren	17
7	Third Lanark	17
8	Dundee	15
9	Leith Athletic	10
10	Renton	4

1894–95

1	Hearts	31
2	Celtic	26
3	Rangers	22
4	Third Lanark	21
5	St Mirren	19
6	St Bernard's	17
7	Clyde	16
8	Dundee	14
9	Dumbarton	7
10	Leith Athletic	7

1895–96

1	Celtic	30
2	Rangers	26
3	Hibernian	24
4	Hearts	22
5	Dundee	16
6	Third Lanark	15
7	St Bernard's	15
8	St Mirren	13
9	Clyde	11
10	Dumbarton	8

1896–97

1	Hearts	28
2	Hibernian	26
3	Rangers	25
4	Celtic	24
5	Dundee	22
6	St Mirren	19
7	St Bernard's	14
8	Third Lanark	11
9	Clyde	8
10	Abercorn	3

1897–98

1	Celtic	33
2	Rangers	29
3	Hibernian	22
4	Hearts	20
5	Third Lanark	18
6	St Mirren	18
7	Dundee	13
8	Partick Thistle	13
9	St Bernard's	9
10	Clyde	5

1898–99

1	Rangers	36
2	Hearts	26
3	Celtic	24
4	Hibernian	23
5	St Mirren	20
6	Third Lanark	17
7	St Bernard's	12
8	Clyde	12
9	Partick Thistle	6
10	Dundee	4

Scottish Cup Winners 1874–1899

1874	Queen's Park
1875	Queen's Park
1876	Queen's Park
1877	Vale of Leven
1878	Vale of Leven
1879	Vale of Leven
1880	Queen's Park
1881	Queen's Park
1882	Queen's Park
1883	Dumbarton
1884	Queen's Park
1885	Renton
1886	Queen's Park
1887	Hibernian
1888	Renton
1889	Third Lanark
1890	Queen's Park
1891	Hearts
1892	Celtic
1893	Queen's Park
1894	Rangers
1895	St Bernard's
1896	Hearts
1897	Rangers
1898	Rangers
1899	Celtic

1900–1919
The National Sport

Football in the Edwardian era continued to provide rich entertainment for very little outlay. Sixpence was the typical entrance fee, and working men in their droves flocked to matches. Lifelong allegiances were developed, passions aroused. These sometimes manifested themselves in ways that earned rebuke. An over-exuberant crowd invaded the pitch in a Cup-tie between Spurs and Villa in 1904, causing the match to be abandoned. The FA ordered a replay at Villa Park and fined the London club £350. Some years later, when Europe was plunged into war, politicians expressed concern that munitions workers were preoccupied by football when their minds should have been on the war effort.

1901 A maximum wage for footballers introduced

1902 Sheffield United's Alf Common is transferred to Sunderland for £500

1902 A stand collapses at a Scotland v England match at Ibrox Park killing 25 people

1902 Manchester United founded when brewer John Davies bought up a bankrupt team, Newton Heath. The team did not enter the League until 1904

1903 Hampden Park built

1904 FIFA, Federation of International Football Associations is formed with seven members

1905 England joins FIFA

1905 Alf Common is transferred from Sunderland to Middlesbrough for a fee of £1000

1905 Billy Meredith of Manchester City is suspended after attempting to bribe Aston Villa's captain to help his team win the League

1905 After Fulham turned down an offer to buy Stamford Bridge the owners decided to create

Chelsea FC to play there

1905 Despite being created by staff at the Royal Exhibition in 1861, Crystal Palace did not turn professional until 1905 because the FA opposed the idea that a team could play an FA Cup Final on their home ground, which was used as the location for FA Cup Finals at the time

1905 Celtic beat Rangers in a Championship play-off after they finish level on points. Had goal average or goal difference been

used as a tie-breaker, Rangers would have won

1906 Prevention of Corruption Act passed making bribery and match fixing a punishable offence

1907 Wales win the Home International Championship for the first time

1907 Celtic become Scotland's first double winners

1908 England plays Austria in Vienna; their first international against foreign opposition

1908 Football was first introduced as an Olympic sport at the London

LEFT: At the end of the 19th century, Sunderland, dubbed "team of all the talents" was the most successful club in the north-east. However, by 1900 Newcastle United began to make its mark. Like its neighbour, the Newcastle team contained many Scottish players. In the 1901–02 season Sunderland regularly fielded 9 Scots.

OPPOSITE: Supporters of Everton and Sheffield had a long way to travel for the 1907 Cup Final at Crystal Palace. Here supporters are going past St Paul's as they make their way to South London. 84,000 fans watched Wednesday win the match 2-1.

Meredith leads players' challenge against maximum wage

Burgeoning interest inevitably meant that football was no longer simply sport and entertainment but also big business. Some of the top clubs started to show extremely healthy balance sheets, and it wasn't long before players began to demand a bigger slice of the cake. In April 1901 a new maximum wage of £4 a week was introduced. This compared favourably with other skilled tradesmen of the day, but players began to recognise their worth and started to express dissatisfaction. Matters came to a head in 1907 with the formation of a Players' Union. The League and FA were worried about footballers becoming organised, possibly even affiliating to the Trade Union movement. They threatened to impose a ban on players who took up union membership. Manchester United star Billy Meredith was one of a vociferous group unwilling to be browbeaten. While many players lost their nerve and fell into line, Meredith led a group of players who

threatened to withdraw all their labour. Prior to the 1909–10 season they began training independently under the banner of The Outcasts. Just before the season got under way the authorities caved in. The maximum wage was subsequently increased to £5 a week. The principle of player power was established.

First £1000 transfer

Another manifestation of the way in which football was now a huge enterprise was in the transfer market. 1905 saw Sunderland and England inside-forward Alf Common join Middlesbrough for £1000, the first four-figure fee. This landmark deal polarised opinion. Boro fans were jubilant after Common helped the club finish clear of relegation. But to some the buying and selling of players in such a way smacked of human trafficking, something that was morally questionable. The game's administrators may not have taken such an extreme view, but they were apprehensive. In 1908 the League tried to impose a £350 cap on transfers. It lasted just four months. The authorities realised that the ruling was unenforceable. Pragmatism won the day, as it had over the issue of professionalism some 20 years earlier.

Olympics in White City. England went on to win the gold medal beating Denmark 2-0

1908 First FA Charity Shield match played; the idea for a match between the winners of the FA Cup and the League for charity was that of Charles Clegg the then Vice President of the FA

1909 Walter Tull becomes the first black outfield player in the First Division, playing for Tottenham

Rangers and Celtic in the Scottish Cup Final, fans rioted at Hampden Park when it was announced that there would be no extra-time. There was no third match; it was the only peacetime year since 1874 that the Cup was not awarded

1912 It becomes illegal for goalkeepers to handle the ball outside the penalty area

1912 Danny O'Shea of West Ham is

1912 The Stockholm Olympics sees England take their second gold by beating Denmark 4-2 in the final

1913 Woolwich Arsenal moves from South-East to North London in a bid to gain more supporters amid financial difficulties

1914 Ireland win the Home International Championship outright for the first time

1915 Football League games suspended for the duration of the

1915 FA Cup Final still played and won by Sheffield United. The event became known as the Khaki Cup Final on account of the large number of servicemen in the crowd

1919 Leeds City are expelled from the Football League for allegedly making illegal payments to players. The club was replaced with Leeds United

1919 Football League enlarged to hold

Newcastle dominant

On the field of play one team stood out in the early years of the new century: Newcastle United. In the 13 seasons 1899–1900 to 1911–12 Newcastle finished in the top 6 eleven times and won the championship on three occasions, in 1905, 1907 and 1909. Their Cup record was, if anything, even more remarkable. Between 1905 and 1911 they reached the Final five times. In 1909 the team went down to Manchester United in the semis, so 1907 was the only year in which the club failed to reach the last four. And that season of "failure"

was dramatic indeed – a home defeat by Crystal Palace, then a Southern League outfit.

Unfortunately, Newcastle's record after reaching the Final was not so impressive. Crystal Palace, the venue for each of them, was not a happy hunting ground. Newcastle failed to record a single victory in five attempts. Their best effort came in 1910, when they managed a 1-1 draw with Second Division Barnsley before beating the Yorkshire side in a replay at Goodison Park.

Villa thwart Double hopes

1904–05 saw Newcastle come agonisingly close to the Double. Aston Villa spoiled the party in the Cup Final. Villa were not quite the force they'd been in the 1890s, but spearheaded by new young striking sensation Harry Hampton they ran out 2-0 winners. Hampton scored both goals. Newcastle picked themselves up and won 3-0 at Middlesbrough on the last day of the season, enough to pip Everton for the Championship by a point.

BELOW: A scene from the 1907 Cup Final between Everton and Sheffield Wednesday. Just one year earlier Everton were 1-0 victors over Newcastle, but on this occasion were beaten 2-1 by Wednesday. The middle years of the decade were highly successful for both Merseyside teams. Alec Young's goal gave Everton the FA Cup in 1906 and Liverpool's Scottish centre-half Alex Raisbeck helped them secure victory in the League in the same year.

Rise of Liverpool and Manchester United

ABOVE: The 1911 Cup Final played at Crystal Palace ended in a 2-2 draw forcing a mid-week replay at newly-completed Old Trafford. Newcastle were unlucky again being defeated by Bradford by one goal to nil. The Tyneside team had reached the Final 5 times in the last 7 years but had only lifted the trophy once – in 1910.

During the 1909–10 season Manchester United took up residence at Old Trafford and Arsenal's new stadium at Highbury was completed in 1913.

Liverpool and Manchester United also made their mark in this period, winning the title four times between them. Liverpool had come a long way since their League baptism in 1893. Just six years later they were on course for the Double, but were hammered 5-0 by Villa in a title showdown, then lost an FA Cup semi-final to Sheffield United. That was the year that Liverpool changed their colours from blue-and-white quarters to red. It didn't help them then, but two years later, 1900–01, the title went to Anfield for the first time. On that occasion, instead of riding high, then falling away, as they had done two years earlier, the team went on a tremendous late run, which included nine wins and three draws in 12 games. A 1-0 victory at relegated West Bromwich Albion clinched the Championship.

Raisbeck stars at Anfield

Liverpool's star was Alex Raisbeck. In his third season at the club, the Scottish international was tigerish in the tackle and outstanding in the air, despite standing only 5ft. 9in. tall. Raisbeck was still the linchpin when Liverpool won their second title five years later, 1905–06. The intervening period had been something of a rollercoaster, the club having been relegated in 1903–04. But they made their mark in the record books by winning the Second and First Division Championships in consecutive seasons. 1905–06 was also noteworthy for the fact that Everton beat Newcastle in the FA Cup Final; Liverpool's journalists made much capital out of their city's footballing supremacy that year.

Billy Meredith

Billy Meredith, the "Welsh Wizard", is widely regarded as the game's first superstar. Meredith came from Welsh mining stock, and he himself was working underground by the age of 12. His parents were eventually persuaded to allow him to pursue a career in football and Meredith joined Manchester City in 1894. He quickly established himself as a skilful, free-scoring winger, and became known for the fact that he never took to the field without a toothpick to chew on.

By 1904 30-year-old Meredith was City's captain, and scored the only goal of the game in that year's FA Cup Final win over Bolton. Meredith was banned for eight months after allegedly attempting to bribe an Aston Villa player before a vital League match in April 1905. He denied the charge and when the ban was lifted he moved across the city to join Manchester United. He helped United to win the FA Cup in 1909 and the Championship in 1910–11. He rejoined Manchester City in 1921 as a player-coach. He finally hung up his boots three years later, when he was four months short of his 50th birthday. His swansong came in City's 1924 FA Cup semi-final defeat by Newcastle. He had played 48 times for Wales between 1895 and 1920, winning the last of his caps when he was 45.

Meredith was at the forefront of a campaign to end the £4 maximum wage that was in force in the early 1900s. That figure was increased to £5 as a result, and the roots of the PFA can be traced back to the Welshman's early efforts to establish a Players' Union.

The "Welsh Wizard"

Wales made a stuttering start on the international front, suffering seven defeats in five years before recording a 1-0 win over England in 1881. A first home championship success came in 1906–07, when "Welsh Wizard" Billy Meredith was in his pomp. Meredith was still there when Wales notched their second win in 1920, 45 years old when he took to the field against England in March that year. The successes continued even after Meredith's retirement, Wales racking up seven wins in all during the inter-war period, six of those outright wins.

ABOVE INSERT: Billy Meredith, a tough, talented and controversial player who captained Wales and played for both Manchester City and Manchester United in a 30-year career which ended in 1924. Instrumental in setting the foundations for a Players' Union, he was also banned for a season for reportedly attempting to bribe an Aston Villa player in a match-fixing scandal.

RIGHT: In the first decade of the 20th century Wednesday won the League twice in the 1902–03 and 1903–04 seasons and the FA Cup in 1907, beating Everton 2-1 at Crystal Palace.

League Division One 1900–1919
Top 10 League Positions

1899–1900
1	Aston Villa	50
2	Sheffield United	48
3	Sunderland	41
4	Wolverhampton W.	39
5	Newcastle United	36
6	Derby County	36
7	Manchester City	34
8	Nottingham Forest	34
9	Stoke	34
10	Liverpool	33

1900–01
1	Liverpool	45
2	Sunderland	43
3	Notts County	40
4	Nottingham Forest	39
5	Bury	39
6	Newcastle United	38
7	Everton	37
8	The Wednesday	36
9	Blackburn Rovers	33
10	Bolton Wanderers	33

1901–02
1	Sunderland	44
2	Everton	41
3	Newcastle United	37
4	Blackburn Rovers	36
5	Nottingham Forest	35
6	Derby County	35
7	Bury	34
8	Aston Villa	34
9	The Wednesday	34
10	Sheffield United	33

1902–03
1	The Wednesday	42
2	Aston Villa	41
3	Sunderland	41
4	Sheffield United	39
5	Liverpool	38
6	Stoke	37
7	West Bromwich Albion	36
8	Bury	35
9	Derby County	35
10	Nottingham Forest	35

1903–04
1	The Wednesday	47
2	Manchester City	44
3	Everton	43
4	Newcastle United	42
5	Aston Villa	41
6	Sunderland	39
7	Sheffield United	38
8	Wolverhampton W.	36
9	Nottingham Forest	31
10	Middlesbrough	30

1904–05
1	Newcastle United	48
2	Everton	47
3	Manchester City	46
4	Aston Villa	42
5	Sunderland	40
6	Sheffield United	40
7	Small Heath	39
8	Preston	36
9	The Wednesday	33
10	Woolwich Arsenal	33

1905–06
1	Liverpool	51
2	Preston	47
3	The Wednesday	44
4	Newcastle United	43
5	Manchester City	43
6	Bolton Wanderers	41
7	Birmingham City	41
8	Aston Villa	40
9	Blackburn Rovers	40
10	Stoke	39

1906–07
1	Newcastle United	51
2	Bristol City	48
3	Everton	45
4	Sheffield United	45
5	Aston Villa	44
6	Bolton Wanderers	44
7	Woolwich Arsenal	44
8	Manchester United	42
9	Birmingham City	38
10	Sunderland	37

1907–08
1	Manchester United	52
2	Aston Villa	43
3	Manchester City	43
4	Newcastle United	42
5	The Wednesday	42
6	Middlesbrough	41
7	Bury	39
8	Liverpool	38
9	Nottingham Forest	37
10	Bristol City	36

1908–09
1	Newcastle United	53
2	Everton	46
3	Sunderland	44
4	Blackburn Rovers	41
5	The Wednesday	40
6	Woolwich Arsenal	38
7	Aston Villa	38
8	Bristol City	38
9	Middlesbrough	37
10	Preston	37

1909–10
1	Aston Villa	53
2	Liverpool	48
3	Blackburn Rovers	45
4	Newcastle United	45
5	Manchester United	45
6	Sheffield United	42
7	Bradford City	42
8	Sunderland	41
9	Notts County	40
10	Everton	40

1910–11
1	Manchester United	52
2	Aston Villa	51
3	Sunderland	45
4	Everton	45
5	Bradford City	45
6	The Wednesday	42
7	Oldham	41
8	Newcastle United	40
9	Sheffield United	38
10	Woolwich Arsenal	38

1911–12
1	Blackburn Rovers	49
2	Everton	46
3	Newcastle United	44
4	Bolton Wanderers	43
5	The Wednesday	41
6	Aston Villa	41
7	Middlesbrough	40
8	Sunderland	39
9	West Bromwich Albion	39
10	Woolwich Arsenal	38

1912–13
1	Sunderland	54
2	Aston Villa	50
3	The Wednesday	49
4	Manchester United	46
5	Blackburn Rovers	45
6	Manchester City	44
7	Derby County	42
8	Bolton Wanderers	42
9	Oldham	42
10	West Bromwich Albion	38

1913–14
1	Blackburn Rovers	51
2	Aston Villa	44
3	Oldham	43
4	Middlesbrough	43
5	West Bromwich Albion	43
6	Bolton Wanderers	42
7	Sunderland	40
8	Chelsea	39
9	Bradford City	38
10	Sheffield United	37

1914–15
1	Everton	46
2	Oldham	45
3	Blackburn Rovers	43
4	Burnley	43
5	Manchester City	43
6	Sheffield United	43
7	The Wednesday	43
8	Sunderland	41
9	Bradford PA	41
10	West Bromwich Albion	40

FA Cup Finals

1900	Bury	v	Southampton	4-0
1901	Tottenham Hotspur	v	Sheffield United	3-1
1902	Sheffield United	v	Southampton	2-1
1903	Bury	v	Derby County	6-0
1904	Manchester City	v	Bolton Wanderers	1-0
1905	Aston Villa	v	Newcastle United	2-0
1906	Everton	v	Newcastle United	1-0
1907	Sheffield W.	v	Everton	2-1
1908	Wolverhampton W.	v	Newcastle United	3-1
1909	Manchester Utd	v	Bristol City	1-0
1910	Newcastle United	v	Barnsley	2-0
1911	Bradford City	v	Newcastle United	1-0
1912	Barnsley	v	West Bromwich Albion	1-0
1913	Aston Villa	v	Sunderland	1-0
1914	Burnley	v	Liverpool	1-0
1915	Sheffield United	v	Chelsea	3-0
1916–1919			no competition	

Newton Heath reformed as Manchester United

Manchester United also scaled the heights after some lean times at the turn of the century. By 1901 the Newton Heath club was in a parlous state, both on and off the field. The team was languishing in the Second Division and facing crippling debts. A winding-up order was issued and the team had to rely on fund-raising through bazaars and the like in order to fulfil its fixtures. In 1902 things improved dramatically when some wealthy local businessmen pumped much-needed funds into the club. The Phoenix-like revival prompted a call for a new name. Manchester Celtic and Manchester Central were considered; Manchester United was settled upon.

Mangnall masterminds title win

Legendary manager Ernest Mangnall arrived the following year, and after three top six finishes in Division Two, United won promotion in 1905–06 and made their debut in the top flight the following season. The team that was promoted already boasted Charlie Roberts, one of the outstanding half-backs of his day. Apart from his dominance on the pitch, Roberts was noted for bucking the usual trend regarding length of shorts, preferring to wear his well above the knee. This act of rebelliousness, together with his vocal support of the Players' Union, was said to be one of the reasons why he won only three caps.

Mangnall knew he had to strengthen the team for an assault on the Championship. He signed Billy Meredith from neighbours Manchester City, one of the transfer coups of the period. Meredith, who had scored the goal that beat Bolton in the 1904 Cup Final, was an established star but arrived at United under a cloud. There had been allegations of illegal payments at Manchester City and Meredith himself was implicated in a bribery scandal. All that was forgotten two years later when Manchester United became champions for the first time. Ten straight wins early in the 1907–08 season, including a 6-1 thrashing of defending champions Newcastle, gave United a lead that proved decisive. As champions, United took part in the inaugural Charity Shield match, in which they faced Southern League winners Queen's Park Rangers. The match took place at Stamford Bridge, United winning 4-0 after a replay.

United relocate to Old Trafford

The following season was disappointing as far as the League went, but it brought a first FA Cup success. In the Final United beat mid-table side Bristol City 1-0, but along the way they had accounted for Newcastle, Everton and Blackburn, who occupied three of the top four places in the League that year.

1909–10 saw United finish empty-handed but it was noteworthy as the season in which the club took up residence at Old Trafford. The move to the new stadium, which cost £60,000 and could hold 100,000, was timely; for as United played host to Liverpool on 19 February 1910 to mark the beginning of a new era, part of the old Bank Street ground collapsed in a gale. In 1910–11, United's first full season at Old Trafford, they were crowned champions for the second time.

Spurs set new record

Teams from the Midlands and the North continued to dominate. Sunderland, Sheffield Wednesday, Blackburn and Everton were the other clubs which won League titles between 1900 and 1915. In that final campaign before war brought a 4-year hiatus, one of Lancashire's lesser lights very nearly made it to the top of the tree. Oldham would have won the Championship had they beaten Liverpool in their final match; they lost and Everton snatched the title by a point.

For the emerging teams from the South success was sporadic. However, in 1901 it was a London team which created a record that will surely remain unequalled. Spurs, then in the Southern League, won the FA Cup, the only non-League side ever to win the trophy. They disposed of three Division One sides en route: Preston, West Bromwich Albion and holders Bury. They faced Sheffield United in the final, and most observers thought they were on the receiving end of a bad decision when 'keeper Clawley was adjudged to have made a save behind his line. A goal was given and the game ended 2-2. A 3-1 victory in the replay at Bolton meant that any error hadn't been too costly. Sandy Brown was the Spurs' hero, netting a record 15 times during the Cup run, including three in the two Finals. 110,000 watched the first encounter at Crystal Palace, a record that has been beaten only twice since. Some commentators did note that the team consisted entirely of players from the provinces and Scotland, and as such the victory could hardly be regarded as a revival of the capital's footballing fortunes. Spurs were elected to the league in 1908, winning promotion to Division One at the first attempt.

Arsenal's rise was more steady. It wasn't until 1904–05 – 11 years after becoming a League club – that the Gunners made it into the top flight. Several seasons of consolidation followed before the club was relegated in 1912–13. This proved to be a blessing in disguise, as it precipitated Chairman Henry Norris's decision to relocate to Highbury. New neighbours Spurs were none too pleased with the decision, creating a rivalry that continues unabated.

Chelsea win League status in five months

Chelsea's entry into the League was remarkable in itself. At the start of 1905 the club didn't exist, yet just five months later it was elected to Division Two. Founder Gus Mears was behind this amazing rise up the ladder. He acquired the Stamford Bridge Athletic ground, signed a group of players and then, in May, saw the club's application to join the Second Division accepted. Both divisions were expanded from 18 to 20 clubs, and Chelsea joined the ranks with a club that would have rather less of an impact on the game, Clapham Orient. Chelsea finished third in their debut season, while Clapham Orient propped up the table. Chelsea were promoted to the First Division the following year.

"Khaki Final"

In 1914–15 Chelsea finished second from bottom in the League but reached their first Cup Final. They failed to reproduce their best form, however, and went down 3-0 to Sheffield United. The Yorkshire club hoisted a brand-new trophy aloft, the third in the competition's history. The design of the previous cup had been copied by a regional competition, and the FA decided to present it to Lord Kinnaird for his services to the game and have a brand new one made.

The Chelsea-Sheffield United match was dubbed "The Khaki Final" because of the number of uniformed spectators present that afternoon. Football had come in for a lot of criticism for completing the 1914–15 programme, hostilities having broken out the previous August. Questions had been asked in the House of Commons over the issue, but the game did serve as an effective recruiting sergeant. Rousing speeches were made at matches, and both players and supporters enlisted in droves, long before conscription was introduced. At the end of the Khaki Final Lord Derby gave a speech, saying: "You have played with one another and against one another for the Cup. Play with one another for England now."

Brief moment in the limelight

The period immediately prior to World War One saw some unheralded clubs enjoy a brief moment in the spotlight. Apart from Oldham's agonising experience in the 1914–15 Championship race, Yorkshire clubs Bradford City and Barnsley also tasted success. In 1910–11 Bradford finished 5th in the League and beat Newcastle in the Cup Final. Division Two side Barnsley made it to two Finals in three seasons, losing to Newcastle in 1910 and beating West Bromwich Albion in 1912. Between those two appearances the club had finished 19th in Division Two and been forced to apply for re-election.

Both of Barnsley's Cup appearances and Bradford's 1911 victory had gone to replays, prompting the FA to institute extra time from 1913. It wasn't needed that year – a 1-0 win for Villa over Sunderland – or the next, when Burnley ran out 1-0 winners over Liverpool. That 1914 Final marked the first time that a reigning monarch attended football's showpiece. King George V handed Burnley's skipper Tommy Boyle the Cup and at the same time rang down the curtain on the Crystal Palace as a Cup Final venue.

OPPOSITE: Spectators climb trees to watch the 1912 Cup Final between Barnsley and West Bromwich Albion, that ended in a no-score draw. Second Division Barnsley finally defeated West Brom by a single goal scored during extra time in the replay. Three successive drawn Cup Finals convinced the FA to change the rules of the competition to allow extra time to be played should the first match be tied.

LEFT ABOVE: A record crowd of over 120,000 gather outside the Crystal Palace ground for a view of the 1913 FA Cup Final between Aston Villa and Sunderland.

LEFT: The 1914 Cup Final in which Burnley defeated Liverpool by one goal scored in the 58th minute. This was the fourth year in succession that the Final had ended with a 1-0 scoreline.

Decline of gentlemen-amateurs

Until the early 1900s the England side invariably included a number of amateurs. The cream of the public-school and university systems could still hold their own against the professionals. Players such as Charles Burgess Fry and Gilbert Oswald Smith were outstanding performers. The latter was rated a better goalscorer than the legendary Steve Bloomer.

Many of the top gentlemen-amateurs turned out for Corinthians, who regularly beat the top League sides they came up against. In 1900 Corinthians put eight past Wolves and in 1904 thrashed Cup holders Bury 10-3. In March 1902 England fielded just one amateur in the side that drew with Wales in Wrexham. In April 1905 Spurs' centre-forward Vivian Woodward was the sole amateur in the side which beat Scotland 1-0 at Crystal Palace. The decline of the amateur international was hastened in 1907, when the FA sought to bring all players under their jurisdiction. The amateurs demurred and formed the Amateur Football Association. This marked a parting of the ways, and as top sides, such as Corinthians, were now prevented from testing themselves against League opposition, they soon lost their edge and a proud tradition was consigned to the history books.

Ibrox disaster

On the international front this period is remembered chiefly for a tragedy. When Scotland and England met at Ibrox Park on 5 April 1902, 25 people were killed when a section of the stand collapsed. The game eventually continued and ended 1-1 but the result was later expunged from the record books.

ABOVE: Over 70,000 people officially attended the Cup Final in 1914 but many preferred to spectate from vantage points outside the ground. This was the last time that Crystal Palace was to play host to the Final, the first time being in 1895 when Aston Villa's John Devey scored a goal forty seconds into the game. Among the crowd at the 1914 Cup Final was King George V, the first monarch ever to attend the event. Ironically, the public schools that had done so much to develop the game of football had now adopted rugby as their sport and football became the passion of the working classes.

OPPOSITE: The 1915 Cup Final was a subdued affair, held in Manchester on a damp afternoon before a crowd of only 50,000, many of whom were servicemen displaying signs of the injuries sustained in battle.

Football becomes Olympic sport

International football was still largely confined to fixtures against the other home nations. But in 1908 football made its official debut as an Olympic sport. An England side was chosen to represent the United Kingdom and took the gold medal. England retained the Olympic crown in 1912; on both occasions the beaten finalists were Denmark.

FIFA founded

Bohemia had sought entry into the 1912 Olympic tournament but had been unable to compete since the country was not a member of FIFA. The Fédération Internationale de Football Association had been formed in Paris on 21 May 1904. France, Belgium, Switzerland, Denmark, the Netherlands, Sweden and Spain were the founding members of world football's new governing body, England joining the following year.

Football in the trenches

As the 1914–15 season drew to a close it was clear that football could not continue. The decision to suspend the League and Cup competition came as no surprise, and the global conflict brought forth the heroic and less seemly side of the footballing fraternity. The unsavoury element occurred in a game between Manchester United and Liverpool on 2 April 1915. The political uncertainties prompted a number of players to conspire and rig the result – a 2-0 win for United – and make a killing at the bookmaker's. Suspicions were aroused and the subsequent inquiry resulted in eight players receiving life bans. After the war the Football League took a more charitable view of those who had fought for their country. The exception was Manchester United's Enoch "Knocker" West, whose ban remained in force after he continued to deny all charges.

Greater nobility was shown in the famous Christmas Day truce of 1914, when German and British soldiers played an impromptu game in No-Man's-Land. And even in the height of battle football was often used as a morale booster. Members of some regiments invoked the names of their beloved clubs as they advanced, and even dribbled balls onto the battlefield. Back in England, regional football replaced the traditional competitions between 1915 and 1918. These were low-key affairs and fixtures were organised so as not to interfere with the war effort. After Armistice Day on 11 November 1918 the appetite of both clubs and supporters to reinstate the official programme was huge. There was even talk of getting a truncated FA Cup competition off the ground immediately. In the end the authorities decided in favour of starting afresh the following season, and 1919–20 thus became the first postwar campaign.

> *Football served as an effective recruiting sergeant. Rousing speeches were made at matches, and both players and supporters enlisted in droves.*

Celtic and Rangers dominate

Football took a back seat at the start of the new century. On 5 April 1902 over 80,000 fans packed out Ibrox Park, eager to see if Scotland could beat England and make it three wins out of three in the Home International series. The stadium was barely two years old, built at a cost of £20,000, supposedly to state-of-the-art standards. But the wooden decking and timber joists in the West Stand failed when the game was a few minutes old. A gaping hole opened up and 25 people fell to their deaths, with hundreds more injured. The game was eventually played out to a subdued 1-1 draw, an irrelevance that was later expunged from the records. The teams met at Villa Park the following month, a 2-2 draw enough to give Scotland the Championship outright for the ninth time.

"The Mighty Quinn"

On the domestic front, Rangers and Celtic continued to exert the grip established in the latter years of the previous century. The Old Firm shared the League spoils in 18 out of 20 seasons, Celtic holding sway a record six times in a row up to 1910, and adding four more titles on the spin from 1914. At the end of the 1915–16 season a fixture pile-up meant they had to play Raith and Motherwell on the same day, winning 6-0 and 3-1. The star of the era was Jimmy Quinn, a brave, bullocking centre-forward who banged in over 200 goals for the club he joined in 1900. Perhaps "Mighty Quinn's" greatest day was the 1904 Cup Final, when a hat-trick turned the match against a Rangers side that had taken a 2-0 lead.

The 1904–05 League campaign went to a play-off after Celtic and Rangers both took 41 points from their 26 matches. Rangers had scored more goals and conceded fewer, but Celtic prevailed in the decider. Rangers also went down to Third Lanark in the Cup Final,

Scottish Cup Finals

1900	Celtic	v	Queen's Park	4-3
1901	Hearts	v	Celtic	4-3
1902	Hibernian	v	Celtic	1-0
1903	Hearts	v	Rangers	1-1
	Hearts	v	Rangers	0-0
	Rangers	v	Hearts	2-0
1904	Celtic	v	Rangers	3-2
1905	Rangers	v	Third Lanark	0-0
	Third Lanark	v	Rangers	3-1
1906	Hearts	v	Third Lanark	1-0
1907	Celtic	v	Hearts	3-0
1908	Celtic	v	St Mirren	5-1
1909	Celtic	v	Rangers	2-2
	Celtic	v	Rangers	1-1
1910	Clyde	v	Dundee	2-2
	Clyde	v	Dundee	0-0
	Dundee	v	Clyde	2-1
1911	Celtic	v	Hamilton	0-0
	Celtic	v	Hamilton	2-0
1912	Celtic	v	Clyde	2-0
1913	Celtic	v	Clyde	2-0
1914	Celtic	v	Hibernian	0-0
	Celtic	v	Hibernian	4-1
1914–1919			no competition	

so finished the season empty handed having been in contention to become Scotland's first double-winners. That honour went to their great rivals in 1907, a feat the Bhoys promptly repeated a year later. Celtic might have made it a hat-trick in 1909, but failed to add Cup glory to yet another League triumph – despite being unbeaten! Once again it was an Old Firm clash, and after two games the sides could not be separated. There were ugly scenes at Hampden when fans learned that there would be a third meeting rather than extra-time. That game never took place and the Cup was withheld, the only peacetime year that no name was etched on the trophy.

Breaking the stranglehold

Hibernian and Third Lanark broke the Celtic-Rangers stranglehold on the Championship in 1903 and 1904, respectively, with Dundee and Hearts taking the runners-up spots. It would be another 56 years before the top two didn't include at least one of the Glasgow giants. Dundee landed their first silverware in 1910, lifting the Cup after a marathon 10-game run over the five rounds. They needed a replay to beat Beith, and three games to overcome both Hibs in the semis and Clyde in the final. Falkirk also had their first taste of glory. They and Aberdeen were elected to the First Division in 1905 – justifiably so in Falkirk's case as they finished Division Two runners-up. The Dons, however, ended the season mid-table. Champions Clyde were probably not too enamoured with the discretionary system then in place, though they themselves were elected to the top flight 12 months later. After two seasons of consolidation, Falkirk finished runners-up to Celtic twice in three years. They slipped to fifth in 1912–13, but won the Cup with a 2-0 win over Raith, having beaten Rangers on their own patch along the way.

By 1920 it was clear that it took some doing to dislodge Rangers and Celtic in the League, and a Cup run offered the other clubs the likelier route to success. This pattern was emphatically reinforced over the next decade.

Scottish League 1900–1919
Top 10 League Positions

1889–1900
1	Rangers	32
2	Celtic	25
3	Hibernian	24
4	Hearts	23
5	Kilmarnock	18
6	Dundee	15
7	Third Lanark	15
8	St Mirren	12
9	St Bernard's	12
10	Clyde	4

1900–01
1	Rangers	35
2	Celtic	29
3	Hibernian	25
4	Greenock Morton	21
5	Third Lanark	18
6	Kilmarnock	18
7	Dundee	17
8	Queen's Park	17
9	St Mirren	16
10	Hearts	14

1901–02
1	Rangers	28
2	Celtic	26
3	Hearts	22
4	Third Lanark	19
5	St Mirren	19
6	Hibernian	16
7	Kilmarnock	16
8	Queen's Park	14
9	Dundee	13
10	Greenock Morton	7

1902–03
1	Hibernian	37
2	Dundee	31
3	Rangers	29
4	Hearts	28
5	Celtic	26
6	St Mirren	22
7	Third Lanark	21
8	Partick Thistle	19
9	Kilmarnock	16
10	Queen's Park	15

1903–04
1	Third Lanark	43
2	Hearts	39
3	Rangers	38
4	Celtic	38
5	Dundee	28
6	St Mirren	27
7	Partick Thistle	27
8	Queen's Park	21
9	Port Glasgow Athletic	20
10	Hibernian	19

1904–05
1	Celtic	41
2	Rangers	41
3	Third Lanark	35
4	Airdrieonians	27
5	Hibernian	26
6	Partick Thistle	26
7	Dundee	25
8	Hearts	25
9	Kilmarnock	23
10	St Mirren	22

1905–06
1	Celtic	49
2	Hearts	43
3	Airdrieonians	38
4	Rangers	37
5	Partick Thistle	36
6	Third Lanark	34
7	Dundee	34
8	St Mirren	31
9	Motherwell	26
10	Greenock Morton	26

1906–07
1	Celtic	55
2	Dundee	48
3	Rangers	45
4	Airdrieonians	42
5	Falkirk	41
6	Third Lanark	39
7	St Mirren	37
8	Clyde	36
9	Hearts	35
10	Motherwell	33

1907–08
1	Celtic	55
2	Falkirk	51
3	Rangers	50
4	Dundee	48
5	Hibernian	42
6	Airdrieonians	41
7	St Mirren	36
8	Aberdeen	35
9	Third Lanark	33
10	Motherwell	31

1908–09
1	Celtic	51
2	Dundee	50
3	Clyde	48
4	Rangers	45
5	Airdrieonians	41
6	Hibernian	39
7	Aberdeen	36
8	St Mirren	36
9	Falkirk	33
10	Kilmarnock	33

1909–10
1	Celtic	54
2	Falkirk	52
3	Rangers	46
4	Aberdeen	40
5	Clyde	37
6	Dundee	36
7	Third Lanark	34
8	Hibernian	34
9	Airdrieonians	33
10	Motherwell	32

1910–11
1	Rangers	52
2	Aberdeen	48
3	Falkirk	44
4	Partick Thistle	42
5	Celtic	41
6	Dundee	41
7	Clyde	39
8	Third Lanark	39
9	Hibernian	36
10	Kilmarnock	34

1911–12
1	Rangers	51
2	Celtic	45
3	Clyde	42
4	Hearts	40
5	Partick Thistle	40
6	Greenock Morton	37
7	Falkirk	36
8	Dundee	35
9	Aberdeen	35
10	Airdrieonians	32

1912–13
1	Rangers	53
2	Celtic	49
3	Hearts	41
4	Airdrieonians	41
5	Falkirk	40
6	Hibernian	37
7	Motherwell	37
8	Aberdeen	37
9	Clyde	35
10	Hamilton	32

1913–14
1	Celtic	65
2	Rangers	59
3	Hearts	54
4	Greenock Morton	54
5	Falkirk	49
6	Airdrieonians	48
7	Dundee	43
8	Third Lanark	36
9	Clyde	33
10	Ayr United	33

1914–15
1	Celtic	65
2	Hearts	61
3	Rangers	50
4	Greenock Morton	48
5	Ayr United	48
6	Falkirk	39
7	Hamilton	38
8	Partick Thistle	38
9	St Mirren	36
10	Airdrieonians	35

1915–16
1	Celtic	67
2	Rangers	56
3	Greenock Morton	51
4	Ayr United	48
5	Partick Thistle	46
6	Hearts	46
7	Hamilton	41
8	Dundee	40
9	Dumbarton	37
10	Kilmarnock	35

1916–17
1	Celtic	64
2	Greenock Morton	54
3	Rangers	53
4	Airdrieonians	50
5	Third Lanark	49
6	Kilmarnock	43
7	St Mirren	40
8	Motherwell	38
9	Partick Thistle	35
10	Dumbarton	35

1917–18
1	Rangers	56
2	Celtic	55
3	Kilmarnock	43
4	Greenock Morton	43
5	Motherwell	41
6	Partick Thistle	40
7	Queen's Park	34
8	Dumbarton	34
9	Clydebank	33
10	Hearts	32

1918–19
1	Celtic	58
2	Rangers	57
3	Greenock Morton	47
4	Partick Thistle	41
5	Motherwell	38
6	Ayr United	38
7	Hearts	37
8	Kilmarnock	35
9	Queen's Park	35
10	Clydebank	32

1920–1929
Expanding the Game

Once the Great War was over, the appetite to quickly reinstate the League and Cup competitions proper was huge. The early months of 1919 saw all the clubs take stock. After a four-year interruption they had to assess their playing staffs and effect repairs to their stadiums. The administrators were also busy. Divisions One and Two were immediately expanded to 22 clubs, and within two years two regional Third Divisions had been formed. This meant that the Football League in 1921–22 comprised 86 clubs compared with just 40 prior to World War One.

1920 A Third Division of the football league is formed

1920 England resigns from FIFA unable to tolerate dealing with former enemies but rejoin in 1924

1921 Third Division divided into the Third Division South and the Third Division North

1921 The English FA bans women's football

1921 Cardiff City gain promotion to Division One in their first season in League football, the first Welsh club to play in the top flight

1922 Syd Puddefoot becomes the first player to be transferred for a fee

of £5000 in a move from West Ham to Falkirk

1922 The maximum wage for professional footballers is reduced from £9 to £8 per week

1923 Wembley hosts the FA Cup for the first time when Bolton beat West Ham 2-0

1923 The football pools is introduced

1925 The offside rule is updated to allow only two players, not the previous three, to be between the player with the ball and the goal

1926 The BBC broadcast the FA Cup Final over radio for the first time

Controversy as 5th-placed Arsenal gain promotion

The way in which Division One was expanded in 1919–20 got the new era off to a controversial start. The expectation was that the top two Second Division sides from the 1914–15 season, Derby and Preston, would simply be promoted. But the Football League decided that Arsenal would go up too. The Gunners had finished only 5th in that final pre-war season, and Chairman Henry Norris was said to have engaged in some feverish behind-the-scenes lobbying in order to get the club elected to the top table. Three promoted teams meant that a First Division club had to go. Tottenham had finished bottom in 1914–15 and they were the obvious candidates. It took Spurs just one season to bounce back, but the circumstances in which they had swapped places with their north London rivals did nothing to promote harmony between the two clubs.

Leeds expelled over illegal payments

The early drama of the 1919–20 campaign took place off the field, when Second Division side Leeds City were expelled from the League for making illegal payments. City, managed by Herbert Chapman, had won the Northern Regional Championship in 1918 and seemed to be a team on the up. After the allegations were made Chapman chose to put a match to the club's books rather than submit them for scrutiny. He was suspended and Port Vale took over Leeds' fixtures. For Chapman and Leeds it was the parting of the ways, though both would rise again after a brief period in the wilderness. In 1920 the club reconstituted itself as Leeds United and returned to the fold. That same year Chapman, after a short spell with an engineering firm, also returned to the game. Over the next 14 years, first with Huddersfield Town and then with Arsenal, Chapman would take club management into a different realm.

OPPOSITE: A typical band of Cup-tie enthusiasts who paraded the streets on their way to Stamford Bridge plentifully bedecked with rosettes and ribbons, and keeping up their spirits with rattles and other noisy instruments. Stamford Bridge, an impressive stadium built in 1904 by Chelsea with a capacity of 100,000 was to be the venue for the postwar Cup Finals until Wembley Stadium was completed in 1923.

RIGHT TOP: Aston Villa collect the Cup at Stamford Bridge in 1920.

RIGHT CENTRE: Cantrell, the Spurs centre-forward, and Bliss (right) inside-left, battling with defenders in the Wolves' goalmouth during the 1921 Cup Final.

RIGHT BELOW: Going for goal: Decades before Denis Law perfected the art Bliss executes an overhead kick for Tottenham in the 1921 Cup Final against Wolves.

The rise of Huddersfield

In 1920 Huddersfield were in dire straits. The club was the poor relation to the town's rugby league side, and had even contemplated relocating lock, stock and barrel to Leeds. Things improved after the club acquired several of the players auctioned off by Leeds City. Huddersfield then made the most important signing of all: Herbert Chapman himself. In 1920 Huddersfield won promotion to the top flight for the first time and also made it to the FA Cup Final, in which they went down 1-0 to Aston Villa. This was no flash in the pan; the best was yet to come. Chapman set to work using his uncanny knack for buying the right player at the right time and moulding individuals into a formidable unit. Probably the key acquisition was Villa's inside-forward Clem Stephenson, who arrived in March 1921 in a £4000 deal. Many thought 30-year-old Stephenson's best years were behind him, but Chapman made him captain and in the autumn of his career he enjoyed a golden period as he led Huddersfield on an extraordinary run of success. The first silverware came in 1922, when the Yorkshire club lifted the FA Cup. It was a dour affair, with Preston providing the opposition. The only goal came from the penalty spot after Huddersfield winger Billy Smith was brought down. Preston seemed to have a legitimate case that the foul had been committed outside the box, but the referee waved this away and Smith himself stepped up to score. This game marked the last of three postwar finals to be contested at Stamford Bridge. By the following April the new Wembley Stadium would be ready.

Mathematicians needed to determine Championship

In the next six seasons Huddersfield finished no lower than third in the League, and the club's remarkable run included a famous hat-trick of championships starting in 1923–24. This first League title was also the most dramatic. At the end of the season Huddersfield and Cardiff both had 57 points. Huddersfield's goals column read 60-33, Cardiff's 61-34. This was an era in which goal average decided such issues and Huddersfield's was superior by a wafer-thin 0.024. Cardiff would not have needed to trouble the mathematicians had they converted a last-minute penalty in their final match at Birmingham. But a nervous Len Davies fired wide, the game ended in a goalless draw and Cardiff had to settle for the runners-up spot. Under the modern goal difference system, of course, the placings would have been reversed, Cardiff having scored one more goal than their rivals.

Chapman moves to Arsenal

Huddersfield retained their title in 1924–25, conceding just 28 goals all season. No club had ever won the Championship with a better defensive record than that. Wednesday had been equally miserly in 1903–04 but that was in the days of a 34-match season.

Herbert Chapman laid the foundations for Huddersfield's hat-trick of League titles but before the third crown had been claimed he had taken up a new challenge. It would take him longer to shape his new club, Arsenal, into a championship-winning side, but by the end of the decade the Gunners would be setting the standards all other clubs had to measure themselves by.

OPPOSITE: Herbert Chapman pictured with Huddersfield Town in 1921. Chapman is one of a select group of managers who have won the League Championship with different clubs: Huddersfield Town in 1924 and 1925, Arsenal in 1931 and 1933.

ABOVE LEFT: Supporters of both Aston Villa and Huddersfield seemed full of confidence on their way to the 1920 Cup Final. Villa, who eventually won a closely fought contest 1-0 after extra time, had now won the Cup six times. They would only win the competition once more in the 20th century – beating Manchester United in 1957.

ABOVE RIGHT: W.H. Smith of Huddersfield scores the winning goal from a disputed penalty in the 1922 Final. Smith had been brought down by the Preston defence but it was generally agreed that the action took place outside the box.

RIGHT: Stamford Bridge 1922: The Duke of York shakes hands with the Huddersfield team with Prince George and Wilson, the Huddersfield captain, behind him. Chapman's most important addition to his new team was Aston Villa's inside-forward Clem Stephenson for whom he paid £4000.

Rise and fall of West Brom and Burnley

Huddersfield apart, no club enjoyed a sustained period of success in the 1920s. West Bromwich Albion won the first postwar Championship, 1919–20, for the only time in their history. Long before the decade was out the Midlands club was languishing in the Second Division. Burnley had finished runners-up to West Brom, and they took over the mantle in 1920–21. A 30-match unbeaten run – 21 wins and 9 draws – between early September and late March carried the Lancashire club to its first title. But once again decline quickly set in. After six seasons in the bottom half of the table Burnley finally suffered the drop in 1929–30.

Scott marshals mean Liverpool defence

Liverpool were the only club apart from Huddersfield to win two Championships in this period. The team's success was built on a resilient defence, with the huge Irish goalkeeper Elisha Scott performing heroics and establishing himself as an Anfield legend. In 1921–22 Liverpool found the net just 63 times. Six teams had bettered that but none could match the 36 in the Goals Against column. The following year Liverpool held off the challenge of a skilful Sunderland side to retain their crown, and this time their defence was even more impenetrable: only 31 goals conceded in their 42 games, a new record. Liverpool didn't suffer the same fate as West Bromwich Albion and Burnley thereafter, but their form for the rest of the 1920s was erratic and they didn't mount another serious title challenge.

Gallacher becomes toast of Tyneside

Huddersfield then took charge, and their vice-like grip on the League was not broken until Newcastle claimed their 4th title in 1926–27. Their star was diminutive Scottish striker Hughie Gallacher, widely regarded as the greatest finisher of his era. Gallacher, who had joined Newcastle from Airdrie for £5500, hit 36 of the team's 96 League goals. Having missed four matches, this very nearly gave him a scoring ratio of a goal a game.

Herbert Chapman

Herbert Chapman was the most successful manager of the 1920s and early 1930s, his influence on the game continuing long after his death in 1934. He had had an undistinguished playing career at Northampton, Sheffield United and Spurs, standing out more for his trademark yellow boots than for the quality of his play. He made his name during the First World War as manager of Leeds City, but in 1919 he was suspended over financial irregularities. He took over an ailing Huddersfield Town side in 1920 and within four years he transformed the club into Championship winners. After retaining the title, Chapman moved to Highbury in 1925. Along with veteran inside-forward Charlie Buchan, Chapman reacted to a change in the offside law by introducing a fluid WM system, replacing the rigid 2-3-5 formation that most teams played. This involved the centre-half dropping into a purely defensive role, abandoning his usual role of providing the link between defence and attack. That "schemer's" job was filled by an inside forward, which meant a revolutionary 3-3-4 formation.

Chapman had an uncanny knack for spotting potential. He signed Cliff Bastin and paid a world record £10,890 for David Jack. It is said that when he met his opposite number at Bolton to discuss Jack's transfer, he arranged for the hotel waiter to keep the drinks coming – but instructed that his own glass should contain nothing alcoholic. By the time the men got down to business the atmosphere was very convivial. Bolton did get a world record fee but Chapman still thought his underhand tactic had given him the better of the deal.

Alex James was acquired for slightly less than Jack, but it was his arrival from Preston in 1929 that sparked a phenomenal run of success.

With James playing that key schemer's role, Arsenal went on to win the Championship three times in four years, and finished runners-up to Everton in 1931–32. There was also an FA Cup victory over Chapman's former club, Huddersfield, in 1930.

Chapman died just before Arsenal confirmed their third Championship, but all the pieces were in place for further success. The Gunners' League titles of 1935 and 1938, together with another FA Cup victory in 1936, also owed much to the groundwork Chapman laid. His influence also spread to the international side, notably when England beat Italy in November 1934. Chapman's Arsenal provided seven of the players who beat the reigning World Champions 3-2.

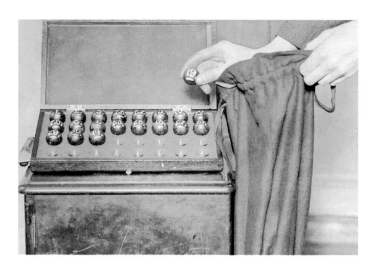

OPPOSITE: Herbert Chapman made his name as manager of Leeds City during the First World War. After transforming Huddersfield he went on to even greater success at Arsenal.

ABOVE: "The Cup Draw" was already part of tradition by the 1920s.

RIGHT: Frank Barson was one of the game's best-known characters. He played 353 League games for five clubs, most notably for Aston Villa and Manchester United. He was considered one of the first "hard" men in football and was often sent off and suspended. As a commanding centre-half who liked to go forward he was powerful in the air. On Boxing Day in 1921 he scored with a header from almost 30 yards to give Aston Villa victory over Sheffield United.

BELOW: A panoramic photograph of the last Cup Final at Stamford Bridge before the move to Wembley. Smith's winning penalty kick for Huddersfield was the first to decide a Cup Final. Preston's goalkeeper, James Mitchell, had tried to distract Smith as he prepared to take the kick by moving about on the goal line. Following this incident, the rule was brought in which required the goalkeeper to remain still until the ball was kicked.

New offside law brings goal avalanche

Newcastle's record of 96 goals scored and 58 conceded in 1926–27 made for an interesting comparison with Huddersfield's performance two years earlier. In their second Championship-winning season the Yorkshire club's goals column read 69-28, their defence proving even meaner than Liverpool's. For Newcastle to have scored 27 more goals but let in 30 more suggests a cavalier approach. But the chief reason for the surge in goalscoring was a change in the offside rule, which had been brought in in 1925.

Since the 1870s three players were required between the attacker and the goal for him to be onside. Over that 50-year period defences had got the offside trap down to a fine art. Newcastle themselves were arch-exponents. It is said that when one visiting team pulled into the city's train station and heard a guard's whistle, a wag chimed: "Blimey! Offside already!"

Under the new law only two players were now required between the attacking player and the goal for him to be onside. As most teams played the traditional 2-3-5 formation, forwards could now be onside with just the two full-backs to beat. There was a goal avalanche, which was exactly what the FA had wanted. On 29 August 1925 the first matches took place under the new system and the effect was immediate and dramatic. Villa beat Burnley 10-0, and in the following weeks there was a plethora of high-scoring games. 1703 goals were scored in Division One in 1925–26, an increase of over 500 on the previous season. Sterile, negative play might have been eliminated but not everyone was thrilled by the goal-fest. Some felt that goalscoring had become devalued and that the ingenuity and skill required to find the back of the net before the rule change was somewhat lacking under the revised system.

Villa beat Burnley 10-0, and in the following weeks there was a plethora of high-scoring games. 1703 goals were scored in Division One in 1925–26.

60-goal Dean fires Everton to title

Everton rattled in 102 goals on their way to the 1927–28 Championship. They weren't the first team to hit the magic ton mark, but it was a record-breaking campaign for one man: Dixie Dean. When Everton went into their final League fixture, a home clash with Arsenal, they were already confirmed as Champions. Nevertheless, a vast crowd turned up to see if Dean, who had hit 57 goals, could break the individual scoring record. That was held by George Camsell, who had hit 59 for Second Division Champions Middlesbrough a year earlier. Dean got the hat-trick he needed, ending the campaign with a phenomenal 60 goals to his name. Herbert Chapman wanted Dean to spearhead the Arsenal side he was building and asked Everton to name their price. Unsurprisingly, the Merseyside club was in no hurry to part with its prized asset.

Everton slipped to 18th the following season, and the decade ended with Wednesday on top of the pile. Having finished 16th and 14th in the two previous campaigns, Wednesday edged out Leicester and Villa to claim their third Championship. It was to be their last appearance under the Wednesday banner; by the time they began the defence of their title in the summer of 1929 the club had officially been renamed Sheffield Wednesday.

BELOW: The 1923 Cup Final, played at the new Empire Stadium at Wembley between West Ham United and Bolton Wanderers, attracted the largest crowd ever seen at a football match in the country. The King was present and was one of the most keenly interested spectators. Here the nearest fans are seen cheering as the National Anthem is played.

Dixie Dean
1907–1980

Middlesbrough's George Camsell is unfortunate that his name is not better known in footballing circles. Camsell scored 59 goals for Boro in 1926–27 as they won the Division Two title. His record lasted just one year. William "Dixie" Dean hit 60 for Everton the following season, a record which stands to this day.

Dean moved to Goodison Park for £3000 in 1925, having scored 27 goals in as many games for Tranmere Rovers. Everton were languishing in mid-table at the time, but Dean's phenomenal strike rate soon changed all that. Everton already had the Championship sewn up when Arsenal came to Goodison on the last day of the 1927–28 season. 48,000 turned up to see if their 21-year-old goal machine, who had netted 57 times, could beat Camsell's record. Dean scored a hat-trick, the third goal, fittingly, coming from a towering far-post header eight minutes from time. He was imperious in the air, despite the fact that he stood just 5ft 10in tall.

Dean also hit 44 goals as Everton won the League title in 1931–32. He ended his career with 473 goals from 502 appearances in all competitive matches. 379 of those came in the League, putting him second to Arthur Rowley on the all-time list.

His 18 games for England yielded 16 goals. He ended his career at Notts County, then went to play in Ireland, but Everton was his greatest love. Dean died after watching his beloved team play Liverpool at Goodison Park on 1 March 1980.

International Caps	16
International Goals	18
Total Appearances	502
Total Goals	473

FA Cup moves to Wembley

The first three postwar FA Cup competitions were staged at Stamford Bridge. This was not a popular venue and in 1919–20 nearly proved embarrassing for the FA as Chelsea won through to the semi-finals. Villa saved the authorities from the headache of having one of the finalists playing at home. They beat Chelsea and went on to score a 1-0 win over Huddersfield in the Final. It was the Midland club's 6th win, a record for the competition. The next two Finals, won by Spurs and Huddersfield, respectively, were uninspiring affairs which were also decided by a single goal. By the time Bolton met West Ham on 28 April 1923 the new Wembley Stadium was ready.

200,000 see first Wembley Final

With a capacity of 127,000, Wembley was capable of holding 70,000 more fans than had turned up to watch the previous year's showpiece. Few thought there would be a problem. But West Ham were a popular Second Division side and the occasion captured the public's imagination. Estimates vary as to how many flooded into Wembley that day, the figure put anywhere from 150,000 to 200,000–plus. The official gate of 126,047 didn't take into account the thousands who poured into the stadium by climbing walls and shinning up drainpipes. The game was held up for 45 minutes as fans spilled onto the pitch. PC George Scorey and his white horse Billy were in the thick of things trying to restore order and duly took their place in the annals of the sport. A grateful FA gifted the officer complimentary tickets for subsequent finals but Scorey, who was not a football fan, never took up the offer.

ABOVE: A crowded street scene in Wembley which was to host the FA Cup Final for the rest of the century.

TOP: Dixie Dean; his record 60 goals in a season still stands today.

1923:
The White Horse Final

Bolton Wanderers 2 – West Ham United 0

West Ham, in contention for promotion to Division One, played exciting, fast-moving football and their 5-2 defeat of Derby in the Cup semi-final enhanced this reputation. However, once the match got underway, it was only two minutes before Bolton's Jack opened the scoring and from then on West Ham never regained their stride. The game was disrupted after 11 minutes when the crowd surged back onto the pitch and after order was restored, the police rode along the touchline to prevent a recurrence. Just minutes after half-time, during which the teams were unable to leave the field, Bolton's J.R. Smith headed the ball, hitting the underside of the West Ham crossbar. The ball bounced inside the goal, then back onto the field and although West Ham protested, the goal was given. The match ended in a 2-0 victory for Bolton whose keeper, Pym, was scarcely tested during the contest. Smith, scorer of the second goal, completed a personal "double" having already won a Scottish Cup medal. Jack's contribution to his club's Cup run had been crucial to their success; he was the only man to score in four of their matches leading up to the Final and his early goal at Wembley set Bolton on their way.

Top: A spectacular aerial view of PC George Scorey and his white horse, Billy, trying to restore order. Admission by ticket was not even considered because it was thought there was room for all. Ever since the showpiece game has been an all-ticket affair.

With the postwar expansion of the Leagues and the ever-increasing popularity of the game, the FA wanted a prestigious stadium to host national and Cup games. After rejecting the idea of developing Crystal Palace the decision was made to move to Wembley. Work didn't commence until January 1922 but the stadium was ready for the legendary 1923 Final.

Above: Seymour setting the seal on Newcastle United's victory in the 1924 Cup Final just before the final whistle. Although the Cup Final was between Newcastle and Aston Villa, the most successful club of the middle part of the decade was Herbert Chapman's Huddersfield Town who topped the League in 1924, 1925 and 1926. Huddersfield had been on the verge of bankruptcy after the war and narrowly escaped a forced merger with Leeds United.

Future Cup Finals to be all-ticket

The West Ham camp were rather less enamoured with Billy and the other police horses on duty that day in 1923. The Hammers claimed the pitch was badly churned up as a result, something which didn't suit their nimble forwards. Bolton's attackers seemed to cope well enough, however. David Jack scored Wembley's first-ever goal and Bolton ran out 2-0 winners. After the game the FA quickly realised that only good fortune had prevented a catastrophe. Cup Finals thereafter became all-ticket affairs to prevent a recurrence of the 1923 situation.

Bolton went on to lift the Cup in 1926 and 1929. Amazingly, in those three triumphs over a seven-year spell only 17 players were used. In 1926 Manchester City were the beaten side. City went on to lose their last League match at Newcastle the following week and were relegated. It was the first time that a club had had that particular double disappointment.

ABOVE: Sheffield United's goalkeeper, Sutcliffe, punches clear.

TOP RIGHT: Cardiff's goal under siege. Thousands of Welsh fans flocked to London in 1925 to support Cardiff City's bid to bring the FA trophy back with them to Wales. Strong defences on both sides meant that the final score was 1-0 and Sheffield United won the cup for the fourth time in their history.

LEFT: A Bolton player heads the ball at a critical moment following a corner forced by West Ham. Within two minutes of the late kick-off David Jack put Bolton ahead and Smith scored their second early in the second half. Bolton went on to win the Cup twice more before the end of the decade – in 1926 and 1929.

David Jack

David Jack was 29 years old when Herbert Chapman targeted him as the man to replace Charlie Buchan after the latter retired at the end of the 1927–28 season. Jack had already had a glittering career at Bolton, with whom he won two FA Cup winners' medals. An inside-forward with terrific ball skills and a keen eye for goal, Jack scored the first-ever goal in a Wembley showpiece, the famous "White Horse Final" in which Bolton beat West Ham 2-0.

Chapman caused a stir when he paid £10,890 to bring Jack to Highbury, doubling the previous transfer record. It proved an astute move, however, as Jack was a key figure in the all-conquering Arsenal side of the 1930s. He picked up three Championship medals and also made it a hat-trick of Cup successes when Arsenal beat Huddersfield in the 1930 Final.

ABOVE RIGHT: David Jack watches the ball soar into the net as he scores the goal that won the Cup for Bolton Wanderers in 1926.

RIGHT: England's Billy Walker scores against Scotland in the last international match of the 1924 season played at Wembley before 65,000 spectators. Harper, Scotland's goalkeeper rushes out in an attempt to save. The game finished all square at 1-1. Scotland's next visit to Wembley 4 years later ended in a famous 5-1 victory.

BELOW: An aerial photograph of the crowded Wembley Stadium during the Cup Final in which Bolton defeated Manchester City by 1-0 watched by 92,000 people. Despite reaching the Cup Final and scoring 89 goals in the 1925–26 season, Manchester City were relegated to the Second Division along with Notts County and Leeds.

A change in the offside rule came into effect in the 1925–26 season. Three defenders between the attacker and the goal were no longer necessary to remain onside, two would suffice. The tally of goals scored soared at the beginning of the season until defenders learned to cope with the change.

Bolton and Jack again

The 1926 Cup Final between Lancashire sides Bolton and Manchester City kept the crowds on tenterhooks right until the last minutes of the game. Bolton had the better of the match and the Manchester side seemed to be nervous at the outset. But Pym, the Bolton keeper was called upon to make many saves during the afternoon, most spectacularly when he stopped a dangerous header from Manchester's Johnson in the second half. With just minutes to go, David Jack, standing in front of the Manchester goal, received the ball from Vizard. Jack grasped the opportunity and launched the ball into the back of the net, scoring his second goal in an FA Cup Final and winning the trophy for Bolton.

ABOVE: Goalmouth action: A late goal gave Bolton the Cup for the second time in three years.

RIGHT: The heroes of the day receive boisterous congratulations as they leave the Wembley grandstand with the FA Cup.

FA Cup goes to Wales

One of the big Cup stories of the decade came in 1926–27. Arsenal and Cardiff were both mid-table sides when they won through to the Wembley Final. Cardiff boasted eight internationals, all of whom were well known to Gunners' 'keeper Dan Lewis, who had also been capped by Wales. The game was settled when Lewis fumbled a speculative shot by Cardiff centre-forward Hugh Ferguson. It rolled agonisingly over the line and the FA Cup left England for the only time in its history. Lewis later blamed the slippery sheen on his new jersey for the blunder, and thereafter Arsenal always made sure that new kit was washed before it was worn.

Welsh club football

Cardiff City's FA Cup win in 1927 put Welsh club football firmly on the map just seven years after its premier sides took their Football League bow in the postwar reorganisation. The Bluebirds were admitted to Division Two in 1920 – gaining promotion and reaching the Cup semi-final at the first time of asking – while Swansea, Newport and Wrexham were among the Southern League clubs adopted wholesale as the new third tier of English football. Led from the half-back line by the great Fred Keenor, Cardiff came within a whisker of being crowned champions in 1923–24, and paid their first visit to Wembley the following year, losing 1-0 to Sheffield United in the Cup Final. It was a remarkable success story for a club formed as recently as 1899 under the banner Riverside FC. Rapid decline soon set in, though, and by the mid-30s Cardiff were propping up the Third Division (South) and seeking re-election.

There were two interesting footnotes to Cardiff's successes of the 1920s. The victorious Cup run of 1926–27 included a quarter-final win over Chelsea. During that match, City goalkeeper Tom Farquarson rushed off his line to block a penalty, an incident that led to a law change requiring 'keepers to stay at home until the ball was kicked. The second fascinating fact came in the relegation season of 1928–29, when Cardiff boasted the best defensive record in the division despite finishing bottom of the pile. 59 goals conceded was three fewer than champions Wednesday!

LEFT: Wales and England shared the points in a 1927 international game that finished 3-3 in Wrexham. Dixie Dean scored twice for England while Len Davies did the same for Wales. Davies remains the record career goalscorer for Cardiff City.

BELOW: Cardiff defend as Arsenal look for a way back in the 1927 FA Cup Final. The game is most remembered for Arsenal goalkeeper Dan Lewis's mistake, which led to the only goal of the game. It was also the first ever Cup Final to be broadcast by BBC Radio. During the decade Cardiff were one of the strongest sides in the English League, finishing runners-up in 1923–24 and also losing 1-0 to Sheffield United in the FA Cup Final of 1925.

"Wembley Wizards" thrash England

International football in the 1920s began on a sour note. The FA withdrew from FIFA over the question of rejoining competition with the defeated Axis powers, a rift that rumbled on until 1924. The late 1920s saw the England team suffer two reverses, which became milestones in the record books. The first came on 31 March 1928, when Scotland came to Wembley and handed England a 5–1 thrashing. Alex Jackson, Alex James and Hughie Gallacher were among the stars who would go down in history as the "Wembley Wizards".

Continental football on the rise

Perhaps an even more significant defeat came on 15 May the following year. England went to Madrid and lost 4–3 to Spain, their first-ever defeat at the hands of a foreign side. This didn't surprise everyone. There were already rumblings from some commentators, who argued that English teams would do well to look to their continental cousins, who put greater emphasis on coaching and training. This was an era in which many English coaches were adherents of the "ball starvation" philosophy, denying players too much ball-work during the week so that they would be hungry for it on match days.

RIGHT: Portsmouth goalkeeper Gilfillan makes a good save under pressure from a Bolton attacker in the 1929 Cup Final. His outstanding performance, however, couldn't stop Bolton running out 2-0 winners.

BELOW: 1928: Blackburn's Roscamp charges towards Mercer, the Huddersfield keeper, and seconds later scored when Mercer lost the ball. The 1928 Cup Final brought fewer surprises and upsets than that held the previous year when Cardiff City defeated Arsenal and carried the cup to Wales, but Roscamp's first goal scored in the opening minutes of the match was an exciting start. Huddersfield were outplayed by the Blackburn team, losing the match by three goals to one.

League Division One 1920–1929

1919–1920

1	West Bromwich Albion	60
2	Burnley	51
3	Chelsea	49
4	Liverpool	48
5	Sunderland	48
6	Bolton Wanderers	47
7	Manchester City	45
8	Newcastle United	43
9	Aston Villa	42
10	The Arsenal	42
11	Bradford PA	42
12	Manchester United	40
13	Middlesbrough	40
14	Sheffield United	40
15	Bradford City	39
16	Everton	38
17	Oldham	38
18	Derby County	38
19	Preston	38
20	Blackburn Rovers	37
21	Notts County	36
22	The Wednesday	23

1920–21

1	Burnley	59
2	Manchester City	54
3	Bolton Wanderers	52
4	Liverpool	51
5	Newcastle United	50
6	Tottenham Hotspur	47
7	Everton	47
8	Middlesbrough	46
9	The Arsenal	44
10	Aston Villa	43
11	Blackburn Rovers	41
12	Sunderland	41
13	Manchester United	40
14	West Bromwich Albion	40
15	Bradford City	39
16	Preston	39
17	Huddersfield	39
18	Chelsea	39
19	Oldham	33
20	Sheffield United	30
21	Derby County	26
22	Bradford PA	24

1921–22

1	Liverpool	57
2	Tottenham Hotspur	51
3	Burnley	49
4	Cardiff	48
5	Aston Villa	47
6	Bolton Wanderers	47
7	Newcastle United	46
8	Middlesbrough	46
9	Chelsea	46
10	Manchester City	45
11	Sheffield United	40
12	Sunderland	40
13	West Bromwich Albion	40
14	Huddersfield	39
15	Blackburn Rovers	38
16	Preston	38
17	The Arsenal	37
18	Birmingham City	37
19	Oldham	37
20	Everton	36
21	Bradford City	32
22	Manchester United	28

1922–23

1	Liverpool	60
2	Sunderland	54
3	Huddersfield	53
4	Newcastle United	48
5	Everton	47
6	Aston Villa	46
7	West Bromwich Albion	45
8	Manchester City	45
9	Cardiff	43
10	Sheffield United	42
11	The Arsenal	42
12	Tottenham Hotspur	41
13	Bolton Wanderers	40
14	Blackburn Rovers	40
15	Burnley	38
16	Preston	37
17	Birmingham City	37
18	Middlesbrough	36
19	Chelsea	36
20	Nottingham Forest	34
21	Stoke	30
22	Oldham	30

1923–24

1	Huddersfield	57
2	Cardiff	57
3	Sunderland	53
4	Bolton Wanderers	50
5	Sheffield United	50
6	Aston Villa	49
7	Everton	49
8	Blackburn Rovers	45
9	Newcastle United	44
10	Notts County	42
11	Manchester City	42
12	Liverpool	41
13	West Ham United	41
14	Birmingham City	39
15	Tottenham Hotspur	38
16	West Bromwich Albion	38
17	Burnley	36
18	Preston	34
19	The Arsenal	33
20	Nottingham Forest	32
21	Chelsea	32
22	Middlesbrough	22

1924–25

1	Huddersfield	58
2	West Bromwich Albion	56
3	Bolton Wanderers	55
4	Liverpool	50
5	Bury	49
6	Newcastle United	48
7	Sunderland	48
8	Birmingham City	46
9	Notts County	45
10	Manchester City	43
11	Cardiff	43
12	Tottenham Hotspur	42
13	West Ham United	42
14	Sheffield United	39
15	Aston Villa	39
16	Blackburn Rovers	35
17	Everton	35
18	Leeds United	34
19	Burnley	34
20	The Arsenal	33
21	Preston	26
22	Nottingham Forest	24

1925–26

1	Huddersfield	57
2	The Arsenal	52
3	Sunderland	48
4	Bury	47
5	Sheffield United	46
6	Aston Villa	44
7	Liverpool	44
8	Bolton Wanderers	44
9	Manchester United	44
10	Newcastle United	42
11	Everton	42
12	Blackburn Rovers	41
13	West Bromwich Albion	40
14	Birmingham City	40
15	Tottenham Hotspur	39
16	Cardiff	39
17	Leicester City	38
18	West Ham United	37
19	Leeds United	36
20	Burnley	36
21	Manchester City	35
22	Notts County	33

1926–27

1	Newcastle United	56
2	Huddersfield	51
3	Sunderland	49
4	Bolton Wanderers	48
5	Burnley	47
6	West Ham United	46
7	Leicester City	46
8	Sheffield United	44
9	Liverpool	43
10	Aston Villa	43
11	The Arsenal	43
12	Derby County	41
13	Tottenham Hotspur	41
14	Cardiff	41
15	Manchester United	40
16	The Wednesday	39
17	Birmingham City	38
18	Blackburn Rovers	38
19	Bury	36
20	Everton	34
21	Leeds United	30
22	West Bromwich Albion	30

1927–28

1	Everton	53
2	Huddersfield	51
3	Leicester City	48
4	Derby County	44
5	Bury	44
6	Cardiff	44
7	Bolton Wanderers	44
8	Aston Villa	43
9	Newcastle United	43
10	Arsenal	41
11	Birmingham City	41
12	Blackburn Rovers	41
13	Sheffield United	40
14	The Wednesday	39
15	Sunderland	39
16	Liverpool	39
17	West Ham United	39
18	Manchester United	39
19	Burnley	39
20	Portsmouth	39
21	Tottenham Hotspur	38
22	Middlesbrough	37

1928–29

1	The Wednesday	52
2	Leicester City	51
3	Aston Villa	50
4	Sunderland	47
5	Liverpool	46
6	Derby County	46
7	Blackburn Rovers	45
8	Manchester City	45
9	Arsenal	45
10	Newcastle United	44
11	Sheffield United	41
12	Manchester United	41
13	Leeds United	41
14	Bolton Wanderers	40
15	Birmingham City	40
16	Huddersfield	39
17	West Ham United	39
18	Everton	38
19	Burnley	38
20	Portsmouth	36
21	Bury	31
22	Cardiff	29

FA Cup Finals

1920	Aston Villa	v	Huddersfield Town	1-0
1921	Tottenham H.	v	Wolverhampton W.	1-0
1922	Huddersfield T.	v	Preston N.E.	1-0
1923	Bolton Wanderers	v	West Ham United	2-0
1924	Newcastle United	v	Aston Villa	2-0
1925	Sheffield United	v	Cardiff City	1-0
1926	Bolton Wanderers	v	Manchester City	1-0
1927	Cardiff City	v	Arsenal	1-0
1928	Blackburn Rovers	v	Huddersfield Town	3-1
1929	Bolton Wanderers	v	Portsmouth	2-0

Bolton's third triumph in six years

1929 was a remarkable year for Bolton Wanderers who appeared in their third Cup Final since the fixture had first been staged at Wembley in 1923. The game, against Portsmouth, ended in 2-0 victory for the northern team and Pym, the Bolton keeper, kept a clean sheet for the third time in the Final. This victory in 1929 brought Lancashire's tally of Cup wins to 17 since the competition was established in 1871.

However, the trophy didn't leave the capital straight away because the team, taking the Cup with it, attended a concert at the London Palladium before returning. In response to calls from the audience, Bolton's captain Seddon came up on to the stage so that the crowd would have a better view.

RIGHT: Thirteen minutes before the final whistle Gilfillan, the Portsmouth goalkeeper, stumbles when he rushes out to intercept a shot and the ball is deflected off his team-mate Mackie and crosses the line. Here, Mackie is trying to control the spinning ball but can't prevent the goal.

BELOW: Bolton's goalkeeper Pym stops a shot by Weddle, the Portsmouth centre forward.

Arsenal's first major honour

Fittingly, the 1930 FA Cup Final saw Huddersfield take on Arsenal, the team of the 1920s against the team which would dominate the 1930s. By now Herbert Chapman had forged a side capable of beating his former club. Arsenal won the match 2-0, Highbury's first major honour. Since Chapman's arrival five years earlier, Arsenal had spent much of the time in mid-table, saving their best form for the Cup. That was all about to change.

BELOW: The Portsmouth team is introduced to the Prince of Wales before the start of the 1929 Cup Final. Bolton are without their 29-year-old star player David Jack on this occasion having agreed to sell him to Arsenal for the record sum of £10,890.

RIGHT: Eddie Hapgood, a key defender in Herbert Chapman's Arsenal side who were to dominate the next decade.

Football takes to the airwaves

The excitement of domestic football continued to draw huge crowds. The minimum entrance fee had been raised from sixpence to one shilling, but football remained cheap entertainment for the masses. Inevitably, it also attracted the new broadcast media. 22 January 1927 saw the first radio commentary of a football match, a clash between Arsenal and Sheffield United. To enable the listeners to visualise proceedings, a pitch divided into numbered squares was published in *The Radio Times*. As the commentators described the play they also reported in which square the action was taking place.

RIGHT: Part of the excited crowd at the 1929 Cup Final. Football remained cheap entertainment and now commentary could be followed on the radio.

ABOVE: The Prince of Wales presents the Cup to Seddon, the captain of Bolton Wanderers in 1929.

Scottish League 1920–1929

1919–1920

1	Rangers	71
2	Celtic	68
3	Motherwell	57
4	Dundee	50
5	Clydebank	48
6	Greenock Morton	45
7	Airdrieonians	44
8	Third Lanark	43
9	Kilmarnock	43
10	Ayr United	40
11	Dumbarton	39
12	Queen's Park	38
13	Partick Thistle	38
14	St Mirren	38
15	Clyde	37
16	Hearts	37
17	Aberdeen	35
18	Hibernian	33
19	Raith Rovers	32
20	Falkirk	31
21	Hamilton	29
22	Albion Rovers	28

1920–21

1	Rangers	76
2	Celtic	66
3	Hearts	50
4	Dundee	49
5	Motherwell	48
6	Partick Thistle	46
7	Clyde	45
8	Third Lanark	44
9	Greenock Morton	44
10	Airdrieonians	43
11	Aberdeen	42
12	Kilmarnock	42
13	Hibernian	41
14	Ayr United	40
15	Hamilton	40
16	Raith Rovers	37
17	Albion Rovers	34
18	Falkirk	34
19	Queen's Park	33
20	Clydebank	28
21	Dumbarton	24
22	St Mirren	18

1921–22

1	Celtic	67
2	Rangers	66
3	Raith Rovers	51
4	Dundee	49
5	Falkirk	49
6	Partick Thistle	48
7	Hibernian	46
8	St Mirren	46
9	Third Lanark	46
10	Clyde	44
11	Albion Rovers	44
12	Greenock Morton	42
13	Motherwell	39
14	Ayr United	38
15	Aberdeen	35
16	Airdrieonians	35
17	Kilmarnock	35
18	Hamilton	34
19	Hearts	32
20	Dumbarton	30
21	Queen's Park	28
22	Clydebank	20

1922–23

1	Rangers	55
2	Airdrieonians	50
3	Celtic	46
4	Falkirk	45
5	Aberdeen	42
6	St Mirren	42
7	Dundee	41
8	Hibernian	41
9	Raith Rovers	39
10	Ayr United	38
11	Partick Thistle	37
12	Hearts	37
13	Motherwell	36
14	Greenock Morton	35
15	Kilmarnock	35
16	Clyde	33
17	Third Lanark	30
18	Hamilton	29
19	Albion Rovers	26
20	Alloa Athletic	23

1923–24

1	Rangers	59
2	Airdrieonians	50
3	Celtic	46
4	Raith Rovers	43
5	Dundee	43
6	St Mirren	42
7	Hibernian	41
8	Partick Thistle	39
9	Hearts	38
10	Motherwell	37
11	Greenock Morton	37
12	Hamilton	36
13	Aberdeen	36
14	Ayr United	34
15	Falkirk	32
16	Kilmarnock	32
17	Queen's Park	31
18	Third Lanark	30
19	Clyde	29
20	Clydebank	25

1924–25

1	Rangers	60
2	Airdrieonians	57
3	Hibernian	52
4	Celtic	44
5	Cowdenbeath	42
6	St Mirren	40
7	Partick Thistle	38
8	Dundee	36
9	Raith Rovers	36
10	Hearts	35
11	St Johnstone	35
12	Kilmarnock	33
13	Hamilton	33
14	Greenock Morton	33
15	Aberdeen	32
16	Falkirk	32
17	Queen's Park	32
18	Motherwell	30
19	Ayr United	30
20	Third Lanark	30

1925–26

1	Celtic	58
2	Airdrieonians	50
3	Hearts	50
4	St Mirren	47
5	Motherwell	46
6	Rangers	44
7	Cowdenbeath	42
8	Falkirk	42
9	Kilmarnock	41
10	Dundee	37
11	Aberdeen	36
12	Hamilton	35
13	Queen's Park	34
14	Partick Thistle	33
15	Greenock Morton	31
16	Hibernian	30
17	Dundee United	28
18	St Johnstone	28
19	Raith Rovers	26
20	Clydebank	22

1926–27

1	Rangers	56
2	Motherwell	51
3	Celtic	49
4	Airdrieonians	45
5	Dundee	43
6	Falkirk	42
7	Cowdenbeath	42
8	Aberdeen	40
9	Hibernian	39
10	St Mirren	37
11	Partick Thistle	36
12	Queen's Park	36
13	Hearts	35
14	St Johnstone	35
15	Hamilton	35
16	Kilmarnock	32
17	Clyde	29
18	Dunfermline Athletic	28
19	Greenock Morton	28
20	Dundee United	22

1927–28

1	Rangers	60
2	Celtic	55
3	Motherwell	55
4	Hearts	47
5	St Mirren	44
6	Partick Thistle	43
7	Aberdeen	43
8	Kilmarnock	40
9	Cowdenbeath	39
10	Falkirk	37
11	St Johnstone	36
12	Hibernian	35
13	Airdrieonians	35
14	Dundee	35
15	Clyde	31
16	Queen's Park	30
17	Raith Rovers	29
18	Hamilton	28
19	Bo'ness	26
20	Dunfermline Athletic	12

1928–29

1	Rangers	67
2	Celtic	51
3	Motherwell	50
4	Hearts	47
5	Queen's Park	43
6	Partick Thistle	41
7	Aberdeen	40
8	St Mirren	40
9	St Johnstone	38
10	Kilmarnock	36
11	Falkirk	36
12	Hamilton	35
13	Cowdenbeath	33
14	Hibernian	32
15	Airdrieonians	31
16	Ayr United	31
17	Clyde	30
18	Dundee	29
19	Third Lanark	26
20	Raith Rovers	24

Scottish Cup Finals

1920	Kilmarnock	v	Albion Rovers	3-2
1921	Partick Thistle	v	Rangers	1-0
1922	Greenock Morton	v	Rangers	1-0
1923	Celtic	v	Hibernian	1-0
1924	Airdrieonians	v	Hibernian	2-0
1925	Celtic	v	Dundee	2-1
1926	St Mirren	v	Celtic	2-0
1927	Celtic	v	East Fife	3-1
1928	Rangers	v	Celtic	4-0
1929	Kilmarnock	v	Rangers	2-0

Scotland's League expanded

The Scottish league was expanded to 22 clubs in 1919–20, the second tier dispensed with for two seasons. The extra four matches allowed Rangers to amass over 100 goals and 71 points in winning the Championship. They raised the bar a year later, winning 35 of the 42 games and suffering just one defeat. Celtic, runners-up in both campaigns, reversed the positions in 1921–22, the season that saw three clubs relegated and one promoted from the newly restored Second Division. That made for two 20-strong divisions, with a short-lived third tier introduced in 1923.

The promoted side in 1921–22 was Alloa Athletic, who ran away with the Division Two Championship in their first season of League football. After just one top-flight campaign they were back in the Second Division, where they would remain for over half a century. Among the three clubs to suffer the drop in Alloa's glory year was Queen's Park. Scotland's crack side of yesteryear had long been a declining force, finishing bottom of the heap no less than four times since joining the League in 1901. Queen's had been spared relegation on those occasions, but now had to face life outside the elite for the first time. They bounced back immediately, though Hampden's famous amateurs were usually to be found in the lower reaches of the top echelon.

Airdrie push for honours

Rangers and Celtic continued their carve-up of the League spoils, with the former in the ascendancy. Celtic's 1925–26 Championship win broke a remarkable run of success for their Old Firm rivals, who took the title eight times in nine years. In the midst of that sequence Airdrieonians enjoyed their best years, occupying the runners-up spot four seasons running from 1923 and beating Hibs in the 1924 Cup Final. Airdrie's star performer was the legendary Hughie Gallacher. Signed from non-League Queen of the South in 1921, the diminutive Gallacher netted 100 times for the Lanarkshire club before joining Newcastle United in 1925. He also hit 23 goals in 20 games for Scotland, putting him third on the all-time list but with an unrivalled strike rate of 1.15 goals per game. Gallacher's prowess limited the opportunities for Celtic's Jimmy McGrory, another pint-sized goal machine. McGrory set a new top-flight record with 49 goals in 1926–27, many coming from the head of the player nicknamed "Mermaid".

First Cup Final dismissal

There were plenty of Cup shocks in the 1920s. St Mirren beat champions Celtic in the 1926 Final, while Partick Thistle, Morton and Kilmarnock all upset the odds by beating Rangers. Killie finished 31 points adrift of Rangers in 1929 but prevailed 2-0 in the Hampden showpiece. The champions were frustrated, and in Jock Buchanan's case it boiled over; he became the first player to be sent off in a Cup Final. Talk of a Cup hoodoo for Rangers was dispelled when they got their hands on the trophy in 1928, the club's first double-winning season. Falkirk didn't get among the honours, despite setting a new world record with the £5000 acquisition of West Ham's star striker Syd Puddefoot in 1922.

The talent pool around in the 1920s made it a golden era for the national side. Of the 33 matches played during the decade, there were 23 wins and five draws. Among the victories was a 7-3 win over Norway in Bergen, Scotland's first foreign international. But for fans and players alike the big one was the 5-1 win at Wembley on 31 March 1928. With a hat-trick from Huddersfield's Alex Jackson and a brace from Preston's Alex James, Scotland gave a masterclass on that famous away day. The team picked up just one point from the other two games, and Wales took the Championship laurels that season, but the decade as a whole belonged to Scotland with seven wins, six of them outright.

Hughie Gallacher

Hughie Gallacher stood barely 5ft 6in tall, yet he is rated as one of the best centre-forwards of all time. He played for Queen of the South and Airdrie before heading south to join Newcastle for £5500 in 1926. He quickly established himself as an idol on Tyneside after firing Newcastle to the Championship in 1926–27, his first full season with the club. He hit 36 goals in 38 games during the campaign, which remains a club record. Gallacher was a complete striker and amazingly powerful in the air considering his lack of inches. He was capped 23 times for Scotland, scoring 22 goals. Gallacher's private life was more turbulent. He ended his days in straitened circumstances and threw himself under a train in 1957.

1930–1944
A Shift in Power

English football in the 1930s was dominated by one club: Arsenal. The Gunners won the championship five times, and only once, in 1929–30, did they fail to finish in the top six. There were also three FA Cup Final appearances, two of them victorious, and five wins in the Charity Shield. Under Herbert Chapman, Arsenal took professional football to a new level, and even after the legendary manager's death the Gunners continued to set the pace in the domestic game.

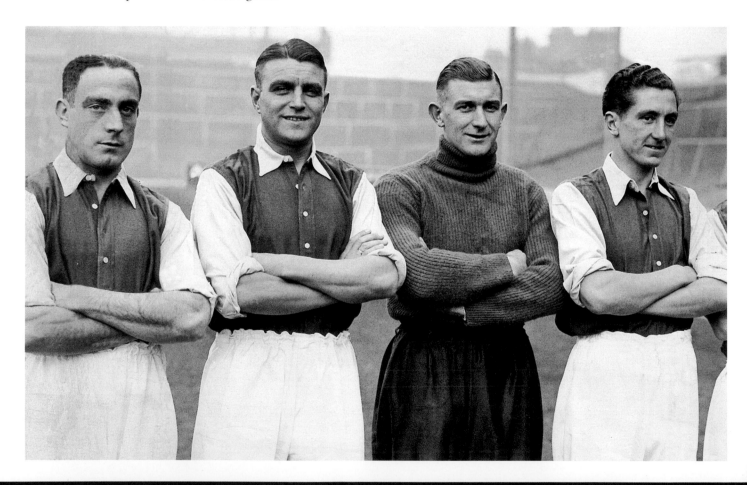

1930 The first Football World Cup is won by Uruguay; England are not one of the 13 teams participating

1931 22-year-old Celtic 'keeper John Thomson dies from injuries sustained in an Old Firm clash

1932 Motherwell's sole Championship win breaks a 28-year run of Old Firm dominance

1933 Numbers first required to be worn on the back of players' shirts for the FA Cup Final between Everton, who were numbered 1 to 11, and Manchester City, numbers 12 to 22

1934 Herbert Chapman, the successful manager who took Arsenal to 1930 FA Cup glory, dies suddenly

1934 Second World Cup competition takes place in Italy, again England do not compete and the host nation win

1935 Football managers are banned from the touchline

1936 Luton Town score a 12-0 victory over Bristol Rovers, with Joe Payne scoring 10

1936 Football highlights shown for the first time by the BBC of a match between Arsenal and Everton

1937 The first foreign professionals enter the British game when Barrow sign two players from Argentina

1937 Wales win the Home International Championship for the third time in five years

Cameras at Highbury

Fittingly, the team of the decade became the first to be filmed for television. In 1937, a decade after radio coverage of football had been established, the cameras rolled for a practice match at Highbury. With the age of television still in its infancy, and the ownership of a set a rarity, it is doubtful whether those present that day realised the role that televised football would come to play in the nation's cultural landscape.

Championship goes south for the first time

In 1930–31 Arsenal not only won the Championship for the first time but also became the first southern club to do so since the inception of the League 43 years earlier. The team lost just four games and notched up 66 points, a record that would stand for 38 years. In only one of their 42 League fixtures did they fail to score. Interestingly, the Gunners' home and away records were identical: Won 14, Drew 5, Lost 2. Jack Lambert top-scored with 38 goals, but all the forwards made handsome contributions. David Jack hit 31 goals, while the brilliant wingers Cliff Bastin and Joe Hulme scored 28 and 14, respectively.

An aggregate 127 goals was not quite enough to set a new record, however. That honour went to runners-up Aston Villa, for whom Tom "Pongo" Waring netted 49 times. Villa scored 128 goals in that campaign, which remains a record in English football's Premier Division.

OPPOSITE. Four of the Arsenal players named for the England team to meet World Champions Italy at Highbury in November 1934. L-R; Copping, Hapgood, Moss and Bowden. The contest, later dubbed "The Battle of Highbury", ended in a 3-2 win for England but commentators were critical of the Italians' behaviour. Copping, Drake, Moss and Bastin all needed treatment for injuries incurred and Hapgood's nose was broken when he was hit in the face.

TOP: 1931: West Bromwich Albion v Birmingham: Pearson, the Albion goalkeeper, dashes across to meet a shot that went past the post.

ABOVE: Eddie Hapgood was Arsenal's powerful full-back who led his team to five Championship medals and two FA Cup victories. He also captained England 21 times in the 1930s.

1938 The first game to be broadcast live on BBC television is the FA Cup Final between Preston North End and Huddersfield. However, only 10,000 people watched compared with 90,000 present in the stadium

1938 The third World Cup is won by Italy for a second tournament running; England still do not participate

1938 England beat Nazi Germany 6-3. The game became infamous because the English team gave a Nazi salute before the game

1938 Aston Villa beat a German select XI the day after the national game but is jeered off the pitch for failing to follow suit and give the Nazi salute

1939 The Football League makes numbers on the back of players' shirts compulsory

1939 The FA suspends all normal competition at the outbreak of war; although the 1939–40 season was started it was cancelled the day after the outbreak of war on 3 September

ABOVE LEFT: Officials of the Football Association meet at their headquarters in Lancaster Gate to make the draw for the fourth round of the FA Cup.

ABOVE RIGHT: Would-be referees take a practical examination using chess pawns to represent players before they appear in front of the Essex County FA Referees Committee.

MIDDLE: Victory – and the Cup. West Brom captain Glidden, surrounded by his elated teammates, carries the Cup after defeating their neighbours Birmingham 2-1. Second Division West Brom were the first team to win promotion and the FA Cup in the same year. Aston Villa also entered the record book in 1931, finishing the season with 128 goals, 49 of which were attributed to Pongo Waring, the season's top marksman.

BELOW: December 1932: Viennese goalkeeper Hiden stops an attack on the Austrian goal by England's Jimmy Hampson at Stamford Bridge. Austria, coached by ex–Bolton player Jimmy Hogan, and recognised as one of the most impressive teams in Europe, were defeated by 4 goals to 3 in an exciting contest. Had Herbert Chapman had his way, Austrian keeper Rudi Hiden would have joined Arsenal in 1930 but the Ministry of Labour refused to allow his transfer from Wiener Sportklub to protect the jobs of British goalkeepers.

Promotion and Cup "double" for West Brom

That season's Cup Final was an all-Midlands affair. Second Division side West Bromwich Albion came out on top against Division One strugglers Birmingham City, becoming the first club to win promotion and the Cup in the same season.

West Brom went up after finishing runners-up to Everton. The following season, 1931–32, the Liverpool club continued an extraordinary run of fluctuating fortunes. Champions in 1928, relegated in 1930, promoted in 1931, Everton lifted the title again in their first season back in the top flight. In winning the Second and First Division championships in successive seasons, Everton emulated the achievement of their city rivals Liverpool between 1904 and 1906. Unsurprisingly, the key to Everton's revival was their goalscoring hero Dixie Dean, whom the club had managed to hold on to despite suffering the drop. Dean couldn't quite match his feat of 1927–28, but his 44 goals were enough to make him the number one marksman once again.

> *Dixie Dean is top scorer again with 44 goals.*

RIGHT: England's goalkeeper, Pearson, keeping out a determined attack from Scotland's forwards in the 1932 Wembley international. England won the game 3-0. Even though England had not competed in the inaugural World Cup, most spectators considered English football to be the best in the world.

BELOW: 50,000 fans packed into Highbury to watch the League Champions.

FIFA unveils World Cup

The main event in international football in the inter-war period was the establishment of a World Cup competition. In 1930, when the inaugural tournament was staged in Uruguay, the prevailing attitude in England was that the country which had given football to the world remained its pre-eminent exponent. The defeat by Spain in 1929 was dismissed as an aberration, and a 7-1 win over the same opposition in 1931 seemed to confirm that view. A few lone voices suggested that English football could learn a thing or two from overseas opposition, but when FIFA unveiled its new tournament, none of the home countries was champing at the bit to be included.

England side run by committee

England certainly lagged behind some of the Continental sides regarding the employment of a manager for the national team. While other countries saw the value in having a single supremo responsible for international team affairs, the England side was still chosen by the International Selection Committee, which had been formed in 1888. The vagaries of this unwieldy system included political manoeuvrings. Committee members who favoured a particular player would try to garner support for their man, and some horse-trading undoubtedly went on. There was little consistency, and in the 1930s nearly a hundred players were capped, although many of these may have played just once or twice before being discarded.

Herbert Chapman was quick to recognise the shortcomings of this system and he persuaded the FA to allow him to take charge of the England side, which toured Italy and Switzerland in May 1933. Chapman thus became the international side's only pre-war manager. England drew with Italy and beat Switzerland, but it would be another decade before the authorities took the idea on board seriously.

Newcastle's controversial victory

At the end of the 1931–32 season Arsenal fans were left to reflect on what might have been. Having faded in the League and seen their crown pass to Everton, the Gunners also lost in the FA Cup Final, and in highly controversial circumstances. Bob John put Arsenal 1-0 up against Newcastle United but it was the equalising goal which provided the game's talking point. The Arsenal defenders momentarily stopped as Jimmy Richardson crossed from the right, the ball appearing to have gone well over the bye-line. Jack Allen pounced to score and the referee allowed the goal to stand. Allen went on to hit the winner 20 minutes from time. Photographic evidence subsequently showed that Arsenal had been hard done by but that was scant consolation. At one point the Gunners looked like becoming the first 20th-century team to achieve the coveted Double; in fact, Chapman's men ended the campaign empty-handed.

ABOVE: Sagar, the Everton goalkeeper, makes a remarkable save in the 1933 Cup Final. Creswell, in white, is nearest the camera, behind him is White and on the left is Herd, Manchester City's centre-forward. This was the first Cup Final in which players wore numbers on the backs of their shirts. Everton was allocated numbers 1–11, printed in black on their white shirts, and Manchester City was given 12–22, written in white on red shirts.

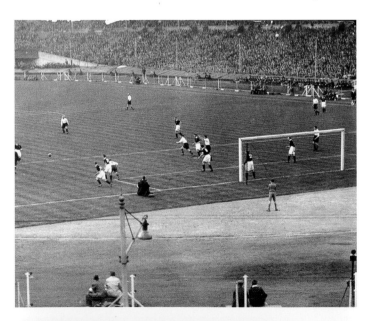

ABOVE LEFT: Play around Manchester City's goal in the 1933 Cup Final. 93,000 people watched as Everton defeated a nervous-looking Manchester City by 3 goals to 0. The 1930s was a successful period in the history of Everton; having been promoted back into Division One in the 1931–32 season the Merseyside team finished the year at the top of the League, pushing Arsenal into second place.

LEFT: The "over the line" Final: Jack, the Arsenal inside-right, gets his head to the ball in front of the Newcastle goal, but McInroy is ready to save the shot. The 1932 Cup Final was a battle between the North and the South remembered for Newcastle's equaliser, which came in the 42nd minute after John had put Arsenal ahead. Arsenal defenders thought the ball had crossed the bye-line before Allen scored for Newcastle but referee Mr W.P.Harper thought otherwise and the goal was given. Allen scored again in the 71st minute and Newcastle took the Cup for the first time since 1924.

League Division One 1930–1944

1930–31

1	Arsenal	66
2	Aston Villa	59
3	Sheffield Wednesday	52
4	Portsmouth	49
5	Huddersfield	48
6	Derby County	46
7	Middlesbrough	46
8	Manchester City	46
9	Liverpool	42
10	Blackburn Rovers	42
11	Sunderland	41
12	Chelsea	40
13	Grimsby	39
14	Bolton Wanderers	38
15	Sheffield United	38
16	Leicester City	36
17	Newcastle United	36
18	West Ham United	36
19	Birmingham City	36
20	Blackpool	32
21	Leeds United	31
22	Manchester United	22

1931–32

1	Everton	56
2	Arsenal	54
3	Sheffield Wednesday	50
4	Huddersfield	48
5	Aston Villa	46
6	West Bromwich Albion	46
7	Sheffield United	46
8	Portsmouth	45
9	Birmingham City	44
10	Liverpool	44
11	Newcastle United	42
12	Chelsea	40
13	Sunderland	40
14	Manchester City	38
15	Derby County	38
16	Blackburn Rovers	38
17	Bolton Wanderers	38
18	Middlesbrough	38
19	Leicester City	37
20	Blackpool	33
21	Grimsby	32
22	West Ham United	31

1932–33

1	Arsenal	58
2	Aston Villa	54
3	Sheffield Wednesday	51
4	West Bromwich Albion	49
5	Newcastle United	49
6	Huddersfield	47
7	Derby County	44
8	Leeds United	44
9	Portsmouth	43
10	Sheffield United	43
11	Everton	41
12	Sunderland	40
13	Birmingham City	39
14	Liverpool	39
15	Blackburn Rovers	38
16	Manchester City	37
17	Middlesbrough	37
18	Chelsea	35
19	Leicester City	35
20	Wolverhampton W.	35
21	Bolton Wanderers	33
22	Blackpool	33

1933–34

1	Arsenal	59
2	Huddersfield	56
3	Tottenham Hotspur	49
4	Derby County	45
5	Manchester City	45
6	Sunderland	44
7	West Bromwich Albion	44
8	Blackburn Rovers	43
9	Leeds United	42
10	Portsmouth	42
11	Sheffield Wednesday	41
12	Stoke	41
13	Aston Villa	40
14	Everton	40
15	Wolverhampton W.	40
16	Middlesbrough	39
17	Leicester City	39
18	Liverpool	38
19	Chelsea	36
20	Birmingham City	36
21	Newcastle United	34
22	Sheffield United	31

1934–35

1	Arsenal	58
2	Sunderland	54
3	Sheffield Wednesday	49
4	Manchester City	48
5	Grimsby	45
6	Derby County	45
7	Liverpool	45
8	Everton	44
9	West Bromwich Albion	44
10	Stoke	42
11	Preston	42
12	Chelsea	41
13	Aston Villa	41
14	Portsmouth	40
15	Blackburn Rovers	39
16	Huddersfield	38
17	Wolverhampton W.	38
18	Leeds United	38
19	Birmingham City	36
20	Middlesbrough	34
21	Leicester City	33
22	Tottenham Hotspur	30

1935–36

1	Sunderland	56
2	Derby County	48
3	Huddersfield	48
4	Stoke	47
5	Brentford	46
6	Arsenal	45
7	Preston	44
8	Chelsea	43
9	Manchester City	42
10	Portsmouth	42
11	Leeds United	41
12	Birmingham City	41
13	Bolton Wanderers	41
14	Middlesbrough	40
15	Wolverhampton W.	40
16	Everton	39
17	Grimsby	39
18	West Bromwich Albion	38
19	Liverpool	38
20	Sheffield Wednesday	38
21	Aston Villa	35
22	Blackburn Rovers	33

1936–37

1	Manchester City	57
2	Charlton Athletic	54
3	Arsenal	52
4	Derby County	49
5	Wolverhampton W.	47
6	Brentford	46
7	Middlesbrough	46
8	Sunderland	44
9	Portsmouth	44
10	Stoke	42
11	Birmingham City	41
12	Grimsby	41
13	Chelsea	41
14	Preston	41
15	Huddersfield	39
16	West Bromwich Albion	38
17	Everton	37
18	Liverpool	35
19	Leeds United	34
20	Bolton Wanderers	34
21	Manchester United	32
22	Sheffield Wednesday	30

1937–38

1	Arsenal	52
2	Wolverhampton W.	51
3	Preston	49
4	Charlton Athletic	46
5	Middlesbrough	46
6	Brentford	45
7	Bolton Wanderers	45
8	Sunderland	44
9	Leeds United	43
10	Chelsea	41
11	Liverpool	41
12	Blackpool	40
13	Derby County	40
14	Everton	39
15	Huddersfield	39
16	Leicester City	39
17	Stoke	38
18	Birmingham City	38
19	Portsmouth	38
20	Grimsby	38
21	Manchester City	36
22	West Bromwich Albion	36

1938–39

1	Everton	59
2	Wolverhampton W.	55
3	Charlton Athletic	50
4	Middlesbrough	49
5	Arsenal	47
6	Derby County	46
7	Stoke	46
8	Bolton Wanderers	45
9	Preston	44
10	Grimsby	43
11	Liverpool	42
12	Aston Villa	41
13	Leeds United	41
14	Manchester United	38
15	Blackpool	38
16	Sunderland	38
17	Portsmouth	37
18	Brentford	36
19	Huddersfield	35
20	Chelsea	33
21	Birmingham City	32
22	Leicester City	29

1939–40

1	Liverpool	57
2	Manchester United	56
3	Wolverhampton W.	56
4	Stoke	55
5	Blackpool	50
6	Sheffield United	49
7	Preston	47
8	Aston Villa	45
9	Sunderland	44
10	Everton	43
11	Middlesbrough	42
12	Portsmouth	41
13	Arsenal	41
14	Derby County	41
15	Chelsea	39
16	Grimsby	38
17	Blackburn Rovers	36
18	Bolton Wanderers	34
19	Charlton Athletic	34
20	Huddersfield	33
21	Brentford	25
22	Leeds United	18

FA Cup Finals

1930	Arsenal	v	Huddersfield Town	2-0
1931	West Bromwich A.	v	Birmingham	2-1
1932	Newcastle United	v	Arsenal	2-1
1933	Everton	v	Manchester City	3-0
1934	Manchester City	v	Portsmouth	2-1
1935	Sheffield Wed.	v	West Bromwich A.	4-2
1936	Arsenal	v	Sheffield United	1-0
1937	Sunderland	v	Preston North End	3-1
1938	Preston North End	v	Huddersfield	1-0
1939	Portsmouth	v	Wolverhampton W.	4-1
1940–45			no competition	

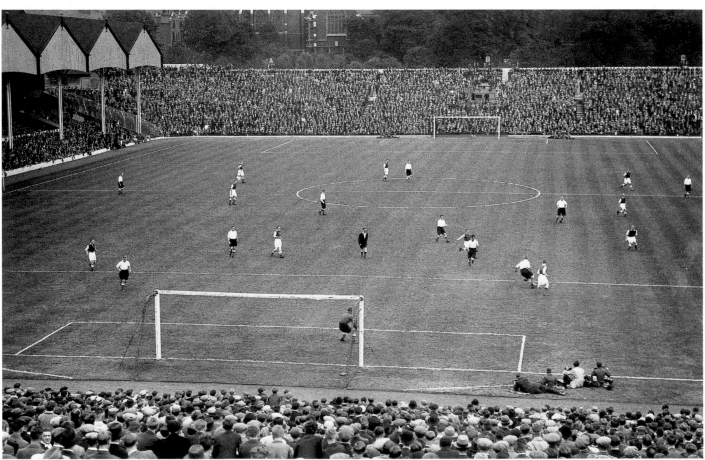

Arsenal follow Huddersfield into record books

The following three seasons saw Arsenal – and Chapman – equal Huddersfield's achievement of the previous decade. The Gunners' record over those three Championship-winning campaigns was impressive: they won 73 of their 126 League matches, were beaten just 24 times and scored over 300 goals.

> *Chapman's Arsenal were quick to turn defence into attack.*

Chapman's sudden death in January 1934 meant that he did not see the triumphant completion of the hat-trick with either club. Yet no one was in any doubt as to who masterminded both achievements. Chapman was known for his attention to detail, and it was typical of the man that he insisted on watching his juniors play, despite the adverse conditions and the fact that he was already running a temperature. He contracted pneumonia and succumbed to the illness on 6 January. He was 62 years old.

Chapman, the visionary manager

Chapman's legacy stretched far beyond another domestic Championship for the Gunners. He was a prescient manager and many of the ideas he championed came to fruition long after his death. These included the advent of night matches under floodlights, the use of numbered shirts and even the Champions League!

In many ways Chapman's Arsenal side played in the modern style. The team was well schooled in the art of absorbing pressure, then quickly turning defence into attack. Swift counter-attacking football is one of the hallmarks of the modern era, yet to the fans in the 1930s it often seemed that the Gunners won matches when they appeared to be on the back foot. This gave rise to the "Lucky Arsenal" jibe, which stuck for so long.

Chapman was also ahead of his time as far as transfer dealings were concerned. In 1930 he signed goalkeeper Rudi Hiden from Wiener Sportklub for £2600. International transfers of this type were almost unheard of, and this one sparked a row which is all too familiar more than 70 years later. The Ministry of Labour refused to sanction Hiden's entry into the country, on the grounds that he would put a British goalkeeper out of work.

OPPOSITE ABOVE: Frank Swift, Manchester City's 19-year-old goalkeeper clears from a corner kick in the 1934 Final at Wembley. After Cup Final nerves disrupted their performance in the previous year's tie, Manchester City defeated Portsmouth 2-1 in a dramatic game. Portsmouth led until almost the last 15 minutes of the match when Allen was knocked unconscious in the penalty area. While he recovered Tilson scored two goals in quick succession for City.

OPPOSITE BELOW: 1934: Arsenal's first practice match of the season. Arsenal were the most successful team of the era. League Champions in 1930–31 and 1932–33 and narrowly missing winning the Double in 1932 when they came second in the League and were runners-up in the Cup. However, disaster struck on 6 January when Herbert Chapman, manager and driving force behind their achievements, died suddenly. Director George Allison took on management duties and Arsenal finished the season on top of the First Division. Allison continued Chapman's work in strengthening the side, signing centre-forward Ted Drake and wing-halves Crayston and Copping.

BELOW: During a game against Chelsea at Stamford Bridge in 1934, Blackburn players appeal to the referee after a goal was given against them – proving that some aspects of the game remain unchanged more than 70 years later.

Walsall in giant-killing act

Almost inevitably, fans of rival clubs envied and resented Arsenal's success in equal measure. Any ill-feeling was not simply down to the club's dominance on the pitch. This was a period of depression and high unemployment, and while the industrial heartlands of the Midlands and the North were hit hard, Highbury epitomised the affluence of a capital, which seemed impervious to the economic climate.

Thus, in 1933 there was a widespread feeling of schadenfreude as Arsenal fell victim to one of the great giant-killing acts of all time. The team was weakened by the loss of several players through illness and injury, but no one expected an upset when mighty Arsenal went to Walsall for a third round FA Cup-tie. There were three new faces in the Gunners' line-up and each of them had a nightmare. One of the trio, defender Tommy Black, gave away the penalty which resulted in the Third Division side going 2-0 up. That was how it finished. Black had no chance to make amends; he was transfer-listed immediately.

Chapman's successor was George Allison, a club director who was best known as a radio commentator. He had no playing experience, but the organisation at Highbury was so well established that this hardly proved a handicap, at least not in the short term. Allison had the benefit of inheriting Tom Whittaker as his right-hand man. Whittaker was an excellent coach and also a top physiotherapist. His methods meant that injured players were back in action in days rather than weeks, another factor in the club's success.

LEFT: Arsenal stars (r-l) Alex James, goalkeeper Frank Moss and Eddie Hapgood admire the juvenile prowess of Hapgood's son, Tony. All three players had international experience: Hapgood and Moss with England and James representing Scotland. Of the three, Hapgood was most capped, making 30 appearances during 1933–39. Moss's recurring shoulder injury forced him to retire in 1937 to take up the post of manager of Heart of Midlothian in Edinburgh.

BELOW: Amazing scenes were witnessed at Arsenal with huge numbers of people hoping to attend the clash between Spurs and Arsenal in January 1934. In the background is the vast crowd who were unable to get into the game. In 1936 a new East Stand was opened at Highbury, which provided seating for a further 8000 spectators.

Drake keeps Gunners on top

Allison had mixed fortunes in the transfer market as he sought to keep Arsenal at the top of the pile. He told a young Len Shackleton that he wouldn't make the grade, and it was Sunderland and Newcastle who would benefit from the services of one of the great inside-forwards of the postwar era. If Allison made a long-term mistake with Shackleton, he certainly made an inspired signing shortly after Chapman's death. The acquisition of Ted Drake from Southampton undoubtedly helped maintain the club's supremacy. In 1934–35, his first full season at Highbury, Drake hit 42 League goals, making him the First Division's top marksman. In December 1935 Drake hit all seven of Arsenal's goals when they won 7–1 at Villa Park, and he also scored the goal which beat Sheffield United in the 1936 Cup Final.

RIGHT ABOVE: While the other members of the team are in Brighton preparing for their FA Cup-tie with Bolton Wanderers, George Hunt (left) and Ted Drake remain at Highbury for treatment. They are seen in the electrical room where Drake is receiving infrared rays. Hunt played with Arsenal for just one season, coming from Spurs in October 1937 for a fee of £7500 and transferring to Bolton for £4000 in March 1938.

RIGHT CENTRE: A disputed goal at the Burnley end of the field when Sheffield Wednesday met Burnley in the semi-final of the FA Cup at Villa Park in 1935. Wednesday went on to win 3–0, having defeated Arsenal in the previous round.

BELOW LEFT: West Brom attack the Sheffield Wednesday goal in the 1935 FA Cup Final. It was a six-goal thriller, the highest goal tally in the showpiece since Bury's 6–0 win over Derby County in 1903. The crowd had hardly settled after kick-off before Wednesday took the lead, while Rimmer's final goal for the Midlands team came in the last minute. Sheffield Wednesday won 4–2.

BELOW RIGHT: Action around the Spurs goal in the 1935 Cup-tie between Spurs and Bolton Wanderers. Bolton narrowly missed out on a place in the Final, losing to West Brom in the replay of the semi-final. In the 1934–35 season there were still only four southern teams in Division One: Arsenal, Chelsea, Portsmouth and Spurs.

LEFT: Manchester City playing Portsmouth at Maine Road in January 1936. City finished ninth that season but went on to win the League the following year, losing only seven times.

BELOW LEFT: Alex James supported by his teammates holds the 1936 FA Cup aloft, Arsenal having overcome Sheffield United in the Final by one goal to nil. The London club's goal was scored by Ted Drake who had recently rejoined the side after a knee operation. The victorious team returned to Islington Town Hall in North London driving through two miles of cheering crowds. In response to the demands of the fans, James and Drake stood on the roof of the motor vehicle holding the cup between them.

BELOW: Magnall heads Millwall's first goal in the 1937 Cup-tie against Manchester City. Millwall became the first Third Division team to reach the semi-final of the Cup and were eventually eliminated by winners Sunderland.

OPPOSITE: Arsenal's Kirchen leaps to challenge Strong, the Portsmouth keeper at Highbury in April 1937. Television coverage of football began with a practice match transmitted from Highbury in 1937, but it wasn't until the 1940s that those with television sets could expect regular transmissions of games.

Sunderland hold off Gunners

It was Sunderland who halted Arsenal's run of Championship successes. The Wearsiders' star was inside-forward Horatio "Raich" Carter, and he inspired the club's title-winning campaign of 1935–36, their first since 1913. Sunderland couldn't maintain their form, slipping to 8th the following season, but there was compensation in the form of a first FA Cup triumph. They came from a goal behind against Preston to win 3-1 in 1937. A Preston side including Bill Shankly made it to Wembley again the following year, with Huddersfield as their opponents. A drab, goalless 90 minutes meant that this became the first Wembley Final to go into extra time. It was also the first to be decided by a penalty, George Mutch scoring from the spot with the last kick of the match.

Swift is City star

Manchester City were another side that tasted both League and Cup success in the 1930s. In the 1933 FA Cup Final City were thumped 3-0 by Everton, who thus completed a remarkable treble, following their Championship wins in the Second and First Divisions in the previous two seasons. The 1933 Final was unique in that the teams wore numbered shirts for the first time, but not in the familiar manner. The Everton shirts were numbered 1 to 11, City's 12 to 22.

City bounced back to reach the Final the following year, and this time they got their hands on the Cup with a 2-1 win over Portsmouth. The City side boasted a fine wing-half called Matt Busby, but it was 19-year-old goalkeeper Frank Swift who made the headlines. Swift blamed himself for the goal which gave Portsmouth a half-time lead. Fred Tilson scored twice for City after the break, but when reporters behind Swift's goal began counting down the minutes, it all proved too much. At the final whistle he collapsed with nervous exhaustion. Three years later Swift helped City to win their first Championship, 44 years after the club entered the League. He went on to become one of the all-time great keepers, spending his entire playing career at Maine Road. After retiring from the game he turned his hand to journalism and was among those killed in the Munich air crash in 1958.

> *Manchester City and Everton wear numbered shirts for the first time.*

World football catches up

England's claim to footballing supremacy was dented in the early 1930s. There were defeats against France, Czechoslovakia and Hungary, albeit all away from home. In December 1933 Hugo Meisl's much-vaunted Austrian "Wunderteam" came to Stamford Bridge. England played to their strengths and won the match 4-3, but the Austrians had displayed some dazzling skills and were on top for long periods.

A year later, 14 November 1934, Vittorio Pozzo's Italy, the newly crowned World Champions, came to Highbury to try to become the first team to win on English soil. Pozzo, like Hugo Meisl, believed in meticulous preparation. In contrast, the England players all turned out for their clubs the previous Saturday, and there were several withdrawals before the team was announced, 24 hours before the game. There was hardly any time for practice, but England at least benefited from the fact that seven Arsenal players were in the line-up.

"Battle of Highbury"

It was an ugly game, one which would go down in the annals as the "Battle of Highbury". The scene was set in the opening moments when Ted Drake clashed with Italy's centre-half Luisito Monti. The latter came off worse, breaking a bone in his foot and eventually having to leave the field. His team-mates were bent on retribution for what they regarded as a blatant foul. As the World Champions took their eye off the ball – quite literally – England eased into a 3-0 lead. In the second half the visitors regained their composure and began to play. They scored twice, both from the great Giuseppe Meazza, but couldn't complete the comeback. England's record remained intact, but at a cost. Eric Brook and Eddie Hapgood had to go to hospital and there was a queue of players for the treatment table.

No stroll for England in Vienna

Eighteen months later, 6 May 1936, England went to Vienna and lost to Austria, in circumstances which showed up the international team's lack of an overseer. On the day of the match the players accepted Hugo Meisl's "generous" offer of a walking tour of the city, and it was only after they had pounded the streets for some miles that the players realised that the hospitality was perhaps not as gracious as it first appeared. England lost the game 2-1.

In May 1938 England went to Berlin to face Germany in the Olympic Stadium. The players reluctantly agreed to perform the Nazi salute prior to the game, and although they ran out convincing 6-3 winners, the occasion was overlaid with political rather than sporting significance.

LEFT: A large crowd gathered to watch Arsenal – Brentford on Good Friday morning, 1938. Arsenal won the League again that year while Brentford repeated the sixth position from the previous year's campaign.

BELOW LEFT: Gurney, in stripes, scores Sunderland's equaliser.

BELOW RIGHT: Cup Final 1937: O'Donnell, the Preston centre-forward and scorer of their first-half goal, receives attention after an injury. Despite holding 6 League titles, it was not until 1937 that Sunderland were successful in the Cup. After being 1-0 down through the whole of the first half, the team from the north-east came back to win the match 3-1 with goals from Gurney, Carter and Burbanks.

Tommy Lawton

Celebrated by Stanley Matthews as "a brilliant header of the ball", centre-forward Tommy Lawton also had two good feet and blistering pace. When he joined Third Division Notts County in 1947, attendances at Meadow Lane soared. The affection was mutual, with Bolton-born Lawton naming Nottingham his adopted city. He collected 103 goals in 166 run-outs for the club, and was also capped for England – one of the few lower division players ever to wear the national colours. In all his career, he was never booked or sent off.

A teenage sensation at Burnley, he was quickly signed up to a bigger club, Everton, for the then remarkable fee of £6500. As part of Everton's 1938–39 Championship-winning side, he scored 35 goals and seemed set to be the next Dixie Dean. But the outbreak of war prevented Lawton from playing other than unofficial internationals, and he moved to Chelsea when he was demobbed. It was a golden time: in 1946–7 he broke the club's scoring record, with 26 goals in 34 matches.

Joining Brentford as player-manager in 1952, aged 33, he admitted to finding it a struggle, but he bowed out of the Football League in fine style with a spell in dangerously good form at Arsenal. He died of pneumonia in 1996.

TOP: Thousands on the terraces watch as Wolverhampton's Dorsett scores in the 10th minute of the second half of the 1939 Cup Final.

MIDDLE: A dramatic moment in the League Cup Final at Blackburn. Gallimore, Preston's right-back, was trying to stop the ball but instead kicked it into his own goal. Despite this, Preston beat Arsenal 2-1.

BOTTOM: England thwarted by the Wales goalkeeper in their international match at Middlesbrough in 1937. England went on to win the game 2-1. There were growing concerns that England needed a full-time manager in order to play a dominant role in world football.

Arsenal buy Wolves star

In 1937–38 Arsenal became champions for the fifth time in eight seasons. Even so, the Gunners' air of invincibility was beginning to fade. The great Alex James retired at the end of the 1936–37 campaign, and in August 1938 Allison splashed out £14,000 on a replacement.

The man with the new British record price tag on his head was Bryn Jones. No doubt Wolves were reluctant to sell their Welsh international, not least because they had a burgeoning side and had just finished runners-up to Arsenal by a single point. The depth of the Highbury coffers proved decisive, however, and Arsenal got their man. Whether the weight of expectation rested heavily on his shoulders, Jones was not at his best in 1938–39, which would be the last full season for seven years. Arsenal slipped to 5th in the League, Everton taking top honours, with Wolves once again having to settle for the runners-up spot.

Pompey hold the cup for seven years

The season turned into a double agony for Wolves as they went down in the Cup Final, too. They faced Portsmouth, a team languishing in the bottom half of the table, and were red-hot favourites to lift the trophy. Portsmouth used all manner of lucky omens and superstitions to aid their cause, as they had done in 1934. Bringing in comedian Bud Flanagan to relax the team hadn't worked back then, but manager Jack Tinn continued to put a lot of faith in his "lucky spats". There had been a lot of publicity surrounding Wolves' use of so-called "monkey gland" treatment to aid the performance of their players. It didn't help them on the big day. It is said that when the Pompey camp saw the spidery scrawl of their opponents in the official autograph book, they knew they had a golden opportunity. The hands that had signed the book had obviously been shaking, and those feelings of anxiety accompanied the Wolves' players onto the pitch. Portsmouth ran out comfortable 4-1 winners and would remain Cup holders for seven years.

BELOW LEFT: Portsmouth beat the odds when they outplayed favourites Wolverhampton Wanderers to lift the F A Cup in 1939. Such was the quality of their play the 4-1 victory didn't flatter the victors. Jimmy Guthrie is chaired off the field carrying the trophy.

BELOW RIGHT: Now for the homecoming: Pompey captain, Guthrie, carries off the FA Cup under escort. With the outbreak of war just months away Portsmouth would remain Cup holders for seven years.

OPPOSITE ABOVE: A scene at Upton Park where West Ham United played Leicester City showing the usual football fans watching the game – in Army uniform. This picture was taken the day before war was declared and emphasises the degree to which the war was becoming inevitable.

OPPOSITE BELOW LEFT: Manchester United's stadium after a bomb had dropped through the roof of the main stand.

OPPOSITE BELOW RIGHT: All factories and institutions had their own roof-spotters, usually members of staff who did an extra shift. The roof-spotter's job was to act as an early warning to those inside the building of the approach of a raid. Here the roof spotter works on while West Ham play Chelsea in December 1940, at the height of the Blitz. The gate was less than 2000.

Wartime football boosts morale

The 1939–40 season was just three games old when it was aborted due to the outbreak of war. Initially, all forms of football ceased, but Winston Churchill was among those who appreciated the morale-boosting role that the game could play. The Board of Trade even issued coupons to cover the purchase of football kit, effectively recognising that here was a commodity that had to be rationed, but not dispensed with entirely. Regional football was introduced, and although there were both League and Cup competitions, the honours were hardly something to be coveted. Travel restrictions meant that clubs were allowed to field guest players, and those which had large numbers of soldiers stationed nearby reaped the benefit. Aldershot, for example, regularly fielded international players, thanks to this highly flexible system.

Wartime internationals

After war was declared, in September of the following year, international football continued. But as with the revamped League competition, the matches were inevitably a victim of circumstance. In 1943, for example, Blackpool's young centre-forward Stan Mortensen made his debut – against England! Mortensen had been a substitute for the match against Wales and came on for the opposition after one of the Welsh players was injured.

30 games were played during the conflict, together with five "Victory" internationals between September 1945 and May 1946. These were not accorded official international status in the record books.

Hampden roars as fans flock back to the game

As had happened in 1918, the end of the global conflict brought the fans flocking back to football. The clubs had to assess the state of their stadiums and check on their players. Inevitably, war had claimed the lives of some, and those who did return for duty were seven years older. It was a chaotic period, with many clubs forced to try out players who might otherwise never have been given an opportunity. There was no time to restart a League programme in 1945–46, but the FA Cup made a welcome return to the sporting calendar. Football was back.

RIGHT: Part of the vast crowd of 133,000 spectators at Hampden Park who watched England play Scotland on 22 April 1944.

BELOW: An England v Scotland game at Wembley in October 1941 gives fans some relief from the austerity and the trauma of the hostilities. Scotland's goalkeeper, Dawson, has a hard job to prevent England's forwards scoring from this clear-cut opportunity.

Scottish League 1930–1940

1929–1930

1	Rangers	60
2	Motherwell	55
3	Aberdeen	53
4	Celtic	49
5	St Mirren	41
6	Partick Thistle	41
7	Falkirk	41
8	Kilmarnock	39
9	Ayr United	38
10	Hearts	37
11	Clyde	37
12	Airdrieonians	36
13	Hamilton	35
14	Dundee	34
15	Queen's Park	34
16	Cowdenbeath	33
17	Hibernian	29
18	Greenock Morton	27
19	Dundee United	22
20	St Johnstone	19

1930–31

1	Rangers	60
2	Celtic	58
3	Motherwell	56
4	Partick Thistle	53
5	Hearts	44
6	Aberdeen	41
7	Cowdenbeath	41
8	Dundee	39
9	Airdrieonians	39
10	Hamilton	37
11	Kilmarnock	35
12	Clyde	34
13	Queen's Park	33
14	Falkirk	32
15	St Mirren	30
16	Greenock Morton	29
17	Leith Athletic	27
18	Ayr United	27
19	Hibernian	25
20	East Fife	20

1931–32

1	Motherwell	66
2	Rangers	61
3	Celtic	48
4	Third Lanark	46
5	St Mirren	44
6	Partick Thistle	42
7	Aberdeen	41
8	Hearts	39
9	Kilmarnock	39
10	Hamilton	38
11	Dundee	38
12	Cowdenbeath	38
13	Clyde	35
14	Airdrieonians	32
15	Greenock Morton	31
16	Queen's Park	31
17	Ayr United	29
18	Falkirk	27
19	Dundee United	19
20	Leith Athletic	16

1932–33

1	Rangers	62
2	Motherwell	59
3	Hearts	50
4	Celtic	48
5	St Johnstone	44
6	Aberdeen	42
7	St Mirren	42
8	Hamilton	42
9	Queen's Park	41
10	Partick Thistle	40
11	Falkirk	36
12	Clyde	35
13	Third Lanark	35
14	Kilmarnock	35
15	Dundee	33
16	Ayr United	30
17	Cowdenbeath	25
18	Airdrieonians	23
19	Greenock Morton	21
20	East Stirlingshire	17

1933–34

1	Rangers	66
2	Motherwell	62
3	Celtic	47
4	Queen Of The South	45
5	Aberdeen	44
6	Hearts	44
7	Kilmarnock	43
8	Ayr United	42
9	St Johnstone	40
10	Falkirk	38
11	Hamilton	38
12	Dundee	36
13	Partick Thistle	33
14	Clyde	31
15	Queen's Park	31
16	Hibernian	27
17	St Mirren	27
18	Airdrieonians	26
19	Third Lanark	25
20	Cowdenbeath	15

1934–35

1	Rangers	55
2	Celtic	52
3	Hearts	50
4	Hamilton	48
5	St Johnstone	46
6	Aberdeen	44
7	Motherwell	40
8	Dundee	40
9	Kilmarnock	38
10	Clyde	38
11	Hibernian	36
12	Queen's Park	36
13	Partick Thistle	35
14	Airdrieonians	33
15	Dunfermline Athletic	31
16	Albion Rovers	29
17	Queen Of The South	29
18	Ayr United	29
19	St Mirren	27
20	Falkirk	24

1935–36

1	Celtic	66
2	Rangers	61
3	Aberdeen	61
4	Motherwell	48
5	Hearts	47
6	Hamilton	37
7	St Johnstone	37
8	Kilmarnock	35
9	Third Lanark	35
10	Partick Thistle	34
11	Arbroath	33
12	Dundee	32
13	Queen's Park	32
14	Dunfermline Athletic	32
15	Queen Of The South	31
16	Albion Rovers	30
17	Hibernian	29
18	Clyde	28
19	Airdrieonians	27
20	Ayr United	25

1936–37

1	Rangers	61
2	Aberdeen	54
3	Celtic	52
4	Motherwell	51
5	Hearts	51
6	Third Lanark	46
7	Falkirk	44
8	Hamilton	41
9	Dundee	39
10	Clyde	38
11	Kilmarnock	37
12	St Johnstone	36
13	Partick Thistle	34
14	Arbroath	31
15	Queen's Park	30
16	St Mirren	29
17	Hibernian	25
18	Queen Of The South	24
19	Dunfermline Athletic	21
20	Albion Rovers	16

1937–38

1	Celtic	61
2	Hearts	58
3	Rangers	49
4	Falkirk	47
5	Motherwell	44
6	Aberdeen	39
7	Partick Thistle	39
8	St Johnstone	39
9	Third Lanark	35
10	Hibernian	35
11	Arbroath	35
12	Queen's Park	34
13	Hamilton	33
14	St Mirren	33
15	Clyde	33
16	Queen Of The South	33
17	Ayr United	33
18	Kilmarnock	33
19	Dundee	32
20	Greenock Morton	15

1938–39

1	Rangers	59
2	Celtic	48
3	Aberdeen	46
4	Hearts	45
5	Falkirk	45
6	Queen Of The South	43
7	Hamilton	41
8	St Johnstone	40
9	Clyde	39
10	Kilmarnock	39
11	Partick Thistle	38
12	Motherwell	37
13	Hibernian	35
14	Ayr United	35
15	Third Lanark	32
16	Albion Rovers	30
17	Arbroath	30
18	St Mirren	29
19	Queen's Park	27
20	Raith Rovers	22

1940–1945   No Competition.

Scottish Cup Finals

1930	Rangers	v	Partick Thistle	0-0
	Rangers	v	Partick Thistle	replay 2-1
1931	Celtic	v	Motherwell	2-2
	Celtic	v	Motherwell	replay 4-2
1932	Rangers	v	Kilmarnock	1-1
	Rangers	v	Kilmarnock	replay 3-0
1933	Celtic	v	Motherwell	1-0
1934	Rangers	v	St Mirren	5-0
1935	Rangers	v	Hamilton	2-1
1936	Rangers	v	Third Lanark	1-0
1937	Celtic	v	Aberdeen	2-1
1938	East Fife	v	Kilmarnock	1-1
	East Fife	v	Kilmarnock	replay 4-2
1939	Clyde	v	Motherwell	4-0
1940–1945			no competition	

Motherwell break Old Firm grip

Since surviving relegation by the skin of their teeth in 1924–25, Motherwell had been on an upward curve. The Steelmen finished third behind Rangers and Celtic twice at the back end of the decade, and split the Old Firm with a runner-up spot in 1926–27. Manager John 'Sailor' Hunter also organised a highly successful Continental tour, in which the men from Fir Park beat Real Madrid and drew with Barcelona.

By 1930 Motherwell were on the cusp of a breakthrough, scenting major honours for the first time since the club's formation in 1886. The next five seasons saw the team take the League runners-up spot on three more occasions, to Rangers each time. But in 1931–32 they turned the tables on the men from Ibrox, taking the title by five points. It was an era that brought an avalanche of goals. A forward line including Willie McFadyen and George Stevenson helped Motherwell to top the 100-goal mark four years running, the division's most potent attack in each of those campaigns. McFadyen hit 52 of Motherwell's 119 goals during the Championship-winning season, beating Jimmy McGrory's record for the top division.

Motherwell also made three Cup Final appearances in the 30s, losing twice to Celtic, then having put out the men from Parkhead in the quarters in 1938–39, they crashed 4–0 to Clyde in the Final. Clyde's first silverware came when they were a mid-table side, but Motherwell, too, had by now begun to slide as the great team of the early 30s was broken up.

BELOW: Even with Gallacher in the strike force Scotland couldn't score and went down 3-0 at Wembley in 1934.

McPhail stars for Rangers

Motherwell's title success of 1931–32 broke a 28-year grip on the Championship exerted by the Old Firm. It brought no sea change in fortune, though; Rangers and Celtic would go on to share the League spoils for the next 16 years. Rangers had the whip hand, taking a seventh title in 10 years in 1938–39, when hostilities brought League football to an end for seven years. In that final season before the outbreak of war, Rangers finished the campaign 11 points clear of Celtic, the biggest margin since the 16-point gulf of 1928–29. The Cup also went to Ibrox five times during the 30s, making Rangers the dominant force in knockout, football too. In 1933 they boasted 10 Scottish internationals on their books, plus three who had been capped for Ireland. One of the stars of the era was inside-forward Bob McPhail, who joined the club in 1927. He won six Cup medals in all with Rangers, and was a teenager in the Airdrie side that lifted the trophy in 1924.

Celtic were crowned League Champions twice during the decade, and added three Cup wins to the Parkhead honours board. Jimmy Delaney was in the side that beat Aberdeen in the 1936–37 Cup Final, the first leg of a remarkable personal treble. Delaney would add Cup wins with Manchester United (1948) and Derry City (1954) to his medal haul, and collected a fourth, losing the FAI final while playing for Cork Athletic in 1956.

Celtic's successes of this period were overshadowed by the death of 22-year-old 'keeper John Thomson, who died from head injuries sustained during an Old Firm clash at Ibrox, 5 September 1931. Famed for diving fearlessly at the feet of onrushing attackers, the man dubbed the "Prince of Goalkeepers" received the fatal blow after tangling with Rangers' Sam English.

LEFT: Scotland had their revenge the following year with a resounding 2-0 win at Hampden in 1935 with Aberdeen-born Douglas "Dally" Duncan scoring both goals. Here, Hibbs, the England goalkeeper, prepares to save as Gallacher, the Scotland centre-forward, rushes in to follow up.

Cup glory for Fifers

Special mention goes to East Fife, who along with Motherwell and Clyde were the only club outside the Old Firm to land a piece of silverware during the decade. In 1937–38 the Fifers became the first team from outside the top tier to lift the Cup. The draw was kind: they faced four other Second Division sides en route to Hampden, but there was also a fine win over Aberdeen, a top six team in League One. The Fifers needed five replays in all, including the final against Kilmarnock, which they won 4-2 after extra-time.

One of East Fife's Cup victims that year was Raith Rovers, another Division Two side on the record-breaking trail. Raith hit 142 goals in their 34-match League programme, netting 27 more than any other club that term. They went up as Champions by a country mile, but found life among the elite a lot harder: 26 defeats in 1938–39 meant a swift return from whence they had come. A British record in the Goals For column was some consolation.

A record 149,547 crowd pack Hampden

The national side fared less well than in the previous decade, recording just one outright win in the Home International Championship. On 17 April 1937 England came to Glasgow with just second place up for grabs, Wales having already sewn up the Championship with maximum points. That was more than enough incentive for the Scots. A world record 149,547 people crammed into Hampden Park to see Scotland beat the Auld Enemy 3-1, McPhail hitting two late goals. Two years later, this was the only fixture on the calendar, Scotland and England playing out 15 wartime internationals between December 1939 and April 1945. The League programme was dropped in favour of regional competition, clubs vying for honours such as the Scottish Emergency Cup and the Scottish Summer Cup. When normal service was restored in 1946–47, there was a third domestic trophy up for grabs.

Alex James

Alex James was the outstanding player of Herbert Chapman's mighty Arsenal side of the 1930s. Probably the most complete player of his generation, James was equally adept in the scheming role or as a finisher. Chapman paid Preston £8750 for his services in 1929. It proved to be money well spent. Over the next eight years James was the orchestrator-in-chief in a phenomenally successful spell, which included four Championships and two FA Cup victories. James was a wayward star, however, and that contributed to the fact that he won a meagre eight caps for Scotland. One of those came in March 1928, when Scotland took on England at Wembley. James was outstanding, scoring twice in a 5-1 victory and cementing his place in the annals as one of the famous "Wembley Wizards".

1945–1959
The Golden Era

The early postwar years were a golden era for English football. The global conflict might have been over but Britain faced years of austerity and rationing. Ex-servicemen had money burning a hole in the pockets of their demob suits and precious little to spend it on. When it came to mass entertainment and escapism, football had few rivals. More than 35 million people crammed into football grounds all around the country when the League programme was relaunched in 1946–47. Within a couple of years the 40-million mark was surpassed.

1945 With Old Trafford a bomb site, Matt Busby is appointed manager of Manchester United

1946 Walter Winterbottom becomes the first National Coach

1946 33 spectators are killed when crowd barriers collapse at a Cup tie between Bolton and Stoke City

1946 England rejoins FIFA after the dispute in 1928

1946 England teams up with the other home nations to field a one-off postwar National side against the Rest of Europe, resulting in a 6-1 victory for Great Britain

1946 Derby County win the first FA Cup in the aftermath of the war by beating Charlton Athletic 4-1 in the Final

1946 Scottish League Cup introduced

1947 First £20,000 transfer – Tommy Lawton from Chelsea to Notts County

1947 Charlton beat Burnley 1-0 in the FA Cup Final

1948 Stanley Matthews wins the first Football Writers' Association Footballer of the Year award

1949 1,272,155 spectators make a record Football League attendance on 27th December

1949 Fred Wall and Stanley Rous are knighted for their services to football

1949 Sports Report is broadcast by BBC Radio for the first time

1949 Rangers become the first Scottish club to do the domestic treble

1950 The Football League increases the number of clubs from 88 to 92

1950 England compete in the World Cup for the first time. The event is held in Brazil, but won by Uruguay and England fail to clear the group stages

1950 Portsmouth win the League Championship for a second consecutive year. The unexpected postwar success of the club was due to many ex-servicemen stationed in the town joining the team

1950 Scotland qualify for the World Cup but refuse to participate after finishing runners-up to England in the Home International Championship

1950 Sheffield Wednesday gain promotion to Division One at the expense of neighbours United, thanks to a 0.008 superior goal average

1951 The increased use of floodlights, which were banned between 1930 and 1950, prompted the introduction of the white football

1953 Hungary beat England 6-3 at Wembley, England's first official defeat on home soil

1954 UEFA, Union of European Football Associations is formed

1954 Fifth World Cup competition is held in Switzerland and won by West Germany. England compete but lose to Uruguay in the quarter finals

League grows to 92 clubs

The huge wave of popularity led to many minor clubs seeking League status. In 1950 four applications were accepted. Colchester, Scunthorpe, Gillingham and Shrewsbury were added to the Division Three ranks, thereby increasing the League from 88 to 92 clubs.

The football that the fans flocked to see in those early postwar years was not always of the highest standard. The players that survived from the pre-war era were seven years older. Clubs were squeezed, since young talent could not be developed overnight. In an effort to steal a march on their rivals, many clubs tried out players on an unprecedented scale, giving opportunities to some who would scarcely have merited a look in days gone by. By the end of the 1946–47 campaign, a number of clubs had fielded more than thirty players in an effort to find a winning formula.

OPPOSITE: Lawton scores the fourth goal for Britain when they faced the Rest of Europe at Hampden Park in May 1947. Britain defeated the Continental team comprising players from 9 countries by 6 goals to one; Mannion netting 3, Lawton 2 and Scotland's Billy Steel scoring one.

ABOVE: King George VI presents the Cup to Harris, the Chelsea captain after they defeated their London rivals Millwall in the 1945 Southern League Cup Final. Public demand for the resumption of fixtures was high, encouraging the FA to alter the rules for the 1946 FA Cup so that teams played 2 legs at each round until reaching the semi-finals.

LEFT: A capacity crowd watches Chelsea play Moscow Dynamo when the Russian team toured Britain in the winter of 1945. The match ended in a draw with three goals scored by each side. Dynamo went on to defeat Cardiff, draw with Rangers and, in a match full of controversies, defeated an Arsenal side containing many guest players, by 4 goals to 3.

1954 England suffer their biggest ever defeat when Hungary win 7-1 in Budapest

1954 Scotland make their World Cup debut in Switzerland, where the team is eliminated at the group stage

1955 First floodlit England international – England v Spain at Wembley

1955 First floodlit FA Cup-tie between Brierley Hill and Kidderminster

1955 Birmingham City become the first English club to participate in a European competition when it enters the Inter-City Fairs Cup (now UEFA Cup) reaching the semi finals but losing to Barcelona

1956 Portsmouth v Newcastle

becomes the first League game to be played under floodlights

1956 Real Madrid win the first European Cup; there were no English teams in the 16 teams participating in the competition after Chelsea were instructed to decline the invitation to compete. Hibernian flew the flag for Scotland, beaten by Stade Reims in the semi-final

1956 ITV's first televised game is a Cup-tie between Bedford Town and Arsenal

1956 The four home nations share the International Championship, the only four-way tie in the competition's history

1957 Juventus buy John Charles from

Leeds for a record £67,000

1957 Manchester United is the first English team to enter the European Cup competition

1957 Chelsea become the first team to be transported to a League match by aeroplane when they travelled up to meet Newcastle

1957 Jimmy Hill is elected as Chairman of the Professional Footballers' Association

1958 Sixth World Cup held in Sweden; the competition won by Brazil after England lost to the USSR in the play-offs between the group stage runners-up. This tournament became the first World Cup to be televised

1958 Everton introduce under-soil

heating to protect pitch from frost, the first club to do so

1958 Manchester United lose 8 of their players as the team's plane crashes at Munich Airport on the return flight from a European Cup match against Red Star Belgrade

1958 Hearts hit a record 132 goals in winning their first Championship of the 20th century. Goal difference of 103 is also a record

1959 Billy Wright, the England captain wins his 100th international cap and retires on 105

1959 The Third Division North and South divide is scrapped in favour of one, national Third Division

LEFT: Charlton face Bolton in the semi-final of the FA Cup at Villa Park in 1946.

BELOW: Prime Minister Clement Attlee shakes hands with Stanley Matthews as England line up to meet Belgium at Wembley in 1946. The postwar years brought greater interest in international football and England not only played abroad but entertained Continental teams more frequently. The national team travelled to Switzerland at the end of the 1946 season winning 1-0, but chalked up a remarkable victory in Portugal defeating their opponents by 10-0 with Lawton and Mortensen scoring 4 goals apiece.

OPPOSITE: On a blisteringly hot day, Charlton's Duffy scores the winning goal in the 1947 Cup Final against Burnley. The goal, scored in the last minutes of extra time, averted the threat of a replay, which had last been necessary in 1912 when Barnsley drew with West Brom.

Cullis and Busby turn to management

Of the 1930's stars, Tommy Lawton, Joe Mercer, Billy Liddell, Tom Finney and Bob Paisley were among those who successfully bridged the seven-year gap. And, of course, the incomparable Stanley Matthews, who had turned 30 but still had nearly twenty years of League football left in him. Wolves stalwart Stan Cullis managed just one more season before hanging up his boots.

Traditional rivalries are put aside as clubs share facilities.

Former Manchester City and Liverpool half-back Matt Busby was 36 when the war ended and his thoughts had already turned to management. Cullis and Busby would become two of the dominant figures in the 1950s, locking horns as bosses of Wolves and Manchester United, respectively, as they had done in their pomp as players. Each would lead his side to three Championships, though their footballing philosophies could hardly have been more different.

Tragedy at Burnden Park

1945–46 saw all the clubs take stock of their playing staffs and facilities. Many grounds had been damaged during the war, and while repairs were carried out some ground-sharing went on. Old Trafford was one of those affected, and for some time Manchester United played their home matches at Maine Road. Arsenal and Spurs also put aside their traditional rivalry to share facilities in the early peacetime months.

There may have been no League fixtures that year but the Cup returned to provide the players and fans with some competitive football. As this was the only competition of the season the FA decided to increase the number of matches by making each tie up to the semi-final a two-legged affair. It was in the second leg of a sixth-round tie between Bolton and Stoke at Burnden Park that football saw one of its worst-ever tragedies. The gates were closed on this eagerly awaited match, but thousands forced their way in by every conceivable means. In the resulting crush some of the steel barriers gave way and there were 33 fatalities. There was little appetite for the game to go ahead, but after some delay the teams played out a goalless draw, Bolton going through thanks to their 2-0 win in the first leg.

Jackie Milburn

Few Newcastle United players are held in greater affection by the fans than Jackie Milburn, or "Wor Jackie" as he was known. A gifted centre-forward, Milburn had a winger's pace, having played out on the flanks in his early days. This talent, combined with his great shooting power and brilliance in the air, made him the foremost central striker in the country in the 1950s.

Milburn achieved a scoring rate of a goal every other game with 178 goals in 11 years at the Tyneside club. He led the attack as Newcastle won the FA Cup three times in five seasons, in 1951, 1952 and 1955. He scored both goals in the team's 2-0 win over Blackpool in the 1951 FA Cup Final, and put away a classic header, rifled into the net just seconds into the game at Wembley, to set up a 3-1 win over Manchester City four years later.

As the natural successor to Tommy Lawton in the England centre-forward position, Milburn scored 10 goals in his 13 international appearances. Part of a footballing family, with brothers who were also professionals, his nephews, Bobby and Jackie Charlton, were to follow him into the England team in the 1960s.

Charlton lose a Cup match but make it to Wembley

Bolton were beaten by Charlton in the semi-final, and the London club faced Derby at Wembley. For both sides it had been a marathon campaign. Derby needed a semi-final replay to beat Birmingham, and so played ten matches to reach the final. Charlton's run was unique. Having been beaten by Fulham in the away leg of their third-round tie, Charlton thus became the first club to reach the Cup Final having lost a match. Derby had just splashed out to sign Raich Carter from Sunderland and he helped the Rams to their first major honour. Charlton's Bert Turner scored at both ends to take the game into extra time, when the classier Derby side scored three times without reply.

Agonising wait for Liverpool

The first postwar FA Cup whetted the appetite for the return of League action. The 1946–47 fixture list replicated that of the aborted 1939–40 season, trying to give a semblance of continuity. Liverpool became the first postwar champions, inheriting the title Everton had won eight years earlier. At the beginning of the season the two clubs had both vied for the signature of Newcastle hotshot Albert Stubbins. Both offered £12,500 and Stubbins is said to have opted for Anfield by tossing a coin. He proved his worth to the Reds, scoring 26 goals as Liverpool became involved in an exciting Championship run-in.

The worst winter in living memory meant that the season ran into June. Liverpool went top after a 2-1 away win at Wolves, ending the latter's own title hopes. They then had an agonising two-week wait to see if Stoke could overhaul them by beating Sheffield United. The Potteries club lost and Liverpool were crowned champions for the fifth time.

OPPOSITE ABOVE: Some of the 90,000 spectators at the Burnley v Charlton Cup Final in 1947.

OPPOSITE BELOW: Manchester United captain Johnny Carey is carried on the shoulders of his enthusiastic team-mates after receiving the FA Cup from the King. United had a difficult road to the Final, facing Division One teams in every round, the 6-4 defeat of Aston Villa in the third round being one of the highlights of the 1947–48 season.

RIGHT: Compton, the Manchester United goalkeeper, pressed by Blackpool's Mortensen makes a spectacular save in the 1948 Final. Mortensen and the newly acquired Stanley Matthews presented a danger to the Manchester defence, but United were triumphant, winning by 4 goals to 2 in a classic Final.

BELOW: Middlesbrough gives Chelsea an anxious moment at Stamford Bridge in 1948.

RIGHT: Arsenal, the 1950 Cup winners, parade the trophy in Islington after defeating Liverpool 2-0, both goals scored by Reg Lewis. The Gunners were the first club to reach Wembley without playing outside their own city and the first to allow their players to spend the night before the Final at home.

BELOW: Goring scores the first of Arsenal's goals against Manchester City in their 4-1 victory in April 1950.

ABOVE: Players rush to the rescue as Arsenal team-mates Mercer and Leslie Compton collide during their match with Blackpool in 1949.

"Stop-gap" Mercer captains Arsenal to Cup glory

Arsenal won the League in 1947–48, and did so again five years later. The FA Cup also went to Highbury in 1950, but this was not a period of dominance to match the 1930s. The team included Joe Mercer and the Compton brothers, Denis and Leslie. Mercer had played in Everton's Championship-winning side of 1939, and Arsenal regarded him as a short-term acquisition after the war. The irrepressible Mercer played on for eight seasons and was named Footballer of the Year in 1950, when he lifted the Cup as the Gunners' captain.

The Compton brothers could not have been more different. The flamboyant Denis played on the wing with a devil-may-care style. In that 1950 Wembley Final, against Liverpool, Compton was looking weary when someone handed him a tot of brandy. He perked up immediately and provided the cross, which led to the second goal in Arsenal's 2-0 win.

Elder brother Leslie, a rugged centre-half, carved his name in the record books by winning his first cap for England at the age of 38 years 2 months, the oldest player to make his England debut.

LEFT: Arsenal pictured with the Cup before their match with Portsmouth in 1950. The south-coast team were League Champions in two consecutive seasons, finishing five points ahead of their nearest rivals Manchester United in the 1948–49 season. The margin was much tighter the following year when Portsmouth finished above Wolves on goal difference.

Nat Lofthouse

Nat Lofthouse is a legend at Bolton Wanderers, the club where he spent his entire playing career between 1946 and 1960. With 255 goals scored during that period, he is still the club's highest League scorer. A powerful centre-forward, he scored in every round of the FA Cup in the 1952–53 season, and although he finished on the losing side in the "Matthews Final", he had the consolation of picking up the Footballer of the Year award. Five years later he was on the winning side at Wembley, scoring both goals in Bolton's 2-1 win over a Manchester United side devastated by the Munich air disaster.

Lofthouse made 33 appearances in an England shirt, scoring an astonishing 30 goals, placing him joint third on the all-time list of England scorers. He is best remembered for his heroic contribution to England's victory away to Austria in the 1951–52 season. Having already scored one goal against the team ranked the best in Europe, he hit a second-half winner but was knocked unconscious in the process. His bravery and commitment earned him the tag the "Lion of Vienna". Lofthouse was Wanderers' club president at the time of his death in 2011, aged 85.

England
back in FIFA fold

This period was also notable for England's return to the international fold. The hatchet was finally buried on the row with FIFA over payments to amateurs, a dispute going back to 1928. The reconciliation was celebrated with a match between a Great Britain XI and a side representing Europe. Wilf Mannion was the star of the show, hitting a hat-trick, with Tommy Lawton grabbing a brace. Great Britain won the match 6-1.

*England
are World Cup
favourites.*

In May 1947 England went to Lisbon and thrashed Portugal 10-0, debutant Stan Mortensen hitting four goals. In the next 12 months there were wins over Belgium and Sweden, and a dazzling 4-0 victory over Italy in Turin. Such results no doubt suggested to some that England were ready to reassume their position as world-beaters. The 1950s would disabuse the optimists of any such feelings.

England make their World Cup debut

Throughout the 1950s, when he was well into his 30s, Stanley Matthews remained a regular in the international side. In 1950 he got his chance to grace a World Cup, along with stars such as Mannion, Mortensen, Milburn, Wright and Finney. FIFA declared that the Home International Championship would constitute a qualifying group for the tournament, which was staged in Brazil. England won, and Scotland also earned a place as runners-up. The Scots declined, however, one of a number of withdrawals. Other notable absentees included Hungary, Austria, Germany, France and Russia. Just 13 teams took part, and England were installed as joint-favourites.

BELOW: Argentina score against England at Wembley when the teams meet for the first time in May 1951. Argentina's defence held on to their 1-0 lead until Mortensen equalised from a header and Milburn hit the back of the net 10 minutes before time.

ABOVE: Stanley Matthews is presented to the Duke of Edinburgh before the 1953 Cup Final. It looked as though Matthews would be on the losing side for the third time when Blackpool was trailing 3-1 at the end of the first half. However, after the break Bolton faded and Blackpool's Mortensen scored 2 so that the teams were level at the start of injury time. In the final moments of the game Perry crashed the ball into the net and Blackpool won a thrilling 4-3 victory. A crowd of 200,000 lined the streets to welcome the team home.

OPPOSITE BELOW: Tommy Lawton playing for Chelsea in 1946 before his departure for Third Division Notts County the following year. Lawton soon returned to top-flight football, signing for Arsenal at the start of the 1953–54 season. The Gunners had just won a record seventh League title but manager Tom Whittaker realised the need to bring new blood into the team.

OPPOSITE ABOVE INSERT: Tom Finney trains with the England team at Stamford Bridge.

Lawton signs for Third Division side

The shock of the 1947–48 season occurred off the pitch, when Chelsea and England centre-forward Tommy Lawton moved to Third Division Notts County in a record £20,000 deal. County quickly began recouping their huge investment with gates of 30,000, a three-fold increase on what they were used to. Lawton subsequently moved on to Brentford, and looked set for a career in management. But the man who had inherited Dixie Dean's mantle made a dramatic return to the top flight with Arsenal, and showed that even in his mid-30s he was still a fearsome competitor. His 231 League goals came in at well under a goal every other game, and he scored 23 goals for England in just 22 full internationals.

Busby's first trophy

In the first five postwar seasons Manchester United finished Division One runners-up four times, and fourth on the other occasion. The club finally got its hands on some silverware by winning the Cup in 1948. United twice came from behind against Blackpool to win 4–2, a match that was described as a classic for the purists. Blackpool's Stanley Matthews, who had been honoured with the inaugural Footballer of the Year award, was now 33 and all neutrals wanted to see him get a winners' medal. But two goals from Jack Rowley helped United to victory and ended the "Wizard of the Dribble" hopes for another year.

Matt Busby had inherited some good players when he took over as manager at Old Trafford in October 1945. He also bought wisely and moulded a side which was immediately challenging for top honours. The team was led by Johnny Carey, who played in every position except left-wing. Carey also had the unusual distinction of having played for both the Republic of Ireland and Northern Ireland, the latter thanks to his service in the British Army.

Tom Finney

Dubbed the "Preston Plumber", Tom Finney was a brilliant ball-playing winger. A contemporary of Stanley Matthews, he shared many of Matthews' creative and skilful qualities. However, he was a much more versatile player; Matthews concentrated on being simply the best outside-right of his era. Finney was two-footed and could operate on either wing, and he also played as a central striker.

He played throughout his career for Preston North End and his 187 goals in 24 seasons for the club remains a record at Deepdale – testimony to his clinical finishing; but Finney was also a provider for other strikers. His loyalty to his home-town club probably cost him in terms of silverware, for he ended his illustrious career with no major honours.

Nevertheless, his talents did not go unnoticed and he earned 76 England caps. During his service for the national side he bagged 30 goals, setting a new record. Even now, on the list of all time record England scorers he lies at joint fifth, alongside Nat Lofthouse and Alan Shearer.

He received a rare footballing accolade in being twice named Footballer of the Year, in 1954 and 1957. And Bill Shankly, a former team-mate, once famously said that Finney would have been brilliant in any era, "even if he'd been wearing an overcoat". Rewarded for his loyalty to Preston and his services to football, Tom Finney became club president at Deepdale, and was knighted in 1998. He died in February 2014.

Stanley Matthews

Stanley Matthews enjoyed a playing career spanning 32 years 10 months, and was over 50 by the time he retired from top-class football. He is the oldest player ever to appear in English football's top flight. He is also the oldest England player, winning his last cap, at the age of 42, against Denmark in May 1957. He did not score in that match but his last goal in an international came against Northern Ireland in October 1956; he was 41 years 248 days, making him the oldest player to score for England. While it is conceivable that some of his records might be broken, it is inconceivable that Stanley Matthews' achievements will ever be eclipsed.

At the age of 15 Matthews joined his local side Stoke City and made his debut two years later. Matthews spent 17 years at the club, establishing himself as the best outside-right in world football and earning himself the tag "Wizard of the Dribble".

In his debut game for England in September 1934, he scored, helping the side to a 4-0 win over Wales. This was the start of a 20-year international career during which he won 84 caps, playing in the 1950 and 1954 World Cups. In the 1950 tournament in Brazil Matthews missed the humiliating 1-0 defeat at the hands of the USA; the selectors had decided to alternate Matthews and Tom Finney on the right wing and it was Finney who played that day in Belo Horizonte.

In 1947 Matthews joined Blackpool in a £11,500 transfer deal, but found himself on the losing side in the FA Cup Finals of 1948 and 1951. When Blackpool made it to Wembley again in 1953, all neutral supporters hoped he would finally get a winners' medal. Things looked bleak when opponents Bolton went 3-1 ahead, but 38-year-old Matthews inspired a terrific comeback, Blackpool triumphing as 4-3 winners. The match went down in footballing annals as the "Matthews Final".

Matthews was 46 when he left Blackpool, in October 1961, but incredibly he chose to return to Stoke as a player rather than retire. Four more years at the Potteries club saw Matthews play his last competitive match on 6 February 1965, five days after his 50th birthday. He had just received a knighthood in the New Year's Honours List and went out in style, with a 3-1 win over Fulham.

Matthews was twice Footballer of the Year, in 1948 and 1963, and was also the inaugural European Footballer of the Year in 1956. He died in February 2000, aged 85.

The "Matthews Final"

If Manchester United and Wolves were the most consistent performers in the League during this period, Newcastle United were the most successful Cup side. Spearheaded by Jackie Milburn–"Wor Jackie"– and George Robledo, Newcastle won the Cup three times in five years. Blackpool were the first of their Wembley victims in 1951. Two goals from Milburn won the match, leaving Stanley Matthews to rue yet another missed opportunity.

Blackpool made it to Wembley again in 1953, their third appearance in six seasons. Trailing 3–1 to Bolton with 20 minutes left, it looked like a third agonising defeat. But in this most dramatic of all finals Blackpool drew level. Matthews crossed for Mortensen to score, and three minutes from time Mortensen crashed home a free-kick to level. With extra time looming, Matthews weaved yet another piece of magic on the right wing and crossed for Perry to rifle the ball into the net. The 38-year-old maestro finally got his hands on an FA Cup winners' medal, and the match would be forever known as the "Matthews Final".

BELOW: Lofthouse opens the scoring for Bolton after 90 seconds as the ball flies past Farm and into the net.

OPPOSITE INSERT: The winning goal: While the tremendous crowd urges him on, the "Wizard of the Dribble", Stanley Matthews, streaks down the wing to beat Bolton's Wheeler (4), and puts the ball across to Bill Perry who scored the fourth and winning goal, giving Blackpool the FA Cup and Matthews his first winners' medal.

RIGHT: Matthews pictured in 1952, 22 years after his debut for Stoke.

Shock defeat by USA

After a 2-0 win over Chile, England took on the USA in Belo Horizonte. The Americans rode their luck and scored the only goal of the game, a header by Larry Gaetjens. Matthews didn't play in the game that would go down as the blackest moment in England's 80 years of international football. The selectors decided that he and Finney should alternate on the right wing, an extraordinary decision given the fact that Finney was equally potent on the left or through the middle. Matthews returned for the last group match, but even his magic couldn't save the day. A 1-0 defeat by Spain wrapped up a miserable World Cup debut, and England didn't even stay to watch the remaining matches.

> *First international defeat on home soil.*

Magyars teach England a lesson

Any doubts that England were no longer guaranteed a place at football's top table were ended three years later, when a brilliant Hungary side came to Wembley. The Mighty Magyars, including Puskas, Hidegkuti and Kocsis, taught England a painful lesson in a match that ended 6-3. It was the country's first defeat on home soil. A return match in Budapest six months later showed it was no fluke; Hungary won that encounter 7-1. England full-back Alf Ramsey had witnessed this 13-goal fusillade at close quarters. It was an experience which left an indelible memory on him and would inform his views when he turned his thoughts to management.

At the 1954 World Cup England went down 4-2 to reigning Champions Uruguay at the quarter-final stage. In Sweden four years later, Walter Winterbottom was hampered by the loss of the Manchester United stars killed in the Munich disaster. England finished level on points with Russia and the two teams had to play off for the right to go through with Brazil. Russia, won 1-0; England's third World Cup ended in disappointment once again.

BELOW: England's goalkeeper lies prostrate as Johnston retrieves the ball from the net after Hungary score for the fourth time.

OPPOSITE LEFT: Billy Wright and Hungarian captain Puskas exchange flags before the start of their Wembley clash in November 1953. England's record of never having been beaten at home by a Continental team was shattered when the Magyars scored six goals with only three in reply.

OPPOSITE RIGHT: The England International football team as they appeared in a friendly match against the Rest of Europe at Wembley on 21 October 1953, when they drew 4-4. Alf Ramsey is second from the left in the back row, and Stanley Matthews is on the far left of the front row.

OPPOSITE BELOW: Brazil's number 8, Valente, walks away with the ball followed by his team-mates and the referee after a penalty was awarded against the South Americans when they played England in May 1956. The Brazilians entertained the crowd with their ball skills but England won by 4 goals to 2, scoring two within the first few minutes of the game.

Wales' World Cup adventure

The 1950s, the era of John Charles and Ivor Allchurch, was a golden one for Wales. The national team shared in three more Home Championship successes during the decade, but the crowning glory was a first World Cup adventure in 1958. There was a degree of good fortune over the qualification route, Wales having finished group runners-up to Czechoslovakia. A play-off victory over Israel provided back-door entry into the competition, Wales accepting the lifeline when several other countries had refused to take the pitch with a perceived pariah state. Unbeaten in their three group matches at the finals, Wales faced Hungary in yet another play-off, this time for a place in the last eight. Goals from Allchurch and Spurs winger Terry Medwin were enough to beat the 1954 runners-up. Wales met mighty Brazil without the talismanic Charles, who was injured, and went out to a late goal from Pelé.

John Charles

One of the first British players to ply his trade on the Continent, John Charles was dubbed "The Gentle Giant" by Juventus fans, the club he joined in 1957. It was an affectionate and appropriate nickname, for Charles, with a magnificent physique, was a strong and powerful footballer. Yet, despite his strength and the many physical battles he fought in a 16-year career, both as a centre-half and centre-forward, he was never once booked.

Charles began his career at Leeds United as a central defender. It was in the 1953–54 season that he showed his credentials as a striker, hitting 42 League goals for Leeds, a record to this day.

When he joined Juventus for a record £67,000, he made an immediate impact, hitting 28 goals in 34 games in his first season in Italy. He became Serie A's top marksman and his goals helped Juventus to win the Italian Championship. By the time he left Italy in 1962, he had a tally of 93 goals in 155 games. During Charles's five years at the club Juventus won the League title three times and the Cup twice.

He became the youngest player ever to be capped for Wales. Even though he had played only a few games for Leeds, he was picked to join the line-up for what turned out to be a goalless draw against Northern Ireland at Wrexham on 8 March 1950; he was just 18 years 71 days old. Although he missed Wales's greatest moment in international football, Charles was a key figure in his country's achievement in reaching the quarter-finals of the 1958 World Cup. An injury sustained during a tough play-off battle with Hungary meant that Wales had to face the competition's eventual winners, Brazil, without Charles, going down 1-0.

After a spell back at Elland Road, Charles wound down his career with Roma and Cardiff City. He died in 2004.

The "Babes" make their bow

By 1950 the Manchester United side was ageing. There was also disquiet in the ranks as some of the players wanted the club to break the wage cap so that they could cash in during the twilight of their careers. Busby refused, and had already set his sights on a major rebuilding job. He was nurturing a crop of excellent youngsters at the Old Trafford academy, and these represented the future. The old guard had one last moment of glory, finally taking the title in 1951–52. The Championship was secured with a 6-1 win over Arsenal, who themselves had a mathematical chance of winning the League. Afterwards, the transition process gathered pace. 18-year-old Jackie Blanchflower and 21-year-old Roger Byrne were the first to make the breakthrough into the senior side, in November 1951. A local journalist commented that the "babes" had acquitted themselves well and, much to Busby's annoyance, this celebrated term soon became part of footballing folklore.

Busby begins building process.

No stars proves no handicap for Pompey

While the Busby Babes were busy winning the FA Youth Cup five years in succession and slowly being incorporated into the first team, other sides were grabbing the headlines. Portsmouth peaked for two marvellous seasons, winning back-to-back Championships in 1949 and 1950. The team had no real stars, not even an international in their line-up, showing that an outstanding unit could more than compensate for individual brilliance. The season in which they retained their crown, 1949–50, saw Pompey edge out Wolves on goal average. But as Portsmouth's bubble burst—they would be a Division Two side by the end of the decade—Wolves went on to rival Manchester United as the team of the era.

OPPOSITE BELOW INSERT: John Charles (right) trains with his brother Mel who also represented Wales.

BELOW: Manchester United's Taylor jumps to convert a corner but is beaten by the Birmingham keeper in 1955.

OPPOSITE ABOVE: The captains lead out their teams at Wembley in 1955. In a repeat of the 1952 Final, Newcastle's opponents, this time Manchester City, were forced to play a man short for most of the 90 minutes. Newcastle won 3-1 and collected the trophy for the sixth time.

League Division One 1946–1959

1946–47

1	Liverpool	57
2	Manchester United	56
3	Wolverhampton W.	56
4	Stoke	55
5	Blackpool	50
6	Sheffield United	49
7	Preston	47
8	Aston Villa	45
9	Sunderland	44
10	Everton	43
11	Middlesbrough	42
12	Portsmouth	41
13	Arsenal	41
14	Derby County	41
15	Chelsea	39
16	Grimsby	38
17	Blackburn Rovers	36
18	Bolton Wanderers	34
19	Charlton Athletic	34
20	Huddersfield	33
21	Brentford	25
22	Leeds United	18

1947–48

1	Arsenal	59
2	Manchester United	52
3	Burnley	52
4	Derby County	50
5	Wolverhampton W.	47
6	Aston Villa	47
7	Preston	47
8	Portsmouth	45
9	Blackpool	44
10	Manchester City	42
11	Liverpool	42
12	Sheffield United	42
13	Charlton Athletic	40
14	Everton	40
15	Stoke	38
16	Middlesbrough	37
17	Bolton Wanderers	37
18	Chelsea	37
19	Huddersfield	36
20	Sunderland	36
21	Blackburn Rovers	32
22	Grimsby	22

1948–49

1	Portsmouth	58
2	Manchester United	53
3	Derby County	53
4	Newcastle United	52
5	Arsenal	49
6	Wolverhampton W.	46
7	Manchester City	45
8	Sunderland	43
9	Charlton Athletic	42
10	Aston Villa	42
11	Stoke	41
12	Liverpool	40
13	Chelsea	38
14	Bolton Wanderers	38
15	Burnley	38
16	Blackpool	38
17	Birmingham City	37
18	Everton	37
19	Middlesbrough	34
20	Huddersfield	34
21	Preston	33
22	Sheffield United	33

1949–50

1	Portsmouth	53
2	Wolverhampton W.	53
3	Sunderland	52
4	Manchester United	50
5	Newcastle United	50
6	Arsenal	49
7	Blackpool	49
8	Liverpool	48
9	Middlesbrough	47
10	Burnley	45
11	Derby County	44
12	Aston Villa	42
13	Chelsea	40
14	West Bromwich Albion	40
15	Huddersfield	37
16	Bolton Wanderers	34
17	Fulham	34
18	Everton	34
19	Stoke	34
20	Charlton Athletic	32
21	Manchester City	29
22	Birmingham City	28

1950–51

1	Tottenham Hotspur	60
2	Manchester United	56
3	Blackpool	50
4	Newcastle United	49
5	Arsenal	47
6	Middlesbrough	47
7	Portsmouth	47
8	Bolton Wanderers	45
9	Liverpool	43
10	Burnley	42
11	Derby County	40
12	Sunderland	40
13	Stoke	40
14	Wolverhampton W.	38
15	Aston Villa	37
16	West Bromwich Albion	37
17	Charlton Athletic	37
18	Fulham	37
19	Huddersfield	36
20	Chelsea	32
21	Sheffield Wednesday	32
22	Everton	32

1951–52

1	Manchester United	57
2	Tottenham Hotspur	53
3	Arsenal	53
4	Portsmouth	48
5	Bolton Wanderers	48
6	Aston Villa	47
7	Preston	46
8	Newcastle United	45
9	Blackpool	45
10	Charlton Athletic	44
11	Liverpool	43
12	Sunderland	42
13	West Bromwich Albion	41
14	Burnley	40
15	Manchester City	39
16	Wolverhampton W.	38
17	Derby County	37
18	Middlesbrough	36
19	Chelsea	36
20	Stoke	31
21	Huddersfield	28
22	Fulham	27

1952–53

1	Arsenal	54
2	Preston	54
3	Wolverhampton W.	51
4	West Bromwich Albion	50
5	Charlton Athletic	49
6	Burnley	48
7	Blackpool	47
8	Manchester United	46
9	Sunderland	43
10	Tottenham Hotspur	41
11	Aston Villa	41
12	Cardiff	40
13	Middlesbrough	39
14	Bolton Wanderers	39
15	Portsmouth	38
16	Newcastle United	37
17	Liverpool	36
18	Sheffield Wednesday	35
19	Chelsea	35
20	Manchester City	35
21	Stoke	34
22	Derby County	32

1953–54

1	Wolverhampton W.	57
2	West Bromwich Albion	53
3	Huddersfield	51
4	Manchester United	48
5	Bolton Wanderers	48
6	Blackpool	48
7	Burnley	46
8	Chelsea	44
9	Charlton Athletic	44
10	Cardiff	44
11	Preston	43
12	Arsenal	43
13	Aston Villa	41
14	Portsmouth	39
15	Newcastle United	38
16	Tottenham Hotspur	37
17	Manchester City	37
18	Sunderland	36
19	Sheffield Wednesday	36
20	Sheffield United	33
21	Middlesbrough	30
22	Liverpool	28

1954–55

1	Chelsea	52
2	Wolverhampton W.	48
3	Portsmouth	48
4	Sunderland	48
5	Manchester United	47
6	Aston Villa	47
7	Manchester City	46
8	Newcastle United	43
9	Arsenal	43
10	Burnley	43
11	Everton	42
12	Huddersfield	41
13	Sheffield United	41
14	Preston	40
15	Charlton Athletic	40
16	Tottenham Hotspur	40
17	West Bromwich Albion	40
18	Bolton Wanderers	39
19	Blackpool	38
20	Cardiff	37
21	Leicester City	35
22	Sheffield Wednesday	26

1955–56

1	Manchester United	60
2	Blackpool	49
3	Wolverhampton W.	49
4	Manchester City	46
5	Arsenal	46
6	Birmingham City	45
7	Burnley	44
8	Bolton Wanderers	43
9	Sunderland	43
10	Luton	42
11	Newcastle United	41
12	Portsmouth	41
13	West Bromwich Albion	41
14	Charlton Athletic	40
15	Everton	40
16	Chelsea	39
17	Cardiff	39
18	Tottenham Hotspur	37
19	Preston	36
20	Aston Villa	35
21	Huddersfield	35
22	Sheffield United	33

FA Cup Finals

1946	Derby County	v	Charlton Athletic	4-1
1947	Charlton Athletic	v	Burnley	1-0
1948	Manchester Utd	v	Blackpool	4-2
1949	Wolverhampton W.	v	Leicester	3-1
1950	Arsenal	v	Liverpool	2-0
1951	Newcastle United	v	Blackpool	2-0
1952	Newcastle United	v	Arsenal	1-0
1953	Blackpool	v	Bolton W.	4-3
1954	West Bromwich A.	v	Preston N. E.	3-2
1955	Newcastle United	v	Manchester City	3-1
1956	Manchester City	v	Birmingham City	3-1
1957	Aston Villa	v	Manchester United	2-1
1958	Bolton Wanderers	v	Manchester United	2-0
1959	Nottingham Forest	v	Luton Town	2-1

1956–57

1	Manchester United	64
2	Tottenham Hotspur	56
3	Preston	56
4	Blackpool	53
5	Arsenal	50
6	Wolverhampton W.	48
7	Burnley	46
8	Leeds United	44
9	Bolton Wanderers	44
10	Aston Villa	43
11	West Bromwich Albion	42
12	Birmingham City	39
13	Chelsea	39
14	Sheffield Wednesday	38
15	Everton	38
16	Luton	37
17	Newcastle United	36
18	Manchester City	35
19	Portsmouth	33
20	Sunderland	32
21	Cardiff	29
22	Charlton Athletic	22

1957–58

1	Wolverhampton W.	64
2	Preston	59
3	Tottenham Hotspur	51
4	West Bromwich Albion	50
5	Manchester City	49
6	Burnley	47
7	Blackpool	44
8	Luton	44
9	Manchester United	43
10	Nottingham Forest	42
11	Chelsea	42
12	Arsenal	39
13	Birmingham City	39
14	Aston Villa	39
15	Bolton Wanderers	38
16	Everton	37
17	Leeds United	37
18	Leicester City	33
19	Newcastle United	32
20	Portsmouth	32
21	Sunderland	32
22	Sheffield Wednesday	31

1958–59

1	Wolverhampton W.	61
2	Manchester United	55
3	Arsenal	50
4	Bolton Wanderers	50
5	West Bromwich Albion	49
6	West Ham United	48
7	Burnley	48
8	Blackpool	47
9	Birmingham City	46
10	Blackburn Rovers	44
11	Newcastle United	41
12	Preston	41
13	Nottingham Forest	40
14	Chelsea	40
15	Leeds United	39
16	Everton	38
17	Luton	37
18	Tottenham Hotspur	36
19	Leicester City	32
20	Manchester City	31
21	Aston Villa	30
22	Portsmouth	21

ABOVE: Newcastle's right back Cowell clears off the line to preserve The Magpies' two goal advantage in the 1951 FA Cup Final against Blackpool at Wembley on 28 April 1951.

Long-ball game reaps dividends for Wolves

Unlike Busby, who encouraged his talented players to express themselves, Wolves boss Stan Cullis favoured a much more regimented approach. He regarded over-elaboration as a sin. The emphasis was on getting the ball as quickly and as often as possible into the opposition's box. Some denigrated this tactic as simply "kick and rush", yet it reaped considerable dividends. Anchoring the side was the redoubtable Billy Wright, who would go on to make nearly 500 appearances in the famous Old Gold shirt. Wright set a new world record by making 70 consecutive international appearances, and he went on to become the first England player to win one hundred caps.

Wright makes 70 consecutive appearances for England.

Apart from the Championships of 1954, 1958 and 1959, Wolves also enjoyed some sparkling triumphs over top European opposition. In two memorable floodlit matches during the 1954–55 season, Wolves came out on top against Moscow Spartak and a Honved side that boasted Puskas, Kocsis and several other members of Hungary's all-star team. As Honved was regarded as the supreme club side of the day, Cullis was quick to acclaim his men as World Champions. This piece of self-publicity is said to have prompted Gabriel Hanot, a sports reporter with *L'Équipe*, to seek support for his idea to stage a cup competition for Europe's leading clubs. UEFA quickly took the idea on board and in September 1955 the first European Cup matches were held.

Drake makes history at Chelsea

Wolves could only finish runners-up in 1954–55, and it was Chelsea who earned the right to play in the first Champions Cup. Under pressure from the Football League, who were concerned that the new competition would undermine the domestic programme, Chelsea declined to enter. The only League success in the club's history did earn a special place in the record books, however. Ted Drake had won the Championship with Arsenal in the 1930s and had now repeated that success as a manager, the first man to do that particular double.

OPPOSITE RIGHT: The young Chelsea player, Jimmy Greaves, in training for his match against Wolverhampton in October 1957.

OPPOSITE LEFT: England and Russia line up at Wembley before the start of the international in October 1956, which the home team won by five goals to nil.

OPPOSITE BELOW: The moment when England defeated Scotland by 1 goal to nil at Wembley on 11 April 1959. England captain Billy Wright celebrated receiving his 100th international cap, appearing as captain for the 85th time.

BELOW: Jackie Henderson, signed twenty-four hours previously from Wolves for £18,000, paid dividends to his new club Arsenal when he scored a goal against West Bromwich Albion just ten minutes into the match.

Structural problems highlighted

The experience of the 1950s showed that England would have to work hard to match the skills of the top Continental and South American sides. There were also structural and organisational problems. In 1950 Stanley Matthews was with an FA touring side in Canada when his team-mates arrived in Brazil. When the food was discovered to be unpalatable, Winterbottom found himself in charge of the catering! In 1958 the team arrived in Sweden to find there were no training facilities, and Winterbottom had to chase round looking for a suitable venue. There was a minor step forward in that senior players were given a voice on selection matters, but overall the running of the international side left a lot to be desired. Success at international level could no longer be achieved with a part-time manager who had responsibility without power. It was not until the next decade that things changed dramatically for the better. A man of vision was brought in, and freed from the shackles of the Selection Committee he was able to put his ideas into practice.

Duncan Edwards

Duncan Edwards was the jewel in the crown of the young and gifted Manchester United side that Matt Busby fashioned in the 1950s – the "Busby Babes" as they became known. Edwards came into the side as a half-back, but his athleticism and all-round ability meant that his influence spread all over the pitch. His tragic death from injuries sustained in the 1958 Munich air crash robbed football of what undoubtedly would have been one of the most outstanding players in the world game in the 1960s; he would probably have figured in the 1966 World Cup, when he would have been 29 years old.

Honours came early to Edwards. He made his debut for Manchester United at the age of 16, winning two Championship medals, in 1956 and 1957 with Busby's talented team. When he won his first England cap in 1955 in a 7-2 victory over Scotland, he was just 18 years and 183 days old, a record which stood for more than 40 years until Michael Owen's England debut against Chile in February 1998. In his sadly short career, Edwards notched up 18 caps and scored five goals.

United romp to title by 11 points

Chelsea's decision to decline to enter the 1956 competition meant that Manchester United became the country's first Champions to contest the European Cup. Busby's team earned the right by romping to the 1955–56 title by 11 points, equalling the biggest winning margin in the League's 68-year history. When Dennis Viollet scored the only goal of the match against Portsmouth on 21 April 1956, United were uncatchable.

Duncan Edwards makes his debut.

By now the pieces of the jigsaw were all in place. Duncan Edwards had made his debut as a 16-year-old in 1953, with Tommy Taylor moving to Old Trafford from Barnsley in the same year for £29,999. Busby deliberately pitched the deal just short of £30,000 to try and ease the anxiety that might have accompanied a big-money move. Mark Jones, Eddie Colman, David Pegg and Bobby Charlton were others among the precociously talented crop of young players that Busby had assembled. In four years he had transformed a veteran side into one in which the average age was just 22.

"Push and run" brings success to Spurs

United retained their crown the following season, finishing eight points ahead of Tottenham. In style the Spurs side was closer to United than Wolves. Under Arthur Rowe the team had developed a marvellous "push and run" technique, which had brought the club the Championship in 1951. Bill Nicholson and Alf Ramsey were

TOP INSERT: Duncan Edwards, one of the central figures in Matt Busby's new team. United won the League in 1952 but Busby looked towards the future, devoting attention to finding a new crop of juniors who could be moulded to make a formidable unit. By 1956 this new team was ready to compete on the world stage, and Busby had bought just three players: Tommy Taylor, Johnny Berry and Ray Wood.

ABOVE: Members of the Manchester United team travel from Blackpool to London in 1957 (l-r: McGuinness, Foulkes, Jones, Colman and Wood).

members of that side, and the former joined the coaching staff at White Hart Lane when he finished playing. Spurs were also twice runners-up in the 1950s but their greatest moment, with Nicholson at the helm, still lay ahead.

United's European dream ended by Real Madrid

Meanwhile, United's first sortie into European competition ended at the semi-final stage, when they were beaten by holders Real Madrid. Tommy Taylor and Bobby Charlton earned United a 2-2 draw at Old Trafford, not enough to overturn a 3-1 defeat at the Bernebeu Stadium. Busby wasn't unduly worried. Earlier in the competition his team had beaten Anderlecht 12-0 on aggregate, and also put out Borussia Dortmund and Atletico Bilbao before going out to the best side in Europe. Youth was on United's side and they would be even stronger the following season.

BELOW: Bobby Charlton on the training ground. Charlton, Viollet, Gregg and Foulkes were all fit to represent Manchester United in the 1958 FA Cup Final just months after the Munich air disaster. Despite a spirited fight by United, Bolton won the match 2-0.

Sir Matt Busby

Matt Busby built three brilliant Championship-winning sides in a glorious 26-year reign at Old Trafford. Busby spent his playing career at two of United's arch-rivals, neighbours Manchester City and Liverpool, winning an FA Cup winners medal with City in 1934.

He took over at Old Trafford after the Second World War and built a side which finished runners-up four times in five years. The title finally arrived in 1951–52, adding to an FA Cup victory over Blackpool in 1948.

As that ageing side was broken up, Busby scoured the country for the finest young players in the land. By the mid-1950s his outstanding young team, dubbed the "Busby Babes", looked as if it would dominate football for many years. There were successive League Championships in 1956 and 1957. The team also twice made it to the semi-fiinals of the fledgling European Cup competition. It was on a return trip from a successful European quarter-final tie against Red Star Belgrade that the side was all but wiped out. Eight players lost their lives at Munich on 6 February 1958, and Busby himself was given last rites. He recovered to build yet another superb side in the 1960s. The likes of George Best and Denis Law were added to Munich survivors Bobby Charlton and Bill Foulkes. United lifted the FA Cup in 1963 and won the Championship in 1965 and 1967. The latter success gave Busby yet another crack at the trophy he desperately wanted to win. The realisation of a long-held dream came at Wembley on 29 May 1968, when his side beat Benfica 4-1 in the European Cup Final. Busby became only the second British club manager to win the trophy. He was knighted for his achievements in the same year, retiring three years later. Busby died in 1994, an avid watcher of his beloved United right up to the end.

"Villain" McParland makes it seven Cup wins

Before then there was the prospect of the coveted Double. Having wrapped up the League, United faced Aston Villa in the FA Cup Final. The key moment came after just six minutes, when Villa's Peter McParland clattered into United keeper Ray Wood, breaking the latter's cheekbone. Jackie Blanchflower took over in goal, badly disrupting United's rhythm. McParland rubbed salt into United's wounds by scoring both Villa goals in a 2–1 win. It was Villa's seventh victory, a record for the competition.

The incident involving Wood was one of a succession of injuries, which cast a shadow over Wembley Finals in the 1950s. In 1956 Manchester City keeper Bert Trautmann suffered a broken neck in the 3–1 win over Birmingham City. In 1959 Nottingham Forest winger Roy Dwight was carried off with a broken leg, and Blackburn full-back Dave Whelan suffered the same injury a year later. Some dubbed it the "Wembley hoodoo", while others put the number of injuries down to the fact that the turf was too soft.

BELOW: Aston Villa goalkeeper Sims leaps but fails to stop Taylor's strike in the closing minutes of the 1957 Cup Final. A head-on charge by Villa's McParland on the Manchester goalkeeper left Wood unable to continue playing in goal. Despite the valiant efforts of Jackie Blanchflower who took his place, Manchester, playing with ten men, could not overcome the Villa defence.

RIGHT: Villa captain Johnny Dixon holds the trophy aloft.

Eight United players killed in Munich tragedy

On 1 February 1958 United went to Highbury and won a sparkling match 5-4. The result kept them in second place in the League, looking ominously good to equal Huddersfield's and Arsenal's achievement of a hat-trick of Championships. The team then headed to Belgrade to take on Red Star in the second leg of their European Cup-tie. Having won 2-1 at home, a 3-3 draw was enough to put United into the semis once again. On the return journey the plane stopped to refuel at Munich. In atrocious weather two attempted take-offs were aborted. The third attempt ended in disaster, the plane failing to get off the ground and slewing into the perimeter fence. There were 23 fatalities, including seven of the Babes. An eighth, Duncan Edwards, lost his battle for life two weeks later. Johnny Berry and Jackie Blanchflower survived but never played football again.

> *Having built two Championship-winning sides, Busby immediately set about creating a third.*

No sentiment as United go down fighting

The heart had been ripped out of United, yet amazingly, a side made up of reserve and youth team players, together with a couple of emergency signings, reached that year's FA Cup Final. There was no fairytale, however; two goals from Nat Lofthouse won the trophy for Bolton Wanderers.

Some suggested that the European Cup should be awarded to United as a mark of respect to the great players who had perished at Munich. But sentiment was not allowed to prevail and United's semi-final clash with AC Milan went ahead as scheduled. United lost 5-2 on aggregate. Having built two Championship-winning sides, Busby immediately set about creating a third.

BOTTOM: Manchester United's Cup finalists in 1957. Busby's team narrowly failed to win the trophy but had topped the League at the end of 1956 and 1957, qualifying for the embryonic European Cup. Playing against the wishes of the FA, United reached the semi-finals of the competition, eventually being knocked out by Real Madrid. l-r, Back row: Inglis, Geoff Bent, Ray Wood, Mark Jones, Billy Foulkes, Dennis Viollet and Tom Curry. Front row: Jackie Blanchflower, Colin Webster, Wilf McGuinness, Tommy Taylor, Bill Whelan and David Pegg. With ball: Johnny Berry.

BELOW: The wreckage of the plane following the Munich crash. There were 23 fatalities, including seven United players. Duncan Edwards lost his battle for life two weeks later.

Scottish League 1946–1959

1946–47

1	Rangers	46
2	Hibernian	44
3	Aberdeen	39
4	Hearts	38
5	Partick Thistle	35
6	Greenock Morton	34
7	Celtic	32
8	Motherwell	29
9	Third Lanark	28
10	Clyde	27
11	Falkirk	26
12	Queen Of The South	26
13	Queen's Park	22
14	St Mirren	22
15	Kilmarnock	21
16	Hamilton	11

1947–48

1	Hibernian	48
2	Rangers	46
3	Partick Thistle	36
4	Dundee	33
5	St Mirren	31
6	Clyde	31
7	Falkirk	30
8	Motherwell	29
9	Hearts	28
10	Aberdeen	27
11	Third Lanark	26
12	Celtic	25
13	Queen Of The South	25
14	Greenock Morton	24
15	Airdrieonians	21
16	Queen's Park	20

1948–49

1	Rangers	46
2	Dundee	45
3	Hibernian	39
4	East Fife	35
5	Falkirk	32
6	Celtic	31
7	Third Lanark	31
8	Hearts	30
9	St Mirren	30
10	Queen Of The South	30
11	Partick Thistle	27
12	Motherwell	25
13	Aberdeen	25
14	Clyde	24
15	Greenock Morton	22
16	Albion Rovers	8

1949–50

1	Rangers	50
2	Hibernian	49
3	Hearts	43
4	East Fife	37
5	Celtic	35
6	Dundee	31
7	Partick Thistle	29
8	Aberdeen	26
9	Raith Rovers	26
10	Motherwell	25
11	St Mirren	25
12	Third Lanark	25
13	Clyde	24
14	Falkirk	24
15	Queen Of The South	16
16	Stirling Albion	15

1950–51

1	Hibernian	48
2	Rangers	38
3	Dundee	38
4	Hearts	37
5	Aberdeen	35
6	Partick Thistle	33
7	Celtic	29
8	Raith Rovers	28
9	Motherwell	28
10	East Fife	28
11	St Mirren	25
12	Greenock Morton	24
13	Third Lanark	24
14	Airdrieonians	24
15	Clyde	23
16	Falkirk	18

1951–52

1	Hibernian	45
2	Rangers	41
3	East Fife	37
4	Hearts	35
5	Raith Rovers	33
6	Partick Thistle	31
7	Motherwell	31
8	Dundee	28
9	Celtic	28
10	Queen Of The South	28
11	Aberdeen	27
12	Third Lanark	26
13	Airdrieonians	26
14	St Mirren	25
15	Greenock Morton	24
16	Stirling Albion	15

1952–53

1	Rangers	43
2	Hibernian	43
3	East Fife	39
4	Hearts	30
5	Clyde	30
6	St Mirren	30
7	Dundee	29
8	Celtic	29
9	Partick Thistle	29
10	Queen Of The South	28
11	Aberdeen	27
12	Raith Rovers	26
13	Falkirk	26
14	Airdrieonians	26
15	Motherwell	25
16	Third Lanark	20

1953–54

1	Celtic	43
2	Hearts	38
3	Partick Thistle	35
4	Rangers	34
5	Hibernian	34
6	East Fife	34
7	Dundee	34
8	Clyde	34
9	Aberdeen	33
10	Queen Of The South	32
11	St Mirren	28
12	Raith Rovers	26
13	Falkirk	25
14	Stirling Albion	24
15	Airdrieonians	15
16	Hamilton	11

1954–55

1	Aberdeen	49
2	Celtic	46
3	Rangers	41
4	Hearts	39
5	Hibernian	34
6	St Mirren	32
7	Clyde	31
8	Dundee	30
9	Partick Thistle	29
10	Kilmarnock	26
11	East Fife	24
12	Falkirk	24
13	Queen Of The South	24
14	Raith Rovers	23
15	Motherwell	22
16	Stirling Albion	6

1955–56

1	Rangers	52
2	Aberdeen	46
3	Hearts	45
4	Hibernian	45
5	Celtic	41
6	Queen Of The South	37
7	Airdrieonians	36
8	Kilmarnock	34
9	Partick Thistle	33
10	Motherwell	33
11	Raith Rovers	33
12	East Fife	31
13	Dundee	30
14	Falkirk	28
15	St Mirren	27
16	Dunfermline Athletic	26
17	Clyde	22
18	Stirling Albion	13

1956–57

1	Rangers	55
2	Hearts	53
3	Kilmarnock	42
4	Raith Rovers	39
5	Celtic	38
6	Aberdeen	38
7	Motherwell	37
8	Partick Thistle	34
9	Hibernian	33
10	Dundee	32
11	Airdrieonians	30
12	St Mirren	30
13	Queen's Park	29
14	Falkirk	28
15	East Fife	26
16	Queen Of The South	25
17	Dunfermline Athletic	24
18	Ayr United	19

1957–58

1	Hearts	62
2	Rangers	49
3	Celtic	46
4	Clyde	42
5	Kilmarnock	37
6	Partick Thistle	37
7	Raith Rovers	35
8	Motherwell	32
9	Hibernian	31
10	Falkirk	31
11	Dundee	31
12	St Mirren	30
13	Aberdeen	30
14	Third Lanark	30
15	Queen Of The South	29
16	Airdrieonians	28
17	East Fife	23
18	Queen's Park	9

1958–59

1	Rangers	50
2	Hearts	48
3	Motherwell	44
4	Dundee	41
5	Airdrieonians	37
6	Celtic	36
7	St Mirren	35
8	Kilmarnock	34
9	Partick Thistle	34
10	Hibernian	32
11	Third Lanark	32
12	Stirling Albion	30
13	Aberdeen	29
14	Raith Rovers	29
15	Clyde	28
16	Dunfermline Athletic	28
17	Falkirk	27
18	Queen Of The South	18

OPPOSITE ABOVE: Born in Grangemouth, George Young started his career with junior side Kirkintilloch Rob Roy before moving to Rangers in 1941. Although primarily considered a centre half, he was often played at right back during his 16 years with Rangers (1941–1957), to accommodate Willie Woodburn in Rangers' renowned Iron Curtain defence.

OPPOSITE BELOW: Jock Stein was club captain until his Celtic playing career ended due to injury in 1956. He captained Celtic to their first League Championship since 1938 and first League and Scottish Cup Double since 1914.

Rangers achieve the treble

In April 1946 Aberdeen beat Rangers 3-2 in the final of the Scottish Southern League Cup. This had greater cachet than some of the other wartime competitions, and remained on the schedule simply as the League Cup when normal service resumed in 1946–47. There was a group stage, with four of the 16 top-flight sides seeded to meet lower-league opposition in the knockout phase. Aberdeen and Rangers contested the first final, too; this time Rangers scored a convincing 4-0 victory. Rangers were also winners of the rebranded "Division A", but it was third-placed Aberdeen who lifted the Scottish Cup, beating League runners-up Hibs 2-1 at Hampden. Scottish football had seen several doubles; the race was on to see which club could complete the domestic treble.

There was a mere two-year wait, for in 1948–49 Rangers enjoyed a clean sweep of the silverware. The Scottish Cup was won at a canter, Rangers putting at least three past Motherwell, Partick, East Fife and finalists Clyde. Division B champions Raith were overcome 2-0 in the League Cup Final, but the title race was tight, Rangers edging Dundee by a point. Dundee held a one-point advantage on the last day, but lost at Falkirk, while Rangers cruised to victory away to an Albion Rovers side that finished 14 points adrift at the bottom of the table.

Scottish Cup Finals

1947	Aberdeen	v	Hibernian	2-1
1948	Rangers	v	Greenock Morton	1-1
	Rangers	v	Greenock Morton	1-0
1949	Rangers	v	Clyde	4-1
1950	Rangers	v	East Fife	3-0
1951	Celtic	v	Motherwell	1-0
1952	Motherwell	v	Dundee	4-0
1953	Rangers	v	Aberdeen	1-1
	Rangers	v	Aberdeen	1-0
1954	Celtic	v	Aberdeen	2-1
1955	Clyde	v	Celtic	1-1
	Clyde	v	Celtic	1-0
1956	Hearts	v	Celtic	3-1
1957	Falkirk	v	Kilmarnock	1-1
	Falkirk	v	Kilmarnock	2-1
1958	Clyde	v	Hibernian	1-0
1959	St Mirren	v	Aberdeen	3-1

Gers retained two of their trophies the following season, but were denied successive trebles by East Fife, the team they beat in the Scottish Cup Final. The Fifers prevailed in the League Cup semis, and it was no great shock, for they had twice finished in the top four since being promoted as Division B Champions in 1947–48. The Fifers won the League Cup in promotion year, and made it two wins in three seasons by beating Dunfermline in the 1950 Final. A third success followed in 1953–54 during what was undoubtedly the club's golden period.

Hibs's "Famous Five"

Another team on the march was Hibernian, who save for a couple of Cup Final appearances had been starved of success since the early years of the century. Between 1947 and 1956 Hibs finished no lower than sixth, winning the Championship in 1948, 1951 and 1952. They were also runners-up three times to Rangers, losing out narrowly on goal average in 1952–53. This was the era of the "Famous Five" forward line – Smith, Johnstone, Reilly, Turnbull and Ormond – who made Hibs the most potent attacking force in the land, the division's top scorers six years running. They were less impressive in the Cups, losing in the final of each during this period, but the club did have the distinction of becoming the first British

representative in the battle for European honours. Hibs's 1955–56 European Cup run was ended by Stade Reims in the semis, though by then the team had passed its peak.

It was a good time for Edinburgh football. Hearts were a force to be reckoned with throughout the 1950s, never outside the top four and Champions in 1958. There was also a first Scottish Cup win in half a century, and two League Cup successes. The "Terrible Trio" of Alfie Conn, Willie Bauld and Jimmy Wardhaugh were the goalscoring heroes, the Maroons hitting 132 goals in the Championship-winning

Rangers' success was founded on the famous "Iron Curtain" defence.

season, a record for the top division. Runners-up Rangers were next highest scorers with 89, and finished 13 points behind. Hearts' goal difference was a remarkable 103, and defeat at Clyde the only reverse of the season. Dave Mackay was the driving force until he left for White Hart Lane in March 1959.

For Celtic, who had been led by former Parkhead legend Jimmy McGrory since 1945, it was something of a lean time. There were back-to-back League Cup wins, the second of those a 7-1 trouncing

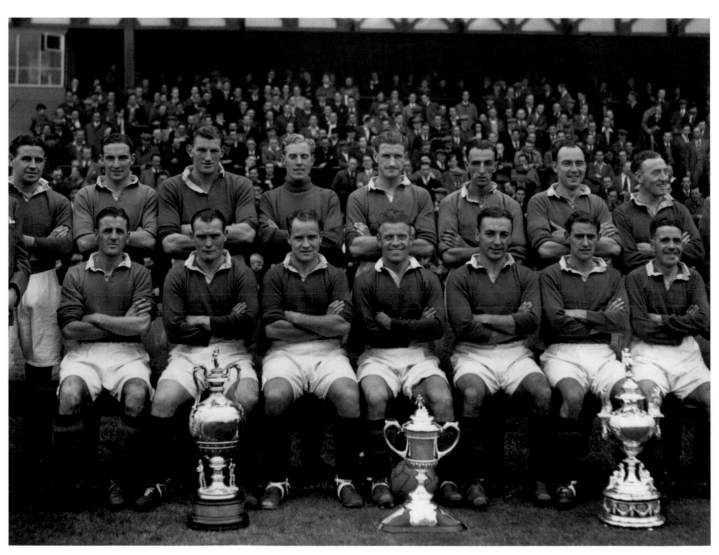

of Rangers at Hampden, the biggest margin in any major British final. The Hoops also notched two Scottish Cup successes, but the Championship went to Celtic Park just once in 13 years. Celtic's average League position during this period was a shade better than sixth. Rangers, by contrast, were Champions seven times in that period, and only twice dropped out of the top two. Their success was founded on the famous "Iron Curtain" defence, which included stalwarts George Young and Sammy Cox. And it continued even after Bill Struth, manager for 34 glory-filled years, stepped down in 1954. He died two years later, aged 81.

SFA refuse World Cup place

Scotland had withdrawn from FIFA twice over the issue of the status of amateur players. Along with the other home countries, Scotland rejoined the fold in 1946, and should have featured in the first postwar World Cup, staged in Brazil in 1950. FIFA had offered the top two finishers in the 1949–50 Home International Championship a place in the finals, but the SFA refused to go unless it was as champions. That made England's visit to Glasgow on 15 April a showdown, both sides having already beaten Wales and Northern Ireland. Chelsea's Roy Bentley scored the only goal of the game, and Scotland passed up the chance of a trip to Rio.

The SFA took a more pragmatic view when Scotland finished second in the 1953–54 Home Championship, this time allowing the country to take its place at the fifth World Cup, held in Switzerland. It was a shambolic affair. Team manager Andy Beattie, who shared national team duties with his role as Huddersfield Town boss, was only allowed to take 13 players, when the rules permitted 22-man squads. He resigned before a ball was kicked. Scotland went down to Austria and were hammered 7-0 by Uruguay, the country's heaviest defeat. Sweden '58 was little better, although Scotland at least claimed their first point in the competition, courtesy of a draw with Yugoslavia. The year ended on a bright note, Huddersfield's Denis Law scoring on his international debut, a 3-0 win against Wales. At 18 years 236 days, he became the youngest player to win a senior cap.

OPPOSITE: Rangers became the first side to win all three trophies in the same season in 1948–49. Back row: Waddell, McColl, Young, Brown, Woodburn, Findlay, Watkins, Rutherford, Simpson (Trainer). Front row: Rutherford, Gillick, Thornton, Shaw (captain), Williamson, Cox, Caskie.

BELOW: Celtic 1948. Back row: McGuire, R Milne, Milne, McPhail, Boden, McAuley. Front row: Weir, Evans, Johnston, Gallacher, Tully.

1960–1969
The World Stage

As the new decade got into its stride football faced a number of problems. Hooliganism, corruption and falling gates all gave cause for concern. On the pitch there was a marked increase in foul play, and fewer goals were scored as defences got on top. On a brighter note, Matt Busby built his third great side, English clubs made the breakthrough in European competition and the national side were crowned World Champions.

1960 The Soviet Union win the inaugural European Nations Cup, beating Yugoslavia 2-1 in the final. None of the home nations participate	**1960** Real Madrid lift the European Cup for the fifth successive year	Ipswich Town are League Champions	**1963** Alf Ramsey appointed England manager
1960 Burnley become League Champions. They didn't head the table until the final day of the season	**1961** Tottenham become the first club since the turn of the century to do the double	**1962** Denis Law joins Manchester United from Torino for a British record £115,000	**1963** The High Court rules the "retain and transfer" system to be a restraint of trade
1960 Football League Cup launched. Aston Villa are the first winners, though several clubs decline to enter	**1961** England beat Scotland 9-3 at Wembley	**1962** At the seventh World Cup, staged in Chile, England lose to Brazil in the quarter-finals	**1964** Spain are crowned European Champions after a 2-1 win over the Soviet Union
	1961 Rangers lose to Fiorentina in the final of the inaugural Cup Winners' Cup competition	**1963** Spurs beat Atletico Madrid 5-1 in the Cup Winners' Cup final, the first British club to win a European trophy	**1965** Kilmarnock edge out Hearts on goal average to claim their sole Scottish Championship
	1961 Abolition of the maximum wage		**1965** Jock Stein appointed Celtic manager
	1962 Alf Ramsey's newly promoted		

Changing attitudes

By the 1960s people were enjoying greater affluence and had many more options when it came to spending their "leisure pound". The demand for cars and foreign holidays went up, while every form of entertainment had to compete with television. In the Swinging Sixties England was at the cutting edge of the pop-music and fashion industries, and these were yet more diversions as the Baby Boomers came of age. There was also a distinct change in attitude, women no longer being content with playing a domestic role while the menfolk went off to the match.

BELOW LEFT: Forwards Johnny Haynes, Bobby Smith and Jimmy Greaves on England duty.

BELOW RIGHT: The score changes but the outcome is not in doubt at an exhibition match in May 1961. Commentators attributed England's recent run of victories to Walter Winterbottom's newly adopted 4-2-4 formation introduced in the face of current tactics.

OPPOSITE: Jimmy Greaves scores his first league goal for Chelsea against Tottenham Hotspur.

Fears over televised matches

The effect of all these factors was reflected in declining attendances, particularly for struggling clubs or those perceived as unglamorous. As the footballing authorities sought ways to encourage more people through the turnstiles, the one avenue they naturally fought shy of was the televising of matches. In 1960 negotiations between the Football League and the Independent Television Authority fell through over fears that broadcasting a live game might have an adverse effect on attendances. Concerns were not allayed by the proposal to schedule the matches so that they didn't clash with any other football taking place. Within a couple of years, however, the broadcasting companies persuaded the Football League that a highlights package would not be detrimental to the game, and indeed could help to generate more interest and a wider fan base.

When *Match of the Day* took to the airwaves in 1964, it quickly became an institution. Television turned the top players into celebrities as well as sportsmen. The authorities' fears that TV would lead to an army of armchair fans proved largely unfounded. However, seeing the likes of Greaves, Charlton and St John in action on the small screen did persuade a considerable number to switch their allegiance or to forge a new one. In short, the glamour clubs flourished at the expense of the rest.

> *When Match of the Day took to the airwaves in 1964, it quickly became an institution.*

1965 10 players are found guilty of match-fixing. Among those jailed and given life bans are ex-England internationals Peter Swan and Tony Kay

1965 Substitutes allowed for the first time, initially only to replace injured players

1965 West Ham beat 1860 Munich 2-0 in the Cup-Winners' Cup Final

1966 England win the eighth World Cup on home soil, beating West Germany 4-2 in the Final

1967 Scotland beat World Champions England 3-2 at Wembley

1967 Celtic's "Lisbon Lions" beat Inter Milan 2-1 to become the first British club to win the European Cup. A clean sweep of the three domestic trophies gives Celtic an unprecedented quadruple

1968 Manchester City pip neighbours United for the League crown, City's second Championship

1968 Manchester United become the first English club to lift the European Cup, beating Benfica 4-1 in the Wembley Final

1968 Alan Mullery becomes the first to be sent off while playing for England, in a European Championship semi-final against Yugoslavia. England lost 1-0

1968 Italy beat Yugoslavia 2-0 in the final of the European Championship

1968 Leeds beat Ferencvaros in the UEFA Cup Final, 1-0 on aggregate

1969 Leeds United's Championship-winning tally of 67 points sets a new top-flight record. Two defeats is also a record for a 42-match League programme

1969 Newcastle United beat Ujpest Dozsa in the Inter-Cities Fairs Cup Final, 6-2 on aggregate

Hill leads campaign to end wage cap

The cult of celebrity had another important knock-on effect: the rise of player power. In the early 1960s players became aware of their worth, and realised that they were being sorely undervalued. Before 1960 even the sport's greatest names reaped little financial reward for the pleasure they brought to millions of fans. After hanging up their boots there was no life of luxury. The lucky ones found alternative employment. Tommy Lawton and Hughie Gallacher both ended up on the dole, the latter committing suicide by throwing himself under a train in 1957. In that same year the Players' Union got a new chairman, Fulham's Jimmy Hill. Hill led the campaign to end the wage cap, which stood at £20 a week, £17 during the close season.

Haynes becomes first £100-a-week footballer

It took Hill four years to garner the support he needed to act. This was because the Players Union had been emasculated by mass resignations over the same issue more than 30 years earlier. In the depression of the 1920s the Union had been unable to prevent clubs from reducing the maximum wage to £8 a week. In the intervening years the Football League hardly condescended to meet with players' representatives. But in January 1961 the threat of strike action made the authorities sit up and take notice. In June of that year the maximum wage was abolished. England captain Johnny Haynes became the first £100-a-week footballer, his chairman Tommy Trinder declaring that he was delighted at finally being able to properly reward his star performer, who was worth every penny to the club.

ABOVE: Fulham's Jimmy Hill and Parker of Everton find themselves in the net while the ball sails past in January 1960.

BELOW: The Blackburn goalkeeper fails to save and Deeley scores a second goal for Wolves in the 1960 Final. Blackburn fans were disappointed when left-back Wheelan broke his leg forcing their team to play more than half the match with only 10 men. The game ended in a 3-0 win for Wolves.

OPPOSITE ABOVE LEFT INSERT: Johnny Haynes, who succeeded Billy Wright as England captain, leads his team out of the tunnel.

OPPOSITE ABOVE RIGHT: Prolific scorer Jimmy Greaves lashes the ball into the net when England met Spain in October 1960.

OPPOSITE BELOW: Haffey, Scotland's goalkeeper, is beaten by Bobby Smith's shot, England's fifth goal.

Johnny Haynes

Johnny Haynes was ardently loyal to Fulham, his only club, and that loyalty cost him dearly in terms of honours. At the time – Haynes was at Craven Cottage from 1952 to 1969 – the club was either in the Second Division or struggling in the lower reaches of the First.

England captain

Despite playing for an unfashionable and relatively unsuccessful club, Haynes established himself in the England side in the mid-1950s. An inside-forward who was noted for his wonderful passing, Haynes was a regular on the scoresheet. In his 56 England appearances he bagged 18 goals and, in 1959, took over the captaincy of the national side after Billy Wright's retirement. He was an essential player in both the 1958 and

1962 World Cups, helping England to the quarter-final in the latter tournament.

Soon after the World Cup in Chile, in 1962, a serious car crash ended his international career. But loyal to the end, he turned out for Fulham for another seven years. A reward for that loyalty and an indication of how valued Haynes was can be seen in the fact that he became the first £100-a-week footballer after the maximum wage was abolished in 1961. He ended his footballing days as player-manager of Durban City after emigrating to South Africa. He died in 2005.

England 9
Scotland 3

The early form of the international side in the 1960s was encouraging. After defeats in Spain and Hungary, England went on a fine run in the next six games. They rattled in 40 goals, including an 8-0 home win over Mexico and a 9-0 victory in Luxembourg. But the outstanding result was undoubtedly the 9-3 demolition of Scotland on 15 April 1961. It was a strong Scotland side – including Law, Mackay and St John – which came to Wembley for what was the decider in the Home International Championship. A Greaves hat-trick, together with two goals each from Johnny Haynes and Bobby Smith, contributed towards the Scots' worst-ever result in international football.

Ramsey takes over from Winterbottom

Performances such as these boded well for the 1962 World Cup in Chile, but the tournament proved to be something of a disappointment. England did reach the last eight, squeezing through their group after a win, a draw and a defeat, but they were unconvincing. After a 3-1 defeat against holders Brazil they were on their way home.

The tournament marked the end of Walter Winterbottom's 16-year reign as England manager. In came Alf Ramsey, who had worked wonders at Ipswich, although he was said to be only third choice for the job.

Defeats against France and Scotland got the new regime off to an inauspicious start. Even so, Ramsey was soon predicting victory in the 1966 World Cup. Despite home advantage, England were not fancied to do well. The international side had lost just four times on home soil against overseas opposition, but as the optimists rested their hopes on fortress Wembley, the doom-mongers pointed to England's World Cup record since 1950.

BELOW: Haffey falls to the ground in despair as England scores a seventh.

RIGHT: Despite a run of successes, England's lacklustre performance in the 1962 World Cup spelled the end of Winterbottom's tenure as manager. Mindful of the need to make a good showing in the next World Cup to be staged in England, the FA employed new manager Alf Ramsey and granted him autonomy in team selection.

Spurs become the century's first Double winners

On the pitch the decade got off to a sparkling start as Bill Nicholson's Spurs side became the first of the century to achieve the Double. The strength of the side was epitomised by the two wing-halves: granite-hard Dave Mackay and the cultured, cerebral Danny Blanchflower. Spurs began with a record run of 11 straight wins, and their 31 victories in all was another League best. 66 points equalled Arsenal's total of 1931. The team banged in 115 goals, a postwar record, and that was before the incomparable Jimmy Greaves had joined the club. Nicholson thus became only the second man to win the Championship as both player and manager. The season took its toll in the latter stages of the Cup. Spurs needed a replay to beat Division Two side Sunderland in the 6th round, and they were below par when they took on Leicester City at Wembley. But top scorer Bobby Smith and Terry Dyson both beat City keeper Gordon Banks and history was made. Following the Cup successes of 1901 and 1921, and the championship in 1951, fans were already noting the club's peculiar affinity with the second year of the decade.

BELOW: Blanchflower lifts the Cup. Following in the footsteps of Preston and Aston Villa, Spurs become the first side to complete the Double since 1897. Nicholson's team had secured the League title in mid-April but had to wait three weeks before meeting Leicester in the Cup Final. Spurs won 2-0.

Bill Nicholson

Bill Nicholson spent his entire career at Tottenham, joining the club as a 16-year-old. When his playing days were over, Nicholson became a coach under Arthur Rowe, the architect of the "push and run" side that had won the title in 1951. He took over as manager in 1959, and assembled a team which took Rowe's ideas to dazzling new heights. His team combined superb ball skills with steely resolve, featuring players of the stature of Blanchflower and Mackay. In 1960–61 he guided Spurs through a glorious campaign, which saw the team win 31 of their 42 League games, scoring 115 goals in the process. They secured the Championship by an eight-point margin, then beat Leicester City 2-0 in the FA Cup Final, despite going into the game with an injury-ravaged squad. No 20th-century team had won the Double, and many thought the demands of the modern game meant that it was unachievable. Nicholson proved the doubters wrong.

Spurs retained the Cup the following season, and in 1963 Nicholson became the first manager of a British club to win a European trophy. Spurs beat holders Atletico Madrid 5-1 in the Cup Winners' Cup Final in Rotterdam. Victory over Chelsea in the 1967 FA Cup Final meant that Nicholson had brought the trophy to White Hart Lane three times in seven years.

Nicholson stepped down during the 1974–75 season but remained associated with the club into his 80s. He died in 2004, aged 85.

ABOVE INSERT: Bill Nicholson and Danny Blanchflower. Nicholson celebrated a personal double having played in the 1951 Tottenham side that won the League before going on to manage the team that triumphed ten years later.

Eastham takes Newcastle to court

Clubs might have had to pay their top players more but they still had the whip hand by dint of the "retain-and-transfer" system that was in place. Under this arrangement players were bound to their clubs even at the end of their contracts. In 1963 England international George Eastham was seeking a move away from Newcastle United and challenged this restriction of his freedom in the courts. The ruling went in his favour, with the prevailing system condemned as an "unreasonable restraint of trade".

ABOVE: 23 November 1963: Arsenal players wear black armbands and stand in silent tribute to the late President Kennedy before the start of their match against Blackpool. (l-r) Eastham, Barnwell, McCullogh, Anderson, Clarke, MacLeod, Strong, Brown, Baker, Ure and Furnell.

BELOW LEFT: The Wales team that beat Scotland 2-0 in Cardiff, 1960 – a first victory in the annual fixture for 23 years.

BELOW RIGHT: Adamson of Burnley and Fulham's Cook and O'Donnell go for the ball as the teams fight for a place in the 1962 Cup Final. Burnley finished as runners-up, losing in the Final to Spurs.

Cup Winners' Cup takes off

Spurs kept the Cup the following year, beating Burnley 3-1 in the Final, but slipped to third in the League. Their European Cup campaign ended at the semi-final stage, when they went down 4-3 on aggregate to holders Benfica. Retaining the Cup in 1962 gave Spurs entry into the following season's Cup Winners' Cup competition. This had been launched in 1960, the brainchild of a group of European Football Federations. In just two seasons it had made more impact than the third European trophy up for grabs, the Inter-Cities Fairs Cup. Under the rules of the Fairs Cup, which had been launched in the mid-1950s, industrial towns and cities competed with each other, matches arranged to coincide with trade fairs. This meant that the first two tournaments took five years to complete! Moreover, a city could enter a club side or a representative XI. Between 1955 and 1958 Barcelona beat a London side including Kelsey (Arsenal), Blanchflower (Spurs), Greaves (Chelsea) and Haynes (Fulham). By the mid-1960s the competition had severed its connections with trade fairs and become a sought-after trophy for the top European clubs who failed to win their domestic league or cup.

Danny Blanchflower

Danny Blanchflower joined Tottenham Hotspur from Aston Villa for £30,000 in 1954. Over the next ten years Blanchflower, an intelligent wing-half with a sharp tactical brain, became a legend at White Hart Lane. He was the brains and the driving force of the side, which, in the 1960–61 season, won the much sought-after Double; he was the first captain of the century to lift both trophies in one season. Following on from that unparalleled success it was fitting that Blanchflower won his second Footballer of the Year award — only Tom Finney had managed that achievement at the time.

Blanchflower steered Spurs to FA Cup victory the following season, even getting on the scoresheet himself in the team's 3-1 win over Burnley in the Final at Wembley. In what was to be his last but one season before retirement, Blanchflower inspired Tottenham to a 5-1 win over Atletico Madrid in the European Cup Winners' Cup Final, becoming the first captain of a British side to lift a European trophy.

Blanchflower was born in Belfast and played 56 times for Northern Ireland, where he also took on the captain's role. His most memorable moment with the national side was probably in the 1958 World Cup, when he led the side to the quarter-finals. He died in 1993, aged 67.

ABOVE: After 10 years with Spurs, Danny Blanchflower retired in 1964. Alan Mullery, bought from Fulham, was Nicholson's choice to fill the gap left by Blanchflower.

LEFT ABOVE: Dave Mckay and his fellow Spurs players can't hide their astonishment as White's corner swings in without anyone touching it.

LEFT: Fulham's Johnny Haynes in action.

First British side to win European trophy

In 1962–63 Spurs became the first British side to win a European trophy when they lifted the Cup Winners' Cup. They put out Rangers, Slovan Bratislava and OFK Belgrade en route to the final, where they faced holders Atletico Madrid. Despite missing Mackay through injury, Spurs ran out 5-1 winners. The key moment came in the second half when Spurs were 2-1 up. Terry Dyson floated a cross into the box and it swirled over keeper Madinabeytia into the net.

Nicholson ends Greaves's Italian nightmare

Jimmy Greaves scored two of the goals that night in Rotterdam. Greaves had been one of a number of high-profile players lured to the Continent by a bigger wage-packet and better lifestyle. His time at AC Milan following an £80,000 move from Chelsea had not been a happy one and he was only too pleased when Bill Nicholson paid £99,999 to bring him back to the First Division. It was a British transfer record, although Nicholson kept it below the six-figure mark so that Greaves wouldn't be burdened with the tag of the first £100,000 player. Denis Law had an equally unhappy time after leaving Manchester City to join Torino. The one outstanding success story in this regard was John Charles, the Leeds United and Wales star who was lionised by Turin fans after his move to Juventus in 1957.

ABOVE: Players parade the Cup Winners' Cup through the streets of Tottenham. l-r: Cliff Jones (rear), Bill Brown (front), Ron Henry, Jimmy Greaves (holding cup) and Terry Dyson.

Jimmy Greaves

Jimmy Greaves was a slightly built inside-forward with lightning-fast feet, a razor-sharp brain and a killer instinct in front of goal. Throughout the 1960s Greaves was the foremost goal-poacher in English football. Although closely associated with Tottenham Hotspur, he started his career at Chelsea where he became a teenage prodigy before joining AC Milan in 1961. His failure to settle in Italy, where he played just 15 games, enabled Spurs' boss Bill Nicholson to bring him to White Hart Lane for what was then the hefty price tag of £99,999.

Record goalscorer

During the following nine years Greaves hit 220 league goals for Spurs, including 37 in the 1962–63 season, both of which are still club records. He was the First Division's top scorer six times in that nine-year period. Despite a much-publicised, and ultimately victorious, battle with alcoholism, his goalscoring talents were evident throughout his career. By the time he retired, after playing for a number of seasons for another London club, West Ham, he had scored a total of 357 league goals, all in the First Division.

44 goals for England

Unfortunately for Greaves, in a decade which witnessed many of his most incredible achievements, he chose the worst possible moment to suffer a drop in form. He was Alf Ramsey's first-choice striker as the England team went into the 1966 World Cup, but was replaced by Geoff Hurst in the latter stages of the tournament. Despite missing several of the 1966 World Cup games, including the Final, he scored 44 times for England, putting him third behind Bobby Charlton and Gary Lineker in the all-time list of England strikers. But Greaves's haul came from just 57 international appearances, far fewer than either Lineker or Charlton, who won 80 and 106 caps, respectively – testament to his magnificent goal-scoring talents.

Mackay suffers two broken legs in a year

After 1963 the great Spurs side broke up very quickly. It was a new-look team which brought the club its only other piece of silverware of the decade, a third FA Cup win in 1967. Of the eleven who had won the Cup Winners' Cup only Greaves was on the pitch when Spurs beat Chelsea 2-1. Most of the changes had been organic but one was the result of a tragedy: John White, the 27-year-old Scottish international inside-forward, was killed by lightning on a London golf course in July 1964. In the same year Dave Mackay broke his left leg twice within ten months, something which would have ended the career of a player with less resolve. But having missed out on that European glory night, Mackay battled back to play on for eight more years, including the Wembley Final of 1967.

RIGHT INSERT: Alan Mullery and captain Dave Mackay (right) hold the FA Cup after a 2-1 win over Chelsea in the 1967 Cup Final. Mackay and Greaves were the only representatives of the Tottenham side that won the Cup in 1962.

BELOW: Bobby Charlton and his manager Matt Busby talk with a young fan.

BOTTOM: Accrington Stanley skipper Bob Wilson reads the bill for a match that was never to take place, the club being forced to resign from the league because of financial difficulties. Ironically, Exeter, too, was suffering from crippling debts.

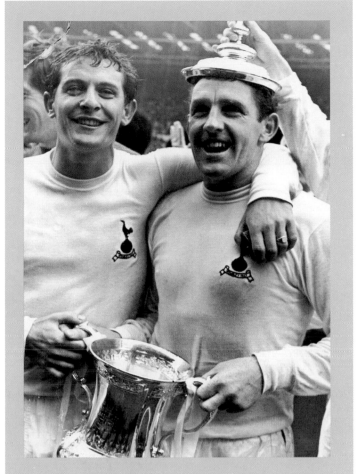

Dave Mackay

After starting his career with Heart of Midlothian, Dave Mackay joined Tottenham Hotspur in 1959. As a dynamic and inspirational half-back he provided the steel and drive in the great Spurs side of the early 1960s.

Although he was already an established Scotland international before he joined Tottenham, it was at club level that Mackay enjoyed his greatest successes. Spurs' celebrated Double was achieved in the 1960–61 season, and the team retained the FA Cup the following year. Injury forced him to miss the final of the European Cup Winners' Cup in 1963, when Spurs beat holders Atletico Madrid 5-1.

Footballer of the Year

His career looked in serious doubt as a result of two broken legs, sustained within a ten-month period in 1964, but the indomitable Mackay fought back to captain Spurs' to another FA Cup triumph in 1967. The following season he transferred to Derby County where he led the team to the Division Two championship in 1968–69, an achievement which earned him the Footballer of the Year award, an honour he shared with Manchester City's Tony Book.

Ramsey's Ipswich take First Division by storm

The team that took the title from Spurs in 1962 was Alf Ramsey's unheralded Ipswich Town. The East Anglia club had risen from the Third Division (South) to English Champions in just five years. Ramsey's men won the Division Two and Division One titles in successive seasons, the fourth club to record that particular achievement. Ramsey the player had been schooled in Spurs' great "push and run" side of the previous decade, and it was outstanding team play rather than brilliant individuals that carried Ipswich to the title. It would put Ramsey's name in the frame when the England job became vacant following the 1962 World Cup.

Exit Accrington Stanley

While Ipswich were riding high, one of the famous names in the English game was making a sad exit. Accrington Stanley, one of the League's founder members, had mounting debts and was forced to resign from the Fourth Division. This was yet another sign of the polarisation between the haves and have-nots, a trend that was set to continue.

BELOW: Spectators and staff show their feelings, as Ramsey's Ipswich are one goal away from winning the League title in 1962. Ramsey's side, recently languishing in the Third Division and with its absence of star players, were unlikely champions, tipped by pundits for relegation rather than triumph.

BOTTOM: Manchester United 'keeper Gaskell goes to full stretch to snatch the ball from Leicester's Cross in the 1963 Cup Final. David Herd and later Denis Law, back from Turin, had reinforced Busby's side at the start of the '61–2 season. Both players paid dividends in the 1963 Final – Herd chalking up two goals and Law the third.

Everton champions in year of the big freeze

Accrington's demise was in sharp contrast to Everton, whose boss Harry Catterick had been on a spending spree in a bid to bring the glory days back to Goodison. The spine of the side was strong: keeper Gordon West, centre-half Brian Labone and centre-forward Alex Young. Everton didn't secure the title until 11 May 1963, when it became mathematically impossible for Spurs to catch them. The late finish to the season had been caused by a three-month winter freeze, which had played havoc with the fixture lists. Over 400 games had to be postponed, disrupting the season even more than the big freeze of 1946–47. The Pools companies initially suffered like everyone else, before coming up with a novel solution to the problem. A Pools Panel made up of pundits decided the outcome of postponed matches. Punters were thus still able to have a flutter, although some of the experts' decisions were as controversial as any dubious offside.

Everton would remain top-six contenders for the remainder of the decade but would not clinch the title again until the start of the next.

Meanwhile, there were two FA Cup appearances, against Sheffield Wednesday in 1966 and West Bromwich Albion two years later. Everton were favourites to win both. They had to come back from 2-0 down to beat Wednesday, Mike Trebilcock hitting two and Derek Temple grabbing the winner. In 1968 they went down to an extra-time goal from Albion's Jeff Astle.

Match-fixing scandal

By that time one of Catterick's early acquisitions had left the game in disgrace. Wing-half Tony Kay, who was capped once for England, was one of a number of players implicated in a match-rigging scandal, a story that broke in *The People* in April 1964. Kay, along with former Sheffield Wednesday team-mate Peter Swan was found guilty of conspiring to throw a match against Ipswich in 1962. Swan was also an England player, and went to Chile as part of the 1962 World Cup squad. Investigations revealed that the problem was even more widespread than at first thought, with an ex-player named Jimmy Gauld the chief orchestrator of the scam. Gauld received a four-year prison sentence and ten players were given life bans.

Bobby Charlton

Bobby Charlton won just about every honour in the game, at both club and international level. Football was in his blood; his brother Jack also became a professional footballer and his uncle was Jackie Milburn, a legend on Tyneside in the 1950s. A true gentleman of football, he was famed for playing the game in the spirit of genuine sportsmanship. Indeed, in a sparkling 20-year career he was booked just once – for time-wasting when his side was losing!

Charlton was signed to Manchester United in 1955 as part of Matt Busby's grand scheme to comb the country for the best young talent in the land. In a wonderfully ironic turn, he scored twice against Charlton Athletic on his debut in 1956. He and the other "Busby Babes", as Busby's young team became known, looked set to dominate football for many years but on 6 February 1958 the team was all but wiped out in the Munich air crash. Charlton survived and recovered sufficiently to receive the first of his 106 England caps just a few weeks after the tragedy.

Deep-lying centre-forward

Originally a winger or inside-forward, Charlton developed into a deep-lying centre-forward and during the 1960s he was a key player in Busby's exciting new United side, and was equally influential for England. He distributed passes with pinpoint accuracy or burst forward to unleash thunderous shots with either foot. He helped England to World Cup glory in 1966; during the campaign, Mexico and Portugal both found themselves on the receiving end of his scoring power. His performances in that season won him the European Footballer of the Year award.

Triumph for Charlton

Two years later, in 1968, Charlton captained the United side, which lifted the European Cup, scoring two goals in a 4-1 victory over Benfica at Wembley. It was an emotional and powerful triumph for Charlton, the team and Busby, as it was during a campaign to win in Europe that so many of the "Busby Babes" had lost their lives in the Munich air crash, ten years earlier. Charlton played his 606th and final League game for United at Stamford Bridge in 1973.

During the 1970 World Cup in Mexico he played his final game for England in the quarter-final against West Germany. Many believe that England manager Alf Ramsey's decision to substitute Charlton in the second half, when England were 2-1 ahead, was a crucial factor in the team's defeat. His record 106 caps was subsequently overhauled, but his 49 goals has yet to be beaten. In 1994 he was honoured for his services to football – Sir Bobby Charlton.

The Shankly era

After Everton's 1963 championship, three clubs dominated the domestic game: Liverpool, Leeds and Manchester United. Liverpool had had a miserable time of things in the 1950s, much of it spent in the Second Division. Manager Phil Taylor was sacked in November 1959 and a month later a new messiah arrived. 46-year-old Bill Shankly was persuaded to leave Huddersfield and take over the reins at Anfield on a £2500 salary. Over the next three years he let some players go, revitalised the careers of others and made some key signings. These included Ron Yeats from Dundee United, Ian St John from Motherwell and Gordon Milne from Preston. The Reds stormed to the Second Division championship in 1961–62 and after just one year of consolidation in the top flight became champions in 1964. After a slow start that season, Liverpool took 47 points from 30 games to secure their 6th championship. Defensive football was on the way, yet Liverpool were in irresistible goalscoring form, particularly at Anfield. They banged in 60 goals in front of their home fans, an average of nearly three per game. Roger Hunt was again the goalscoring hero, hitting 31 of the team's 92 league goals.

First FA Cup win for Liverpool

The following season Liverpool suffered a reaction in their League form, slipping to 7th, but the club had two memorable Cup runs. They finally got their name on the FA Cup, thanks to a 2-1 win over a Leeds side, which had just finished as runners-up in the League. After a cagey 90 minutes in which defences were on top, Liverpool scored through Hunt. Bremner hit an equaliser, then St John confirmed his status as an Anfield legend by heading in an Ian Callaghan cross. However, the hero of the hour was Gerry Byrne, who played for most

of the match with a broken collarbone following an early clash with Bobby Collins. The use of substitutes was finally allowed the following season, initially just for injuries and then for tactical purposes, too. After all the debilitating injuries that had dogged Wembley finals in recent years it was a decision that was long overdue.

ABOVE: The Cup is held aloft by Liverpool skipper Ron Yeats and Gordon Milne, who had to stand down from the team because of injury, in the lap of honour at Wembley in 1965. Others are: (l-r) Hunt who scored Liverpool's first goal, Smith and Stevenson. Shankly's team triumphed over Leeds by 2-1, all three goals being scored in extra-time.

RIGHT: Ron Yeats and Ian St John at Euston Station, taking the Cup back to Anfield for the first time in Liverpool's 73-year history.

OPPOSITE BELOW: Liverpool pose in 1965 with the FA Cup and the Charity Shield. However, having started the 1964–65 season as reigning champions, the club's performance in the League was less impressive. Liverpool finished in 7th place and Manchester United, the previous year's runners-up took the title, with Leeds hot on their heels.

OPPOSITE ABOVE: When Bill Shankly arrived at Anfield in 1959 his first task was to help Liverpool regain its place in the First Division, and this was achieved by the beginning of the 1962–63 season.

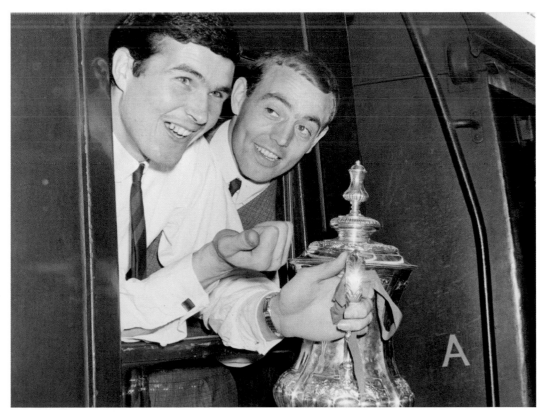

Reds lose two finals

New Cup-holders Liverpool barely had time to draw breath before facing World Club champions Inter Milan in the semi-final of the European Cup. Liverpool pulled off a sensational 3-1 win over Helenio Herrera's much-vaunted side at home, but three controversial goals by the Italians at the San Siro turned the tie on its head. The ball was kicked out of keeper Tommy Lawrence's hands for one of Inter's goals, and the fact that such incidents went unpunished led Shankly and others to suspect that the officials had been bribed.

Liverpool recovered to lift the title again the following season. They also made it to the final of the Cup Winners Cup, following a titanic struggle with Celtic in the semis. They faced Borussia Dortmund at Hampden Park in the final, the German side winning 2-1 in extra-time.

RIGHT: George Best and Manchester City's Mike Summerbee pose for photographers outside their boutique, Edwardia. Busby gave Best his first game for United on 14 September 1963 against West Bromwich Albion. It was not until December that Best was offered another opportunity to play and the famous line-up of Charlton, Law and Best was born.

Denis Law

Playing alongside George Best and Bobby Charlton at Manchester United in the 1960s, Denis Law was the King of the Stretford End, an unstoppable firebrand, exciting and unpredictable going forward, a showman with one arm raised exultantly when he found the net, which he did so often – 236 goals in 399 appearances for the club. He scored the first, and created the other two, in United's 3-1 FA Cup Final victory over Leicester City in 1963, and his skill and infectious enthusiasm for winning helped the club to the league title in both 1964–65 and 1966–67. He was named European Footballer of the Year in 1964. In United's European campaigns, he scored four hat-tricks, but missed the 1968 European Cup-winning final with an injured knee.

30 goals for Scotland

Born in Aberdeen in 1940, he'd turned professional at Huddersfield Town in 1957, only to be poached by Manchester City in 1960, for a then record fee of £55,000. Another record fee, £100,000, took him to Torino the next year, but by 1962 he had joined United. On his international debut in 1958 aged 18, he was the youngest Scot to be capped since 1899, and his tally of 30 goals for Scotland (in 55 outings) was equalled only by Dalglish. The characteristic impish grin was broadly on display when he played in the Scottish side that beat England 3-2 at Wembley.

A passionate United man, Law found himself out of favour with manager Tommy Docherty in the declining side of the early 1970s, and in 1973 went back to rivals Manchester City, on a free transfer. There was to be no cockiness, pleasure or one-armed saluting when his backheeled goal against United sent his old club down to the Second Division in 1974. He called it a day at the end of that season, going out of the game he loved while he was still at the top of his form.

Bobby Moore

An Essex boy, Bobby Moore was West Ham's, and England's, gentleman-footballer. His modesty belied the inspirational leadership he showed when captaining club and country. Famed for his incisive tackling, timing and sureness in defence, he was also one of the most accurate passers of the ball the English game has ever seen.

Moore joined the Hammers in 1958 at the age of 17 and showed tenacious loyalty, playing 545 games for the club. He led them to their first-ever FA Cup Final win, over Preston North End in 1964, and the European Cup Winners' Cup the following year, in a 2-0 victory over 1860 Munich.

England's youngest-ever captain

His international career was stellar. After a record 18 outings for England's youth team, Moore joined the senior side in 1962. He played in that year's World Cup in Chile, when England lost to Brazil in the quarter-finals. A year later, with Alf Ramsey in charge, Moore became England's youngest-ever captain, and in 1966 led his team out at Wembley to their historic 4-2 World Cup win against West Germany. Four years later, he captained the defending champions in Mexico, where in the group-stage game against Brazil he had one of his most memorable games. Moore and Pelé's embrace at the end of the match, which Brazil won 1-0, was eloquent – full as it was of genuine mutual respect.

Classically skilful

In the 1970s, after a series of disagreements with manager Ron Greenwood, Moore left West Ham to join Fulham and helped the team to reach the 1975 FA Cup Final – ironically, against 2-0 winners West Ham. He ended his playing days in the United States, then went into management, but with little success, first at Oxford City and then Southend.

Moore had seemed to have it all in the optimistic era of the 1960s – he was blond, handsome, gracious and classically skilful, with an uncanny ability to read the game. Tragically, he died at the age of 51, in 1993, from bowel cancer.

RIGHT: Bobby Moore led West Ham to their first-ever FA Cup Final win, when they beat Preston North End in 1964

1966 World Cup: England's finest hour

The ex-defender Ramsey brought a solid look to the England side. Nobby Stiles was the defensive anchor in front of a solid back four. Ramsey had wingers Ian Callaghan, John Connelly and Terry Paine in his squad but as the tournament progressed he decided to dispense with wide players altogether. That added to the defensive solidity of the team; the question now was whether they would be able to break the opposition down and score themselves.

Progress to the knockout stage was unspectacular. A dull, goalless draw against Uruguay was followed by 2-0 wins over Mexico and France. The quarter-final clash with Argentina was an explosive affair. The turning point came when Argentine captain Antonio Rattin was ordered off for verbally abusing the German referee after he had already been booked. There was a long delay as Rattin refused to leave the field. Geoff Hurst scored the game's only goal, a glancing header 13 minutes from time. The Hurst-Hunt strike partnership would continue for the rest of the tournament. Jimmy Greaves, the most prolific striker in the squad with 43 goals in just 51 appearances, had chosen the worst possible moment to suffer a loss of form.

The sporting semi-final

Ramsey branded the Argentine players "animals" and refused to let his players swap shirts at the final whistle. This was just one of many ill-tempered encounters. Pelé had come in for very rough treatment as Brazil failed to make it beyond the group stages. By contrast, England's semi-final against Portugal was an oasis of sportsmanship. In a fast, free-flowing game Bobby Charlton scored twice, but England had to live on their nerves in the last few minutes as Eusebio pulled one back from the penalty spot.

Weber forces extra time

England's opponents in the final were West Germany. They had beaten a Uruguay side reduced to nine men in the quarter-finals, and in the semis Russia had also had a man sent off. Helmut Haller opened the scoring in the final, capitalising on a weak clearance from Ray Wilson after 13 minutes. Within minutes the teams were level as Bobby Moore flighted a free-kick onto the head of his West Ham team-mate Hurst, who powered the ball past Tilkowski. The third of the Hammers' contingent, Martin Peters, put England ahead with less than 15 minutes to go. The man whom Ramsey had described as "10 years ahead of his time" scored from close range after a Hurst shot was blocked. A West Germany free-kick in the last minute somehow found its way through a crowded box and Wolfgang Weber squeezed the ball in at the far post. It meant that extra time would be played for the first time since 1934, which was also the last occasion that the host nation had won the tournament.

Hurst's controversial goal

20-year-old Alan Ball was still full of running, and it was his right-wing cross 10 minutes into extra time that led to the most controversial moment in World Cup history. Hurst controlled the ball, turned and let fly, only to see his shot hit the underside of the bar. It bounced

OPPOSITE ABOVE: A clash of headgear as an England supporter reaches to shake hands with a Mexican supporter wearing a giant sombrero before the opening match of the World Cup tournament between England and Uruguay on 11 July 1966.

OPPOSITE BELOW. Greaves runs towards goal pursued by Uruguay's Ubinas in an inglorious beginning to England's World Cup campaign. Despite winning 16 corners and making 15 shots on goal, England did not score and the match ended in a draw.

ABOVE: Gordon Banks takes control in the World Cup Final. Banks did not concede a goal in the competition until the semi-final against Portugal.

down and was cleared, but had the ball crossed the line? The referee consulted his Russian linesman who was in no doubt that it had. Hurst sealed victory by hammering in a fourth for England in the last minute. It also made him the only man to score a hat-trick in a World Cup final. Technology later suggested that he was fortunate not to have his second goal ruled out, but that didn't detract from the jubilant scenes at Wembley on 30 July 1966. England were World Champions. For Bobby Moore it was the completion of a memorable hat-trick of his own. He had captained the West Ham side, which won the FA Cup in 1964 and the Cup Winners' Cup the following year. It was thus the third time in as many years that Moore had raised a trophy aloft at Wembley.

World Cup 1966 Results

Group 1

England	0	Uruguay	0
France	1	Mexico	1
Uruguay	2	France	1
England	2	Mexico	0
Uruguay	0	Mexico	0
England	2	France	0

	P	W	D	L	F	A	Pts
England	3	2	1	0	4	0	5
Uruguay	3	1	2	0	2	1	4
Mexico	3	0	2	1	1	3	2
France	3	0	1	2	2	5	1

Group 2

W. Germany	5	Switzerland	0
Argentina	2	Spain	1
Spain	2	Switzerland	1
Argentina	2	Switzerland	0
W. Germany	2	Spain	1
W. Germany	1	Argentina	1

	P	W	D	L	F	A	Pts
W. Germany	3	2	1	0	8	2	5
Argentina	3	2	1	0	4	1	5
Spain	3	1	1	1	2	3	3
Switzerland	3	0	1	2	1	7	1

Group 3

Brazil	2	Bulgaria	0
Portugal	3	Hungary	1
Hungary	3	Brazil	1
Portugal	3	Bulgaria	0
Portugal	3	Brazil	1
Hungary	3	Bulgaria	1

	P	W	D	L	F	A	Pts
Portugal	3	3	0	0	9	2	6
Hungary	3	2	0	1	7	5	4
Brazil	3	1	0	2	4	6	2
Bulgaria	3	0	0	3	1	8	0

Group 4

Sov. Union	3	N. Korea	0
Italy	2	Chile	0
Chile	1	N. Korea	1
Sov. Union	1	Italy	0
N. Korea	1	Italy	0
Sov. Union	2	Chile	1

	P	W	D	L	F	A	Pts
Sov. Union	3	3	0	0	6	1	6
N. Korea	3	1	1	1	2	4	3
Italy	3	1	0	2	2	2	2
Chile	3	0	1	2	2	5	1

Quarter-Finals

England	1	Argentina	0
W. Germany	4	Uruguay	0
Portugal	5	N. Korea	3
Sov. Union	2	Hungary	1

Semi-Finals

| W. Germany | 2 | Sov. Union | 1 |
| England | 2 | Portugal | 1 |

3rd Place Play-off

| Portugal | 2 | Sov. Union | 1 |

Final July 30 – Wembley Stadium

England	4	W. Germany	2
(Hurst 19, 100, 119, Peters 77)		(Haller 13, Weber 89)	
Aet ht: 1-1 90 min 2-2.		Ref: Dienst (Swi)	
Att: 96,924.			

England:
Banks, Cohen, Wilson, Stiles, J Charlton, Moore,
Ball, Hunt, R Charlton, Hurst, Peters
West Germany:
Tilkowski, Höttges, Schnellinger, Beckenbauer, Schülz, Weber, Haller,
Overath, Seeler, Held, Emmerich.

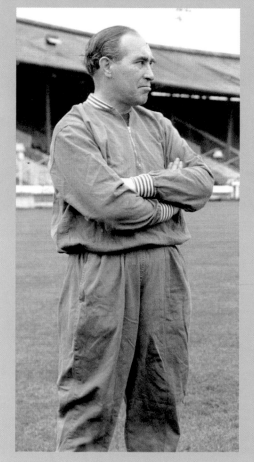

Sir Alf Ramsey

Alf Ramsey was a cultured full-back in the famous Spurs' "push and run" side, which won the Championship in 1951. He was capped 32 times for England between 1949 and 1954. After his playing days were over, Ramsey took over as manager of Ipswich Town. In seven years Ramsey took the unfashionable East Anglia club from the Third Division to the top flight, culminating in the League Championship in 1961–62. It was on the strength of this achievement that he was offered the England manager's job in 1963. Ramsey was the first full-time incumbent and he insisted on being given sole responsibility for selection, a freedom that his predecessor had not enjoyed.

Early in his tenure as national team boss he predicted that England would win the 1966 World Cup. That looked a long way off when his side was hammered 5-2 by France in his first game in charge. Three years later, Ramsey fulfilled his promise as his "wingless wonders" triumphed, beating West Germany in the Final.

After going out at the semi-final stage of the 1968 European Championship, England went to Mexico to defend their world crown. Many thought that Ramsey's squad in 1970 was even stronger than that which had won the tournament four years earlier. West Germany ended England's hopes at the quarter-final stage, coming back from 2-0 down to win 3-2. Some thought Ramsey's decision to take off both Charlton and Peters was instrumental in the defeat.

He survived that disappointment, and another quarter-final exit in the 1972 European Championship, when the Germans again proved to be the stumbling-block. He was finally dismissed after England drew with Poland at Wembley in 1973, a result which meant that England failed to qualify for the 1974 World Cup. Ramsey was knighted in the 1967 New Year's Honours list. He died in 1999.

Rise of Leeds

Don Revie's transformation of Leeds United was if anything even more dramatic than Shankly's at Liverpool. The Yorkshire club was flirting with relegation to the Third Division in 1962, yet by the middle of the decade they were a formidable footballing machine. Revie had been a deep-lying centre-forward in the Manchester City side of the mid-1950s, and Footballer of the Year in 1955. Ten years later he was the architect behind a powerhouse Leeds side which was universally respected if not always admired. Players of the stature of Billy Bremner, Bobby Collins, Jack Charlton and Norman Hunter took Leeds to the top – or, more often, second place. 1964–65 was to prove all too typical: runners-up in the League and beaten finalists in the Cup.

New points record as defences get on top

After three more seasons of finishing in the top four, and defeat in the 1966 Fairs Cup Final, Leeds finally won the title in 1968–69. And they did it in fine style, losing just twice in the League. 67 points set a new record, eclipsing Arsenal's 1931 tally by one. Leeds' goals column that season made interesting reading: 66 scored, just 26 conceded. At the beginning of the decade Spurs' Double-winning side had scored 115 and let in 55. In that year even relegated Newcastle scored 86! English teams were now regularly coming up against Continental opposition, and in particular the miserly "catenaccio" system operated by Italian sides. Tight defence was seen as the key to success.

BELOW LEFT: Referee Ken Burns hears the views of the disgruntled Leeds players (l-r: Greenhoff, Bremner, Giles and Bell) after he disallows Leeds' equaliser in the semi-final of the 1967 FA Cup. Their opponents, Chelsea, reached the Final, defeating Leeds by 1 goal to nil. But Don Revie's team were to take the league in the following season, losing only twice. Revie's contribution was recognised: he was awarded Manager of the Year in both 1969 and 1970, the preceding recipients being Matt Busby and Jock Stein.

BELOW RIGHT: Crowds at Craven Cottage cause officials to order the gates to be closed before the start of Fulham's derby with Chelsea.

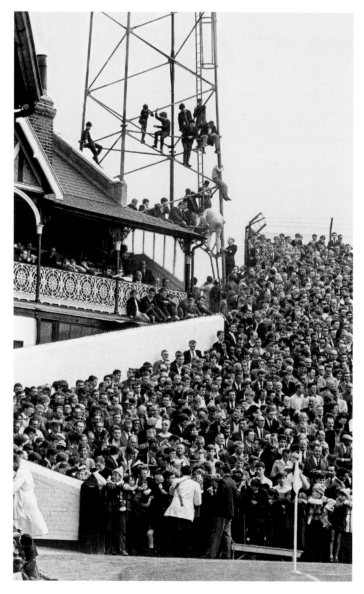

Geoff Hurst

West Ham striker Geoff Hurst, knighted in 1998, has the proud distinction of being the only man ever to score a hat-trick in a World Cup Final – and the only first-class cricketer to win a World Cup medal at football. He batted for Essex against Lancashire in 1962 and, of course, played for England in their 1966 victory over West Germany.

Over 400 games for the Hammers

The 24-year-old Hurst had come into form at exactly the right time – even if many Germans still believe his second goal, which came off the underside of the bar, never crossed the line. He hadn't even played in England's opening game of the tournament, but having taken the place of the injured Jimmy Greaves and scored the winner against Argentina in the quarter-final, he kept his place.

Between 1959 and 1972, Hurst made over 400 League appearances for the Hammers, helping them to win the FA Cup in 1964 and the European Cup Winners' Cup the following year. In 1972 he moved to Stoke City, then after a period at West Bromwich Albion, went into management and helped with the national squad.

TOP: West Ham and England World Cup heroes Bobby Moore and Martin Peters.

ABOVE: North London rivalries are put aside for a moment when Spurs' Terry Venables (left) acts as best man for Arsenal centre-forward George Graham.

Faltering start for League Cup

Despite their reputation as "nearly men", Leeds did pick up two other trophies in the 1960s, a Fairs Cup and League Cup double in 1968. The latter competition had had a chequered history since Football League Secretary Alan Hardaker had championed it at the beginning of the decade. In the early years the top clubs boycotted the League Cup, feeling that it was an unwelcome addition to the fixture list. With three European trophies to aim for, a second domestic cup competition hardly set the pulse racing. When Second Division Norwich City beat Fourth Division Rochdale over two legs in the 1962 final, the competition was in danger of withering on the vine.

Cup honours for Third Division sides

The turning point came in 1967, when the final became a one-legged affair at Wembley. The status was further enhanced with the award of a Fairs Cup place to the winners, provided they were in the First Division. That stipulation meant that Queen's Park Rangers and Swindon, winners in 1967 and 1969, respectively, weren't able to embark on a European adventure. Both were Third Division sides when they lifted the trophy and both came out on top against Division One opposition. Rodney Marsh inspired QPR to come back from a 2-0 deficit to win 3-2 against West Brom. In 1969 two extra-time goals from Swindon winger Don Rogers ended the hopes of an Arsenal side that had finished fourth in the championship. By the end of the decade, the League Cup had become firmly established, although critics pointed out that it remained a poor relation to the premier knockout competition. Certainly, no Third Division side had come close to lifting the FA Cup in the 50 years that those leagues had been in existence.

Gordon Banks

Gordon Banks earned his first cap in 1963 and, following that debut, was a fixture in the England side for nearly a decade, including the glorious 1966 World Cup campaign. But perhaps his most memorable moment came on 7 June 1970 when, as the finest goalkeeper of his age, he thwarted the world's greatest player with probably the best save ever seen. Pelé's crashing downward header was miraculously scooped off the line by Banks ten minutes into the England v Brazil World Cup group match at Guadalajara, Mexico. England lost that game but made it through to the quarter-final, where Banks' late withdrawal through illness was widely seen as a key factor in the team's defeat in the match against West Germany.

Career was cut short

Banks began his career at Chesterfield and established his reputation after a move to Leicester City, which he joined in 1959. In the 1961 FA Cup Final he was on the losing side when his team went down 0-2 to Tottenham Hotspur; he picked up another losers' medal two years later. Banks moved to another unfashionable club, Stoke City, in 1967. Five years later in 1972, soon after he had signed a long-term contract with the Potteries side, his career was cut short by a car accident in which he lost an eye.

LEFT: Spurs players celebrate their second goal, scored by Saul, in the 1967 Cup Final, an all-London affair. Tommy Docherty's Chelsea side were overwhelmed by Spurs' skill and tactics and even a late Chelsea goal, bringing the score to 2-1, didn't loosen Spurs' hold on the game.

League Division One 1960–1969

1959–60

1	Burnley	55
2	Wolverhampton W.	54
3	Tottenham Hotspur	53
4	West Bromwich Albion	49
5	Sheffield Wednesday	49
6	Bolton Wanderers	48
7	Manchester United	45
8	Newcastle United	44
9	Preston N.E.	44
10	Fulham	44
11	Blackpool	40
12	Leicester City	39
13	Arsenal	39
14	West Ham United	38
15	Everton	37
16	Manchester City	37
17	Blackburn Rovers	37
18	Chelsea	37
19	Birmingham City	36
20	Nottingham Forest	35
21	Leeds United	34
22	Luton	30

1960–61

1	Tottenham Hotspur	66
2	Sheffield Wednesday	58
3	Wolverhampton W.	57
4	Burnley	51
5	Everton	50
6	Leicester City	45
7	Manchester United	45
8	Blackburn Rovers	43
9	Aston Villa	43
10	West Bromwich Albion	41
11	Arsenal	41
12	Chelsea	37
13	Manchester City	37
14	Nottingham Forest	37
15	Cardiff	37
16	West Ham United	36
17	Fulham	36
18	Bolton Wanderers	35
19	Birmingham City	34
20	Blackpool	33
21	Newcastle United	32
22	Preston N.E.	30

1961–62

1	Ipswich	56
2	Burnley	53
3	Tottenham Hotspur	52
4	Everton	51
5	Sheffield United	47
6	Sheffield Wednesday	46
7	Aston Villa	44
8	West Ham United	44
9	West Bromwich Albion	43
10	Arsenal	43
11	Bolton Wanderers	42
12	Manchester City	41
13	Blackpool	41
14	Leicester City	40
15	Manchester United	39
16	Blackburn Rovers	39
17	Birmingham City	38
18	Wolverhampton W.	36
19	Nottingham Forest	36
20	Fulham	33
21	Cardiff	32
22	Chelsea	28

1962–63

1	Everton	61
2	Tottenham Hotspur	55
3	Burnley	54
4	Leicester City	52
5	Wolverhampton W.	50
6	Sheffield Wednesday	48
7	Arsenal	46
8	Liverpool	44
9	Nottingham Forest	44
10	Sheffield United	44
11	Blackburn Rovers	42
12	West Ham United	40
13	Blackpool	40
14	West Bromwich Albion	39
15	Aston Villa	38
16	Fulham	38
17	Ipswich	35
18	Bolton Wanderers	35
19	Manchester United	34
20	Birmingham City	33
21	Manchester City	31
22	Leyton Orient	21

1963–64

1	Liverpool	57
2	Manchester United	53
3	Everton	52
4	Tottenham Hotspur	51
5	Chelsea	50
6	Sheffield Wednesday	49
7	Blackburn Rovers	46
8	Arsenal	45
9	Burnley	44
10	West Bromwich Albion	43
11	Leicester City	43
12	Sheffield United	43
13	Nottingham Forest	41
14	West Ham United	40
15	Fulham	39
16	Wolverhampton W.	39
17	Stoke	38
18	Blackpool	35
19	Aston Villa	34
20	Birmingham City	29
21	Bolton Wanderers	28
22	Ipswich	25

1964–65

1	Manchester United	61
2	Leeds United	61
3	Chelsea	56
4	Everton	49
5	Nottingham Forest	47
6	Tottenham Hotspur	45
7	Liverpool	44
8	Sheffield Wednesday	43
9	West Ham United	42
10	Blackburn Rovers	42
11	Stoke	42
12	Burnley	42
13	Arsenal	41
14	West Bromwich Albion	39
15	Sunderland	37
16	Aston Villa	37
17	Blackpool	35
18	Leicester City	35
19	Sheffield United	35
20	Fulham	34
21	Wolverhampton W.	30
22	Birmingham City	27

1965–66

1	Liverpool	61
2	Leeds United	55
3	Burnley	55
4	Manchester United	51
5	Chelsea	51
6	West Bromwich Albion	50
7	Leicester City	49
8	Tottenham Hotspur	44
9	Sheffield United	43
10	Stoke	42
11	Everton	41
12	West Ham United	39
13	Blackpool	37
14	Arsenal	37
15	Newcastle United	37
16	Aston Villa	36
17	Sheffield Wednesday	36
18	Nottingham Forest	36
19	Sunderland	36
20	Fulham	35
21	Northampton	33
22	Blackburn Rovers	20

1966–67

1	Manchester United	60
2	Nottingham Forest	56
3	Tottenham Hotspur	56
4	Leeds United	55
5	Liverpool	51
6	Everton	48
7	Arsenal	46
8	Leicester City	44
9	Chelsea	44
10	Sheffield United	42
11	Sheffield Wednesday	41
12	Stoke	41
13	West Bromwich Albion	39
14	Burnley	39
15	Manchester City	39
16	West Ham United	36
17	Sunderland	36
18	Fulham	34
19	Southampton	34
20	Newcastle United	33
21	Aston Villa	29
22	Blackpool	21

1967–68

1	Manchester City	58
2	Manchester United	56
3	Liverpool	55
4	Leeds United	53
5	Everton	52
6	Chelsea	48
7	Tottenham Hotspur	47
8	West Bromwich Albion	46
9	Arsenal	44
10	Newcastle United	41
11	Nottingham Forest	39
12	West Ham United	38
13	Leicester City	38
14	Burnley	38
15	Sunderland	37
16	Southampton	37
17	Wolverhampton W.	36
18	Stoke	35
19	Sheffield Wednesday	34
20	Coventry	33
21	Sheffield United	32
22	Fulham	27

1968–69

1	Leeds United	67
2	Liverpool	61
3	Everton	57
4	Arsenal	56
5	Chelsea	50
6	Tottenham Hotspur	45
7	Southampton	45
8	West Ham United	44
9	Newcastle United	44
10	West Bromwich Albion	43
11	Manchester United	42
12	Ipswich	41
13	Manchester City	40
14	Burnley	39
15	Sheffield Wednesday	36
16	Wolverhampton W.	35
17	Sunderland	34
18	Nottingham Forest	33
19	Stoke	33
20	Coventry	31
21	Leicester City	30
22	Queen's Park Rangers	18

FA Cup Finals

1960	Wolverhampton W.	v	Blackburn Rovers	3–0
1961	Tottenham H.	v	Leicester City	2–0
1962	Tottenham H.	v	Burnley	3–1
1963	Manchester Utd	v	Leicester City	3–1
1964	West Ham Utd	v	Preston N.E.	3–2
1965	Liverpool	v	Leeds United	2–1
1966	Everton	v	Sheffield W.	3–2
1967	Tottenham H.	v	Chelsea	2–1
1968	West Bromwich A.	v	Everton	1–0
1969	Manchester City	v	Leicester City	1–0

Busby rebuilds again

Many would agree that the accolade of team of the decade belonged to Manchester United. Following the Munich air disaster, Busby embarked on yet another rebuilding process. It proved to be a long journey. In the four seasons from 1959–60 United finished 7th twice, 15th and 19th. Ironically, it was in the season that they flirted with relegation that the new-look side won its first silverware. Opponents Leicester City had finished 4th that year, but two goals from David Herd and one from Denis Law made a mockery of the clubs' respective positions. Four months later 17-year-old George Best made his debut for the club. Pat Crerand also joined United in 1963, while players such as David Sadler and John Aston were showing promise in the youth ranks. And of course, Busby also had Munich survivors Bobby Charlton and Bill Foulkes at his disposal.

European Cup goes to Old Trafford

After finishing runners-up to Liverpool in 1963–64, United won the title twice in three seasons. In 1967–68 United had to be content with the runners-up spot again, this time to neighbours Manchester City. Yet this was to bring the club the proudest moment in its history. In the semi-final of the European Cup United took a slender 1-0 lead to the Bernebeu Stadium. Real Madrid went 3-1 ahead but two unlikely goals from Sadler and Foulkes put United into the final. Ten years on from Munich United went to Wembley to face a Benfica side, which boasted the great Eusebio. He almost won the game for the Portuguese side with a thunderous shot in the dying minutes when the score stood at 1-1. But Alex Stepney made a great save and the game went into extra-time. United hit three in those 30 minutes. The first was a typical piece of virtuoso skill from Best; Brian Kidd, celebrating his 19th birthday, headed United into a 3-1 lead; and Bobby Charlton swept home his second of the match to make the final score 4-1. After the events of 1958 there was an element of natural justice as United became the first English club to win European football's premier trophy.

BELOW: Best displays perfect balance and control.

Top: Players and staff of Manchester United on the pitch at Wembley on 29 May 1968, the day of the European Cup Final.

Above: Pat Crerand (left) shares the moment of glory with Matt Busby. Ten years after the Munich air disaster, Busby's dream is realised and a rebuilt Manchester United defeated Benfica by 4 goals to 1 to win the European Cup. Charlton and Foulkes, survivors of the crash, played at Wembley and Charlton had the satisfaction of scoring 2 of United's goals. In the following season, Busby announced his intention to step down as manager of the team to take on the role of general manager of the club.

Right: United team-mates Law and Kidd celebrate after Best scored in the first leg of the semi-final of the 1968 European Cup against Real Madrid.

George Best

George Best had everything: speed, strength, poise, creativity and incredible ball skills. A two-footed player, he was excellent in the air and fearless in the tackle and a lethal finisher. A team-mate in the Manchester United side of the 1960s once said that Best could have played in any outfield position – and outperformed the man who usually played there. By the time he was 22 he had won a European Footballer of the Year award and had a European Cup Winners' medal. He looked set to win many more honours, yet the pressures of celebrity, combined with a tendency to press the self-destruct button all too often, meant that by his late 20s, his career in the top flight was virtually over.

Belfast Boy

Best was brought to Old Trafford from his home in Belfast in August 1961, when he was 15. Just two years later he made his debut for United and was soon a fixture in an exciting new side that Matt Busby was building. Busby recognised Best's natural talent and reasoned that it was best left alone. Consequently, he had told the coaching staff not to try and teach the youngster anything. Later, despite all the headaches Best gave him, Busby never wavered in his view of the Irishman's ability on the field, claiming that he had never seen any other player who had so many different ways of beating an opponent.

After a stunning individual display in a 5-1 away victory over Benfica in the 1965–66 European Cup, he became the first pop-star footballer and soon came under the most intense media scrutiny. Good-looking and fashionable, he was dubbed "El Beatle" and for a time he managed to combine the life of a high-profile celebrity with outstanding performances on the pitch. But, inevitably, the revelling began to take its toll.

Best leaves United at 25

After United won the European Cup in 1968, it became necessary for Busby to reinforce the ageing team and Best felt that he should be more central to the make-up of the team. Unsurprisingly, this put pressure on relations between him, his team-mates and the club, which were already strained as a result of his high living and media profile. He walked out of Old Trafford in 1972, two days before his 26th birthday. The following decade saw him join a succession of clubs, both in Britain and America, but he would never reproduce the kind of dazzling displays which were a trademark of his younger days.

On the international front, Best was picked for Northern Ireland when he was 17, after just 15 appearances for United. Although he won 37 caps, he never really had the opportunity to show his skills on the world stage.

Long after he had hung up his boots, Best continued to find himself in demand as a football pundit and on the after-dinner circuit. However, his years of alcohol abuse finally caught up with him and in the summer of 2002 he underwent a liver transplant operation. He died in 2005, aged 59.

English clubs make their mark

The year after winning the World Cup England came back to earth with a bump as Scotland came to Wembley and won 3-2, a game in which Jim Baxter was at his mercurial best. The Scots lost little time in claiming to be unofficial World Champions.

England went into the 1968 European Championship as favourites. After beating Spain in the quarter-final, it all went wrong against Yugoslavia. Alan Mullery was sent off for retaliation, the first England player to receive his marching orders, and the team went down 1-0.

At the end of a turbulent decade, English clubs had made their mark in Europe, winning five trophies in all. And the national side was once again on top of the world. The next decade would see continued success at club level, while the national side would find it hard to reach a World Cup, let alone win it.

RIGHT: Manchester United display the European Cup. Back row: Foulkes, Aston, Rimmer, Stepney, Gowling and Herd. Middle row: Sadler, Dunne, Brennan, Crerand, Best, Burns and Crompton. Front row: Ryan, Stiles, Law, Busby, Charlton, Kidd and Fitzpatrick.

ABOVE: Allan Clarke shows his delight after scoring for Leicester in the semi-final of the Cup in 1969. Clarke's goal took Leicester to Wembley, going some way to justifying the new record-breaking transfer fee of £150,000 paid to Fulham.

ABOVE RIGHT: Manchester City players train before the Final of the 1969 FA Cup in the red and black striped shirt they will wear on the day. City won the Cup, for the fourth time in their history, Young scoring the only goal of the match against Leicester. Mercer and Allison's new signings of Mike Summerbee (second from the left), Francis Lee (third from the left) and Colin Bell (fourth from the left) played a crucial role in City's League and Cup success in the late 1960s.

Kilmarnock take League crown

By the time the 1964–65 season kicked off, Kilmarnock fans must have been heartily sick of the bridesmaid's tag. Manager Willie Waddell had shaped Killie into an impressive unit, led from half-back by "Big Frank" Beattie, but the team had fallen just short of bringing the first silverware to Rugby Park since 1929 – not once but on seven occasions since the turn of the decade. Killie had been league runners-up four times in five years, Rangers taking three of those championships, Hearts the other. In 1960–61 they had lost out to the men from Ibrox by a single point. The cups had brought similar agonies: defeat by Rangers in the 1959–60 Scottish Cup, and losses to Rangers and Hearts in League Cup finals. Kilmarnock fans must have feared a similar outcome when the team went to Tynecastle on the last day of the 1964–65 season. Hearts held a two-point lead, and the goals situation was such that even a 1-0 win wouldn't have been enough for Killie. Davie Sneddon and Brian McIlroy put the visitors two up, and they managed to keep a clean sheet, for even a 2-1 defeat would have been enough for Hearts. Killie's wafer-thin 0.042 superior goal average delivered the championship to Rugby Park for the first time in the club's foundation in 1869.

Second treble for Gers

Notwithstanding Kilmarnock's mighty achievements, the first half of the decade belonged to Scot Symon's Rangers. Apart from the three league successes, Gers lifted the Scottish Cup and League Cup four times each. The team peaked in 1963–64, claiming the treble for the second time in the club's – and Scottish football's – history. The League was wrapped up with a six-point gap over Kilmarnock: Division Two winners Morton were swept aside 5-0 in the League Cup final, Jim Forrest hitting four; and Dundee were rocked by two late goals in the Scottish Cup showpiece, 3-1 the final score. Rangers' key acquisition during this period was the mercurial Jim Baxter, signed from Raith Rovers for £17,500 in summer 1960.

Rangers' domestic success in the early 1960s brought European adventures, and in 1960–61 Symon led his side to the inaugural Cup Winners' Cup final. There was only a ten-strong entry, but Gers entered the record books as the first British club to contest a European final. They put 11 past Borussia Moenchengladbach and beat Wolves in the semis, but struggled to pierce the Fiorentina defence in the final, losing 4-1 on aggregate.

Dundee was the only other club to take championship honours in the early 1960s. A side including Ian Ure and Alan Gilzean won in 1961–62, sandwiched between rather less impressive 10th and 9th place finishes. Veteran Dens Park aficionados still recall the day that Dundee went to Ibrox and beat their title rivals 5-1, Gilzean bagging four. Dundee reached the European Cup semi-final the following year, accounting for Cologne, Sporting Lisbon and Anderlecht before losing to eventual winners AC Milan.

ABOVE RIGHT: The Glasgow Rangers team relax before their game in the European Cup Winners' Cup.

BELOW RIGHT: Jock Stein's first day as manager of Celtic in March, 1965.

Scottish League Champions 1960–1969

1959–60

1	Hearts	54
2	Kilmarnock	50
3	Rangers	42
4	Dundee	42
5	Motherwell	40
6	Clyde	39
7	Hibernian	35
8	Ayr United	34
9	Celtic	33
10	Partick Thistle	32
11	Raith Rovers	31
12	Third Lanark	30
13	Dunfermline Athletic	29
14	St Mirren	28
15	Aberdeen	28
16	Airdrieonians	28
17	Stirling Albion	22
18	Arbroath	15

1960–61

1	Rangers	51
2	Kilmarnock	50
3	Third Lanark	42
4	Celtic	39
5	Motherwell	38
6	Aberdeen	36
7	Hearts	34
8	Hibernian	34
9	Dundee United	33
10	Dundee	32
11	Partick Thistle	32
12	Dunfermline Athletic	31
13	Airdrieonians	30
14	St Mirren	29
15	St Johnstone	29
16	Raith Rovers	27
17	Clyde	23
18	Ayr United	22

1961–62

1	Dundee	54
2	Rangers	51
3	Celtic	46
4	Dunfermline Athletic	43
5	Kilmarnock	42
6	Hearts	38
7	Partick Thistle	35
8	Hibernian	33
9	Motherwell	32
10	Dundee United	32
11	Third Lanark	31
12	Aberdeen	29
13	Raith Rovers	27
14	Falkirk	26
15	Airdrieonians	25
16	St Mirren	25
17	St Johnstone	25
18	Stirling Albion	18

1962–63

1	Rangers	57
2	Kilmarnock	48
3	Partick Thistle	46
4	Celtic	44
5	Hearts	43
6	Aberdeen	41
7	Dundee United	41
8	Dunfermline Athletic	34
9	Dundee	33
10	Motherwell	31
11	Airdrieonians	30
12	St Mirren	28
13	Falkirk	27
14	Third Lanark	26
15	Queen Of The South	26
16	Hibernian	25
17	Clyde	23
18	Raith Rovers	9

1963–64

1	Rangers	55
2	Kilmarnock	49
3	Celtic	47
4	Hearts	47
5	Dunfermline Athletic	45
6	Dundee	45
7	Partick Thistle	35
8	Dundee United	34
9	Aberdeen	32
10	Hibernian	30
11	Motherwell	29
12	St Mirren	29
13	St Johnstone	28
14	Falkirk	28
15	Airdrieonians	26
16	Third Lanark	25
17	Queen Of The South	16
18	East Stirlingshire	12

1964–65

1	Kilmarnock	50
2	Hearts	50
3	Dunfermline Athletic	49
4	Hibernian	46
5	Rangers	44
6	Dundee	40
7	Clyde	40
8	Celtic	37
9	Dundee United	36
10	Greenock Morton	33
11	Partick Thistle	32
12	Aberdeen	32
13	St Johnstone	29
14	Motherwell	28
15	St Mirren	24
16	Falkirk	21
17	Airdrieonians	14
18	Third Lanark	7

1965–66

1	Celtic	57
2	Rangers	55
3	Kilmarnock	45
4	Dunfermline Athletic	44
5	Dundee United	43
6	Hibernian	38
7	Hearts	38
8	Aberdeen	36
9	Dundee	34
10	Falkirk	31
11	Clyde	30
12	Partick Thistle	30
13	Motherwell	28
14	St Johnstone	26
15	Stirling Albion	26
16	St Mirren	22
17	Greenock Morton	21
18	Hamilton	8

1966–67

1	Celtic	58
2	Rangers	55
3	Clyde	46
4	Aberdeen	42
5	Hibernian	42
6	Dundee	41
7	Kilmarnock	40
8	Dunfermline Athletic	38
9	Dundee United	37
10	Motherwell	31
11	Hearts	30
12	Partick Thistle	30
13	Airdrieonians	28
14	Falkirk	26
15	St Johnstone	25
16	Stirling Albion	19
17	St Mirren	15
18	Ayr United	9

1967–68

1	Celtic	63
2	Rangers	61
3	Hibernian	45
4	Dunfermline Athletic	39
5	Aberdeen	37
6	Greenock Morton	36
7	Kilmarnock	34
8	Clyde	34
9	Dundee	33
10	Partick Thistle	31
11	Dundee United	31
12	Hearts	30
13	Airdrieonians	29
14	St Johnstone	27
15	Falkirk	26
16	Raith Rovers	25
17	Motherwell	19
18	Stirling Albion	12

1968–69

1	Celtic	54
2	Rangers	49
3	Dunfermline Athletic	45
4	Kilmarnock	44
5	Dundee United	43
6	St Johnstone	37
7	Airdrieonians	37
8	Hearts	36
9	Dundee	32
10	Greenock Morton	32
11	St Mirren	32
12	Hibernian	31
13	Clyde	31
14	Partick Thistle	28
15	Aberdeen	26
16	Raith Rovers	21
17	Falkirk	18
18	Arbroath	16

Scottish Cup Finals

1960	Rangers	v	Kilmarnock	2-0
1961	Dunfermline Ath.	v	Celtic	0-0
	Dunfermline Ath.	v	Celtic	replay 2-0
1962	Rangers	v	St Mirren	2-0
1963	Rangers	v	Celtic	1-1
	Rangers	v	Celtic	replay 3-0
1964	Rangers	v	Dundee	3-1
1965	Celtic	v	Dunfermline Ath.	3-2
1966	Rangers	v	Celtic	0-0
	Rangers	v	Celtic	replay 1-0
1967	Celtic	v	Aberdeen	2-0
1968	Dunfermline Ath.	v	Hearts	3-1
1969	Celtic	v	Rangers	4-0

Stein's Celtic are kings of Europe

If the early 60s belonged to Rangers, the latter half of the decade was dominated by their Glasgow rivals. 1964–65 was the transitional season. Rangers slipped to fifth and Baxter left for pastures new in Sunderland. As that great side broke up, Celtic was on the verge of an unparalleled run of success. The Hoops finished 8th that year, but under new management the club was heading in only one direction. Ex-skipper Jock Stein, who had guided Dunfermline to cup victory over Celtic in 1961, arrived back at the club he graced as a player in the early 50s. Celtic were in the medals almost immediately, a Billy McNeill header giving them a 3-2 win over Dunfermline in the Scottish Cup final. The following year saw the league championship come to Celtic Park for the first time in a dozen years, and there was a narrow defeat to Liverpool in the Cup Winners' Cup semi-final. Then, in 1966–67, Celtic swept all before them, a grand slam rounded off with a European Cup victory over Inter Milan, winners of the competition in two of the previous three years. The "Lisbon Lions" came from behind to win 2-1 with goals from Gemmell and Chalmers, the first British side to be crowned European champions. One of the abiding memories was "Jinky" Johnstone' toying with full-back Burgnich.

By 1969 Celtic had made it four championships in a row, Rangers runners-up each time. In 1967–68 Rangers won 28 of their 34 games and lost just once, yet still finished two points adrift. In 1968 Colin Stein left Hibs for Ibrox for £100,000, a Scottish transfer record, but the Bhoys were relentless. They won five League Cups on the spin from 1966, and a 4-0 Scottish Cup final win over Rangers in 1968–69 brought a second treble. In that game Alex Ferguson, in for Stein at Number 9, was castigated for allowing Billy McNeill to head Celtic's opener from a corner. He was a Falkirk player before the year was out.

TOP: Captain Billy McNeill lifts the cup following Celtic's 2-1 victory over Inter Milan.

ABOVE: The "Lisbon Lions" came from behind to win 2-1 with goals from Gemmell and Chalmers, the first British side to be crowned European champions.

BELOW: Jock Stein, far left, gets a hand on the coveted trophy.

Berwick rock Rangers

If four trophy-less seasons for Rangers wasn't bad enough, there was also a humiliating first-round exit to Berwick Rangers in the 1966–67 Scottish Cup. Berwick, led by player-coach Jock Wallace, belied their position as a mid-table Second Division side to cause one of the biggest shocks in the competition's history. There was a second European final for Rangers – beaten by Bayern Munich in the Cup Winners' Cup – but Symon was soon shown the door.

Scotland defeat World Champions

Considering the array of available Scottish talent, it was remarkable that the national team failed to qualify for any tournament in the 60s. With the likes of Law, Crerand, Bremner, St John and Charlie Cooke plying their trade south of the border, and a galaxy of stars playing on home turf, the return should have been greater. The low point was undoubtedly the 9-3 loss to England at Wembley in April 1961. Six years later, however, Scots gave themselves the "unofficial World Champions" tag after a famous 3-2 victory on the same ground, England's first defeat since the World Cup success of the previous year.

BELOW: Bobby Lennox scores Scotland's second goal in their 3-2 victory over England in 1967.

ABOVE RIGHT: England 5, Wales 1. Even though they beat Scotland and Ireland and had both Ivor Allchurch and John Charles in their line-up, Wales had to settle for second place in the 1961 Home Championship.

Cardiff reach Euro Semi

In Wales, Cardiff's stand-out season was 1967–68. Success in the Welsh Cup gave the country's top sides an easy path into Europe, and that season Jimmy Scoular's men, including a teenage John Toshack, beat Torpedo Moscow to set up a Cup Winners' Cup semi-final clash with Hamburg. Cardiff gained a creditable draw in Germany but were undone at Ninian Park.

1970–1979
Triumph in Europe

English clubs had won five European trophies in the 1960s. In the next decade Liverpool alone almost managed that. The Reds embarked on a period of domination the like of which the game had never seen. As their traditional rivals found it hard to maintain the pace, two new contenders emerged. Derby County and Nottingham Forest won the title three times between them, a remarkable achievement by the controversial manager who took both clubs from the Second Division to the top of the pile: Brian Clough.

1970 Manchester City win the European Cup Winners' Cup and the League Cup

1970 Ninth World Cup is held in Mexico; Brazil win the competition for the third time and win the Jules Rimet trophy outright. England lose to West Germany 3-2 in the quarter finals

1970 First football song to reach No. 1 in the charts – "Back Home" by the England World Cup squad

1970 Chelsea and Leeds meet in the FA Cup Final and draw; the first draw in a Wembley Final caused a rematch which Chelsea won

1970 Celtic lose 2-1 to Feyenoord in the European Cup Final

1971 Chelsea win European Cup Winners' Cup

1971 66 spectators are killed when staircase barriers give way during an Old Firm game at Ibrox on 2 January

1972 UEFA Cup, formally the Fairs Cup, won by Tottenham Hotspur

1972 Rangers beat Moscow Dynamo 3-2 in the Cup Winners' Cup Final in Barcelona

1973 Liverpool become the first club to win the League title and a European trophy when they win the UEFA Cup

1974 Last FA Amateur Cup Final

1974 League football played on Sunday for the first time

1974 England do not qualify for the tenth World Cup held in West Germany. It was won by the host nation. Scotland are unbeaten but eliminated on goal difference

1974 Football hooliganism is fast becoming known as the "English Disease" after 100 Chelsea fans are arrested for rioting at Luton Town and 50 Manchester United fans are arrested in Stoke on the

Division Two teams get to Wembley

If Derby County and Nottingham Forest were the surprise packages in the league, there were several in the cup competitions. Between 1970 and 1980 seven Division Two sides made it to Wembley, while Division One strugglers Stoke and Ipswich also struck a blow for the underdog.

Ironically, as English sides prospered in Europe, the fortunes of the national team declined. After going to Mexico as holders in 1970, England suffered successive failures in the next two World Cup qualification campaigns.

OPPOSITE: Leeds celebrate Mick Jones's goal in the 1970 FA Cup Final, believing that the Cup was theirs. But the celebrations were short-lived. Two minutes later Hutchinson scored to make it 2-2. Extra time at Wembley was followed by extra time in the replay at Old Trafford, where Chelsea ended victorious against a Leeds side recognised as one of the English League's greatest teams.

BELOW RIGHT: Footballers on fashion parade – Bob McNab, Geoff Hurst and Peter Marinello show that they can impress off the pitch as much as on it!

BELOW LEFT: Harris and Hollins parade the FA Cup after Chelsea's 2-1 win in the replay against Leeds United.

Fences go up to counter hooligan threat

The 1970s also saw the introduction of a three-up, three-down system, and red and yellow cards for on-field misdemeanours. From 1974 the players also got to choose their own Player of the Year. It wasn't until the seventh vote took place, in 1980, that their choice, Terry McDermott, coincided with that of the Football Writers Association. On a more worrying note, the twin problems of indebtedness and hooliganism continued to cast a shadow over the game. Fences started to go up to try and counter the threat of pitch invasions, which became an increasingly common occurrence. The fact that few clubs were operating in the black didn't stop transfers from continuing their upward spiral, and before the end of the decade the English game had seen its first million-pound transfer.

Mexico 1970

The decade began with a footballing jamboree in Mexico. Many thought the squad Sir Alf Ramsey took to defend England's world crown was stronger than that which had won the Jules Rimet trophy four years earlier. Things got off to a bad start in Bogotá, where England were acclimatising to the kind of temperatures they would face in Mexico. Bobby Moore was accused of stealing a bracelet and taken into custody. Although the charge was soon dropped, the incident overshadowed the squad's pre-tournament preparations.

> *England are joint favourites.*

England and Brazil were the joint favourites, and they were drawn in the same group. After each side had recorded a victory, the two teams met in Guadalajara. After a bright start by England, Jairzinho beat Cooper on the right wing and picked out Pelé with his cross. Pelé powered a downward header just inside the far post, but somehow Banks managed to scoop it up and over the bar. It was hailed as one of the greatest saves of all time. Pelé set up Jairzinho for the only goal of the match 14 minutes into the second half, but England had reason to be optimistic. Peters and Lee had missed chances, and Astle missed a golden opportunity when he came on as substitute. There was every indication that the two teams would meet again in the final.

England throw away 2-0 lead

That hope disappeared in Leon, where England faced West Germany in the quarter-final. 2-0 up through goals from Mullery and Peters, England looked odds-on to go through. In the second half Beckenbauer beat Peter Bonetti to pull one back for the Germans. The Chelsea keeper had been a late replacement for Banks, who had gone down with stomach cramps before the game. Suddenly, it was the German side that had the momentum. Ramsey took off Bobby Charlton and

Peters, replacing them with Colin Bell and Norman Hunter. A back header from Uwe Seeler looped agonisingly over Bonetti's head, forcing extra time. England's misery was complete when Gerd Müller, who would go on to be the tournament's top scorer, volleyed the winner from close range.

Two years later, West Germany again proved to be the stumbling-block in the quarter-final of the European Championship. Helmut Schoen's side was at its peak, and England had no answer as the Germans cruised to a 3-1 victory at Wembley. Ramsey's men earned a goalless draw in Berlin a fortnight later, but the damage had been done. Worse was to come the following year, and it would be a disappointment too many for the England manager.

LEFT: Members of the England team training at the Atlas Club in Guadalajara as they prepare for their match against Brazil in the 1970 World Cup in Mexico.

ABOVE: As they receive cars and membership of the RAC, some of the England World Cup squad pose for photographs. The 1970s saw the beginnings of sponsorship which was to develop as a major feature in the 1980s.

OPPOSITE LEFT: Martin Chivers scores for Tottenham Hotspur. Spurs had paid £125,000 for Chivers in 1968 and throughout the early 1970s continued to pay big money in transfer deals. However, the decade was not particularly successful for the London club and they spent the 1977–78 season in Division Two.

OPPOSITE BELOW: "The Charlton Brothers". During the 1970s Jackie (left) and Bobby Charlton continued to be successful at both club and national level. Jackie was an important member of the great Leeds team of the early years of the decade while Bobby remained loyal to Manchester United, despite the club's struggle to remain mid-table. At the end of the 1972–73 season Bobby retired, having played 751 games and scored 247 goals for the club.

RIGHT: George Best in happier days. By the early 1970s, his career in the top flight was almost over. In December 1972 he was transfer-listed by the club after a series of failures to turn up for training and matches, as well as disagreements with United's new manager, Frank O'Farrell, who was sacked by the board at the same time as Best was given his marching orders. Ironically on the same day as United told him they no longer wanted him as a player, Best had written to the club saying he no longer wished to play for them.

Double for Arsenal

Domestic football in the new decade got off to a dramatic start, Arsenal coming through with a late burst to record a famous Double in 1970–71. It was ten years on from Spurs' achievement, and fate decreed that the Gunners had to win their last match at White Hart Lane to secure the title. A Ray Kennedy goal settled the issue. Arsenal had been six points off the pace with six weeks to go, but 27 points from the last 16 games was unstoppable championship form. Almost inevitably it was Leeds who missed out, pipped by a single point.

Arsenal also left it late in the Cup. They needed a last-minute penalty to salvage a draw against Stoke in the semi-final before winning the replay 2-0. Five days after the Spurs match Arsenal went to Wembley for the 64th and final match of the campaign.

They were up against a Liverpool side that was in a state of flux. The likes of Tommy Lawrence, Ron Yeats, Peter Thompson, Roger Hunt and Ian St John had all disappeared as Shankly overhauled the squad completely. Teenager Emlyn Hughes had arrived from Blackpool in 1967. He had been joined by John Toshack, Larry Lloyd, Steve Heighway and Brian Hall in a new-look side. There were also two youngsters who would enjoy very different fortunes at the club. Shankly paid Wolves £100,000 for striker Alun Evans. He would show flashes of what he could do at Anfield but overall the verdict was one of disappointment. The same could hardly be said of Shankly's £35,000 buy from Scunthorpe, who sat in the stands to watch his new team-mates take on Arsenal. His name was Kevin Keegan.

Shankly's new-look Liverpool.

LEFT: The Double-winning Arsenal team arrive aboard an open-top bus at Islington Town Hall for a civic reception.

BELOW: In extra time, Charlie George slams the ball into the net past Liverpool's keeper Ray Clemence to provide the goal that won Arsenal the FA Cup and the Double in the 1970–71 season; they had won the League with just one point to spare over Leeds United.

OPPOSITE ABOVE: Members of the Arsenal team that had won the 1970 Fairs Cup (from 1972, the UEFA Cup), set off for the airport for a flight to Rome where they were to play Lazio at the start of their defence of the title.

OPPOSITE BELOW: Goalscorer Martin Peters is lifted in celebration by Martin Chivers as Geoff Hurst rushes to congratulate and Scotland's Frank McLintock shouts in dismay in England's 3-1 win at Wembley in the Home Championships of 1971.

George hits Wembley winner

When Steve Heighway opened the scoring in extra time, it seemed that Keegan was about to take his place in a Cup-winning team. But Eddie Kelly poked in a scrappy equaliser, and Charlie George rifled in a 25-yard winner. It was a special day for Frank McClintock, who had suffered a string of Wembley disappointments. He was named Footballer of the Year for leading Arsenal to the fourth Double in history. Gunners' boss Bertie Mee received many plaudits, although credit was also due to the groundwork laid down by his predecessor, Billy Wright.

Derby take title in sunny Spain

Derby County finished a respectable 9th that year. Brian Clough had been at the Baseball Ground for four years, taking the club up as Division Two champions in 1968–69. 4th place in their first year back in the top flight was an excellent effort by the Rams. 9th this time

> *Clough's team beat Liverpool and Leeds for their first championship.*

round was still respectable. But to a perfectionist such as Clough that was never good enough. In 1972 his side won the title, albeit by the narrowest of margins and in the most dramatic circumstances. Derby beat Liverpool in their last game of the season to go one point clear at the top. Clough and his men then promptly decamped to Majorca, leaving Liverpool and Leeds – who both had one remaining fixture – to do their worst. Leeds needed just a point at mid-table Wolves. If they failed, Liverpool could go top with a win at Arsenal.

In the event neither club could meet its target. Leeds went down 2-1, while Liverpool were held to a goalless draw. Liverpool thought they'd won it with a last-minute goal from Toshack, but it was disallowed. Derby were champions for the first time in their history.

Hereford humble Newcastle

Leeds had the consolation of winning the centenary FA Cup Final, Allan Clarke scoring the only goal of the match against holders Arsenal. The highlight of the 1972 FA Cup came in the third round, when Hereford took on Newcastle United. The Southern League side seemed to have had their moment of glory with a 2-2 draw at St James's Park. In the replay at Edgar Street Hereford rode their luck until ten minutes from the end, when Malcolm Macdonald finally found the back of the net. Ronnie Radford sent the 15,000 crowd delirious with a 30-yard screamer, and Ricky George slotted home the winner in extra time. Hereford went on to draw 0-0 with West Ham before going down 3-1 at Upton Park in a replay. The club's Cup heroics helped to earn them election to the Football League the following season.

Billy Bremner

Despite beginning his career as a winger, it was at the heart of the brilliant Leeds United side of the late 1960s and early 1970s that Billy Bremner made his name and where he enjoyed a phenomenal run of success. He forged a formidable midfield partnership with Johnny Giles and, although Giles was regarded as the skilful artist and canny ball-player, Bremner's superb passing and incisive forward runs made him a vital cog in the Elland Road machine.

54 caps for Scotland

As captain, Bremner led the side to two League Championships, in 1968–69 and 1973–74, and to FA Cup victory over Arsenal in 1972. Leeds United also had two successful Inter-Cities Fairs Cup campaigns, in 1968 and 1971. Regrettably, Bremner's haul of runners-up medals was even bigger: Leeds finished runners-up in the League on five occasions during Bremner's era, and were beaten FA Cup finalists three times. After the team's defeat at the hands of Bayern Munich in the 1975 European Cup Final, Bremner moved to Hull City, and then finished his playing career at Doncaster.

Capped 54 times for Scotland, Bremner's appearances for his national side fell one short of Dennis Law's all-time record. His greatest triumph on the international stage was when he led the Scots in the 1974 World Cup Finals in West Germany, where they were unbeaten and unlucky to be eliminated on goal difference.

No stranger to controversy, he and Liverpool's Kevin Keegan became the first British players to be sent off at Wembley when they exchanged blows during the 1974–75 Charity Shield match. This was followed shortly afterwards by the decision to award a life ban from the Scottish FA following a misconduct charge during a trip to Copenhagen for a European Championship match. He died in 1997.

OPPOSITE: The Leeds squad at the beginning of the 1972–73 season. The early 1970s were a part of the golden age for the club. They won the League in 1974 and were runners-up three years in succession between 1970 and 1972, and also had a series of good Cup runs.

RIGHT: Liverpool's Kevin Keegan races Kenny Burns for the ball in his team's match against Birmingham City in 1973. Keegan won European Footballer of the Year twice in the 1970s.

ABOVE INSERT: Smiles on the faces of Leeds manager Don Revie and club captain Billy Bremner as they hold the FA Cup, which the club won in 1972, the competition's centenary year when they beat Arsenal 1-0.

Stoke win League Cup after 7-hour marathon

The 1971–72 League Cup matched the FA Cup for drama. Entry to the League Cup was now compulsory and competition was fierce. Stoke and West Ham fought out a seven-hour semi-final marathon, a Terry Conroy goal settling the tie after two legs and two replays. Stoke beat Chelsea 2-1 in the final, and had thus played 12 games to get their hands on their first piece of silverware in their 109-year history. 35-year-old George Eastham hit the winner, his first goal for nearly two years. It was also a first medal at club level for 34-year-old Gordon Banks.

Clough quits Derby

Clough and his assistant, Peter Taylor, were the toast of Derby after winning the championship in 1972, yet barely a year later they and the club had parted company. The outspoken and abrasive Clough had not always endeared himself to the directors at the Baseball Ground, who feared that his controversial outbursts might land the club in hot water. In the autumn of 1973 relations worsened and Clough and Taylor resigned. Derby initially fared better than Clough. Former player Dave Mackay took over and he would lead the Rams to another championship in 1975. But by the end of the decade Derby would be back in Division Two, while Clough and Taylor would be managing the European champions.

Brian Clough

Brian Clough was the fans' choice to be given the England manager's job in the 1970s and early 1980s. The accepted wisdom was that it was his outspoken, abrasive style that cost him a chance of getting the top job rather than his footballing credentials, which were of the highest order.

Clough had been a prolific goalscorer with Middlesbrough and Sunderland, and was capped for England before his playing career was cut short through injury. In 1965, 30-year-old Clough became the youngest manager in the league when he took over at Hartlepool, but it was when he moved to Derby County that he established his reputation. He led the Rams to the Division Two championship in 1969, and after two years of consolidation in the top flight, his side won the League title in 1972. The team reached the semi-final of the European Cup the following year, losing 3-1 on aggregate to Juventus. Derby fans were up in arms when Clough left the Baseball Ground following a disagreement with the board. After an infamous 44-day reign at Leeds United at the beginning of the 1974–75 season, Clough embarked on a glorious 18-year association with another unfashionable club, Nottingham Forest. He won the championship in 1977–78, relegating Liverpool to second place for once. In doing so he became only the third manager in history to win the title with two different clubs. In 1979 he won the European Cup with a 1-0 win over Malmö. The goal was scored by Trevor Francis, whom Clough had made the first £1 million player. Forest retained the trophy the following year, a John Robertson penalty giving the team victory over Hamburg. Clough also won the League Cup four times during his reign at the City Ground. He retired after the team was relegated in 1993. Brian Clough died on 20 September 2004.

First European trophy for Liverpool

ABOVE: The 1971 Liverpool squad, pictured with manager Bill Shankly. The seventies was a decade of success for Liverpool with wins in the premier competitions at home and in Europe.

By the 1972–73 season Shankly had completed his rebuilding process. Liverpool stormed to a record 8th championship, using just 16 players all season. They made it a domestic and European double by winning the UEFA Cup, which had replaced the Fairs Cup the previous year.

Toshack and Keegan bring Liverpool first Euro success.

The fact that UEFA wanted to take the competition under its umbrella, as it had the Cup Winners' Cup a decade earlier, made no difference to English clubs' domination. Arsenal, Leeds and Spurs had won the last three finals, adding to Leeds' and Newcastle's victories at the end of the 1960s. Liverpool were thus bidding to bring the trophy back to England for the sixth successive year.

They faced holders Spurs in the semi-final and took a narrow 1-0 lead to White Hart Lane for the second leg. Martin Peters, who had moved to Spurs for a record £200,000 after the 1970 World Cup, scored twice in a 2-1 win, but Heighway's away goal put Liverpool through.

In the final they faced a highly rated Borussia Moenchengladbach side that included Netzer, Bonhof, Heynckes and Vogts. The first leg at Anfield showed Shankly at his cunning best. He played Brian Hall instead of John Toshack, feeling that the smaller, quicker man might get more joy against the German defence. Torrential rain forced an abandonment after 30 minutes, but in that time the Liverpool boss had seen that Moenchengladbach were susceptible to the high ball. 24 hours later Toshack was back in the side champing at the bit after being left out of the original line-up. His flicks created two goals for Keegan and the Reds won 3-0. The German side nearly turned it round, winning the return leg 2-0, but Liverpool had their hands on their first European trophy.

Manchester United relegated

In 1973–74 Southampton finished 20th in the league and became the first Division One side to suffer from the new three-up, three-down system. Manchester United, European champions just six years earlier, finished one place below the Saints and found themselves in Division Two for the first time since 1938. The Manchester derby at Old Trafford has gone down in folklore as the game in which Denis Law, who had returned to his former club, backheeled the goal which put United down. Law, playing his last game before hanging up his boots, did put City one up, and after a pitch invasion that was the score when the game was halted four minutes from time. Several days later, the Football League decided to allow the result to stand. However, in the final table United finished four points behind Southampton and five adrift of Birmingham, the team which just avoided the drop. Manager Tommy Docherty would bring a new young side back to the top flight as Division Two champions the following year.

BELOW: Ian Porterfield's (right) shot flies over Leeds goalkeeper, Harvey, to score the goal that gave Second Division Sunderland a miraculous FA Cup victory against the favourites.

RIGHT: A delighted Sunderland manager, Bob Stokoe, hugs Porterfield after the team's stunning win.

Ramsey sacked after "clown" denies England

Poland end England's 1974 World Cup dream.

The 1973–74 season saw a number of managerial bombshells. Hard on the heels of Clough's acrimonious departure from the Baseball Ground, Sir Alf Ramsey finally paid the price for failure. On 17 October 1973 a 1–1 draw against Poland ended England's hopes of qualifying for the 1974 World Cup. Poland keeper Jan Tomaszewski had been dubbed a "clown" but he was in inspired form on that night at Wembley. England peppered his goal for 90 minutes, but it took an Allan Clarke penalty to beat him. By then Poland were one up, Domarski's shot squeezing under Shilton's body. The fact that Poland went on to be one of the teams of the tournament in Germany, playing some delightful football on their way to finishing third, was of little consolation. Nor could it save Ramsey, who had been sacked a month earlier.

Revie takes England job

Joe Mercer was given temporary charge of the England team, and in July the FA announced that Don Revie would take over. Leeds had just won the title, five points ahead of arch-rivals Liverpool. Revie's men had been under threat from the FA following their appalling disciplinary record in previous seasons. In this campaign it was their footballing qualities which took the eye. Leeds went on a 29-match unbeaten run to win their second championship in style. Revie's decision to take the England job may have had something to do with the fact that he now had an ageing side that would need a major overhaul sooner rather than later. The man who stepped into Revie's shoes was Brian Clough, but he was barely there long enough to claim a car-parking space, let alone put his stamp on the team. Amid rumours of a dressing-room bust-up between manager and players, Clough departed after just 44 days in charge.

BELOW: Allan Clarke scores from a penalty to put England level at one goal apiece with Poland. The draw in this game was not sufficient to take England through to the 1974 World Cup Finals in West Germany.

Johnny Giles

When Johnny Giles joined Leeds United from Manchester United in 1963 they were a Division Two side. Even in those days, at a cost of £35,000, Leeds got a bargain, for over the next 12 years Giles was a major influence in helping turn Don Revie's side into a force to rival Manchester United and Liverpool.

Leeds playmaker

Giles was originally a winger but at Leeds he became a superbly skilled and creative midfield playmaker, forming an almost telepathic partnership with the fiery Billy Bremner. In his first season at the club, 1963–64, Leeds won promotion to the First Division. During the following 10 years Leeds were never out of the top flight – never finishing lower than fourth in the table and twice taking the championship. Giles went on to win the FA Cup with Leeds in 1972, adding to the winners' medal he gained when he was part of Manchester United's victory over Leicester City nine years earlier. He also won two winners' medals in the Fairs Cup, but missed out on a European Cup victory when Leeds lost 2-0 to Bayern Munich in Paris in 1975. Soon after that defeat Giles left Elland Road for West Bromwich Albion.

As a Republic of Ireland international for nearly two decades, playing his 59th and last game in 1979, it was fitting that he ended his playing career with Shamrock Rovers.

Leeds fans riot as Bayern are crowned European champions

Jimmy Armfield took up the reins and although Leeds slipped to 9th in the league, they did make it to the 1975 European Cup Final. Leeds dominated in the early stages against holders Bayern Munich. They were unlucky not to be awarded a penalty and also had a Lorimer strike ruled out. Bayern weathered the storm and won the match with late goals from Roth and Müller. Leeds fans went on the rampage after the game and the club received a three-year ban from European competition. It hardly mattered as it was the end of a glorious era. Leeds were more commonly to be found in mid-table for the rest of the decade and were relegated early in the next.

ABOVE: QPR's Stan Bowles strides confidently away from the goalmouth after scoring against Manchester United; Martin Buchan looks on disconsolately. That season, 1973–74, saw Manchester United relegated to Division Two when they scored only 32 points from 42 games.

OPPOSITE ABOVE: Hero – Kevin Keegan soars in the air to score England's second goal in their 2-0 win over Wales at Cardiff in 1974.

OPPOSITE MIDDLE: Villain – Keegan lands a right to the jaw of Leeds captain Billy Bremner when the pair got into a brawl during the 1974 Charity Shield match.

OPPOSITE BELOW: The 1974 FA Cup Final saw Liverpool win 3-0 against Newcastle United. Here Keegan powers home the opening goal; he would later score the third.

Another World Cup exit for England

If Revie had timed his Elland Road exit well, his decision to take on the England job was to prove no great boost to his managerial career. He failed to establish a settled side, and although the usual club versus country wrangle didn't help matters, Revie himself contributed to the problem with constant changes in personnel. England failed to reach the last eight of the 1976 European Championship, and in July the

> *Fixtures postponed to increase England's chances.*

following year he handed in his resignation. England were on the brink of yet another World Cup exit and Revie headed off to the Middle East with comments that he jumped before he was pushed ringing in his ears.

Ron Greenwood stepped into the breach and that autumn guided England to victories in their last two World Cup qualifying matches. A 2-0 win over Italy merely reversed the result in Rome. It was the victory over Luxembourg by the same score that settled England's fate, the Italians going through on goal difference. As in 1974, England lost out to a side that went on to do well in the tournament – Italy would finish fourth – but after the heady days of 1966, and to a lesser extent 1970, it was a bitter pill to swallow.

The gruelling nature of the domestic season was highlighted as a contributory factor in the national team's fortunes. Grudgingly, the Football League finally accepted the postponement of fixtures prior to key international matches.

League Division One 1970–1979

1969–70

1	Everton	66
2	Leeds United	57
3	Chelsea	55
4	Derby County	53
5	Liverpool	51
6	Coventry	49
7	Newcastle United	47
8	Manchester United	45
9	Stoke	45
10	Manchester City	43
11	Tottenham Hotspur	43
12	Arsenal	42
13	Wolverhampton W.	40
14	Burnley	39
15	Nottingham Forest	38
16	West Bromwich Albion	37
17	West Ham United	36
18	Ipswich	31
19	Southampton	29
20	Crystal Palace	27
21	Sunderland	26
22	Sheffield Wednesday	25

1970–71

1	Arsenal	65
2	Leeds United	64
3	Tottenham Hotspur	52
4	Wolverhampton W.	52
5	Liverpool	51
6	Chelsea	51
7	Southampton	46
8	Manchester United	43
9	Derby County	42
10	Coventry	42
11	Manchester City	41
12	Newcastle United	41
13	Stoke	37
14	Everton	37
15	Huddersfield	36
16	Nottingham Forest	36
17	West Bromwich Albion	35
18	Crystal Palace	35
19	Ipswich	34
20	West Ham United	34
21	Burnley	27
22	Blackpool	23

1971–72

1	Derby County	58
2	Leeds United	57
3	Liverpool	57
4	Manchester City	57
5	Arsenal	52
6	Tottenham Hotspur	51
7	Chelsea	48
8	Manchester United	48
9	Wolverhampton W.	47
10	Sheffield United	46
11	Newcastle United	41
12	Leicester City	39
13	Ipswich	38
14	West Ham United	36
15	Everton	36
16	West Bromwich Albion	35
17	Stoke	35
18	Coventry	33
19	Southampton	31
20	Crystal Palace	29
21	Nottingham Forest	25
22	Huddersfield	25

1972–73

1	Liverpool	60
2	Arsenal	57
3	Leeds United	53
4	Ipswich	48
5	Wolverhampton W.	47
6	West Ham United	46
7	Derby County	46
8	Tottenham Hotspur	45
9	Newcastle United	45
10	Birmingham City	42
11	Manchester City	41
12	Chelsea	40
13	Southampton	40
14	Sheffield United	40
15	Stoke	38
16	Leicester City	37
17	Everton	37
18	Manchester United	37
19	Coventry	35
20	Norwich City	32
21	Crystal Palace	30
22	West Bromwich Albion	28

1973–74

1	Leeds United	62
2	Liverpool	57
3	Derby County	48
4	Ipswich	47
5	Stoke	46
6	Burnley	46
7	Everton	44
8	Queen's Park Rangers	43
9	Leicester City	42
10	Arsenal	42
11	Tottenham Hotspur	42
12	Wolverhampton W.	41
13	Sheffield United	40
14	Manchester City	40
15	Newcastle United	38
16	Coventry	38
17	Chelsea	37
18	West Ham United	37
19	Birmingham City	37
20	Southampton	36
21	Manchester United	32
22	Norwich City	29

1974–75

1	Derby County	53
2	Liverpool	51
3	Ipswich	51
4	Everton	50
5	Stoke	49
6	Sheffield United	49
7	Middlesbrough	48
8	Manchester City	46
9	Leeds United	45
10	Burnley	45
11	Queen's Park Rangers	42
12	Wolverhampton W.	39
13	West Ham United	39
14	Coventry	39
15	Newcastle United	39
16	Arsenal	37
17	Birmingham City	37
18	Leicester City	36
19	Tottenham Hotspur	34
20	Luton	33
21	Chelsea	33
22	Carlisle	29

1975–76

1	Liverpool	60
2	Queen's Park Rangers	59
3	Manchester United	56
4	Derby County	53
5	Leeds United	51
6	Ipswich	46
7	Leicester City	45
8	Manchester City	43
9	Tottenham Hotspur	43
10	Norwich City	42
11	Everton	42
12	Stoke	41
13	Middlesbrough	40
14	Coventry	40
15	Newcastle United	39
16	Aston Villa	39
17	Arsenal	36
18	West Ham United	36
19	Birmingham City	33
20	Wolverhampton W.	30
21	Burnley	28
22	Sheffield United	22

1976–77

1	Liverpool	57
2	Manchester City	56
3	Ipswich	56
4	Aston Villa	51
5	Newcastle United	49
6	Manchester United	47
7	West Bromwich Albion	45
8	Arsenal	43
9	Everton	42
10	Leeds United	42
11	Leicester City	42
12	Middlesbrough	41
13	Birmingham City	38
14	Queen's Park Rangers	38
15	Derby County	37
16	Norwich City	37
17	West Ham United	36
18	Bristol City	35
19	Coventry	35
20	Sunderland	34
21	Stoke	34
22	Tottenham Hotspur	33

1977–78

1	Nottingham Forest	64
2	Liverpool	57
3	Everton	55
4	Manchester City	52
5	Arsenal	52
6	West Bromwich Albion	50
7	Coventry	48
8	Aston Villa	46
9	Leeds United	46
10	Manchester United	42
11	Birmingham City	41
12	Derby County	41
13	Norwich City	40
14	Middlesbrough	39
15	Wolverhampton W.	36
16	Chelsea	36
17	Bristol City	35
18	Ipswich	35
19	Queen's Park Rangers	33
20	West Ham United	32
21	Newcastle United	22
22	Leicester City	22

1978–79

1	Liverpool	68
2	Nottingham Forest	60
3	West Bromwich Albion	59
4	Everton	51
5	Leeds United	50
6	Ipswich	49
7	Arsenal	48
8	Aston Villa	46
9	Manchester United	45
10	Coventry	44
11	Tottenham Hotspur	41
12	Middlesbrough	40
13	Bristol City	40
14	Southampton	40
15	Manchester City	39
16	Norwich City	37
17	Bolton Wanderers	35
18	Wolverhampton W.	34
19	Derby County	31
20	Queen's Park Rangers	25
21	Birmingham City	22
22	Chelsea	20

FA Cup Finals

Year					Score
1970	Chelsea	v	Leeds United		2-1
1971	Arsenal	v	Liverpool		2-1
1972	Leeds United	v	Arsenal		1-0
1973	Sunderland	v	Leeds United		1-0
1974	Liverpool	v	Newcastle United		3-0
1975	West Ham United	v	Fulham		2-0
1976	Southampton	v	Manchester United		1-0
1977	Manchester United	v	Liverpool		2-1
1978	Ipswich Town	v	Arsenal		1-0
1979	Arsenal	v	Manchester United		3-2

End of an era as Shanks steps down

When Ron Greenwood picked his first England side, he named seven Liverpool players. By the middle of the decade they were the team everyone had to beat. In 1973–74, having finished runners-up to Leeds and beaten Newcastle Utd in the FA Cup Final, Liverpool were the latest club to experience a shock managerial resignation. Bill Shankly announced his retirement, ending his 15-year reign at Anfield. After Liverpool's 3-0 demolition of Newcastle at Wembley, Liverpool fans had prostrated themselves at Shankly's feet on the pitch. Two months later he was gone. His final act was a typically shrewd move. The Liverpool way was to strengthen well before it was necessary. Competition was so fierce that players dreaded being sidelined through injury for fear that they might not get back in the team. It was after Shankly unveiled his last signing, Arsenal's Ray Kennedy, that he shuffled off the stage. The Liverpool board may have been worried that the Shankly aura might continue to pervade Anfield in the way that Busby's had at Old Trafford. In the event the break was swift and final, something Shankly was said to have found surprising and hurtful.

ABOVE: The Aston Villa team, with manager Ron Saunders (pointing), inspect the Wembley pitch before their League Cup Final match against Norwich in 1975. Villa won the tie 1-0.

BELOW INSERT: A fan adorns Bill Shankly with a scarf as he bids farewell to Anfield after fifteen years as Liverpool's manager.

Bill Shankly

When Bill Shankly left Anfield for the last time after winning the 1974 FA Cup, it brought down the curtain on a glorious 15-year reign. In that time Shankly had turned Liverpool from a struggling, unambitious club into one of the most formidable sides in world football.

Waking the sleeping giant

Shankly had had success with the other clubs he had managed – Carlisle, Grimsby, Workington and Huddersfield – but was hampered by their lack of vision and unwillingness to invest. Liverpool, on the other hand, was a true sleeping giant, and it was Shankly who woke it up and unleashed it on the world. Promotion to the top flight came in 1961–62, his second full season at the club. After just one season of consolidation Liverpool won the championship. Over the next 10 years he steered the club to two more league titles and two FA Cup victories. He also lifted the UEFA Cup in 1973, Liverpool beating Borussia Moenchengladbach in the final. The man from Glenbuck, Ayrshire was revered by fans and players alike, who loved his dry wit. He certainly laid the foundations for the side which dominated the English game in the 1970s and 1980s. Shankly died in 1981. His name adorns a pair of gates at the entrance to his beloved Anfield and his spirit pervades the club to this day.

Another League and European double for the Reds

In 1975–76 Queen's Park Rangers were the surprise package. Led by England captain Gerry Francis, QPR were top of the league when they'd completed their fixtures. But Liverpool could pip them by winning their last game, at Molineux. Wolves had to win to have any chance of avoiding relegation and they scored first. The Reds came back to win 3-1, however. Wolves were down and Paisley had his first championship under his belt. He also matched Shankly's feat of three years earlier by capturing the UEFA Cup in the same season. Liverpool put out a Barcelona side that boasted Johan Cruyff in the semis, then faced FC Bruges in the final. The Belgians rocked Liverpool by taking a 2-0 lead at Anfield, but the Reds staged a magnificent fightback to win 3-2. Bruges also scored first in the second leg, but a Keegan strike won the trophy for Liverpool.

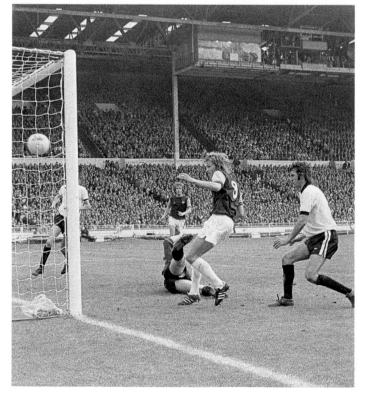

LEFT: Alan Taylor scores the second of his two goals which clinched the FA Cup for West Ham against London rivals Fulham in the 1975 Final.

ABOVE: West Ham's Trevor Brooking is mobbed by fans after the team's defeat of their Second Division rivals.

Strikes bring Sunday football

1974 saw Sunday football played for the first time. This was a tentative move and by no means uncontroversial. A combination of rail and power strikes persuaded the authorities to sanction these matches. Sunday trading laws meant that grounds could not simply open for business as they would on any other day. There were legal restrictions on charging at the gate and clubs circumvented these by selling programmes at the turnstiles for the normal entrance price. These games proved to be very popular with the fans and Sunday soccer would eventually become a way of life.

ABOVE: The Manchester United squad, with manager, Tommy "The Doc" Docherty (far right), at the end of the 1975–76 season. Although the club lost the 1976 FA Cup Final to Southampton, they won the following year and were back on track after their spell in Division Two during 1974–75.

Paisley emerges from "boot room" to take over at Anfield

The famous Anfield "boot room" had been established during the Shankly years. Bob Paisley, Joe Fagan, Ronnie Moran and Reuben Bennett were the key men in the backroom team. Paisley was given the top job, everyone took a step up in the pecking order and a seamless transition was effected.

In Paisley's first season in charge Liverpool finished runners-up to Derby. It was notable for two inspired purchases as Paisley showed he had Shankly's golden touch in the transfer market. Northampton's Phil Neal joined the Reds in a £60,000 deal in October 1974. A month later Terry McDermott, who had played against Liverpool in that year's Cup Final, arrived from Newcastle for £170,000.

United reach successive Cup Finals

1975–76 marked Manchester United's return to the First Division, and Tommy Docherty's young side was immediately chasing the double. They eventually finished third in the league, but in the FA Cup Final they were hot favourites to beat Lawrie McMenemy's Southampton, which had finished only sixth in the Second Division.

> *McMenemy's Southampton lift the Cup.*

Mick Channon and Peter Osgood led the line for Southampton but it was a solitary goal from Bobby Stokes seven minutes from time that brought the club its first major honour.

United returned to Wembley the following year and this time they faced a Liverpool side, which was seeking an unprecedented treble. Having secured a 10th league title, Liverpool had to play two Cup Finals in quick succession. The dream was ended at Wembley, where Docherty's burgeoning young side came out on top. Only Alex Stepney remained from the glory team of the 1960s. Stepney saw a Jimmy Case thunderbolt fly past him, cancelling out a Stuart Pearson shot which had squeezed under Clemence's body. A Lou Macari effort deflected off Jimmy Greenhoff for United's winner. It was an outrageous fluke but after the previous year's disappointment neither United nor the Doc were worried.

ABOVE RIGHT: The "Saints come rolling home"– the Southampton players who won the 1976 FA Cup travel through the streets of their home city, lined by 175,000 people, to attend a civic reception.

RIGHT: West Ham's Frank Lampard sen. and Manchester City's Rodney Marsh race for the ball during a league game at the beginning of the 1975 – 76 season. Despite West Ham's Cup win in 1975, they struggled to avoid relegation at the end of the 1975–76 season.

BELOW: United's Alex Stepney watches the ball go into the net as Bobby Stokes' goal, the only goal of the match, secures the 1976 FA Cup for Southampton.

OPPOSITE INSERT: After Liverpool's European Cup victory in 1977, Kevin Keegan signed for SV Hamburg.

Keegan bows out as Liverpool become champions of Europe

Five days later Liverpool had to pick themselves up as they made their bid to become only the second English side to win the European Cup. Their quarter-final clash with St Etienne had been the key match in their run to the final. St Etienne, the previous year's beaten finalists, had scored a 1-0 win at home, and were outstanding at Anfield. The French side scored to cancel out a Keegan goal, and even after Ray Kennedy restored Liverpool's lead on the night, the Reds still trailed on away goals. Enter David Fairclough, who came on with 20 minutes to go and scored the winner after a breathtaking solo run. "Supersub" had done it again.

Liverpool eased into the final with a win over FC Zurich. They travelled to Rome to face a Borussia Moenchengladbach side for the second time in a major final. The players shrugged off their FA Cup disappointment with an excellent 3-1 victory. It was a great day for two veterans. Tommy Smith, who had made his debut in 1963, headed in a Heighway corner to make it 2-1. Smith was a relative newcomer compared to Ian Callaghan, who had been at Anfield when the club was fighting for promotion to the top flight in the late 1950s.

It was also a special day for Kevin Keegan, playing his last game in the famous No. 7 shirt. His £500,000 move to SV Hamburg had already been agreed. Keegan didn't manage to get on the scoresheet in his final appearance but he gave Berti Vogts a torrid time. The ace German marker finally made a rash challenge, bringing Keegan down inside the box. Penalty king Phil Neal fired in the team's third goal, and Liverpool had equalled Manchester United's achievement of 1968.

Kevin Keegan

For a player who knew he wasn't the most naturally gifted in the game, Kevin Keegan demonstrated that a football career can be built as much on hard work, commitment and self-belief as on virtuoso skills. Surprisingly powerful in the air for a small man, he had a rocketing shot that made him a notable goalscorer, and was always looking to create opportunities for others during six glorious years at Liverpool FC, after Bill Shankly brought him to Merseyside in 1971 from Scunthorpe United, paying just £35,000.

European Footballer of the Year

Keegan scored in his very first game, and he soon made himself vital at the heart of the team. The very next season he netted 22 goals, helping Liverpool to win both the League Championship and the UEFA Cup. He scored twice in Liverpool's 3-0 victory over Newcastle in the 1974 FA Cup Final, and was named the Footballer of the Year in 1976 after the Reds again took the League title and he scored in both legs of the final of the UEFA Cup when they beat Bruges.

The Anfield faithful paid handsome tribute when Keegan was lured to Hamburg in a record £500,000 deal, for he had played 230 games and scored 68 goals in the famous red shirt. Playing in the Bundesliga, he twice won European Footballer of the Year, in 1978 and 1979, the only British player ever to do so.

63 England caps

First appearing for England (against Wales) in 1972, his international career spanned 10 years, during which he won 63 caps (31 of them as captain) and scored 21 goals. The end came when he missed a vital chance in a second-round match against Spain in the 1982 World Cup, and was then dropped for a European Championship qualifying game by

Bobby Robson. Keegan soon quit international football.

But his return to the English League provided a happier swansong. At Southampton and finally at Newcastle, he came right back into form and helped the Geordie side to win promotion to the First Division at the end of the 1983–84 season.

Returning to Tyneside as manager in 1992, he took the Magpies back to the top flight in short order, then made a surprise move to Fulham. Though he confessed to feelings of inadequacy at the end of his tenure as England manager, he showed he could still work his magic at club level, establishing Manchester City as a Premiership force once again before stepping down during the 2004–05 season. A second spell at St James' Park in 2008 lasted just eight months.

Dalglish, the new No.7 hero

Keegan went on to win the European Footballer of the Year award twice while at Hamburg. The blow of losing a player who had become a legend in his six years at Anfield was softened as Paisley went north of the border for a big-name replacement. 26-year-old Kenny Dalglish arrived in Liverpool a month after Keegan's departure. He had scored over a hundred goals for Celtic, the club he had joined at the age of 16. By the end of his first season at Liverpool he had notched 30, putting him well on the way to becoming a double centurion. The Kop had a new idol in the famous number 7 shirt.

Forest storm to the championship

Kenny Dalglish had arrived at Anfield in a blaze of publicity. There had been less of a fanfare when Paisley signed centre-back Alan Hansen from Partick Thistle for £100,000 a couple of months earlier. The 1977–78 season also saw the arrival of a third Scot who would become an Anfield legend. Paisley paid Middlesbrough £350,000 for midfielder Graeme Souness, who provided skill and steel in the heart of the midfield.

Three quality additions to a European Cup-winning side wasn't enough for Liverpool to retain the title in 1977–78. The Reds trailed seven points behind Brian Clough's newly promoted Nottingham Forest. Following the Leeds debacle, Clough had been reunited with Peter Taylor and taken over at Forest. The team only went up in third place behind Wolves and Chelsea and were tipped to make a rapid return to Division Two. Instead, Forest made it a Championship and League Cup double, with mighty Liverpool having to settle for second-best in both cases.

Kenny Dalglish

Already established as a legend at Celtic after a decade of service to the club he joined straight from school, Kenny Dalglish transferred to Liverpool in 1977. A month after Kevin Keegan had left Anfield for SV Hamburg, Liverpool boss Bob Paisley swooped to buy the most feared striker in the Scottish League.

Hundred league goals for Liverpool

Dalglish proved his worth to the club over the next 14 years, both as a player and as a manager; he became the idol of the Kop. In November 1983 he scored his hundredth League goal for Liverpool, the first player to reach that landmark both north and south of the border. He won five championship medals and three European Cups before taking over the reins from Joe Fagan in May 1985, in the wake of the Heysel Stadium disaster. With Dalglish as player-manager, Liverpool won the coveted Double in the 1985–86 season.

On the international stage, the player widely considered to be the greatest ever to wear the red of Liverpool also won a record 102 caps for Scotland, scoring 30 goals at international level to match Denis Law's record. Dalglish had a brief spell as director of football at Celtic, but had been out of the game for almost a decade when he returned to Anfield in 2009 to help run the academy. He returned to the manager's hot seat in January 2011 following Roy Hodgson's departure, initially on a caretaker basis.

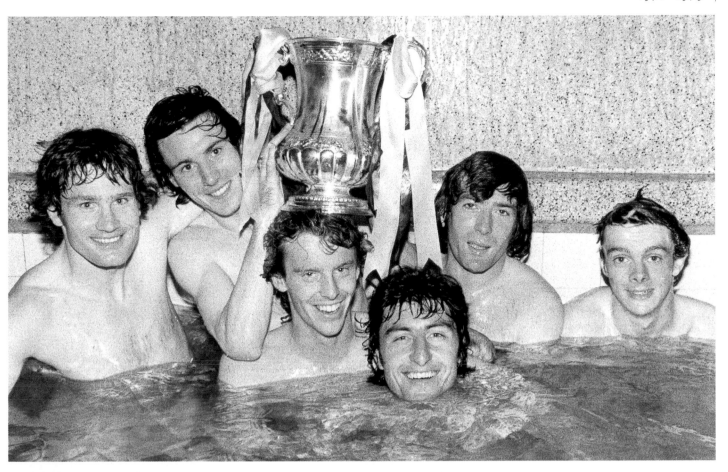

LEFT: Ipswich's Mick Mills holds up the Cup for the fans after the team's 1-0 win over Arsenal in the 1978 FA Cup Final.

ABOVE: Just one year later and Arsenal reverse their fortunes to take the Cup to Highbury in a 3-2 win over Manchester United.

OPPOSITE INSERT: Kenny Dalglish moves in to score the goal that put the holders of the title, Ipswich, out of the 1978–79 FA Cup competition. It was Dalglish's second season at Liverpool and he had proved worthy of the record £440,000 paid to bring the Celtic striker to Anfield as a replacement for Kevin Keegan. In his first season, Dalglish scored 31 goals in 62 appearances for the club.

OPPOSITE LEFT: A Dalglish diving header beats Chelsea's Micky Droy but hits the woodwork in a league game in March during the 1977–78 season when Liverpool turned out runners-up to Nottingham Forest in the championship.

Clough matches Chapman's record

Clough's side included ex-Derby players John McGovern, John O'Hare and Archie Gemmill, together with former Liverpool stopper Larry Lloyd. Clough added Kenny Burns, turning the former Birmingham City bad boy into the Footballer of the Year. There was

Forest lose only three games all season.

also Viv Anderson, a young attacking full-back who became England's first black player when he took the field against Czechoslovakia on 29 November 1978. But the key acquisition was probably Peter Shilton, bought from Stoke for £270,000, the highest amount ever paid for a goalkeeper. Forest lost just three games all season, conceding only 24 league goals, and took the title with four games to spare. Clough followed in the illustrious footsteps of Herbert Chapman in taking two clubs to the championship.

Liverpool retain European Cup

Forest also got the better of Liverpool in the 1978 League Cup Final, a John Robertson penalty settling the issue at Old Trafford after a goalless draw at Wembley. Having been pipped for domestic honours twice, Liverpool made sure they didn't finish the season empty-handed by retaining their European crown. FC Bruges were their Wembley opponents. The Belgians set their stall out defensively, inviting Liverpool to try and break them down. The Reds managed to do so just once, Dalglish chipping the keeper delightfully for his 30th goal of the season.

Osborne overcome as Ipswich lift FA Cup

Between 19 November 1977 and 9 December 1978 Forest were unbeaten in the League. Their only defeat in any competition was an FA Cup quarter-final tie with West Bromwich Albion, who won 2-0. Having beaten the country's form team, West Brom went down to Ipswich in the semis, and it was the East Anglian club who were the surprise winners of the trophy. That game will be remembered for the Roger Osborne goal that beat favourites Arsenal in the final. Osborne was so overwrought with the occasion that he was substituted, apparently through sheer nervous exhaustion. His goal took the Cup to Portman Road for the only time in the club's history.

BELOW: Arsenal's goalkeeper tries to thwart a Liverpool attack as Graeme Souness looks on during a league match in the 1978–79 season when honours were shared – Liverpool won the League and Arsenal the FA Cup.

OPPOSITE ABOVE: Nottingham Forest goalkeeper, Peter Shilton, and team-mate, Tony Woodcock hold the League Cup after the team's 3-2 win against Southampton in 1979. The late 1970s were a golden time for Nottingham Forest. Under manager Brian Clough, they won the league in 1978, the European Cup in 1979 and the League Cup in 1978 and 1979.

ABOVE: Argentinian international, Osvaldo "Ossie" Ardiles pictured in his Tottenham shirt soon after he, and international team-mate, Ricky Villa, joined Spurs. The signing of the two stars of the 1978 World Cup was a coup for Spurs manager, Keith Burkinshaw.

LEFT: Arsenal's Malcolm MacDonald leaves the pitch at Wembley after his team's defeat in the FA Cup Final 1978. His dejection can be understood – he had been on the losing side in a Wembley Final twice before, with Newcastle United, in the FA Cup in 1974 and the League Cup in 1976.

Reds set new defensive record

1978–79 saw Liverpool and Forest dominant once again, although this time their roles were reversed. On 9 December 1978 Liverpool ended Forest's year-long unbeaten run in the League. The Forest bubble didn't burst, however, and they again lost just three times in the League. Incredibly, that was only good enough to earn them second place behind a Liverpool side that was in record-breaking mood. Forest's 60 points would have won the championship on numerous postwar occasions. Liverpool themselves had won with that same points tally in 1973 and 1976, and Derby's two titles had been won with a lesser total. Liverpool lost one more game than Forest but 30 wins and eight draws gave them 68 points, one better than the record set by Leeds in 1968–69. The Reds' defence was phenomenal conceding just 16 goals all season.

Million-pound Francis wins European Cup for Forest
If Liverpool had reclaimed their domestic crown from Forest, it was Clough's men who took Liverpool's mantle as champions of Europe.

The two sides were unlucky to be drawn together in the first round of the European Cup, a game that would have graced the final. New young striking sensation Garry Birtles scored one of the goals as Forest took a 2-0 lead to Anfield. There they fought out a goalless draw and it was Forest who went forward to try and bring Europe's premier cup back to England for the third successive year. They did so, but not without a scare or two. In their semi-final against Cologne, Forest could only draw 3-3 at home. But Clough masterminded a 1-0 win in Germany, Ian Bowyer scoring the goal which put Forest into the final.

They faced Swedish champions Malmö in the Olympic Stadium, Munich. The hero of the hour was Trevor Francis, who headed the only goal of the game just before the break. Francis had become Britain's first million-pound footballer earlier in the season, Birmingham City finally being forced to part with their prize asset. Francis had not been eligible to play in the earlier European ties. His first taste of European football had won the premier trophy and paid off a large chunk of that record fee.

Brady stars in five-goal Wembley thriller

The last FA Cup Final of the decade provided a goal flurry in the dying minutes. Arsenal, with Liam Brady in imperious form, took a 2-0 lead over Manchester United and seemed to be coasting to victory. Some United fans were already making their way to the exits when goals from McQueen and McIlroy, in the 86th and 88th minutes, levelled the match. Man-of-the-match Brady had the final word, setting up the move which ended with Alan Sunderland scoring from a Graham Rix cross.

Liverpool domination set to continue

The 1979 FA Cup Final was refreshing in that it was untypical of the trend, which was for scoring fewer goals and conceding fewer. The decade's champions had, on average, scored 69.9 goals and let in 32.2. In the 1960s the average had been 87.3 and 45.7; in the 1950s it was 92.4 and 51.2. In 1961–62 Ipswich conceded 67 goals on their way to the title, which compared favourably with the number of goals scored by championship-winning sides of the 1970s. The new orthodoxy was getting men behind the ball, denying the opposition space and protecting leads.

15 of the 60 teams that had made it to the finals of the three European competitions over the decade were English, and ten of those had been successful. Liverpool had led the charge, and the Anfield juggernaut showed every sign of rolling on into the 1980s.

OPPOSITE: Trevor Francis and Nottingham Forest captain, John McGovern, hold up the European Cup as the victorious team are driven through the streets of Nottingham in celebration of their superb achievement.

BELOW: Arsenal's Liam Brady leaps over a tackle from David Geddis of Ipswich in the 1978 FA Cup Final. Despite Brady's athleticism, he was on the losing side as Ipswich won with a single goal from Roger Osborne.

BELOW LEFT: The joy on Arsenal's Alan Sunderland's face says it all, after he snatches a last-gasp winner in the 1979 FA Cup Final to beat Manchester United 3-2.

Old Firm game ends in tragedy

Tragedy struck Ibrox for the second time during an Old Firm game on 2 January 1971. A last-gasp equaliser by Colin Stein created a surge among Gers fans heading for the exits. Barriers on the East Terrace gave way and 66 died in the crush.

The new decade brought no change of script. Celtic reeled off five more League successes, making a record-breaking nine in all. Rangers, Hibs and Aberdeen all took supporting honours. The closest race was 1972–73, when Celtic finished a point ahead of Rangers, while in 1969–70 there was a 12-point chasm between first and second, and a ten-point margin in 1971–72. Rangers ended the run under Jock Wallace in 1974–75, and retained the title the following season, when Scottish football was reorganised into a ten-strong Premier Division and two lower leagues with 14 clubs each. The top teams now faced each other at least four times per season. Rangers collected their third treble in 1975–76, and a fourth domestic clean sweep came two years later. Wallace then left abruptly after an internal wrangle and Ibrox legend John Greig took the reins. Celtic trod a similar path, appointing Billy McNeill as Jock Stein's successor. In 1978–79, his first season at the helm, he guided the Bhoys to their seventh League title of the decade, but following a haul of 25 trophies in 13 years was a daunting task.

Thistle upset the odds

The Hoops were also consistent in the Cups, remarkably so in terms of reaching finals. The League Cup success of 1970 made it five in a row in that competition, and in 1978 Celtic featured in their 14th successive final. There were just two wins during the 1970s, though; Celtic were runners-up on seven occasions. Few saw Partick Thistle's 4–1 victory in 1971–72 coming. Thistle fans had to go back 50 years for their only other silverware. Celtic also appeared in seven Scottish Cup finals during the decade, winning five. In 1971–72 they put six past Hibs, something no victorious team had done since 1888, when Renton beat Cambuslang by the same 6–1 scoreline. Dixie Deans hit a hat-trick that day, Lou Macari grabbing a brace. Hibs were on the wrong end of a six-goal beating by Celtic in the 1975 League Cup final, too, but a side including Pat Stanton and Alex Edwards were worthy 2–1 winners over the Bhoys in 1973, the club's sole success of that era. Stanton, lauded by Tommy Docherty as a player to rival Bobby Moore, moved to Celtic Park in 1976, enjoying a couple of post-30 seasons in which he picked up championship and Scottish Cup winners medals, both of which had eluded him during his 13 years at Easter Road.

On the European trail it was Rangers who took the bragging rights. Celtic overcame English champions Leeds United in the European Cup semis in 1969–70 and were favourites to beat Feyenoord to claim a second win in the premier competition. The Dutch champions ran out 2–1 winners after extra-time. Two years later, Rangers made it third time lucky in Cup Winners' Cup finals, beating Moscow Dynamo 3–2 at the Nou Camp. Willie Waddell's team thought they'd been eliminated after losing to Sporting Lisbon on penalties in the second round, until a consultation with the rule-book revealed that they had actually won the tie on away goals! In the final Rangers cruised to a 3–0 lead, with one goal from Stein and two from Willie Johnston. The Russian side pulled two back, the second a couple of minutes from time, but Rangers held out for their first European triumph. The day was marred by crowd trouble – skipper John Greig couldn't receive the trophy on the pitch because of marauding fans. Rangers were hit with a ban that prevented them from defending the title the following year.

LEFT: New Year, 1971, the terraces at Ibrox Park where 66 fans died as a result of a crush when departing spectators tried to make their way back to the stand after Rangers scored a late goal in the Derby Match against Celtic. It raised questions about ground safety in British football stadiums, which were not fully addressed until the end of the next decade.

OPPOSITE: Full-back and Scottish legend Danny McGrain was selected for Celtic's all-time greatest XI. He was part of Jock Stein's 9-in-a-row glory days, winning 8 League Championships, 5 Scottish Cups and two League Cups. McGrain is a member of the Scotland Football Hall of Fame, having won 62 caps. He played for Scotland in the 1974 World Cup, missed the 1978 tournament because of injury and was captain of Scotland at the 1982 World Cup.

Scottish League 1970–1979

1969–70

1	Celtic	57
2	Rangers	45
3	Hibernian	44
4	Hearts	38
5	Dundee United	38
6	Dundee	36
7	Kilmarnock	36
8	Aberdeen	35
9	Greenock Morton	35
10	Dunfermline Athletic	35
11	Motherwell	32
12	Airdrieonians	32
13	St Johnstone	31
14	Ayr United	30
15	St Mirren	25
16	Clyde	25
17	Raith Rovers	21
18	Partick Thistle	17

1970–71

1	Celtic	56
2	Aberdeen	54
3	St Johnstone	44
4	Rangers	41
5	Dundee	38
6	Dundee United	36
7	Falkirk	35
8	Greenock Morton	34
9	Airdrieonians	34
10	Motherwell	34
11	Hearts	33
12	Hibernian	30
13	Kilmarnock	28
14	Ayr United	26
15	Clyde	26
16	Dunfermline Athletic	23
17	St Mirren	23
18	Cowdenbeath	17

1971–72

1	Celtic	60
2	Aberdeen	50
3	Rangers	44
4	Hibernian	44
5	Dundee	41
6	Hearts	39
7	Partick Thistle	34
8	St Johnstone	32
9	Dundee United	31
10	Motherwell	29
11	Kilmarnock	28
12	Ayr United	28
13	Greenock Morton	27
14	Falkirk	27
15	Airdrieonians	26
16	East Fife	25
17	Clyde	24
18	Dunfermline Athletic	23

1972–73

1	Celtic	57
2	Rangers	56
3	Hibernian	45
4	Aberdeen	43
5	Dundee	43
6	Ayr United	40
7	Dundee United	39
8	Motherwell	31
9	East Fife	30
10	Hearts	30
11	St Johnstone	29
12	Greenock Morton	28
13	Partick Thistle	28
14	Falkirk	26
15	Arbroath	26
16	Dumbarton	23
17	Kilmarnock	22
18	Airdrieonians	16

1973–74

1	Celtic	53
2	Hibernian	49
3	Rangers	48
4	Aberdeen	42
5	Dundee	39
6	Hearts	38
7	Ayr United	38
8	Dundee United	37
9	Motherwell	35
10	Dumbarton	29
11	Partick Thistle	28
12	St Johnstone	28
13	Arbroath	27
14	Greenock Morton	26
15	Clyde	25
16	Dunfermline Athletic	24
17	East Fife	24
18	Falkirk	22

1974–75

1	Rangers	56
2	Hibernian	49
3	Celtic	45
4	Dundee United	45
5	Aberdeen	41
6	Dundee	38
7	Ayr United	36
8	Hearts	35
9	St Johnstone	34
10	Motherwell	33
11	Airdrieonians	31
12	Kilmarnock	31
13	Partick Thistle	30
14	Dumbarton	24
15	Dunfermline Athletic	23
16	Clyde	22
17	Greenock Morton	22
18	Arbroath	17

1975–76

1	Rangers	54
2	Celtic	48
3	Hibernian	43
4	Motherwell	40
5	Hearts	35
6	Ayr United	33
7	Aberdeen	32
8	Dundee United	32
9	Dundee	32
10	St Johnstone	11

1976–77

1	Celtic	55
2	Rangers	46
3	Aberdeen	43
4	Dundee United	41
5	Partick Thistle	35
6	Hibernian	34
7	Motherwell	32
8	Ayr United	30
9	Hearts	27
10	Kilmarnock	17

1977–78

1	Rangers	55
2	Aberdeen	53
3	Dundee United	40
4	Hibernian	37
5	Celtic	36
6	Motherwell	33
7	Partick Thistle	33
8	St Mirren	30
9	Ayr United	24
10	Clydebank	19

1978–79

1	Celtic	48
2	Rangers	45
3	Dundee United	44
4	Aberdeen	40
5	Hibernian	37
6	St Mirren	36
7	Greenock Morton	36
8	Partick Thistle	34
9	Hearts	23
10	Motherwell	17

Scottish Cup Finals

1970	Aberdeen	v	Celtic	3-1
1971	Celtic	v	Rangers	1-1
	Celtic	v	Rangers	2-1
1972	Celtic	v	Hibernian	6-1
1973	Rangers	v	Celtic	3-2
1974	Celtic	v	Dundee United	3-0
1975	Celtic	v	Airdrieonians	3-1
1976	Rangers	v	Hearts	3-1
1977	Celtic	v	Rangers	1-0
1978	Rangers	v	Aberdeen	2-1
1979	Rangers	v	Hibernian	0-0
	Rangers	v	Hibernian	0-0
	Rangers	v	Hibernian	3-2

Scotland fly the British flag

Scotland flew the flag at both the 1974 and 1978 World Cups, on each occasion the only British representative. Minnows proved the undoing in each tournament. At West Germany '74 it came down to how many goals the three "established" sides – Scotland, Brazil and Yugoslavia – could put past Zaire. Unfortunately, Willie Ormond's men were first up and gained a modest 2-0 victory, goals from Peter Lorimer and Joe Jordan. Yugoslavia put nine past the Leopards, and Brazil squeezed ahead of Scotland with a 3-0 win. They were unbeaten but on the plane home.

Ally's Army

There were high hopes for Ally MacLeod's talent-rich squad at Argentina '78, cranked up to hubristic levels by the manager himself. Luck seemed to be on their side, for Scotland certainly got the rub of the green in a controversial final qualifier against Wales at Anfield, which they won 2-0. "Ally's Army" were on the march, hoping that the manager could transform the fortunes of the national side, as he had at club level with Ayr United and Aberdeen. Under his watch Ayr had become an established top-flight side, while he had led the Dons to League Cup glory in 1977, beating Celtic in the final. MacLeod's stock rose still further with a 2-1 win over England at Wembley that same year. But flights of fancy involving Scotland actually lifting the trophy had a swift return to earth as the team lost to Peru and could only draw with Iran. In the midst of the unfolding debacle, West Brom winger Willie Johnston was sent home for failing a drug test. Still they had a dog's chance, needing to beat Holland by three goals to progress. The team saved the best for last, but a 3-2 win over an outstanding Dutch side that would go all the way to the final wasn't enough. It was another first-round exit on goal difference, though Archie Gemmill's piece of solo magic in the Holland match would go down as one of the great World Cup goals.

ABOVE: Archie Gemmill scored probably Scotland's greatest-ever World Cup goal at the 1978 tournament in a must-win match against Holland. In a moment of genius after 68 minutes, Gemmill picked up the ball on the right-hand edge of the Dutch box, skipped his way majestically through three despairing tackles before calmly side-footing the ball past advancing keeper Jan Jongbloed.

LEFT: Scotland appeared to be on course against Peru in the 1978 World Cup finals when, after 14 minutes, Jordan snapped up a chance from Quiroga's parry after Rioch had shot from the edge of the area. The opportunity to extend this lead, however, did not arise as Peru came more into the game. On the stroke of half-time Cubillas passed to Cueto, who equalised beyond Alan Rough.

ABOVE: Willie Johnston was a talented player, whose speed and trickery on the left-wing and as an inside-left was a catalyst for the Rangers team which won the European Cup Winners Cup in 1972. He scored twice in the final as Rangers defeated Dynamo Moscow 3–2 in Barcelona.

ABOVE RIGHT: Frank McLintock was born in Glasgow and brought up in the Gorbals. He started his career in the Scottish Juniors and made his debut for Scotland, against Norway in 1963. In October 1964 he was signed by Arsenal and went straight into the first team and in 1971 won the Football Writers' Association Footballer of the Year award. Having only played once for Scotland since 1964, he earned a recall in 1970, winning a further four caps to bring his total to nine.

RIGHT: Another award for Celtic manager Jock Stein supported by Scotland legends Paddy Crerand and Denis Law.

Wales miss out on Argentina '78

Sweden '58 remains Wales's sole appearance in a major tournament, but there have been some near misses. Defeat to Yugoslavia cost them a place in the European Championship semis in 1976, and there followed three agonising World Cup campaigns. A controversial penalty in the crucial group match against Scotland at Anfield helped scupper Wales's hopes of reaching Argentina '78. Doubtless, Joe Jordan still has to keep a low profile in the Principality, for it was he who handled, yet Scotland were awarded a spot-kick.

1980–1989
Glory and Tragedy

In the 1980s Liverpool continued their stranglehold on the English game, their level of performance and trophy haul enduring a number of personnel changes, including two at managerial level. By the middle of the decade it was Everton who posed the greatest threat, and their two Championships meant that only twice in the decade did the title leave Merseyside.

1980 Nottingham Forest win the European Cup for the second year running

1981 Queen's Park Rangers install an artificial playing surface at their home ground, Loftus Road, the first club to do so; however, the pitch was re-turfed in 1987

1981 Liverpool win the European Cup for a third time

1981 Football League introduces three points for a win

1982 The League Cup becomes the Milk Cup under a sponsorship deal with the Milk Marketing Board

1982 Aston Villa win the European Cup after beating Bayern Munich in the Final, meaning six consecutive successes for English clubs in the competition

1982 Twelfth World Cup held in Spain sees Italy winning the competition after England lost in the second group stages to West Germany. Northern Ireland beat the hosts in reaching the second round. Scotland go out at the group stage on goal difference for the third tournament running

1982 England record their greatest victory at Wembley by beating Luxembourg 9-0

1983 The Football League is sponsored by Canon

1983 Tottenham Hotspur becomes the first football club to be floated on the Stock Exchange

1983 Aberdeen beat Real Madrid 2-1 in the Cup Winners' Cup Final in Gothenburg

1983 Dundee United become Scottish League champions for the first time in their 74-year history

1984 Liverpool's fourth win in the European Cup Final

1984 Northern Ireland win the last Home International Championship

1985 Everton win the European Cup Winners' Cup

1985 A fire in a wooden stand at Bradford City's ground kills 56 spectators

1985 39 fans die as a result of rioting during the European Cup Final at the Heysel Stadium in Brussels. As a result UEFA place an indefinite ban on English football clubs entering European competitions, ending a winning streak by British clubs which saw them winning seven out of eight European Cup titles since 1977

Heysel, Hillsborough and Bradford

If the city of Liverpool basked in the glory of being footballing top dogs, it also suffered two horrific tragedies. A total of 135 people lost their lives in the Heysel and Hillsborough disasters. On 11 May 1985, less than three weeks before the Heysel tragedy, Bradford entertained Lincoln City in their last match of the season. It should have been a joyous occasion, Bradford celebrating promotion to Division Two as champions. A discarded cigarette set the wooden stand ablaze and 56 died in the inferno. These three events put the game into its proper perspective. Liverpool boss Kenny Dalglish declared that football was "irrelevant" as the city struggled to come to terms with the tragic events at Hillsborough. These disasters also led the game's administrators to realise that fencing in spectators may have prevented pitch invasions, but it also prevented fans from escaping life-threatening situations.

European victory for Forest

The decade began much as the last one had ended, with Liverpool and Nottingham Forest vying for supremacy at home and in Europe. In 1980 the Reds took the Championship but crashed out of the European Cup at the first hurdle to Dinamo Tbilisi. Forest came through some tough matches, even surviving a home defeat against Dynamo Berlin. A Trevor Francis double helped Forest turn that tie around and they marched on to meet Kevin Keegan's SV Hamburg in the Final. The showcase events were becoming worryingly sterile affairs and this was no great advertisement for the game. John Robertson scored the only goal, cutting in from the left and firing home from 20 yards. Francis had been sidelined through injury and the team was content to sit back and play on the break. When Hamburg did manage to carve an opening, they found Shilton in prime form.

Brooking sets up Hammers

Forest also made it to the League Cup Final, for the third year running. There was no hat-trick of wins, though. A catastrophic mix-up between Shilton and Dave Needham allowed Wolves' Andy Gray to score the game's only goal. Also playing in the famous Old Gold shirt that day was Emlyn Hughes, recently arrived from Liverpool. In his 13 years at Anfield he had won just about every honour in the game – except the League Cup.

The 1980 FA Cup Final was also settled by a solitary goal. Arsenal must have thought their name was on the Cup after coming through a mammoth semi-final against Liverpool, which went to three replays, seven hours of football in total. A Brian Talbot goal finally broke the deadlock and put the Gunners into the Final for the third year running. They faced a West Ham side that had finished 7th in Division Two but a rare header from midfield maestro Trevor Brooking was enough to give the Hammers victory. It was a red-letter day for 17-year-old Paul Allen, the youngest player ever to appear in an FA Cup Final.

OPPOSITE: Liverpool celebrate their win of the 1984 Milk Cup Final against Everton at Maine Road.

LEFT: Goalkeeper Peter Shilton of Nottingham Forest punches the ball clear of the goal as Arsenal attack. Arsenal won the match 1-0, but Forest were in fine form in 1980 and were to beat SV Hamburg in the European Cup Final.

1985 Alex Ferguson's Aberdeen claim a third Scottish Championship in six years

1985 10 September: Scotland manager Jock Stein suffers a fatal heart attack during a World Cup qualifier against Wales at Ninian Park. His assistant Alex Ferguson takes over as national team boss

1985 Manchester United's Kevin Moran becomes the first player to be sent off in an FA Cup Final

1986 Thirteenth World Cup, held in Mexico but won by Argentina but famous for Maradona's "Hand of God" goal against England in the

quarter-finals. Scotland and Northern Ireland are both eliminated at the group stage

1986 Two substitutes allowed in FA and League Cup matches

1986 Aberdeen manager Alex Ferguson becomes the new Manchester United manager

1986 The First Division is reduced to 20 teams

1987 Re-election to the Football League abolished and automatic promotion for the winners of the Conference established

1987 To celebrate its centenary the Football League played a Football

League vs. Rest of the World one-off fixture at Wembley, which saw the Football League win 3-0

1988 Transfer of Ian Rush from Juventus to Liverpool for £2.8m establishes a new record transfer fee

1988 England finish bottom of their group at the European Championship. Holland beat Russia 2-0 in the Final

1989 95 football fans crushed to death at the beginning of an FA Cup semi-final match between Liverpool and Nottingham Forest at Sheffield Wednesday's Hillsborough ground (the total number of deaths became

96 when Tony Bland died four years later). Lord Justice Taylor is commissioned to investigate the tragedy

1989 Former Celtic star Mo Johnston joins Rangers from Nantes, the first high-profile Catholic to play for the club

1989 Arsenal and Liverpool finish level on points and goal difference. The Gunners take the title on goals scored

Arsenal miss out in Cup Winners' Cup

Arsenal's dramatic win over Manchester United the previous year had put them through to the Cup Winners' Cup competition and the Gunners made it through to the Final. Valencia provided the glamorous opposition, but 120 minutes of football produced no goals and this became the first major Final to be decided on penalties. Argentine World Cup hero Mario Kempes missed, but parity was restored when Liam Brady also failed with his spot-kick. Graham Rix was the unlucky man to miss the vital kick and the trophy went to Spain. Arsenal were left with the unique distinction of returning to Highbury empty-handed despite having gone through the tournament unbeaten.

England's Euro failure

In the European Championship England dropped just one point in their eight qualifying matches to reach the finals, which were staged in Italy. A revised format saw the eight countries split into two groups with the winners of each contesting the Final. Tear gas had to be used to quell disturbances as England opened with a goalless draw against Belgium. Marco Tardelli scored the only goal of the game when England met the hosts in the second game. England were out without registering a single goal, although they did manage a 2-1 win against Spain in a meaningless final group match.

Three points for a win

By 1981 concern over the state of the game was being expressed in high places. A lot of the fare on offer was of indifferent quality; hooliganism was a cancer that was proving difficult to excise; and with the country in the grip of recession a match-day ticket became a luxury some fans could ill afford. Liverpool's dominance didn't help matters. Gates were barely above the 20 million mark, half what they had been in the golden postwar years. Several clubs were teetering on the edge of bankruptcy, Wolves among them.

The Football League announce plans to make the game more attacking.

The Football League announced that from 1981–82, there would be three points for a win. The message was clear: football was entertainment as well as sport, and the carrot of three points would surely make teams think twice about putting up the defensive drawbridge.

BELOW: Referee Clive Thomas is mobbed by West Ham players as he overrules the linesman's offside flag in the 1981 League Cup Final.

RIGHT: Ricky Villa holds aloft the FA Cup for the crowds of admiring fans gathered in the streets outside Tottenham Town Hall in 1981. Following a 1-1 draw against Manchester City, Tottenham went on to win the replay at Wembley 3-2.

Villa take the Championship

The intervening season brought plenty of drama, not least of which was the sight of Liverpool languishing in 5th place in the League. The Reds lost just eight games, which was as good as anyone, but had drawn as many as they'd won. It was Ron Saunders' Aston Villa who took the title, for the first time in 71 years. Villa used just 14 players all season and seven of them were ever-present. Ex-Coventry player Dennis Mortimer captained the side, forming an impressive midfield axis with Gordon Cowans and Des Bremner, who provided skill and steel, respectively. Up front Peter Withe and Gary Shaw made up a potent little-and-large strike force. Flying winger Tony Morley was responsible for many assists and was also a regular on the scoresheet himself.

Ardiles and Villa in Cup classic

1981 saw Spurs continue their love affair with years ending in 1. In the FA Cup Final Manchester City's Tommy Hutchinson scored twice, the second of which he would rather not have claimed. A Glenn Hoddle free-kick deflected off him and earned Spurs a replay. Keith Burkinshaw had pulled off the transfer coup of the year when he brought Ricardo Villa and Osvaldo Ardiles to White Hart Lane after Argentina's World Cup victory in 1978. In 1981 the two shared in a spectacular triumph. The teams put on a terrific display when they returned to Wembley for the replay. With minutes to go and the score 2-2, Villa danced his way through the City defence to score what many regard as the best individual goal ever in a Cup Final.

BELOW: Aston Villa's Peter Withe scores against Stoke in a 1-1 draw, gaining an important point for the team, which ended the 1980–81 season at the top of the First Division for the first time in 71 years.

ABOVE: Ipswich Town manager Bobby Robson brings back the UEFA Cup having defeated Dutch side AZ 67 Alkmaar 5-4 on aggregate.

Bob Paisley

Although people often speak of Shankly and Ferguson as the greatest managers to grace the English game, in terms of honours won, nobody can match the achievements of Bob Paisley. He took over from Shankly after the FA Cup victory over Newcastle in 1974, 35 years after joining the club. Paisley had been a member of Liverpool's title-winning side of 1947, joining the coaching staff on his retirement seven years later. But it was for his nine years at the helm that he will be best remembered. He led the club to six Championships and three League Cups, but it was his four European trophies that set him apart from his peers. His team lifted the UEFA Cup in 1976 with a victory over FC Bruges. The following year he made Liverpool the third British side to win the European Cup when Liverpool beat Borussia Moenchengladbach 3-1 at the Olympic Stadium in Rome. Liverpool retained the trophy the following year, beating Bruges once again in a major Final. The hat-trick was completed in 1981, Alan Kennedy scoring the goal which beat Real Madrid. The affable Geordie stepped down in 1983, signing off with a Championship and League Cup double. On the latter occasion, Graeme Souness took the unprecedented step of ushering the manager up the 39 Wembley steps to collect the trophy. Paisley died in February 1996.

Rush signs from Chester

Although the two major domestic honours had escaped them, Liverpool did add two more trophies to the cabinet. The Reds finally added the League Cup to their tally, though they needed a replay to beat West Ham. An Alan Hansen header gave Liverpool a 2-1 victory. Making only his second full appearance that night at Villa Park was young striker Ian Rush, who had signed from Chester City for £300,000 having played just 33 games in Division Four.

Having broken their League Cup duck, Liverpool proceeded to form a firm attachment to it. Victories over Spurs, Manchester United and Everton in the next three Finals set a new record and gave the club outright ownership of the trophy.

Liverpool's third Euro success

1981 also brought Liverpool a third European Cup success. Alex Ferguson's Aberdeen and Bayern Munich were among their scalps en route to the Final. There they met six-time winners Real Madrid, whose side included ex-West Brom star winger Laurie Cunningham. It was a cagey contest, Alan Kennedy breaking the deadlock with a shot from an acute angle nine minutes from time. The victory meant that Liverpool joined Bayern and Ajax as three-time winners of European club football's most prestigious trophy.

Muhren and Butcher lift Robson's Ipswich

Bobby Robson's Ipswich Town made it a European double by lifting the UEFA Cup. Ipswich had finished runners-up in the League, their formidable line-up including Terry Butcher, Paul Mariner, Alan Brazil and John Wark. Like Spurs, the team had two outstanding overseas players, the Dutch midfield duo Frans Thijssen and Arnold Muhren. Ipswich overcame Dutch champions AZ 67 Alkmaar 5-4 on aggregate in the Final. Wark scored a record-equalling 14 goals during the campaign. Wark, Thijssen and Mariner made it an Ipswich clean sweep in the PFA awards, with Thijssen topping the Football Writers poll.

Robson's careful housekeeping at Ipswich showed that success could be had for a modest outlay. Many clubs wielded the chequebook all too readily and huge amounts were changing hands. Some players would prove to be worth every penny. In October 1981 Ron Atkinson paid his former club West Bromwich Albion £1.5 million to bring Bryan Robson to Old Trafford. A decade later that would look a knockdown price. Steve Daley, Kevin Reeves, Justin Fashanu and Gary Birtles were among those whose form – and value – slumped dramatically after high-profile moves.

In one remarkable move Clive Allen joined Arsenal from Queen's Park Rangers, and was sold on to Crystal Palace two months later without having kicked a ball. Allen's cut of the two million-pound deals was around £100,000, players receiving 5% of the fee provided they didn't seek a move.

Swansea's rollercoaster

While Robson was signing for United, an unfamiliar name sat on top of Division One. John Toshack's Swansea had leapt from the Fourth Division to the top flight in just four seasons. They won seven and drew one of their first 10 games and went on to finish 6th in the Championship. Relegation came the following year, however, and by 1986 they were back in the basement, a repeat of the rollercoaster ride Northampton Town had taken in the 1960s.

ABOVE RIGHT: Steve Perryman and John Gregory clash during the 1982 FA Cup Final between Spurs and QPR.

BELOW RIGHT: England's Trevor Francis (left) in action against Scotland at Wembley.

OPPOSITE BELOW RIGHT: The 1981 Charity Shield is shared by Aston Villa and Spurs, following a 2-2 draw. Goalscorers Peter Withe of Villa (left) and Mark Falco of Tottenham pose with the trophy.

Swansea rise to sixth

While John Toshack remains a legend at Cardiff, he is also revered for his achievements at Swansea during the late 70s and early 80s. The club began life as Swansea Town in 1912, changing its name when Swansea was accorded city status in 1971. With Toshack as player-manager, Swansea were promoted three times in four years, and finished sixth in the top flight in 1981–82. The wheels quickly came off, and within five years the club was back in the basement.

Spurs bounce back

Spurs were battling on four fronts in 1981–82. They went down to Barcelona in the Cup Winners' Cup Final and lost to Liverpool in the Final of the League Cup, renamed the Milk Cup after its new sponsor. A late equaliser by Ronnie Whelan took the game into extra time. The Spurs players were visibly deflated. Paisley told his men to look raring to go for another 30 minutes. Whelan and Rush scored to make the final score 3-1 to the holders.

In goal for Spurs that day was Ray Clemence, who had moved to White Hart Lane the previous summer for £300,000. His old team had come back to haunt him, and his new club had tasted Wembley defeat for the first time.

Hoddle's decisive penalty

Spurs finished 4th in the League, 16 points behind champions Liverpool. A possible "quadruple" had been reduced to a single battlefront: the FA Cup. Glenn Hoddle scored the two goals which salvaged Spurs' season. It was his deflected shot which earned Spurs a 1-1 draw against Second Division QPR. He then struck a 6th-minute penalty in the replay to bring the Cup back to White Hart Lane for the second year running.

It was a day of mixed emotions for Ardiles and Villa. Since their semi-final victory over Leicester, Britain had gone to war with Argentina over the Falkland Islands. Under the circumstances it would have been impossible for the two to play in the Final. Both were diplomatically moved on, though Ardiles would return to White Hart Lane when hostilities ended.

LEFT: Watford's John Barnes, and Arsenal's Kenny Sansom struggle for a high-ball in a match that Watford went on to win 2-1.

BELOW: Hoddle scores the penalty in the replay that would win Tottenham the FA Cup in 1982.

League Division One 1980–1989

1979–80

1	Liverpool	60
2	Manchester United	58
3	Ipswich	53
4	Arsenal	52
5	Nottingham Forest	48
6	Wolverhampton W.	47
7	Aston Villa	46
8	Southampton	45
9	Middlesbrough	44
10	West Bromwich Albion	41
11	Leeds United	40
12	Norwich City	40
13	Crystal Palace	40
14	Tottenham Hotspur	40
15	Coventry	39
16	Brighton	37
17	Manchester City	37
18	Stoke	36
19	Everton	35
20	Bristol City	31
21	Derby County	30
22	Bolton Wanderers	25

1980–81

1	Aston Villa	60
2	Ipswich	56
3	Arsenal	53
4	West Bromwich Albion	52
5	Liverpool	51
6	Southampton	50
7	Nottingham Forest	50
8	Manchester United	48
9	Leeds United	44
10	Tottenham Hotspur	43
11	Stoke	42
12	Manchester City	39
13	Birmingham City	38
14	Middlesbrough	37
15	Everton	36
16	Coventry	36
17	Sunderland	35
18	Wolverhampton W.	35
19	Brighton	35
20	Norwich City	33
21	Leicester City	32
22	Crystal Palace	19

1981–82

1	Liverpool	87
2	Ipswich	83
3	Manchester United	78
4	Tottenham Hotspur	71
5	Arsenal	71
6	Swansea	69
7	Southampton	66
8	Everton	64
9	West Ham United	58
10	Manchester City	58
11	Aston Villa	57
12	Nottingham Forest	57
13	Brighton	52
14	Coventry	50
15	Notts County	47
16	Birmingham City	44
17	West Bromwich Albion	44
18	Stoke	44
19	Sunderland	44
20	Leeds United	42
21	Wolves	40
22	Middlesbrough	39

1982–83

1	Liverpool	82
2	Watford	71
3	Manchester United	70
4	Tottenham Hotspur	69
5	Nottingham Forest	69
6	Aston Villa	68
7	Everton	64
8	West Ham United	64
9	Ipswich	58
10	Arsenal	58
11	West Bromwich Albion	57
12	Southampton	57
13	Stoke	57
14	Norwich City	54
15	Notts County	52
16	Sunderland	50
17	Birmingham City	50
18	Luton	49
19	Coventry	48
20	Manchester City	47
21	Swansea	41
22	Brighton	40

1983–84

1	Liverpool	80
2	Southampton	77
3	Nottingham Forest	74
4	Manchester United	74
5	Queen's Park Rangers	73
6	Arsenal	63
7	Everton	62
8	Tottenham Hotspur	61
9	West Ham United	60
10	Aston Villa	60
11	Watford	57
12	Ipswich	53
13	Sunderland	52
14	Norwich City	51
15	Leicester City	51
16	Luton	51
17	West Bromwich Albion	51
18	Stoke	50
19	Coventry	50
20	Birmingham City	48
21	Notts County	41
22	Wolverhampton W.	29

1984–85

1	Everton	90
2	Liverpool	77
3	Tottenham Hotspur	77
4	Manchester United	76
5	Southampton	68
6	Chelsea	66
7	Arsenal	66
8	Sheffield Wednesday	65
9	Nottingham Forest	64
10	Aston Villa	56
11	Watford	55
12	West Bromwich Albion	55
13	Luton	54
14	Newcastle	52
15	Leicester City	51
16	West Ham United	51
17	Ipswich	50
18	Coventry City	50
19	Queen's Park Rangers	50
20	Norwich City	49
21	Sunderland	40
22	Stoke	17

1985–86

1	Liverpool	88
2	Everton	86
3	West Ham United	84
4	Manchester United	76
5	Sheffield Wednesday	73
6	Chelsea	71
7	Arsenal	69
8	Nottingham Forest	68
9	Luton Town	66
10	Tottenham Hotspur	65
11	Newcastle United	63
12	Watford	59
13	Queen's Park Rangers	52
14	Southampton	46
15	Manchester City	45
16	Aston Villa	44
17	Coventry City	43
18	Oxford United	42
19	Leicester City	42
20	Ipswich Town	41
21	Birmingham City	29
22	West Bromwich Albion	24

1986–87

1	Everton	86
2	Liverpool	77
3	Tottenham Hotspur	71
4	Arsenal	70
5	Norwich City	68
6	Wimbledon	66
7	Luton Town	66
8	Nottingham Forest	65
9	Watford	63
10	Coventry City	63
11	Manchester United	56
12	Southampton	52
13	Sheffield Wednesday	52
14	Chelsea	52
15	West Ham United	52
16	Queen's Park Rangers	50
17	Newcastle United	47
18	Oxford United	46
19	Charlton Athletic	44
20	Leicester City	42
21	Manchester City	39
22	Aston Villa	36

1987–88

1	Liverpool	90
2	Manchester United	81
3	Nottingham Forest	73
4	Everton	70
5	Queen's Park Rangers	67
6	Arsenal	66
7	Wimbledon	57
8	Newcastle United	56
9	Luton Town	53
10	Coventry City	53
11	Sheffield Wednesday	53
12	Southampton	50
13	Tottenham Hotspur	47
14	Norwich City	45
15	Derby County	43
16	West Ham United	42
17	Charlton Athletic	42
18	Chelsea	42
19	Portsmouth	35
20	Watford	32
21	Oxford United	31

1988–89

1	Arsenal	76
2	Liverpool	76
3	Nottingham Forest	64
4	Norwich City	62
5	Derby County	58
6	Tottenham Hotspur	57
7	Coventry City	55
8	Everton	54
9	Queen's Park Rangers	53
10	Millwall	53
11	Manchester United	51
12	Wimbledon	51
13	Southampton	45
14	Charlton Athletic	42
15	Sheffield Wednesday	42
16	Luton Town	41
17	Aston Villa	40
18	Middlesbrough	39
19	West Ham United	38
20	Newcastle United	31

FA Cup Finals

Year					Score
1980	West Ham United	v	Arsenal		1-0
1981	Tottenham Hotspur	v	Manchester City		1-1 (3-2)
1982	Tottenham Hotspur	v	QPR		1-1 (1-0)
1983	Manchester United	v	Brighton H.A.		2-2 (4-0)
1984	Everton	v	Watford		2-0
1985	Manchester United	v	Everton		1-0
1986	Liverpool	v	Everton		3-1
1987	Coventry City	v	Tottenham Hotspur		3-2
1988	Wimbledon	v	Liverpool		1-0
1989	Liverpool	v	Everton		3-2

Aston Villa
make it six in a row

The domestic season ended with Aston Villa bringing the European Cup back to England for the 6th year running. Ron Saunders had departed and it was coach Tony Barton who found himself in the hot seat as Villa battled through to play Bayern Munich in the Final. Villa, with just two modest UEFA Cup campaigns in the 1970s behind them, had put out Dynamo Berlin, Dynamo Kiev and Anderlecht

Teenage stand-in keeper Nigel Spink is Villa hero.

along the way. Bayern was the last club to hold the trophy before English sides took over and they were favourites to end that period of domination. It looked even more likely when Villa lost keeper Jimmy Rimmer 10 minutes into the game. 19-year-old rookie Nigel Spink took over and proceeded to have a storming match. A mishit shot by Peter Withe from a Tony Morley cross won the game. It meant that Rimmer – on United's bench for their 1968 triumph – now had two European Cup winners' medals having played a total of 10 minutes in the two finals.

Ron Greenwood's England

30-year-old Peter Withe was the new European champions' only representative in Ron Greenwood's squad that went to Spain for the World Cup. The team's qualification had not been the smoothest.

Defeats in Basel, Oslo and Bucharest left England needing Switzerland to win in Romania. They did, and Greenwood showed his appreciation by donning a Swiss FA tie at the World Cup draw.

England were seeded, somewhat surprisingly, and got off to a dream start. Bryan Robson made World Cup history by scoring after just 27 seconds against France. That set up a 3–1 win over a team that would go on to reach the semi-final. But while France got stronger, England fell away. Victories over Czechoslovakia and Kuwait had put England into the second phase with maximum points, a record matched only by Brazil.

In the second round mini-League England found themselves up against West Germany and hosts Spain. They created the better chances against the Germans but also survived a scare when Rummenigge hit the bar from 25 yards. After Germany beat Spain 2–1, England took on the hosts, needing to win by two goals to go through. Once again they failed to take their chances, against a team that had nothing to play for. The performance was summed up by a glaring miss from substitute Kevin Keegan. The game ended goalless and England were out.

Robson becomes new England boss

It marked the end of Greenwood's reign as national team boss. It was shades of 1962 as the FA named Bobby Robson as his successor. Ramsey had peaked at the right time, taking an unheralded side to the top of the League. Robson had spent relatively little in guiding his team to the runners-up spot in the past two seasons, together with a UEFA Cup victory.

Graham Taylor's Watford finish second

Luton and Watford were promoted to Division One in 1981–82, and the following season were a breath of fresh air in the top flight. They decided that attack was the best form of defence. Only four teams scored more than David Pleat's Luton. Unfortunately, the worst defensive record in the division meant that they finished 18th, surviving with a win over Manchester City on the last day of the season.

Graham Taylor's Watford ended the season second to Liverpool, both in goals scored and League position. Watford had taken five years to get from the basement to Division One, but made a better fist of it than Swansea once they got there. Elton John had taken over as chairman in 1976, when the team was a mid-table Division Four outfit. But it was the appointment of Taylor that was undoubtedly the key to Watford's meteoric rise. The team was always dangerous going forward, Luther Blissett and Ross Jenkins spearheading the attack. Blissett's performances earned him an England call-up, and he scored a hat-trick in his first full appearance, against Luxembourg in December 1982.

Refereeing inconsistencies

The resurgence of attacking football was partly down to the new three-points-for-a-win system. This term the authorities showed their determination to stamp out cynical play by making professional fouls a sending-off offence. This remained a grey area, however, with the seriousness of the misdemeanour left to the referee's discretion. The season was peppered with controversial incidents, some of which resulted in dismissal while others merely earned a caution.

OPPOSITE LEFT: Peter Withe and Nigel Spink of Aston Villa with the European Cup.

OPPOSITE RIGHT: Gary Lineker is among Leicester City players celebrating when Ian Wilson scores against Fulham, helping Leicester pursue promotion to the First Division.

ABOVE: A scene at the opening ceremony of the 1982 World Cup held in Spain. England were to perform well in the initial stages but could not maintain the momentum.

RIGHT: Liverpool goalkeeper Bruce Grobbelaar holds on to this Everton cross during the 1984 Charity Shield, but a later mistake would see Everton win the match 1-0.

Paisley leaves Anfield

1982–83 saw Bob Paisley end his 43-year association with Anfield. Paisley had won 13 major trophies in nine years, plus a string of Charity Shield successes. The FA Cup was missing from his haul, but he was still comfortably the most successful manager in history. He bowed out with two more trophies. By April Liverpool were 16 points clear and had the Championship sewn up. After Ronnie Whelan's extra-time winner against Manchester United in the Milk Cup Graeme Souness pushed his manager up the Wembley steps to accept the trophy, something which had never happened before.

In the 1983 FA Cup Final Brighton took on Manchester United. Brighton were propping up the League and on their way to Division Two. They had the chance of easing the pain of relegation by beating Ron Atkinson's attractive United side which had finished a point behind Watford in third place. They very nearly pulled it off. Gordon Smith headed Brighton into a first-half lead, but Stapleton and Wilkins put United in front after the break. A dramatic late equaliser took the game into extra-time, and in the dying seconds Smith fluffed his lines with only Gary Bailey to beat. Brighton's chance evaporated in that moment; United cruised to a 4-0 win in the replay.

Fagan sets up three in a row

ABOVE: Liverpool, who topped the League in 1982, display the League Cup which they won in the same year.

OPPOSITE BOTTOM: Watford players salute their fans after defeating Birmingham to enter the FA Cup semi-finals.

OPPOSITE ABOVE RIGHT: Everton manager Howard Kendall leaves the pitch after his team's FA Cup Final win over Watford in 1984.

OPPOSITE ABOVE LEFT: The Everton scorers Andy Gray (left) and Graeme Sharp celebrate their Cup win.

Striker Michael Robinson had set up Smith for that golden chance to win the Cup Final for Brighton. He was soon a Liverpool player, one of the first pieces of business concluded by the new Anfield boss, 62-year-old Joe Fagan. Fagan, who had been at the club since the late 1950s, won three trophies in his first season, something that not even Paisley had achieved. Liverpool's 15th Championship was also their third in a row, which meant that the club equalled the achievement of Huddersfield in the 1920s, and Arsenal a decade later.

The Milk Cup Final pitted the Reds against Everton in the first ever Merseyside Final. It was scoreless after 120 minutes, and in the replay at Maine Road Graeme Souness scored the goal which gave Liverpool their fourth successive victory and won the trophy outright.

Fagan's hat-trick was completed at the Olympic Stadium in Rome, where Liverpool overcame a Roma side that enjoyed home advantage. Liverpool took the lead on the quarter-hour, Phil Neal pouncing on a defensive error. Roma equalised on the stroke of half-time and that's the way the scores stood after extra time. Steve Nicol's penalty miss was wiped out by Bruno Conti. Bruce Grobbelaar looked to be the calmest man in the stadium, causing much mirth as he pretended that his knees had turned to jelly. If his clowning was designed to put Graziani off, it worked. He blazed over, leaving Alan Kennedy to calmly slot home the crucial penalty. It was the second time that Kennedy had scored the decisive goal in a European Cup Final.

Kendall's Everton beat Watford

Everton made up for their unlucky defeat in the Milk Cup by beating Watford in the FA Cup Final. After a long time in the doldrums, former Goodison hero Howard Kendall was building a side capable of competing with their neighbours. Kendall had been a key member of the Championship-winning side of 1970, the last major honour that the club had won. Graham Sharpe and Andy Gray scored the goals which left Watford fans in tears – quite literally in the chairman's case.

Forest robbed of UEFA Final place

Spurs made it another English double in Europe by beating holders Anderlecht in the UEFA Cup Final. Both legs ended 1-1 and Spurs came out on top in the first Final to be decided on penalties. This victory was to take a surprising twist 13 years later, when it was revealed that Anderlecht had bribed the referee who took charge of the second leg of their semi-final against Nottingham Forest. In that game Anderlecht overturned a 2-0 deficit to win the tie 3-2. The Belgian side was awarded a dubious penalty, and Forest also had a goal disallowed. These decisions led some in the Forest camp to believe they had been cheated but it was not until 1997 that their suspicions were confirmed. The referee in question had been killed in a car crash by then, but that didn't stop Forest instituting legal proceedings in pursuit of compensation. They came up against UEFA's 10-year statute of limitations regarding retrospective disciplinary action. Financial reparation would hardly have made up for a night of European glory, and to Forest fans 1984 will be remembered as the year they were robbed.

England fail again

The familiar pattern of success in Europe and failure at international level continued as England missed out on the 1984 European Championship. A penalty by former European Footballer of the Year Allan Simonsen gave Denmark a crucial 1-0 win at Wembley, and that country's first-ever victory over England. This result, together with a goalless home draw against Greece, put paid to England's chances and it was the Danes who went to France for the finals.

Barnes dazzles against Brazil

While that tournament was being played out, England went on a three-match tour of South America. There was a defeat by Uruguay and a draw against Chile, but it was the 2-0 win over Brazil which grabbed the headlines. The first goal, a towering header from Mark Hateley, was typically English. The second, a dazzling solo effort by Watford's John Barnes, bore comparison with any Brazil had ever scored.

BELOW: Liverpool's Ian Rush holds the Charity Shield in 1986.

Ian Rush

The Welsh predator Ian Rush was a goal machine while he played for Liverpool FC, with a first touch and pace that gave him a phenomenal strike-rate. Born in 1961, he began his playing career at Chester, moving to Anfield in 1980 and acquiring legendary status with the Kop. In 658 games for Liverpool, he scored an incredible 346 goals.

Apart from the 1987–88 season when he made a brief, ill-fated move to Juventus, he remained at Liverpool for 16 years. With them he won the Championship five times and the FA Cup on three occasions. He scored in each of those three Wembley finals, and his aggregate tally of five goals remains a Cup Final record. Rush won the European Cup with Liverpool in 1984, his 32 goals during that campaign earning him the Golden Boot award. That year was the highpoint of his career, as he was also named double Footballer of the Year.

He also captained Wales, for whom he scored a record 28 goals in 73 games. He joined Leeds in 1996 and later played for Newcastle, Wrexham and Sydney Olympic.

Heysel tragedy rocks English football

1984–85 saw Liverpool fail to win a trophy for the first time in nine years. They lost the European Cup Final to a Michel Platini penalty but that was an irrelevance after it was clear that there had been fatalities at the Heysel Stadium. There had been fighting between Liverpool and Juventus fans before the match, and the collapse of a wall precipitated the tragedy. 39 supporters, mostly Italian, were killed. Liverpool fans were deemed to be primarily responsible and an indefinite ban was imposed on all English clubs competing in European competition.

Everton romp

The Heysel disaster and the Bradford fire, which occurred only weeks earlier, rocked football to the core. The season had also witnessed some of the worst acts of hooliganism ever seen, prompting the government to set up a task force to address the issue.

These events overshadowed the achievements of an Everton side, which won two trophies playing champagne football. Howard Kendall's men romped to the title with a record 90 points, 13 clear of their Liverpool rivals. Kendall joined the select group to have won the Championship as both player and manager.

It was the first leg in a treble, Everton having reached both the Cup Winners' Cup and FA Cup Finals. Having taken the scalp of Bayern Munich 3-1 on aggregate in the semis, Everton faced Rapid Vienna in the Cup Winners' Cup Final. Austria's legendary striker Hans Krankl scored Rapid's consolation goal in a 3-1 defeat and was quick to sing Everton's praises for the quality of their performance. Andy Gray, Trevor Steven and Kevin Sheedy had all been on target.

ABOVE RIGHT: Wimbledon, perhaps the most unconventional and unlikely team in the First Division at the time, celebrate a 3-0 win over Sheffield Wednesday. John Fashanu and Wally Downes embrace Vinny Jones (with his back to the camera), who only three weeks prior to this game had been employed as a hod-carrier.

BELOW LEFT: Chris Waddle of Tottenham rescues his side by scoring against up-and-coming Oxford United to send the game into extra time.

BELOW RIGHT: The pairing of John Barnes and David Bardsley was to prove too much for the Arsenal defence as Watford defeated them 3-1.

First Cup Final dismissal halts Liverpool

The FA Cup proved to be a trophy too far. Everton went down 1-0 to Manchester United, Norman Whiteside curling in a beautiful winner in extra time. The first 90 minutes had been largely uneventful, until with 12 minutes to go Peter Reid pounced onto a loose ball and was upended by Kevin Moran. The referee deemed it a professional

> *Norman Whiteside strike sinks Everton.*

foul and sent the Irishman off, the first Cup Final dismissal. The incident served to galvanise the United side, and they carved out other scoring opportunities apart from the one delightfully taken by Whiteside. Two years earlier he had become the youngest-ever player to score in a Wembley Final – 17 years 324 days – when United lost to Liverpool in the Milk Cup. No doubt this strike gave the Irishman more satisfaction.

Dalglish steps up as player-manager

Joe Fagan had already announced that the 1985 European Cup Final would be his last game in charge. Liverpool made yet another internal appointment, but surprised many by opting for a player-manager: Kenny Dalglish. With the Paul Walsh-Ian Rush strike partnership flourishing, Dalglish was content to spend time in the dugout. His team didn't have things all their own way, and at one point they trailed champions Everton by 11 points. The Reds needed to win their last seven games, five of them away, and hope that others would slip up. On the last day of the season they needed to win at Stamford Bridge and it was Dalglish who scored the game's only goal.

BELOW: Glenn Hoddle of Spurs on the ball in an England World Cup qualifying game.

RIGHT: Goal-scorer Norman Whiteside holds aloft the FA Cup after Manchester United defeat Everton by a goal to nil in extra time in the 1985 Cup Final.

A week later Everton again had to settle for second best in the first Merseyside FA Cup Final. Lineker escaped Hansen's clutches to open the scoring. When Rush equalised, the omens looked bad for Everton, as Liverpool had never lost a game when their Welsh striker was on target. So it proved again. Craig Johnston put the Reds into the lead and Rush rifled in a third six minutes from time. Liverpool thus joined Spurs and Arsenal as the century's only Double winners.

Future stars

Two future Liverpool stars lined up in the Oxford United side, which beat QPR in the Milk Cup Final. Ray Houghton and John Aldridge were in the side, which had climbed from Division Three to Division One in successive seasons. It was an outstanding achievement for a club that had been on the verge of bankruptcy in 1982.

Lineker fires England in Mexico

England were unbeaten in qualifying for the World Cup Finals, although they had been held to a draw by Romania, Finland and Northern Ireland. Defeat by Portugal and a goalless draw against Morocco left Bobby Robson's men facing an early exit. He was hampered by a shoulder injury to his inspirational captain, Bryan Robson, whose tournament was over. Vice-captain Ray Wilkins was sent off against Morocco, the first England player to be given his marching orders in a major tournament. Star striker Gary Lineker, who had topped the scoring chart with 30 goals for Everton, was playing with his arm in plaster. England needed to beat Poland in the final group match and did so in style. Hodge, Reid, Steven and Beardsley came in for Robson, Waddle, Wilkins and Hateley, and the team put on a show guaranteed to wake up the supporters who had dubbed this "the group of sleep". Lineker grabbed the headlines with a hat-trick in a 3-0 win.

Maradona's "Hand of God"

Another brace by Lineker helped England to a 3-0 victory over Paraguay, setting up a quarter-final clash with Argentina. The best and worst of Diego Maradona caused England's downfall. He picked up the ball on the halfway line and beat half the team to score the goal of the tournament and one of the greatest of all time. But before then he had punched the ball into the net when challenging for a high ball with Peter Shilton. Lineker made it 2 1, heading in his sixth goal of the tournament. He would be the tournament's hotshot, but the "Hand of God" along with the genius of Maradona had put paid to England's hopes.

BELOW INSERT: Gary Lineker, by now Everton's star striker, celebrates scoring for England against Northern Ireland in 1986.

Gary Lineker

Sports broadcaster Gary Lineker's role in the consortium that rescued Leicester City was fitting, for it was where, in 1978, his playing career began. Known for lightning acceleration, he scored 26 goals in 1983, helping Leicester back into the First Division. Two years later, he signed for Everton and scored 30 goals in his first season, winning him the PFA and Football Writers' Player of the Year.

He did well initially at Barcelona under Terry Venables, but was later less consistent. Though he contributed to Barça Cup Winners' Cup victory in 1989, he came back to England that summer to join Venables at White Hart Lane. In 1991 Spurs won the FA Cup, beating Nottingham Forest, and in his final season at the club put away a relegation-saving 28 League goals.

It is as a marksman for England, however, that he's most celebrated, with 80 caps and 48 goals – only one fewer than Bobby Charlton. Six of those, including a hat-trick against Poland, came in the 1986 World Cup in Mexico, winning him the Golden Boot. Four years later at Italia '90, it was Lineker's 80th-minute equaliser that kept England in the semi-final against West Germany, though the side went out on penalties. The 1992 European Championships made a frustrating end to Lineker's England career, as he was substituted by Graham Taylor in the final game, against Sweden. He ended his playing days with two seasons in the Japanese League, at Grampus Eight.

Moves abroad

Lineker's World Cup form caught the eye of many big Continental sides, and in the summer of 1986 Barcelona coach Terry Venables paid £4.25 million to see if he could reproduce his scoring form in La Liga. Although Everton no doubt would have preferred to keep Lineker, the fee represented a healthy profit on the £800,000 they had paid Leicester in July 1985.

Venables had already added Mark Hughes to his squad, and Juventus had agreed a £3.2 million deal to take Ian Rush to Turin, although the latter move would not take place until the end of the 1986–87 season.

According to the established principle, Rush should have signed off from Liverpool with a victory in the Littlewoods Cup, which was the League Cup's latest incarnation. Rush put the Reds in front against Arsenal at Wembley in the knowledge that in the previous 143 matches in which he'd got on the scoresheet the team had never lost. The run came to an end in the 144th match. Charlie Nicholas had never recaptured his Celtic form since moving to Highbury but he hit two goals to bring Arsenal their first silverware for eight years.

Ferguson replaces Atkinson at Old Trafford

Liverpool were also knocked off top spot in the League. Everton took their second title in three years, this time by a nine-point margin. The big managerial story of the season came in November, when Ron Atkinson's five-year reign at Old Trafford came to an end. United had won the FA Cup twice and never finished lower than 4th in the League. But with the Championship going to Merseyside with monotonous regularity and a Cup Winners' Cup semi-final their best effort in Europe, it simply wasn't good enough. Aberdeen boss Alex Ferguson was appointed. Ferguson had broken the Celtic-Rangers duopoly, winning the Scottish title on three occasions. He had also led the Dons to Cup Winners' Cup glory in 1983 when they overcame Real Madrid.

Aberdeen boss Alex Ferguson had broken the Celtic-Rangers duopoly, winning the Scottish title on three occasions.

Ferguson's first major signings were Viv Anderson and Brian McClair, in the summer of 1987. United had just ended the season in 11th place, their worst finish since returning to the top flight in 1975.

Wimbledon's meteoric rise

Five places above United at the end of the 1986–87 season was Wimbledon. Dave Bassett's side had gone from non-League to Division One in nine years, and 6th place in their first season represented a phenomenal achievement. Swansea had done exactly the same five years earlier, but the Dons would prove to have much more resilience as a top-division side.

For Coventry and Scarborough 1986–87 was a memorable season, albeit at different ends of the footballing scale. Coventry met Spurs in the FA Cup Final. Spurs had never finished on the losing side in their seven previous appearances. Coventry ended that run and in the process picked up the club's first major honour. Coventry twice came from behind, their second equaliser a spectacular flying header from Keith Houchen. The winner came in extra-time, when Gary Mabbutt deflected a McGrath cross into his net. Coventry coach John Sillett did a Wembley jig to rival Nobby Stiles' effort in 1966.

LEFT: Arsenal captain Kenny Sansom holds aloft the Littlewoods Cup after two goals from Charlie Nicholas saw Liverpool defeated 2-1.

OPPOSITE: Arsenal's Niall Quinn lines up a volley that narrowly misses its target and is just tipped wide by Spurs and former England keeper, Ray Clemence.

Play-offs introduced

Neil Warnock's Scarborough became the first club to win automatic promotion to the Football League. The system of applying for re-election was scrapped; the 4th Division's bottom club would change places with the winners of the Vauxhall Conference.

Play-off matches were also introduced in all divisions. The team which finished just above the automatic relegation spot entered into a play off with the three clubs that had just missed promotion from the division below. Charlton finished in that precarious position in Division One but survived the two-match ordeal.

The play-offs were introduced to make the run-in more exciting, with fewer "dead" matches. It was also designed over two seasons to decrease the size of Division One from 22 clubs to 20.

In the second year Chelsea finished fourth from bottom and lost their Division One status at the expense of Middlesbrough.

Liverpool back on top

Liverpool, meanwhile, were back on top. After three seasons in which the Merseyside clubs had taken the top two spots, in 1987–88 Everton slipped to 4th and Manchester United were the closest challengers. Even then, Ferguson's men finished nine points behind a team that looked stronger than ever. John Barnes, Ray Houghton and Peter Beardsley – bought from Newcastle for a record £1.9 million – all added even more flair to the Anfield machine.

Liverpool went 29 matches unbeaten, equalling Leeds' 1974 record. Everton's Wayne Clark scored the goal which prevented Liverpool from taking the record outright, but the Reds lost just once more in the campaign to match Everton's record points tally. Both finished on 90, although Liverpool had played two games fewer. Their 17th Championship was secured with four matches to spare.

Wimbledon's FA Cup glory

A second double looked a foregone conclusion as Liverpool faced Wimbledon in the FA Cup Final. The Dons had finished a commendable 7th this term but surely they couldn't overturn the mighty Reds. The bookies didn't think so, making Liverpool 1-4 favourites. Wimbledon were fearless, committed and no respecters of reputations. They had already gone to Anfield and won.

Peter Beardsley had the ball in the net, only for the referee to disallow it – for a foul on Beardsley! Laurie Sanchez's glancing header from a Dennis Wise free-kick gave the Dons a 36th-minute lead. After 61 minutes John Aldridge was brought down in the box. Aldridge had a perfect record from his previous 11 spot-kicks that season. The 12th was saved by Dave Beasant. It was the first penalty save in an FA Cup Final and it helped carry the Dons to an unlikely victory.

England eclipsed by Charlton's Ireland

Houghton and Aldridge lined up in the Republic of Ireland side which qualified for the 1988 European Championships. England made it to Germany too, and the two countries met in the opening match of the group stage. Houghton gave the Republic a 1-0 win and although both went out of the competition it was Jack Charlton's men who emerged with more credit. England also lost to eventual finalists the USSR and Holland to finish as wooden spoonists.

A chink of light in a gloomy season for England came in April, when 17-year-old Alan Shearer hit a hat-trick for Southampton against Arsenal, the youngest player ever to do so in the First Division.

Arsenal's last gasp Championship

Liverpool had Ian Rush back in their ranks in 1988–89. Rush scored 14 goals in his season at Juve but failed to settle. He returned for a season which saw the Reds engaged in a terrific Championship battle with Arsenal. At the end of February Liverpool were 8th, 19 points behind the table-topping Gunners. On 26 May Arsenal came to Anfield for the title showdown. Liverpool had eaten away at Arsenal's lead and it was they who held the advantage. Arsenal, who had not won at Anfield for 15 years, needed a victory by two goals to take the title. After a goalless first half, Nigel Winterburn struck an indirect free-kick which Liverpool protested had gone straight into the net. The referee judged that it brushed Alan Smith's head and the goal was given. With seconds to go Michael Thomas burst into the box and flicked the ball past Grobbelaar to give Arsenal the 2-goal margin they needed.

Hillsborough

Second in the League and a 3-2 extra-time win over Everton in the second Merseyside FA Cup Final represented another fine season for Liverpool. But footballing matters had become irrelevant after the events at Hillsborough on 15 April. The eagerly awaited FA Cup semi-final clash with Nottingham Forest was six minutes old when it became clear that there was a tragedy unfolding in the Leppings Lane end. Gates were opened to prevent a crush outside and a mass of fans surged into a part of the ground that was already packed. Perimeter fencing meant that there was no easy outlet. 94 supporters were killed, and the toll rose to 95 a few days later. Tony Bland remained in a coma for four years before his life-support machine was switched off. Lord Justice Taylor was commissioned to head an inquiry into the worst tragedy in British sporting history.

The Taylor Report

In the wake of the tragedy there had been no appetite to complete the competition and an abandonment was considered. But both Liverpool and the bereaved families came to regard the winning of the trophy as a tribute to those who had lost their lives.

In the 1980s the game had been tarnished by hooliganism and touched by tragedy, yet it ended on a note of dignity. The sportsmanship shown in both the FA Cup Final and the Championship decider gave rise to cautious optimism. The game would endure; but as football moved into a new decade the Taylor Report would be a damning indictment of the conditions in which the fans were expected to watch their heroes perform.

> *The sportsmanship shown in both the FA Cup Final and the Championship decider gave rise to cautious optimism.*

LEFT: Peter Beardsley of Liverpool battles with Arsenal's Tony Adams in a title showdown, which saw the Gunners come out on top.

ABOVE: Floral tributes in the Anfield goalmouth commemorating those killed at Hillsborough on 15 April 1989.

Scottish League 1980–1989

1979–80

1	Aberdeen	48
2	Celtic	47
3	St Mirren	42
4	Dundee United	37
5	Rangers	37
6	Greenock Morton	36
7	Partick Thistle	36
8	Kilmarnock	33
9	Dundee	26
10	Hibernian	18

1980–81

1	Celtic	56
2	Aberdeen	49
3	Rangers	44
4	St Mirren	44
5	Dundee United	43
6	Partick Thistle	30
7	Airdrieonians	29
8	Greenock Morton	28
9	Kilmarnock	19
10	Hearts	18

1981–82

1	Celtic	55
2	Aberdeen	53
3	Rangers	43
4	Dundee United	40
5	St Mirren	37
6	Hibernian	36
7	Greenock Morton	30
8	Dundee	26
9	Partick Thistle	22
10	Airdrieonians	18

1982–83

1	Dundee United	56
2	Celtic	55
3	Aberdeen	55
4	Rangers	38
5	St Mirren	34
6	Dundee	29
7	Hibernian	29
8	Motherwell	27
9	Greenock Morton	20
10	Kilmarnock	17

1983–84

1	Aberdeen	57
2	Celtic	50
3	Dundee United	47
4	Rangers	42
5	Hearts	36
6	St Mirren	32
7	Hibernian	31
8	Dundee	27
9	St Johnstone	23
10	Motherwell	15

1984–85

1	Aberdeen	59
2	Celtic	52
3	Dundee United	47
4	Rangers	38
5	St Mirren	38
6	Dundee	37
7	Hearts	31
8	Hibernian	27
9	Dumbarton	19
10	Greenock Morton	12

1985–86

1	Celtic	50
2	Hearts	50
3	Dundee United	47
4	Aberdeen	44
5	Rangers	35
6	Dundee	35
7	St Mirren	31
8	Hibernian	28
9	Motherwell	20
10	Clydebank	20

1986–87

1	Rangers	69
2	Celtic	63
3	Dundee United	60
4	Aberdeen	58
5	Hearts	56
6	Dundee	48
7	St Mirren	36
8	Motherwell	34
9	Hibernian	33
10	Falkirk	26
11	Clydebank	24
12	Hamilton	21

1987–88

1	Celtic	72
2	Hearts	62
3	Rangers	60
4	Aberdeen	59
5	Dundee United	47
6	Hibernian	43
7	Dundee	41
8	Motherwell	36
9	St Mirren	35
10	Falkirk	31
11	Dunfermline Athletic	26
12	Greenock Morton	16

1988–89

1	Rangers	56
2	Aberdeen	50
3	Celtic	46
4	Dundee United	44
5	Hibernian	35
6	Hearts	31
7	St Mirren	29
8	Dundee	28
9	Motherwell	27
10	Hamilton	14

ABOVE: Aberdeen's triumphant homecoming following their victory over Real Madrid in the Cup Winners' Cup Final in Gothenburg, 1983. Eric Black and John Hewitt scored the goals that brought a European trophy to Scotland for only the third time.

Scottish Cup Finals

1980	Celtic	v	Rangers	1–0
1981	Rangers	v	Dundee United	0–0
	Rangers	v	Dundee United	4–1
1982	Aberdeen	v	Rangers	4–1
1983	Aberdeen	v	Rangers	1–0
1984	Aberdeen	v	Celtic	2–1
1985	Celtic	v	Dundee United	2–1
1986	Aberdeen	v	Hearts	3–0
1987	St Mirren	v	Dundee United	1–0
1988	Celtic	v	Dundee United	2–1
1989	Celtic	v	Rangers	1–0

The rise of Aberdeen and Dundee

A new term entered the footballing lexicon during the 1980s: the "New Firm". The rise of Aberdeen and Dundee United upset the old order, particularly Rangers. Ibrox had its share of Cup success, but there was a drought in the League; a couple of third places was the best the club could manage in the seven seasons to 1986.

Aberdeen had won the League Cup under Ally MacLeod in 1976–77 – Willie Miller's first experience of holding a trophy aloft. After MacLeod left to take the Scotland job, and Billy McNeill had come and gone, the Dons turned to St Mirren boss Alex Ferguson, who had steered the mid-table Division One side to the Premier class in 1976–77.

Within two years Aberdeen had secured their first Championship since the mid-1950s. A 5-0 win at Hibs on the final day of the 1979–80 season gave Aberdeen a one-point advantage over Celtic, who were held to a draw by Ferguson's former club. Footballer of the Year Gordon Strachan was the pocket dynamo pulling the strings.

In the next five years Aberdeen won two more titles and were twice runners-up to Celtic, with a hat-trick of Scottish Cup wins thrown in for good measure. Only Rangers had ever done that. And the year that the Dons slipped to third – 1982–83 – was hardly a disappointment as they beat Real Madrid in the Cup Winners' Cup Final in Gothenburg. Eric Black and John Hewitt scored the goals that brought a European trophy to Scotland for only the third time.

In 1985–86 Ferguson brought the League Cup to Pittodrie, the only trophy missing from the cabinet during his tenure. But early the following season he and assistant Archie Knox left for pastures new in the red half of Manchester. Ian Porterfield took over, with just a League Cup Final to show for his brief period in charge.

Silverware for the Terrors

Dundee United's success was perhaps even more noteworthy, given that it was only in the 1960s under Jerry Kerr that they became an established top-division outfit. Jim McLean took the manager's chair at Tannadice in the early 1970s, and at the beginning of the next decade led the Terrors to League Cup victory over Aberdeen. Having waited over 70 years for their first silverware, the fans had just 12 months to hang on before their next arrived, United beating local rivals Dundee to retain the trophy. They were finalists again in 1981–82 but this time went down to Rangers, who also came out on top in their 1980–81 Scottish Cup Final clash.

On the last day of the 1982–83 season United went to Dens Park knowing that victory over Dundee would bring them the title for the first time. A 2-1 win put them a point clear of Celtic and Aberdeen. United let slip a two-goal lead in the European Cup semi-final the following year, Roma turning the tie around at home and going on to face Liverpool. 1986–87 was a case of what might have been as they lost a two-legged UEFA Cup Final to IFK Gothenburg, with a Scottish Cup Final defeat to St Mirren sandwiched between. It was still a marvellous decade: nine Cup finals and a maiden League success.

Rangers' long period in the doldrums – nine years without a Championship – ended in 1987 under new player-manager Graeme Souness. The former Liverpool skipper made it clear from the outset that quality, not sectarianism, would inform his transfer dealings. England internationals figured regularly on his shopping expeditions, the likes of Terry Butcher, Trevor Steven and Gary Stevens. In Souness's first season Rangers landed the League Cup and, more importantly, finished top of the pile in the League. Celtic regained the Championship in 1988, but the decade drew to a close with Rangers in the ascendancy, about to embark on a record-equalling run.

Terrible mix-up

Scotland made it four World Cups in a row by qualifying for both Spain '82 and Mexico '86. In the former a 4-1 defeat by Brazil proved costly. The USSR lost to the South American giants only 2-1, and with both sides beating New Zealand by a three-goal margin, it meant the Scots needed to beat USSR in the final group game; a draw wouldn't be enough. Joe Jordan opened the scoring, Russia levelled, then with time running out a terrible mix-up between Willie Miller and Alan Hansen let the opposition in for a second. Graeme Souness's late strike gave the Tartan Army a glimmer of hope, but the game ended 2-2 and Scotland were eliminated on goal difference yet again.

The 1986 campaign was overshadowed by the death of Jock Stein, who suffered a fatal heart attack during a qualifier against Wales at Ninian Park. Alex Ferguson took over as interim boss, and his side was handed a tough draw. It was no disgrace losing to West Germany and Denmark by the odd goal, though the team might have done better than a goalless draw against a Uruguay side that played most of the game a man short. Scotland had shown once again that it could qualify for major tournaments; the wait continued for a team that could progress beyond the initial stage.

BELOW: The Aberdeen first team pool in 1984 with the club's recent trophy haul.

OPPOSITE BELOW: The Celtic squad that went on to win the 1980–81 title by seven points from Aberdeen, a feat they were to repeat by a two-point margin the following year.

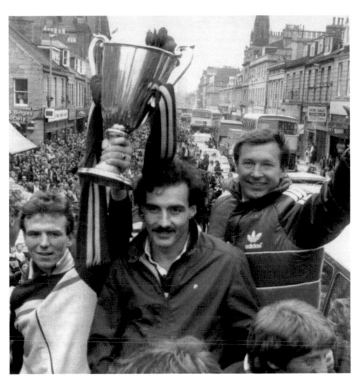

RIGHT: Aberdeen's Eric Black hits the ball with the side of his boot and scores past the helpless Real Madrid goalkeeper Agustin during the first half of the European Cup Winners' Cup Final in 1983.

ABOVE: Alex McLeish holds the European Cup Winners' Cup aloft while Willie Miller and manager Alex Ferguson acknowledge the cheering crowd.

1990–1999
A Premier League

At the start of the 1990s football came in for some harsh criticism. The Taylor Report was scathing about the dilapidated state of the country's stadia. For too long an ethos of "make do and mend" had prevailed. Those days were now over. The prospect of another Hillsborough was unthinkable and intolerable. The report recommended that terraces should be phased out, a view which immediately won government backing.

1990 Fourteenth World Cup held in Italy; England after losing in the semi-finals to eventual winners West Germany, ended up 4th by losing to Italy in the 3/4 place play-offs. The Republic of Ireland qualify for the World Cup for the first time, Jack Charlton's side losing to hosts Italy 1-0 in the quarter-finals

1990 UEFA lifts its ban on English clubs – Manchester United and Aston Villa join European competitions

1990 FA rules that a professional foul should be a sending-off offence

1991 Manchester United win the European Cup Winners' Cup

1991 Artificial pitches withdrawn from First Division

1992 Premier League established

1992 BSkyB win exclusive rights to broadcast Premier League matches

1992 Blackburn buy Alan Shearer for a then record of £3.6 million from Southampton followed by another record buy of Chris Sutton for £5 million, both helped Blackburn to win the 1994-5 Premiership title

1992 England finish bottom of their Euro '92 group. Scotland qualify

for the Championship for the first time, but are also eliminated in the first round

1993 George Graham, Arsenal manager, banned for a year following irregular payments made to him

1993 Alex Ferguson becomes first manager to win Scottish and English Leagues, with Aberdeen and Manchester United, respectively

1994 Tottenham Hotspur fined and banned from the FA Cup following charges of financial irregularities

1994 Arsenal win the European Cup Winners' Cup

1994 Fifteenth World Cup held in USA; Brazil win in an event which saw England fail to qualify for the tournament

1994 Bobby Charlton knighted for services to football

1994 Scottish football reorganised to add a fourth tier. The League now comprises four 10-strong divisions

1995 Stan Collymore is transferred from Nottingham Forest to Liverpool for a record British fee of £8.5 million

The Taylor Report

First and Second Division clubs were required to have all-seater stadia by the start of the 1994–95 season, with lower League clubs following suit by the end of the decade. The cost of improved facilities would be high – running into hundreds of millions – but the cost of doing nothing would be infinitely higher.

The Taylor Report also addressed the hooligan problem and the part played by alcohol in the appalling scenes that had blighted the game. A compulsory ID scheme was considered but rejected. Policing and ticket arrangements needed reviewing. While perimeter fencing, which represented a threat to safety, ought to be removed, harsh penalties were recommended for unwarranted pitch invasions.

The changing face of football
The construction of fabulous new grounds, such as the Reebok, the Stadium of Light and Pride Park, took football into a new era. New facilities such as these would show Wembley in a poor light. By the end of the decade plans would be under way for a new flagship stadium in the capital.

If the face of football was changed with the redevelopment and upgrading of grounds, a shift of equally seismic proportions occurred with the establishment of a Premier League. This coincided with the arrival of satellite broadcasters, who saw football as the main driver for their fledgling business. The game became polarised as never before. At the top level inflation in transfer fees, wages and ticket prices was rampant; meanwhile, the demise of Aldershot, the first League club to go out of business for thirty years, showed that the vast sums of money in the game were not filtering down to the basement.

Merchandise and brand
There was a price to be paid for improved facilities and multimillion-pound TV rights deals, and in the end it was the fans who had to put their hands in their pockets. There were fears that die-hard fans would be priced out of the game and that the sport was undergoing a gentrification process, a return to the kind of constituency it had had in the 19th-century. Perhaps more worryingly, the clubs did not seem to mind. Middle-class supporters with large disposable incomes were highly desirable to clubs which had a product to sell. Nor was the product simply football. Replica strips and all manner of domestic goods bearing the club brand went on sale. Fans could even get financial services from their clubs as football exploited every possible income stream.

A glorious era coming to an end
On the pitch the decade began with yet another League triumph for the team of the 1980s. Liverpool rounded off their season with a 6-1 win at Coventry, though the club's 18th Championship had already been secured by then.

The team that had suffered most heavily at the hands of the Red machine was Crystal Palace, who were on the receiving end of a 9-0 mauling in the early part of the season. There must have been trepidation among Palace fans as the team faced Liverpool again in the FA Cup semi-final at Villa Park. It was a remarkable game and a turning point for Liverpool. Andy Gray equalised to make it 3-3 in the 90th minute, and Alan Pardew headed Palace into the Final in extra time. A glorious era was coming to an end. Over the next few seasons Liverpool would show flashes of their brilliant best, but these would be punctuated by many inept performances. The strong defence of days gone by would become quite porous and Liverpool would be relegated to the role of just another member of the chasing pack.

OPPOSITE: England on the pitch ready to play Germany in the 1990 World Cup semi-final. With the score at 1-1 after extra-time, England lost the game on penalties.

RIGHT: Stuart Pearce, who famously missed his penalty against Germany in the World Cup, scores from this free kick to give Nottingham Forest the lead in the 1991 Cup Final against Spurs.

Ferguson's job on the line

After beating Liverpool, Palace went on to face the team, which was to assume the mantle that had been worn by the Reds for so long. Manchester United had finished 11th and 13th in the past two seasons, and it was said that after four years in charge Alex Ferguson's job was on the line. A Mark Hughes' goal salvaged a replay for United, and Lee Martin scored the goal which brought Ferguson his first piece of silverware.

Italia '90

Before England went to the World Cup in Italy, manager Bobby Robson announced that he would be quitting to return to club management with PSV Eindhoven. Robson's team topped their group, albeit with a one-goal win over Egypt and draws against the Republic of Ireland and Holland. A superb David Platt volley late in extra time accounted for Belgium in the second round. By then it was clear that the team's precocious

Platt's superb volley late in extra-time puts England into the World Cup quarter-final.

young midfielder, Paul Gascoigne, was the star turn. "Gazza" had become the country's first £2 million footballer when he moved from Newcastle to Spurs in 1988. At Italia '90 the raw talent blossomed and he proved that he was a great showman as well as a great player.

England beaten on penalties

Against Cameroon in the quarter-final England were trailing 2-1 with time running out. Lineker was brought down in the box and converted the penalty to take the match into extra time. It was a case of déjà-vu, and Lineker's second spot-kick set up a semi-final clash with West Germany. That match will long be remembered for the tears Gascoigne shed after a rash tackle earned him a booking which would have kept him out of the final. In the end that was academic. An Andreas Brehme free-kick took a wicked deflection and looped over Shilton to put the Germans ahead. Lineker equalised and the game went to penalties. Pearce and Waddle both missed and England were out. There was the consolation of the Fair Play award and the fact that the team had provided rich entertainment and no small amount of drama.

ABOVE LEFT: Paul Gascoigne with Steve Sedgeley and Gary Mabbutt celebrating Spurs' 3-1 victory over Arsenal in the semi-final of the FA Cup in 1991 played at Wembley. The following month Tottenham secured the Cup with a 2-1 win over Nottingham Forest.

MIDDLE LEFT: Spurs' Eric Thorsvedt punches clear in the hard-fought contest that went into extra time.

BELOW LEFT: Gary Mabbutt holds the trophy aloft.

OPPOSITE LEFT: Steve Nicol, Bruce Grobbelaar and Ian Rush with the FA Cup in 1992.

Power Struggle

1990–91 saw the beginnings of a power struggle at the top of the game. Relations between the FA and Football League had never been particularly warm, and when the League suggested that the game should be unified under a single umbrella, the response amounted to exactly the opposite. The FA's blueprint for the future was the establishment of a premier division. This would be the game's gold standard, and would help to improve the fortunes of the national team. Unsurprisingly, the Football League was horrified at the prospect of the glamour clubs seceding in this way. They went to court to challenge the legality of the FA's proposals but found they had no case.

The end of the UEFA ban

This season marked the end of the UEFA ban on English clubs, although Liverpool received a further year's penalty. The six-year ban was said to have put English football down the pecking order in relation to the other traditional powerhouses on the Continent. That didn't stop Manchester United from lifting the Cup Winners' Cup. The 2-1 victory over Barcelona in Rotterdam must have been particularly pleasing for Mark Hughes. His brief spell at the Nou Camp had been a nightmare, and a superb winning goal from a narrow angle showed Barça what an in-form "Sparky" could do. This victory meant that Alex Ferguson joined a select group of managers to have won a European trophy with two different clubs.

Arsenal's title

United had been deducted a point in the League following a brawl in their clash with Arsenal at Old Trafford in October. The Gunners were docked two points, but neither penalty proved costly in the shake-up. United finished 6th, while Arsenal still ended the campaign seven points clear of Liverpool at the top.

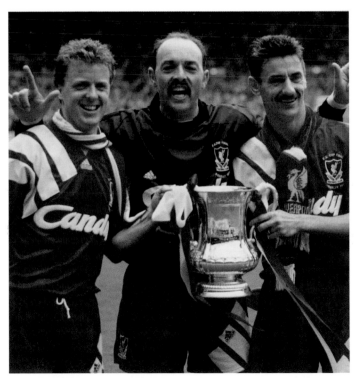

Liverpool had started the season the stronger, recording ten straight wins. The turning point came in a 5th-round FA Cup-tie against Everton. After a goalless draw at Anfield, the two teams met at Goodison. The game ended 4-4, highlighting the fact that Liverpool were still potent up front but far from secure at the back. The following day Kenny Dalglish announced his resignation, citing the strain of the job. The man appointed in his place was an Anfield thoroughbred but he didn't come from within. Graeme Souness was persuaded to leave Rangers and take over the reins at the club he had captained with such distinction.

Alan Shearer

In November 2002, Alan Shearer scored his 100th Premiership goal for his home city club, Newcastle United, and became the first player to achieve this landmark at two clubs, the other being Blackburn Rovers. No wonder that after the 2002–3 season, he was named Player of the Decade – a sweet moment for a striker who had retired from international football after Euro 2000 to make way for younger blood, but could still produce magic in the box.

His career began as a teenager in 1988 with Southampton, who had been tipped off by a North-East scout. Blackburn secured him in the summer of 1992 for a British record transfer of £3.6 million, and Shearer's deadly finishing helped the club to win the Championship three years later. When Rovers signed Chris Sutton from Norwich, the celebrated "SAS partnership" began.

He returned to Newcastle in 1996 for a £15 million fee. Shearer won the first of his 63 caps in February 1990, coming off the bench to score against France. It was the first of a 30-goal haul, putting him joint-fifth in the all-time list. Before the end of the 2004–05 season the Toon Army received the welcome news that their talisman had agreed to stay on for one more campaign. He failed in his final attempt to bring silverware to St James' Park, but did pass Jackie Milburn's all-time scoring record, ending his career with 206 goals for the club.

Arsenal set defensive standard

Although Liverpool maintained their position as League runners-up in 1992, the writing was on the wall. The Reds conceded 40 goals and lost eight games; Arsenal were defeated only once and let in just 18 goals. George Graham had paid QPR £1.3 million for David Seaman the previous summer, a record for a goalkeeper. He took his place behind Adams, Bould, Dixon and Winterburn to form a defensive unit that would set the standard for defensive meanness.

Arsenal faced Spurs in the FA Cup semi-final, the first to be staged at Wembley. Gascoigne stole the show with a stunning 35-yard free-kick, setting up a marvellous 3-1 win. Gazza was again centre stage in the Final, against Nottingham Forest, but this time for the wrong reasons. He had already put in a couple of rash tackles when he challenged Gary Charles on the edge of the Spurs area. Gascoigne conceded the free-kick but it was he who came off worse. He suffered knee ligament damage, which was to put him out of action for months. Stuart Pearce rubbed salt into Spurs' wounds by scoring from the free-kick after Gazza was stretchered off. Paul Stewart hit an equaliser and although Spurs' winner came via a deflection off Des Walker in extra-time, the better team won.

Gazza to Lazio

Lazio had already been chasing Gascoigne's signature, and the deal was finally done in June 1992. It would be six years before Gazza would return to the domestic game. His time in Italy, and subsequently with Glasgow Rangers, would show him in every possible light: flashes of genius one minute, pressing the self-destruct button the next and everything done in his inimitably impish way. Injuries didn't help, but for a player of his gifts there should have been a greater return than his 1992 FA Cup winners' medal with Spurs. That would remain his only honour in the English game.

Eric Cantona

Of all the brilliant players from overseas that found their way into the English game in the 1990s Eric Cantona stands alone as the player who has had the most influence on the teams he played for. Having just helped Marseille to win the French Championship, he joined Leeds halfway through the 1991–92 season. Cantona's success continued as the Yorkshire club went on to win their first Championship since the heady days of the 1970s, in what was the final year of the League system before the introduction of the Premier League. Leeds fans were shocked when Howard Wilkinson sold the 26-year-old to rivals Manchester United in November 1992.

With his incredible vision and majestic touch, and his trademark upturned collar, Cantona performed complex skills with apparent ease. The Old Trafford faithful took him to their hearts and chanting "Oo-ah-Cantona" in praise of their hero became a trademark of the fans. Cantona went on to win four Championships with United, including the Double on two occasions. The second of those came in 1996, when he scored the goal that beat Liverpool in an exciting FA Cup Final. At the end of the 1995–96 season Cantona was named Footballer of the Year for his superb performances during that campaign.

Unfortunately, in the 1994–95 season, Cantona showed the other side to his character. His kung-fu-style kick at a fan after being sent off at Crystal Palace in January 1995 earned him an eight-month ban. It was not the first time Cantona had run into disciplinary problems. His career was punctuated with arguments with players and managers alike, including run-ins with national team coaches, without which he would certainly have won more than 44 caps for France.

To the dismay of United fans Cantona announced his retirement from football at the end of the 1996–97 season, when he was just 30 years old.

Wilkinson's Leeds win the Championship

Leeds were the last winners before the new Premiership era got under way. Howard Wilkinson's side had won promotion in 1990 and finished 4th in their first season back in the top flight. In 1991–92 Leeds held off the challenge of Manchester United to bring the club their first Championship since 1974. Gordon Strachan, who had joined the club from Manchester United in 1989 for just £300,000, had been in sparkling form, despite turning 35 during the season. Alongside him in midfield were Batty, McAllister and Speed, giving a blend of youth and experience, finesse and steel. Midway through the season Wilkinson added more flair by bringing in the controversial French star Eric Cantona. 25-year-old Cantona had had a string of clubs and several run-ins with the authorities in France. He briefly turned his back on the game but decided to start afresh on the other side of the Channel. Sheffield Wednesday boss Trevor Francis had a look at him, but as he vacillated, Howard Wilkinson stepped in to offer terms.

Cantona's Gallic flair

The honeymoon would not last much beyond securing the Championship as far as the club was concerned. For the fans it was a different matter. They warmed to the Gallic flair and air of arrogance Cantona showed on the field. The chant "Oo-ah-Cantona" rang round the Elland Road terraces, but not for long. By the end of the year Cantona had moved to Old Trafford for just £1 million. Over the next five years the Frenchman would become the pivotal player in Ferguson's dream team.

OPPOSITE ABOVE: Manchester United players following their Championship in the 1993–94 season. It was the end of the first full season at the club for Eric Cantona (third from the left).

Taylor's England reign

Graham Taylor had been appointed England manager after the 1990 World Cup. His achievements at Watford and Aston Villa had been considerable. He had taken Villa from 17th in 1989 to runners-up the following year. Qualification for the 1992 European Championship was secured, although not without the odd moment of disquiet. A late Gary Lineker goal in Poland gave England the point they needed to edge out the Republic of Ireland. That strike was Lineker's 48th for England, one short of Bobby Charlton's record. After goalless draws against Denmark and France, Lineker's third chance to equal the record came against hosts Sweden, a game which England needed to win to progress. David Platt volleyed England into an early lead but Sweden hit back to win 2-1. Taylor substituted Lineker with half an hour to go, a decision which mystified many onlookers. It was to be his last game in an England shirt. Taylor came in for fierce criticism for his team selection and tactics. A country which had reached the last four at Italia '90 had finished bottom of their group in the European Championship two years later.

Ryan Giggs

If one-club men are a rare breed in the modern game, it is even more remarkable for an outfield player to spend over two decades as part of the first-team set-up with one of the elite. Remarkable just about sums up the career of English football's most decorated player. As a youngster he was on Manchester City's radar, plucked from under their noses by their local rivals when Giggs was 14. He first pulled on a United shirt in March 1991 – four years before the Reds' latest young flying winger Adnan Januzaj was born – and clocked up 963 appearances, amassing a medal haul that will take some beating. He was part of 13 championship-winning teams, first as a fleet-footed wide player with mesmerising footwork, latterly as a cultured midfield general, orchestrating proceedings with his marvellous range of passing. There were two Doubles in the '90s, as well as that historic night in Barcelona in 1999 when Giggs helped the team snatch victory from Bayern Munich, adding the Champions League to the domestic game's two major prizes. The winner he scored against Arsenal in that year's FA Cup semi-final ranks as one of the great solo goals, the kind that would prompt the Old Trafford faithful to break into their terrace chant, to the tune of the Joy Division song: "Giggs will tear you apart – again."

A decade on from that famous Treble – and with another Champions League success to his name after the shoot-out victory over Chelsea in Moscow – Giggs was named PFA Player of the Year in 2009, adding to the brace of Young Player awards he picked up in the early '90s. The 36-year-old also became only the fifth footballer to be named BBC Sports Personality of the Year. With United the silverware came thick and fast; at international level that was never going to be the case. Cardiff-born Giggs was Wales' youngest capped player when he made his debut for the national side aged 17, but like George Best – with whom he was inevitably compared when he broke into the United first team – Giggs was destined never to grace the finals of a major international tournament. He left the international stage in 2007, with 64 caps and 12 goals to his name.

In 2012-13 he maintained his record of scoring in every season since the Premier League's inception, and though he joined the backroom team for the 2013-14, the first of the post-Ferguson era, he still showed his touch and vision on the pitch when called into action in the year he turned 40. A wonderful ambassador as well as player, Giggs hung up his boots at the end of that campaign, appointed No. 2 to new manager Louis van Gaal with many expecting him to assume the top job after serving an apprenticeship.

Souness makes changes

The 1992 FA Cup went to Liverpool, who beat Sunderland 2-0 in the Final. Souness had been busy in the transfer market, not all of his deals finding favour with the fans. Beardsley and Staunton left for Everton and Villa, respectively. In came Mark Walters from Rangers and the Derby pair, Mark Wright and Dean Saunders. Michael Thomas, the man who had broken Liverpool fans' hearts in 1989, arrived from Arsenal. Thomas hit one of the goals that beat Sunderland. The other came from Rush, a record fifth goal for the Welshman in FA Cup Finals.

For Souness, who had suffered a mild heart attack and was recovering from a bypass operation, FA Cup victory in 1992 would be a false dawn; it would be Liverpool's only trophy in his three-year reign.

OPPOSITE BELOW: Paul Scholes

OPPOSITE ABOVE: Gianfranco Zola

RIGHT: Manchester United celebrate after beating Liverpool in the 1996 Cup Final. Eric Cantona's stunning strike was the difference between the teams.

BELOW INSERT: Republic of Ireland's Roy Keane brings down Holland's Marc Overmars during a World Cup qualifying game.

Roy Keane

It is Roy Keane who Sir Alex Ferguson points to as the most influential of all the superstars that have made Manchester United the dominant force in English football since the inception of the Premiership.

But it was Brian Clough who spotted Keane's potential when he was playing for Cobh Ramblers in the Irish League. Clough paid just £10,000 to take the Irishman to Nottingham Forest in what must rank as one of the bargains of all time. In 1993 Keane moved to Old Trafford from Forest and, at United, his fierce competitiveness, tireless running and great technical ability have enabled him to develop into one of the most complete midfielders in world football. He took over as the driving force in midfield from Bryan Robson, who was a tough act to follow. Since joining United at the age of 21, his footballing skills and superb leadership skills have earned him the captain's position and as such he has helped guide the team in their unprecedented run of success in recent years. In the five seasons between 1996 and 2001, United conceded the Premiership title just once when Arsenal won in 1997–98. Many people have pointed out that during that season Keane missed most of the campaign through injury.

World Cup 1994

On the international front, Keane excelled as part of the Republic of Ireland team in the 1994 World Cup in the USA, where the team progressed respectably before being knocked out by Holland. Although the team failed to qualify for France in 1998, Keane was regarded as a key figure for the Republic's chances in Japan and Korea, 2002. The infamous bust-up between Keane and manager Mick McCarthy meant that Keane was back home before the tournament even started.

Despite the fracas of the World Cup in the summer, 2002–03 saw Keane at his best, driving United on towards yet another title when it looked certain to go to Arsenal for the second successive season. Meanwhile, the arrival of Brian Kerr as the new Republic of Ireland manager prompted Keane to change his mind and return to the international stage. In November 2005 Keane joined Glasgow Celtic, the team he supported as a boy. In his 12 years at Old Trafford he had won seven Championships, four FA Cups and the Champions League, though suspension forced him to miss the memorable 1999 victory over Bayern Munich.

The Premier League

1992–93 ushered in the new era of the Premier League. Squad numbers were introduced and players' shirts sported their names. Sponsorship was now big business, and Carling put their name – and money – into the new venture. Only nine fixtures on the opening Saturday showed that one of the game's great traditions was no longer set in stone. BSkyB wanted football to fit in with its schedule, rather than the other way round. It was a case of he who pays the piper calls the tune.

Manchester United were the inaugural Premiership champions. Ferguson's side romped home 10 points clear of the pack to bring the League crown to Old Trafford for the first time since 1967. Arsenal were left languishing in mid-table, while Liverpool could finish only 6th, failing to qualify for Europe for the first time in 30 years. The Gunners did have the consolation of winning both Cups, beating Sheffield Wednesday in each of the Finals. Bit-part player Steve Morrow scored the winner in the League Cup Final, and suffered a broken arm after Tony Adams hoisted him aloft and then dropped him. It was another fringe player, Andy Linighan, who headed a dramatic winner in the FA Cup Final, which went to a replay.

Keane joins United

United added Roy Keane to their ranks for the defence of their title. His arrival from Nottingham Forest for a British record £3.75 million made the United side even more formidable. This time they went one better, finishing eight points clear of Blackburn in the title race, and completing the double with an FA Cup victory over Chelsea.

England's fortunes went from bad to worse. Defeats against Norway

and Holland left them needing to beat minnows San Marino by seven goals and hope that Holland lost in Poland. England started disastrously, conceding a goal in under ten seconds, which was believed to be an international record. The team recovered to win 7-1 but that was of little consequence as Holland got the win they needed. England had failed to qualify for the World Cup for the first time since 1978. Taylor, who had come in for some vitriolic criticism in the press, fell on his sword.

Venables replaces Taylor

Terry Venables was named as his successor. Venables had been ousted from White Hart Lane in a power struggle with chairman Alan Sugar, a dispute that was being played out in the High Court. With England hosting Euro '96, Venables had no immediate concerns of getting his England side through a competitive series. Graeme Souness's immediate concern was in finding another job as the Liverpool board finally lost patience. He became the first Liverpool manager to be shown the door since the 1950s. The club reverted to their tried and trusted system of appointing from within, Roy Evans being given the task of bringing back the glory days.

George Graham's record

Manchester United's first European Cup campaign since 1967–68 came to an abrupt end as they were beaten by Galatasaray in the Second Round. It was left to Arsenal to fly the flag for England in the 1993–94 European Cup Winners' Cup, and they did so in fine style. An Alan Smith goal was enough to beat Parma in the Final, and although George Graham's side wasn't known for champagne football, six trophies in eight years told its own story.

The following season Graham nearly made it seven when they reached the Final again. A freak 50-yard lob by ex-Spurs player Nayim won the match for Real Zaragoza seconds before the end of extra time.

Sutton and Shearer lead Blackburn to the title

The 1994–95 Championship went to the wire. Kenny Dalglish's Blackburn, spearheaded by the SAS – Sutton and Shearer – went to Anfield on the last day of the season, needing a victory to be sure of the title. Anything less could let in United, who were at West Ham. A last-minute goal by Jamie Redknapp looked to have spoiled Blackburn's party, until news came through that United had been held to a goalless draw. Blackburn thus claimed their first Championship since 1914.

Newcastle go close

United reclaimed top spot in 1995–96, reeling in Kevin Keegan's Newcastle side, who had held a 12-point advantage early in the New Year. The two clubs would finish in the same positions the following season, Alex Ferguson having a distinct edge in the battle of wits that accompanied the on-field skirmishes.

In February 1995 it was revealed that George Graham had received illegal payments in transfer deals brokered by the agent Rune Hauge. Graham's track record couldn't help him; he was sacked by Arsenal and given a one-year ban by the FA. Allegations that Bruce Grobbelaar was involved in match-fixing at the behest of a Far East betting syndicate also hit the headlines. As recently as 1990, Swindon Town had been denied promotion to Division One after being found guilty of betting on the outcome of matches they were involved in.

In January 1995 the game was further tarnished when Eric Cantona lashed out at a fan with a kung-fu-style kick after being red-carded at Crystal Palace. He received an eight-month ban and a community service order. Arsenal's Paul Merson revealed that he had a drug problem, while team-mate Tony Adams had already served a prison sentence for drink-driving. All three players showed that rehabilitation was possible. In Cantona's case he returned to hit the goal which beat Liverpool in the 1996 FA Cup Final. United had won the double again and the Frenchman was named Footballer of the Year.

Paul Gascoigne

Problems with alcohol, injuries and his weight jinxed one of the most dazzling midfield players England has ever seen. "Gazza" grabbed the headlines for both self-destructive behaviour and brilliance. It was a tragedy for him, and for England, that he lacked the mental strength to match his mazy dribbling and slide-rule passes – a great footballing talent was squandered.

A Geordie full of laddish humour, he quickly made an impact at Newcastle United, which he joined in 1985 at 17. Terry Venables paid a record £2 million to bring the prodigious talent to Tottenham Hotspur in 1988. But in the 1991 FA Cup Final, having scored some fabulous goals on the road there, including a blinding 35-yard free-kick against the Gunners in the semi-final, Gascoigne recklessly fouled Forest's Gary Charles and injured his own cruciate ligament, which put him out of the game for a season.

National hero

Italia '90 had seen him emerge as a national hero, with the fans loving his heartfelt emotion when England went out to West Germany on penalties in the semi-final, as much as they'd admired his moments of inspirational genius. He returned to Italy in 1992 for three difficult and injury-beset years at Lazio, but came back to Britain in 1995 for a renaissance at Glasgow Rangers, helping them to the Scottish title with 14 League goals in his first season and becoming Scotland's Footballer of the Year.

Euro '96, held in Britain, was a stage on which Gascoigne shone, and he scored a memorable goal against Scotland – one of the best of the Championship. It was to be his high-water mark, for Glenn Hoddle left him out of the England squad for France '98, and he would never play for his country again.

Gazza struggled for form and fitness in the latter years of his career. In his spells at Middlesbrough, Everton and Burnley he showed only glimpses of his rare talent. There was a brief sojourn in China, and a player-coach stint at Boston Utd. In December 2005 he was sacked after just six weeks in charge of Conference North side Kettering Town.

"Football's Coming Home"

Euro '96 provided welcome relief from a lot of unseemly publicity. The fans sang "Football's Coming Home" and England gave the country something to smile about. A piece of Gascoigne magic helped the team to a 2-0 win over Scotland, and a 4-1 demolition job on the Dutch masters sent the country into a fever of anticipation. David Seaman was the hero in the penalty shoot-out victory over Spain in the quarter-final. When Alan Shearer scored after two minutes against Germany in the semis it looked as if England might go all the way. But the Germans levelled and the two countries went into a shoot-out for the second time in a major tournament. Gareth Southgate had been immaculate in central defence but his spot-kick was saved, leaving Moller to score the goal which put England out.

BELOW: One of the most dramatic moments of Euro '96 when Stuart Pearce scored against Spain. After blasting the kick into the corner, he roared with delight. Pearce had missed from the spot when England were knocked out of the 1990 World Cup semi-finals by West Germany.

BELOW LEFT: Teddy Sheringham shares the moment with an emotional Pearce.

OPPOSITE INSET: Sheringham and Gascoigne celebrate after the midfielder's stunning goal clinched England's victory over Scotland in Euro '96.

OPPOSITE LEFT: Arsene Wenger achieved the Double with Arsenal in only his second season in charge of the team. David Seaman was England's first-choice keeper and fundamental to the Gunners' success.

The Bosman ruling

Jean-Marc Bosman had never set Belgian football alight, let alone the world. But when he took his club Liege to the European Court of Justice on the issue of freedom of contract, he secured a ruling that was to have profound implications for all clubs. From now on contract negotiations – and an eye on the clock – would become of paramount importance when it came to a club's balance sheet. Few businesses had to contend with multi-million-pound assets disappearing overnight, but that wasn't far from the case post-Bosman.

Wenger joins Arsenal

Many Arsenal fans scratched their heads when Arsene Wenger was named as the man to take over at Highbury in 1996, following Bruce Rioch's brief tenure. Wenger couldn't prevent United from taking the title again in his first season, but in 1997–98 he led the Gunners to the Double. It was to be the start of a long battle for supremacy in the domestic game, one involving psychological warfare, as well as battles on the field.

Hoddle at the England helm

Terry Venables had announced before Euro '96 that he would be standing down to devote his energies to sorting out his legal and business affairs. Chelsea's Glenn Hoddle was installed as the new supremo; at 38 he became the youngest-ever England manager. Hoddle's first test came at France '98. England scraped into the Finals, looking far from impressive. A defeat against Romania at the group stage didn't prove costly as it was sandwiched between victories over Tunisia and Colombia. Michael Owen had come off the bench to score against Romania and the clamour among fans for him to start in the second-round match against Argentina was deafening. Hoddle had taken the brave decision to leave Gascoigne out of his final 22; the decision to play Owen was far easier. The 17-year-old Liverpool prodigy scored the goal of the tournament to put England 2-1 ahead. Argentina levelled, and after David Beckham was red-carded for a petulant kick at Diego Simeone it looked to be slipping away from England's grasp. Sol Campbell thought he'd given tenth-man England a "golden goal" winner with a towering header in extra time. It was ruled out for an infringement and England suffered yet another penalty shoot-out exit. Paul Ince and David Batty were the unlucky men to miss from the spot on this occasion.

League Division One and Premiership 1990–1999

1989–90

1	Liverpool	79
2	Aston Villa	70
3	Tottenham Hotspur	63
4	Arsenal	62
5	Chelsea	60
6	Everton	59
7	Southampton	55
8	Wimbledon	55
9	Nottingham Forest	54
10	Norwich City	53
11	Queen's Park Rangers	50
12	Coventry City	49
13	Manchester United	48
14	Manchester City	48
15	Crystal Palace	48
16	Derby County	46
17	Luton Town	43
18	Sheffield Wednesday	43
19	Charlton Athletic	30
20	Millwall	26

1990–91

1	Arsenal	83
2	Liverpool	76
3	Crystal Palace	69
4	Leeds United	64
5	Manchester City	62
6	Manchester United	59
7	Wimbledon	56
8	Nottingham Forest	54
9	Everton	51
10	Tottenham Hotspur	49
11	Chelsea	49
12	Queen's Park Rangers	46
13	Sheffield United	46
14	Southampton	45
15	Norwich City	45
16	Coventry City	44
17	Aston Villa	41
18	Luton Town	37
19	Sunderland	34
20	Derby County	24

1991–92

1	Leeds United	82
2	Manchester United	78
3	Sheffield Wednesday	75
4	Arsenal	72
5	Manchester City	70
6	Liverpool	64
7	Aston Villa	60
8	Nottingham Forest	59
9	Sheffield United	57
10	Crystal Palace	57
11	Queen's Park Rangers	54
12	Everton	53
13	Wimbledon	53
14	Chelsea	53
15	Tottenham Hotspur	52
16	Southampton	52
17	Oldham Athletic	51
18	Norwich City	45
19	Coventry City	44
20	Luton Town	42
21	Notts County	40
22	West Ham United	38

Premier League 1992–93

1	Manchester United	84
2	Aston Villa	74
3	Norwich City	72
4	Blackburn Rovers	71
5	Queen's Park Rangers	63
6	Liverpool	59
7	Sheffield Wednesday	59
8	Tottenham Hotspur	59
9	Manchester City	57
10	Arsenal	56
11	Chelsea	56
12	Wimbledon	54
13	Everton	53
14	Sheffield United	52
15	Coventry City	52
16	Ipswich Town	52
17	Leeds United	51
18	Southampton	50
19	Oldham Athletic	49
20	Crystal Palace	49
21	Middlesbrough	44
22	Nottingham Forest	40

Premier League 1993–94

1	Manchester United	92
2	Blackburn Rovers	84
3	Newcastle United	77
4	Arsenal	71
5	Leeds United	70
6	Wimbledon	65
7	Sheffield Wednesday	64
8	Liverpool	60
9	Queen's Park Rangers	60
10	Aston Villa	57
11	Coventry City	56
12	Norwich City	53
13	West Ham United	52
14	Chelsea	51
15	Tottenham Hotspur	45
16	Manchester City	45
17	Everton	44
18	Southampton	43
19	Ipswich Town	43
20	Sheffield United	42
21	Oldham Athletic	40
22	Swindon Town	30

Premier League 1994–95

1	Blackburn Rovers	89
2	Manchester United	88
3	Nottingham Forest	77
4	Liverpool	74
5	Leeds United	73
6	Newcastle United	72
7	Tottenham Hotspur	62
8	Queen's Park Rangers	60
9	Wimbledon	56
10	Southampton	54
11	Chelsea	54
12	Arsenal	51
13	Sheffield Wednesday	51
14	West Ham United	50
15	Everton	50
16	Coventry City	50
17	Manchester City	49
18	Aston Villa	48
19	Crystal Palace	45
20	Norwich City	43
21	Leicester City	29
22	Ipswich	27

Premier League 1995–96

1	Manchester United	82
2	Newcastle United	78
3	Liverpool	71
4	Aston Villa	63
5	Arsenal	63
6	Everton	61
7	Blackburn Rovers	61
8	Tottenham Hotspur	61
9	Nottingham Forest	58
10	West Ham United	51
11	Chelsea	50
12	Middlesbrough	43
13	Leeds United	43
14	Wimbledon	41
15	Sheffield Wednesday	40
16	Coventry City	38
17	Southampton	38
18	Manchester City	38
19	Queen's Park Rangers	33
20	Bolton Wanderers	29

Premier League 1996–97

1	Manchester United	75
2	Newcastle United	68
3	Arsenal	68
4	Liverpool	68
5	Aston Villa	61
6	Chelsea	59
7	Sheffield Wednesday	57
8	Wimbledon	56
9	Leicester City	47
10	Tottenham Hotspur	46
11	Leeds United	46
12	Derby County	46
13	Blackburn Rovers	42
14	West Ham United	42
15	Everton	42
16	Southampton	41
17	Coventry City	41
18	Sunderland	40
19	Middlesbrough	39
20	Nottingham Forest	34

Premier League 1997–98

1	Arsenal	78
2	Manchester United	77
3	Liverpool	65
4	Chelsea	63
5	Leeds United	59
6	Blackburn Rovers	58
7	Aston Villa	57
8	West Ham United	56
9	Derby County	55
10	Leicester City	53
11	Coventry City	52
12	Southampton	48
13	Newcastle United	44
14	Tottenham Hotspur	44
15	Wimbledon	44
16	Sheffield Wednesday	44
17	Everton	40
18	Bolton Wanderers	40
19	Barnsley	35
20	Crystal Palace	33

Premier League 1998–99

1	Manchester United	79
2	Arsenal	78
3	Chelsea	75
4	Leeds United	67
5	West Ham United	57
6	Aston Villa	55
7	Liverpool	54
8	Derby County	52
9	Middlesbrough	52
10	Leicester City	49
11	Tottenham Hotspur	47
12	Sheffield Wednesday	46
13	Newcastle United	46
14	Everton	43
15	Coventry City	42
16	Wimbledon	42
17	Southampton	41
18	Charlton Athletic	36
19	Blackburn Rovers	35
20	Nottingham Forest	30

FA Cup Finals

1990	Manchester Utd	v	Crystal Palace	3-3	(1-0)
1991	Tottenham H	v	Nottingham F	2-1	
1992	Liverpool	v	Sunderland	2-0	
1993	Arsenal	v	Sheffield Wed	1-1	(2-1)
1994	Manchester Utd	v	Chelsea	4-0	
1995	Everton	v	Manchester Utd	1-0	
1996	Manchester Utd	v	Liverpool	1-0	
1997	Chelsea	v	Middlesbrough	2-0	
1998	Arsenal	v	Newcastle Utd	2-0	
1999	Manchester Utd	v	Newcastle Utd	2-0	

United crowned champions of Europe

In the domestic game the United bandwagon rolled on. Ferguson's men reclaimed the title in 1999, the first in a hat-trick of Championships that would equal Liverpool's feat of the 1980s. European Cup success was still proving elusive, however, a 1997 semi-final defeat by Borussia Dortmund being the nearest United had come to repeating the club's achievement under Busby. In May 1999 the coveted trophy was finally claimed, and in dramatic fashion. United entered the tournament as runners-up, but while Arsenal faltered in their group matches, United emerged to dispose of Inter Milan and Juventus at the knockout stage. A 32-match unbeaten run had carried the club to yet another domestic double and to the Champions' League Final, against Bayern Munich in Barcelona. Trailing 1-0 with a minute to go, Sheringham scored to give United a lifeline. Seconds later Sheringham flicked on a Beckham corner and Solskjaer stabbed the ball into the roof of the net.

ABOVE: United fans swarm the streets of Manchester in celebration of their team's victory, after beating Bayern Munich 2-1 in the European Cup Final in Barcelona.

BELOW: Alex Ferguson proudly parades the European Cup at Manchester Airport.

Alex Ferguson

Alex Ferguson arrived at Old Trafford in 1986 with an impressive record from his eight years at Aberdeen. He succeeded in breaking the Celtic-Rangers stranglehold on Scottish football, winning the Championship three times and the Scottish Cup on four occasions. He also guided the Dons to a famous European Cup Winners' Cup victory over Real Madrid, beating the mighty Spanish side 2-1 in the Final in Gothenburg. He had a brief spell as caretaker manager of Scotland following the death of Jock Stein.

Youth system bears fruit

Ferguson then turned his attention to making Manchester United a powerhouse in England's top flight at a time when Liverpool were the undisputed top dogs. Fortunes in the early days were mixed. His team lifted the FA Cup in 1990 and followed it up with a victory over Barcelona in the European Cup Winners' Cup Final the following year. Shortly afterwards the youth system in which Ferguson had invested so heavily began to bear fruit. Players of the stature of Giggs, Beckham, Scholes and the Neville brothers progressed to the senior side. Ferguson also made some astute signings, notably Peter Schmeichel and Eric Cantona, who together cost just £1.5 million. Ferguson's side proved irresistible, winning the inaugural Premiership title in 1993. A League and Cup Double followed in 1994, and again in 1996. But the crowning moment came in 1999, when Ferguson added the European Cup to his sizeable haul of domestic trophies. He announced that 2002 would be his final season, but had a change of heart and took United to yet another Championship in 2002–03.

Victory over Millwall in the 2004 FA Cup Final gave United their fifth win in the competition in the Ferguson era. A year later it should have been six, but while United dominated the Final, Arsenal left with the silverware. A Carling Cup victory over Wigan in 2005–06 prevented a second trophyless season, United failing to reach the knockout stage of the Champions League for the first time in a decade.

By 2007 United had gone three years without winning the League, the club's worst showing since the Premier League's inception. Ferguson rebuilt yet again and steered United to a hat-trick of Championships for the second time. There was also a second Champions League success in 2008, Barcelona prevented a third win the following year but Premier League title No. 12 came in 2011. Knighted in 1999, Ferguson reached another milestone in 2010 when he overtook Sir Matt Busby to become United's longest-serving manager. After winning a 13th Premier League title, the 49th trophy of his managerial career, Ferguson announced his intention to retire and take up a position on the Manchester United board at the end of the 2012–13 season.

Scottish League 1990–1999

1989–90

1	Rangers	51
2	Aberdeen	44
3	Hearts	44
4	Dundee United	35
5	Celtic	34
6	Motherwell	34
7	Hibernian	34
8	Dunfermline Athletic	30
9	St Mirren	30
10	Dundee	2

1990–91

1	Rangers	55
2	Aberdeen	53
3	Celtic	41
4	Dundee United	41
5	Hearts	35
6	Motherwell	33
7	St Johnstone	31
8	Dunfermline Athletic	27
9	Hibernian	25
10	St Mirren	19

1991–92

1	Rangers	72
2	Hearts	63
3	Celtic	62
4	Dundee United	51
5	Hibernian	49
6	Aberdeen	48
7	Airdrieonians	36
8	St Johnstone	36
9	Falkirk	35
10	Motherwell	34
11	St Mirren	24
12	Dunfermline Athletic	18

1992–93

1	Rangers	73
2	Aberdeen	64
3	Celtic	60
4	Dundee United	47
5	Hearts	44
6	St Johnstone	40
7	Hibernian	37
8	Partick Thistle	36
9	Motherwell	35
10	Dundee	34
11	Falkirk	29
12	Airdrieonians	29

1993–94

1	Rangers	58
2	Aberdeen	55
3	Motherwell	54
4	Celtic	50
5	Hibernian	47
6	Dundee United	42
7	Hearts	42
8	Kilmarnock	40
9	Partick Thistle	40
10	St Johnstone	40
11	Raith Rovers	31
12	Dundee	29

1994–95

1	Rangers	69
2	Motherwell	54
3	Hibernian	53
4	Celtic	51
5	Falkirk	48
6	Hearts	43
7	Kilmarnock	43
8	Partick Thistle	43
9	Aberdeen	41
10	Dundee United	36

1995–96

1	Rangers	87
2	Celtic	83
3	Aberdeen	55
4	Hearts	55
5	Hibernian	43
6	Raith Rovers	43
7	Kilmarnock	41
8	Motherwell	39
9	Partick Thistle	30
10	Falkirk	24

1996–97

1	Rangers	80
2	Celtic	75
3	Dundee United	60
4	Hearts	52
5	Dunfermline Athletic	45
6	Aberdeen	44
7	Kilmarnock	39
8	Motherwell	38
9	Hibernian	38
10	Raith Rovers	25

1997–98

1	Celtic	74
2	Rangers	72
3	Hearts	67
4	Kilmarnock	50
5	St Johnstone	48
6	Aberdeen	39
7	Dundee United	37
8	Dunfermline Athletic	37
9	Motherwell	34
10	Hibernian	30

Scottish Premier League
1998–99

1	Rangers	77
2	Celtic	71
3	St Johnstone	57
4	Kilmarnock	56
5	Dundee	46
6	Hearts	42
7	Motherwell	41
8	Aberdeen	37
9	Dundee United	34
10	Dunfermline Athletic	28

Scottish Cup Finals

1990	Aberdeen	v	Celtic	0-0
1991	Motherwell	v	Dundee United	4-3
1992	Rangers	v	Airdrieonians	2-1
1993	Rangers	v	Aberdeen	2-1
1994	Dundee United	v	Rangers	1-0
1995	Celtic	v	Airdrieonians	1-0
1996	Rangers	v	Hearts	5-1
1997	Kilmarnock	v	Falkirk	1-0
1998	Hearts	v	Rangers	2-1
1999	Rangers	v	Celtic	1-0

Walter Smith's Runaway Rangers

The 1990s belonged to Rangers, who ceded the League title just once. The margin was emphatic more often than not, a 15-point gulf in 1994–95. The exception was 1990–91, when Aberdeen visited Ibrox on the last day of the season needing only a draw to take the title. A brace from Mark Hateley, who had joined Rangers from AC Milan the previous summer, meant the Championship went to Ibrox once again.

Rangers' run had started under Graeme Souness, who demonstrated that he had no truck with sectarianism by signing former Hoops star Mo Johnston from Nantes in summer 1989. He wasn't the first Catholic to turn out for Rangers but his profile put him in a different bracket from those who preceded him. Johnston scored a dramatic late winner against Celtic in November '89 and ended the season as Rangers' top scorer.

Following Souness's departure to Anfield in 1991, with three Championships to his name, Walter Smith took over at Ibrox, a seamless transition as Gers continued to dominate. Smith was recognised with five Manager of the Year awards. Ally McCoist was the League's top marksman with 34 goals in 1991–92 and 1992–93, helping Rangers land a fifth treble in the latter campaign. The team also came within a whisker of a European Cup Final. Having put out Leeds United, Rangers finished a point behind Marseille in the mini-League phase, the winners going on to contest the Final. A year later, only Dundee United's shock 1–0 win in the Scottish Cup Final prevented Rangers from completing successive domestic clean sweeps. Gers boasted the Player of the Year in their ranks six years running from 1992: McCoist, Goram, Hateley, Laudrup (twice) and Gascoigne.

Dons provide main threat

Celtic were feeling the heat, particularly as Rangers closed in on the celebrated nine successive Championships achieved under Jock Stein. But it was Aberdeen who provided the main threat. In 1994 the Dons were runners-up for the fifth time in six years, and finished second to Rangers in all competitions in 1992–93. Liam Brady replaced Billy McNeill as Celtic manager but neither he, Lou Macari nor Tommy Burns could bring back the glory days. After five trophyless seasons, the Hoops finally got their hands on some silverware, beating Airdrieonians in the 1995 Scottish Cup Final. Recent acquisition Pierre van Hooijdonk scored the game's only goal. But fourth in the League and defeat to Division One champions Raith in the League Cup showpiece – Rovers' first-ever Cup win – showed there was still some way to go to compete with Rangers, who finished 18 points ahead of them in the title race.

In 1995–96 Celtic suffered just one League defeat – to Rangers – yet it still wasn't enough. Gers lost three games, but more wins and fewer draws brought an eighth Championship on the spin. The killer stat in Championship No. 9 was Rangers' four wins in the Old Firm encounters. Runners-up Celtic finished five points behind.

One trophy in three years wasn't enough to keep Tommy Burns in a job, and in 1997 Wim Jansen – a member of the Feyenoord team

that beat Celtic in the 1970 European Cup Final – was installed as the new boss. 1970 was soon forgotten as Jansen led Celtic back to the top of the pile, preventing Rangers from achieving the record-breaking 10th successive League success. Celtic also lifted the League Cup for the first time in 15 years with a 3–0 win over Dundee United. Rangers, meanwhile, went down to Hearts in the Scottish Cup Final, thereby finishing the year empty-handed for the first time since 1986.

Walter Smith had already announced he was quitting at the end of the season, Dick Advocaat appointed to try and wrest back the title. It was all change at Celtic, too, with Josef Venglos replacing Jansen, who quit after one season in charge. In 1998–99 Rangers returned to the top with an historic 3–0 win at Celtic Park. Neil McCann scored twice as Rangers secured the title in their rivals' back yard for the first time. Rangers were thus crowned inaugural SPL champions, Scotland's 10 Premier clubs having followed the model of English football's top tier.

St Johnstone finished third in 1998–99, equalling their best-ever League placing, and also reached a major Cup Final for only the second time, going down 2–1 to Rangers in the League Cup. A Rod Wallace goal gave Rangers victory over Celtic in the Scottish Cup Final, allowing Advocaat to bask in the limelight of a first-season treble. Venglos was soon on his way, replaced by a Kenny Dalglish-John Barnes axis, the former directing operations, the latter taking the head-coach role.

Battle of McLean brothers

Other highlights include Aberdeen's 1990 win over Celtic in the Scottish Cup Final, the first to be decided on penalties. The 1991 Final pitted Tommy McLean's Motherwell against brother Jim's Dundee United. The Steelmen prevailed 4–3 in an extra-time thriller, inflicting a sixth Cup Final defeat on Jim. Under rookie coach Alex McLeish, Motherwell finished League runners-up in 1994–95, their best showing since the 30s. Motherwell's Tommy Coyne was the division's top scorer, having previously headed the list with Dundee and Celtic. Kilmarnock's win over Division One side Falkirk in the 1997 Final was the club's first Cup victory for 68 years. Falkirk boss Alex Totten had been sacked by Killie earlier that season. The top flight introduced a short-lived play-off system in 1994–95, ninth placed Aberdeen retaining their top-table status by beating Division One runners-up Dunfermline. That same year, Forfar Athletic won the newly formed Third Division.

On the international stage, Italia '90 marked Scotland's fifth successive appearance in the Finals. Andy Roxburgh's team lost 1–0 to Brazil, and beat group whipping boys Sweden 2–1. The crunch game turned out to be supposed minnows Costa Rica, who won 1–0 and consigned Scotland to another first-round exit. A European Championship debut in 1992 offered no turn of fortune. The team lost by the odd goal to Holland, matched Germany for much of the game and beat the CIS 3–0, with goals from McStay, McClair and McAllister. It wasn't enough to progress. Andy Roxburgh's seven-year stint in charge of the national team ended after Scotland failed to make it to the 1994 World Cup. Under Craig Brown Scotland reached the Finals of Euro '96 and France '98. At the former, Scotland lost out to Holland on goal difference; the Dutch side's consolation in a 4–1 hammering by England proved crucial. Two years later, a Tom Boyd own-goal gave reigning champions Brazil a 2–1 victory. After sharing the honours with Norway, Scotland crashed out with a 3–0 defeat at the hands of Morocco.

OPPOSITE: Rangers' Paul Gascoigne parades the Scottish Coca Cola Cup with Rangers' coach Archie Knox at Celtic Park. Rangers beat Hearts 4-3 to claim the first trophy of the Scottish season.

2000–2009
Living The Dream

The decade began with the first billion-pound TV deal, making Premier League membership more important than ever. A Champions League spot was the big prize, and clubs across the board even began to regard the FA Cup as an unwelcome distraction. Fans added "oligarch" to their vocabulary as football became a playground for the mega-rich. For some the business model was unsustainable. Leeds went from Champions League semi-finalists to fire-sale relegation in double-quick time, and Portsmouth became the first top-flight club to enter administration. Even Manchester United, who added six Championships to the cabinet, carried eye-popping levels of debt.

2000 England appoint Sven-Goran Eriksson as the new manager, the first non-English person to hold the post

2000 Last match at Wembley Stadium before it closes prior to demolition to make way for a new stadium

2001 Manchester United pays £19m to PSV Eindhoven for Ruud van Nistelrooy and £28m to Lazio for Juan Veron

2001 Craig Brown steps down as Scotland boss after eight years and 70 games, the country's longest-serving manager

2002 Seventeenth World Cup is held jointly in Korea and Japan. England lose 2-1 to eventual winners Brazil in the quarter-finals. The Republic of Ireland lose to Spain in the second round

2003 England captain in the seventeenth World Cup, David

Beckham is awarded an OBE shortly before his surprise £24.5-million transfer to Real Madrid from Manchester United

2003 Rangers win their 50th Scottish Championship, edging out Celtic on goal difference

2004 FIFA celebrates its centenary

2004 Greece win the European Championship, staged in Portugal. England lose to the hosts in the quarter-final

2005 Chelsea win the Championship for the first time in 50 years

2005 Liverpool beat AC Milan in the Champions League Final. The game was won 3–2 on penalties, after a 3–3 draw following extra time

2006 Chelsea retain the Premiership title

2006 England lose to Portugal in the quarter-final of the World Cup

Gunners Double Up

In 2001–02 Arsenal won their second Double under Wenger and the third in the club's history. The Gunners began the 2002–03 season like an express train and Wenger tentatively suggested that his side was capable of going through the season unbeaten. Clubs in the chasing pack, looking to strengthen, had the new transfer arrangements to contend with. After the start of the season the "window" would not be open to further deals until January. Arsenal faltered in the second half of the season and in the end they had to settle for retaining the FA Cup and the runners-up spot in the League. United, by contrast, went on a blistering run in the new year to claim their 8th Premiership title in 11 seasons. There was also the prospect of a second European Cup Final appearance, this time at Old Trafford. United managed to beat holders Real Madrid in the home leg of their quarter-final clash, but the damage had already been done at the Bernebeu.

The season ended with the England captain departing to join the team that had knocked United out of the European Cup. David Beckham's name had been linked with several clubs when it became clear that United were prepared to let him go. Real Madrid were one of the few clubs who could afford the £25 million fee as the inflationary bubble had undoubtedly burst. A significant part of Beckham's fee was for the acquisition of a unique brand; Real would expect to recoup the outlay in the sales of merchandise, as well as in his contribution on the pitch.

Football's finances

The financial correction that had occurred since the heady days of the 1990s was stark. The collapse of On Digital showed that football was not a cash cow that could be milked at all levels. Leeds fans watched their Champions League semi-final side of 2001 disintegrate before their eyes, hard proof that gambling on a seat at European football's top table was a high-risk strategy.

The parlous state of football's finances meant that even Champions League qualification was not necessarily a passport to a land of milk and honey. On the final day of the 2002–03 season Chelsea beat Liverpool to secure the fourth Champions League spot. Less than two months later chairman Ken Bates sold his majority shareholding to Russian oil billionaire Roman Abramovich. In seven seasons Chelsea had never finished out of the top six in the Premiership, had twice lifted the FA Cup and also won the Cup Winners' Cup. And yet the club was £80 million in debt and Bates admitted that pockets deeper than his were needed to take Chelsea forward.

Eriksson silences his critics

There was another England-Germany clash at Euro 2000 as the countries were drawn together at the group stage. A Shearer goal gave England victory, but both countries made an early exit. England had let a two-goal lead slip in their opening match against Portugal, losing 3-2. They also led Romania 2-1 in their final match but again failed to press home the advantage and were on the receiving end of another 3-2 defeat.

Failure to qualify for the latter stages led Kevin Keegan to question his ability at the highest level. He stood down with qualification for the 2002 World Cup in Japan and Korea hanging in the balance. The FA looked further afield for their next appointment. Sven-Goran Eriksson was not a universally popular choice, despite his excellent credentials. He silenced many of his critics with a stunning 5-1 win in Germany in September 2001, a result which got England's World Cup campaign back on track.

"Group of Death"

Eriksson succeeded in getting the country out of the "Group of Death", a Beckham penalty against Argentina exorcising the ghost of France '98. A comfortable win over Denmark followed, but England went down to favourites Brazil in the quarter-final. England went ahead through Owen, Rivaldo and Ronaldinho replied for Brazil and Eriksson's men couldn't get back on terms, even when the favourites were reduced to ten men.

ABOVE: The scoreboard records the moment – England's great victory over rivals Germany after having lost the home game of the World Cup qualifying group at Wembley 1-0.

2006 Steve McClaren appointed successor to Sven-Goran Eriksson as England coach

2006 Arsenal lose 2-1 to Barcelona in the Champions League Final

2006 Stevens Inquiry into corrupt transfer dealings

2007 Liverpool lose to AC Milan in the Champions League Final

2007 The new Wembley Stadium opens

2007 Steve McClaren sacked as England manager after the team failed to qualify for Euro 2008

2008 Fabio Capello appointed England coach

2008 Spain crowned European champions with a 1-0 win over Germany in the Final of the tournament, staged in Austria and Switzerland. There is no British representation

2008 Manchester United beat Chelsea in the Champions League Final, the first European Cup Final between two British clubs. The game was won by Manchester

United 6–5 on penalties, after a 1–1 draw following extra time

2008 Rangers lose to Zenit St Petersburg 2-0 in the UEFA Cup Final

2009 Manchester United complete a hat-trick of League titles, drawing level with Liverpool on 18 Championships.

2009 Manchester United lose 2-0 to Barcelona in the Champions League Final staged in Rome.

2009 Cristiano Ronaldo leaves Manchester United for Real Madrid in a world record £80-million deal

2009 Shakhtar Donetsk beat Werder Bremen 2-1 in the Final of the last UEFA Cup before it is revamped as the Europa League

Arsenal match Invincibles

Even established Premiership sides now had to strike a balance between sound investment and over-commitment. For Leeds it was all too late; a string of stars had been sold at knockdown prices and the team propped up the division in 2003-04.

Chelsea, backed by Abramovich's personal fortune, was the one club able to buck the trend. Coach Claudio Ranieri spent over £100 million on a crop of international stars, players of the stature of Makelele, Duff, Crespo and Mutu. Inevitably there were accusations of trying to buy success, and for most of the 2003-04 season it looked as if the strategy was going to bear fruit. Chelsea stayed with the scorching pace set by Arsenal longest, but in the end not even Ranieri's all-stars could match the brilliance of Arsene Wenger's team. The Gunners completed their League programme unbeaten, a feat not achieved in English football's top flight since 1888-89, when Preston's Invincibles won the inaugural League Championship.

Chelsea took revenge over their London rivals with a quarter-final victory in the Champions League, but went down to Monaco in the semis. By most standards Chelsea had had a successful season, but the lack of silverware meant that football's worst-kept secret was finally revealed: out went Ranieri and in came Jose Mourinho, who had just steered Porto to Champions League victory, following a UEFA Cup triumph over Celtic in 2003.

Manchester United was among Porto's scalps in the latter's Champions League campaign. United also trailed in a distant third in the Premiership, 15 points behind Arsenal. Ferguson's side did win the FA Cup semi-final clash between the two giants, and a comfortable 3-0 victory over Millwall in the final gave United their 11th victory in the competition, stretching the club's lead at the top of the all-time list.

Changes at Anfield

The fact that Chelsea had managed to break the Manchester United-Arsenal duopoly in 2003-04 undoubtedly helped to bring down the curtain on Gerard Houllier's reign at Anfield. Liverpool fans saw their team secure Champions League football by finishing fourth in the Premiership, but with a 28-point gulf separating the Reds from Arsenal. In terms of points Liverpool were closer to the relegated clubs, having finished just 26 points ahead of Leeds, Wolves and Leicester. The man charged with bringing the glory days back to Anfield was Rafael Benitez, who had just completed a Primera Liga-UEFA Cup double with Valencia.

Euro 2004

With domestic matters settled, there was the usual pre-tournament mood of buoyant optimism as England departed for Portugal. There was almost a dream start as Sven Goran Eriksson's men led holders and favourites France through a Frank Lampard header in their opening group fixture. Two injury-time goals from Zidane meant that England emerged with considerable credit but no points.

A comfortable 3-0 win over Switzerland followed, Wayne Rooney grabbing a brace and becoming the youngest scorer in the competition's history. That record was taken a few days later by Switzerland's Johan Vonlanthen, but with two more goals in the 4-2 victory over Croatia, it was Rooney's name that was on everyone's lips. He headed the list of the tournament's marksmen and the impact he had made was compared with Pelé's debut on the world stage at the 1958 World Cup.

England qualified for the quarter-finals behind France, the first time that the country had reached the knockout stage of the competition on foreign soil.

The team got off to a dream start against hosts Portugal, Michael Owen silencing his critics with a brilliant strike after three minutes. Rooney limped out with a broken metatarsal midway through the first half, and as the game wore on England fought an increasingly rearguard action. With seven minutes to go the hosts equalised through substitute Helder Postiga, who had all too rarely found the back of the net when turning out for Spurs. There were shades of France '98 as Sol Campbell thought he'd headed England into the semis in the dying seconds, but the Swiss referee spotted an infringement and the game went to extra-time.

Rui Costa's ferocious strike in the second period was cancelled out when Lampard pounced on a knockdown to score his third goal of the tournament. After 120 minutes the teams were locked at 2-2.

Beckham capped a hugely disappointing tournament by blazing over in the penalty shoot-out. Rui Costa did the same to level matters and it went to sudden death. Portuguese 'keeper Ricardo saved from Darius Vassell and then slotted home the decisive spot-kick. In reaching the last eight, and thus only matching the performance at the 2002 World Cup, Euro 2004 was widely regarded as a missed opportunity for England.

LEFT: Thierry Henry celebrates with team-mates Gilberto and Ray Parlour at White Hart Lane in April 2004.

Premiership 2000–2009

1999-2000

1	Manchester United	91
2	Arsenal	73
3	Leeds United	69
4	Liverpool	67
5	Chelsea	65
6	Aston Villa	58
7	Sunderland	58
8	Leicester City	55
9	West Ham United	55
10	Tottenham Hotspur	53
11	Newcastle United	52
12	Middlesbrough	52
13	Everton	50
14	Coventry City	44
15	Southampton	44
16	Derby County	38
17	Bradford City	36
18	Wimbledon	33
19	Sheffield Wed	31
20	Watford	24

2000-01

1	Manchester United	80
2	Arsenal	70
3	Liverpool	69
4	Leeds United	68
5	Ipswich Town	66
6	Chelsea	61
7	Sunderland	57
8	Aston Villa	54
9	Charlton Athletic	52
10	Southampton	52
11	Newcastle United	51
12	Tottenham Hotspur	49
13	Leicester City	48
14	Middlesbrough	42
15	West Ham United	42
16	Everton	42
17	Derby County	42
18	Manchester City	34
19	Coventry City	34
20	Bradford City	26

2001-02

1	Arsenal	87
2	Liverpool	80
3	Manchester United	77
4	Newcastle United	71
5	Leeds United	66
6	Chelsea	64
7	West Ham United	53
8	Aston Villa	50
9	Tottenham Hotspur	50
10	Blackburn Rovers	46
11	Southampton	45
12	Middlesbrough	45
13	Fulham	44
14	Charlton Athletic	44
15	Everton	43
16	Bolton Wanderers	40
17	Sunderland	40
18	Ipswich Town	36
19	Derby County	30
20	Leicester City	28

2002-03

1	Manchester United	83
2	Arsenal	78
3	Newcastle United	69
4	Chelsea	67
5	Liverpool	64
6	Blackburn Rovers	60
7	Everton	59
8	Southampton	52
9	Manchester City	51
10	Tottenham Hotspur	50
11	Middlesbrough	49
12	Charlton Athletic	49
13	Birmingham City	48
14	Fulham	48
15	Leeds United	47
16	Aston Villa	45
17	Bolton Wanderers	44
18	West Ham United	42
19	West Bromwich Albion	26
20	Sunderland	19

2003-04

1	Arsenal	90
2	Chelsea	79
3	Manchester United	75
4	Liverpool	60
5	Newcastle United	56
6	Aston Villa	56
7	Charlton Athletic	53
8	Bolton Wanderers	53
9	Fulham	52
10	Birmingham City	50
11	Middlesbrough	48
12	Southampton	47
13	Portsmouth	45
14	Tottenham Hotspur	45
15	Blackburn Rovers	44
16	Manchester City	41
17	Everton	39
18	Leicester City	33
19	Leeds United	33
20	Wolverhampton W.	33

2004-05

1	Chelsea	95
2	Arsenal	83
3	Manchester United	77
4	Everton	61
5	Liverpool	58
6	Bolton Wanderers	58
7	Middlesbrough	55
8	Manchester City	52
9	Tottenham Hotspur	52
10	Aston Villa	47
11	Charlton Athletic	46
12	Birmingham	45
13	Fulham	44
14	Newcastle United	44
15	Blackburn Rovers	42
16	Portsmouth	39
17	West Bromwich Albion	34
18	Crystal Palace	33
19	Norwich	33
20	Southampton	32

2005-06

1	Chelsea	91
2	Manchester United	83
3	Liverpool	82
4	Arsenal	67
5	Tottenham Hotspur	65
6	Blackburn	63
7	Newcastle United	58
8	Bolton	56
9	West Ham United	55
10	Wigan	51
11	Everton	50
12	Fulham	48
13	Charlton Athletic	47
14	Middlesbrough	45
15	Manchester City	43
16	Aston Villa	42
17	Portsmouth	38
18	Birmingham	34
19	West Bromwich Albion	30
20	Sunderland	15

2006-07

1	Manchester United	89
2	Chelsea	83
3	Liverpool	68
4	Arsenal	68
5	Tottenham Hotspur	60
6	Everton	58
7	Bolton Wanderers	56
8	Reading	55
9	Portsmouth	54
10	Blackburn Rovers	52
11	Aston Villa	50
12	Middlesbrough	46
13	Newcastle United	43
14	Manchester City	42
15	West Ham United	41
16	Fulham	39
17	Wigan	38
18	Sheffield United	38
19	Charlton Athletic	34
20	Watford	28

2007-08

1	Manchester United	87
2	Chelsea	85
3	Arsenal	83
4	Liverpool	76
5	Everton	65
6	Aston Villa	60
7	Blackburn Rovers	58
8	Portsmouth	57
9	Manchester City	55
10	West Ham United	49
11	Tottenham Hotspur	46
12	Newcastle United	43
13	Middlesbrough	42
14	Wigan Athletic	40
15	Sunderland	39
16	Bolton Wanderers	37
17	Fulham	36
18	Reading	36
19	Birmingham City	35
20	Derby County	11

2008-09

1	Manchester United	90
2	Liverpool	86
3	Chelsea	72
4	Arsenal	72
5	Everton	63
6	Aston Villa	62
7	Fulham	53
8	Tottenham Hotspur	51
9	West Ham United	51
10	Manchester City	50
11	Wigan Athletic	45
12	Stoke City	45
13	Bolton Wanderers	41
14	Portsmouth	41
15	Blackburn Rovers	41
16	Sunderland	36
17	Hull City	35
18	Newcastle United	34
19	Middlesbrough	32
20	West Bromwich Albion	32

FA Cup Finals

2000	Chelsea	v	Aston Villa	1-0
2001	Liverpool	v	Arsenal	2-1
2002	Arsenal	v	Chelsea	2-0
2003	Arsenal	v	Southampton	1-0
2004	Manchester United	v	Millwall	3-0
2005	Arsenal	v	Manchester United	0-0
	(aet) Arsenal won 5-4 on penalties			
2006	Liverpool	v	West Ham United	3-3
	(aet) Liverpool won 3-1 on penalties			
2007	Chelsea	v	Manchester United	1-0
2008	Portsmouth	v	Cardiff City	1-0
2009	Chelsea	v	Everton	2-1

Triumphs for Chelsea and Liverpool

2004–05 will be remembered as the season when Manchester United and Arsenal, between them winners of the Premiership title in 11 of the previous 12 years, could do nothing to stop the Chelsea juggernaut. Jose Mourinho's men didn't quite manage to emulate Arsenal's achievement of the previous campaign – defeat at Manchester City prevented that – but it was still a record-breaking season. 29 wins and 95 points eclipsed the previous marks, while Petr Cech's 1025 minutes without conceding broke Peter Schmeichel's record for shut-outs. Chelsea shipped just 15 goals, two fewer than Arsenal in 1998–99. The meanest defence in the land was marshalled by the outstanding John Terry, who edged Frank Lampard for the PFA Player of the Year award, the first defender to be thus honoured since Paul McGrath in 1993. The title came in Chelsea's centenary, and exactly 50 years after Ted Drake delivered Chelsea's only other Championship.

The Carling Cup also went to Stamford Bridge, Chelsea beating Liverpool in the Final. Rafael Benitez's erratic side saved its best performances for Europe. With United and Arsenal both out of the Champions League at the last 16 stage, Liverpool scored excellent wins over Bayer Leverkusen and Juventus to set up a semi-final clash with Chelsea. It was billed as the biggest game in the history of English club football, and also saw the reigning Champions League and UEFA Cup-winning managers go head to head. A Luis Garcia goal at Anfield settled the issue. Liverpool, who would finish 37 points adrift of the champions, were through to their sixth European Cup Final on the 20th anniversary of the Heysel tragedy.

BELOW LEFT: An elated Frank Lampard scores against Bolton Wanderers. The 2-0 victory makes Chelsea winners of the Barclays Premiership for 2004–2005.

BELOW RIGHT: Jose Mourinho, winner of the Premiership at his first attempt.

OPPOSITE: Liverpool's captain, Steven Gerrard, holds the trophy as team mates celebrate after the UEFA Champions League Final at the Ataturk Olympic Stadium in Turkey.

Gerrard leads Reds' revival

Opponents AC Milan were favourites in Istanbul, and odds of 300-1 against the Reds were being quoted at half-time, by which time they were three goals down. Steven Gerrard led from the front as Liverpool fought back to take the game to penalties, and two Dudek saves in the shoot-out saw Liverpool complete the greatest-ever comeback in a European Final. Their fifth win in the competition meant that the Cup would stay at Anfield.

Arsenal beat Manchester United in the Premiership runners-up race, Arsene Wenger maintaining his record of never finishing outside the top two. Third spot for the second year running represented United's "worst" performance since the inception of the Premiership, and came amid the uncertainties created by Malcolm Glazer's take-over of the club.

Gunners win Cup Final shoot-out

Arsenal and United's only hope of silverware rested on the FA Cup, and they met in the Final. United did everything but score, but after a goalless 120 minutes Lehmann's save from Scholes meant that the Gunners won the first Cup Final shoot-out.

Everton, widely tipped as relegation candidates, secured the fourth Champions League spot, earning David Moyes the Manager of the Year award. Everton lost Rooney just before the start of the season, and the influential Gravesen in January, but still secured the club's first European Cup campaign for 34 years. Fifth place Liverpool had to sweat on a dispensation to be allowed to defend their Champions League crown, while Bolton fans looked forward to European football for the first time in the club's history.

On the final day of the season the relegation dogfight provided the greatest drama. Any three of the bottom four could have gone down, and at various times Norwich, Crystal Palace, Southampton and West Brom all occupied the vital 17th place. The Baggies were the only side to win, a 2-0 victory over Portsmouth guaranteeing Premiership football for Bryan Robson's men. Eight points adrift at the foot of the table at Christmas, West Brom made Premiership history by surviving the drop. For Southampton it was the end of a 27-year run in the top flight.

In the Championship, Wigan Athletic won automatic promotion as runners-up to Sunderland. Elected to the League at the end of the 1977–78 season, Wigan had been bought in 1995 by Dave Whelan, 68-year-old founder of the JJB sportswear empire. His money, together with Paul Jewell's shrewd management, had produced a fairytale rise to the top. Alan Pardew, much castigated by West Ham fans, answered his critics by taking the Hammers back to the Premiership via the play-offs.

Chelsea retain Premiership crown

Even before a ball was kicked in the 2005–06 season, Chelsea Chief Executive Peter Kenyon predicted that the champions would come "from a small group of one". Jose Mourinho was singing from the same hymn sheet, insisting that "one Premiership is not enough" as he revealed his aim was not simply to build one or two title-winning sides but to create a dynasty that would dominate English football for a generation. In their bid to emulate Manchester United and become only the second club to retain the Premiership crown, Chelsea splashed out over £50 million on Asier del Horno, Shaun Wright-Phillips and Michael Essien. With Hernan Crespo returning from his loan spell at AC Milan to add extra firepower, the Blues looked ominously strong as they embarked on a nine-month battle to land five trophies.

Lampard breaks record

A brace from Drogba meant that one piece of silverware was in the Stamford Bridge cabinet before August was out, Chelsea completing a 2-1 victory over Arsenal in the Community Shield curtain-raiser. The team's League form was not always scintillating but it was mightily effective. 52 points from 19 games – just five points dropped in the first half of the season – set the standard for the chasing pack. During this run Frank Lampard added another stat to his impressive CV, breaking David James's Premiership record of 159 consecutive games. He clocked up 164 matches before a virus laid him low, an extraordinary achievement for any top-flight player, let alone a combative midfielder.

Liverpool initially looked best placed to run Chelsea close. Rafa Benitez's men also had a summer trophy under their belt, coming from behind to beat UEFA Cup holders CSKA Moscow in the European Super Cup. A brace from Djibril Cisse helped Liverpool to a 3-1 extra-time win, adding to the club's Super Cup victories of 1977

David Beckham

David Beckham has been a villain and he has been a hero. After a bad-tempered kick on Diego Simeone in England's 1998 World Cup clash with Argentina, he was cast as the villain of the piece. But, by the end of the 2002 World Cup, he was universally regarded as England's new hero. His artistry on the ball, superb distribution and the quality of his dead-ball kicks were always acknowledged – what he had gained in the intervening years was a greater maturity and outstanding leadership skills.

When he was still a youngster, Beckham won an award at a Bobby Charlton Soccer Skills school and had trials with his local club, Leyton Orient, but it was Manchester United who signed him just after his 16th birthday. Although he made his debut in a League Cup tie against Brighton in September 1992, Alex Ferguson nurtured his young star carefully and it wasn't until April 1995 that he gave Beckham his Premiership debut. The following season he established himself in United's midfield and in September 1996 Glenn Hoddle gave him a place in the England team.

Three successive Premiership titles

Beckham was a key figure in United's celebrated Treble-winning team of the 1998–99 season and at the end of that season he was narrowly beaten by Rivaldo for the World Footballer of the Year award. "Becks" was instrumental in helping United to their third successive Premiership title in 2001. In October of the same year it was his stunning free-kick in the closing seconds of the game against Greece, which reserved England's place at the 2002 World Cup in Japan & Korea.

His service in that World Cup meant that Beckham had a virtually unassailable position as England captain during the 2002–03 season, yet he was unsure of a place in United's starting line-up. After much speculation on his future, in June 2003 Beckham signed a £25-million deal to take him to Real Madrid, the team that knocked United out of that season's Champions Cup.

He became a "Galactico" at a time when Real's period of dominance was waning, the team failing to land any silverware in his first three seasons at the Bernebeu. There was more disappointment with the national side as Beckham led England to a quarter-final defeat at Germany 2006. He relinquished the captain's armband, but on the verge of becoming only the fifth player to break the 100-cap barrier, he stressed that he wanted to play on under the new Steve McClaren regime.

Beckham added a La Liga championship medal to his haul in 2007 under Fabio Capello, before signing a long-term deal with MLS side LA Galaxy. Thoughts that the 32-year-old was winding down his career in an undemanding League were quashed as Beckham joined AC Milan for two loan spells in Galaxy's off-season. He put himself in contention for a place in England's 2010 World Cup squad, but hopes of a fourth World Cup adventure were dashed by injury. Even so, he had already become England's most capped outfield player with 115 appearances, breaking Bobby Moore's long-standing record. After leaving LA in December 2012, a short spell at the Qatari-backed French Ligue 1 side Paris St Germain meant that Beckham retired at the end of the 2012–13 season with the rare distinction of having league winners' medals from four different countries.

and 2001. The Reds couldn't break their duck in the World Club Championship, though. Liverpool hadn't won the play-off against South America's top dogs following their first four European Cup victories, and in the revamped tournament staged in Japan in December they went down to São Paulo in the Final.

In the Premiership Liverpool went on an autumn run of nine straight wins, despite the fact that £7-million recruit Peter Crouch didn't find the net until December. It was title-winning form – in normal circumstances – but not with Chelsea setting such a scorching pace.

Gunners leave Highbury

After Christmas it was Manchester United who took up the challenge. Alex Ferguson's side recovered from the acrimonious departure of talismanic captain Roy Keane, and some indifferent Champions League performances, which saw the club fail to reach the competition's knockout stage for the first time in a decade. United hit top gear in the second half of the season. They beat Wigan 4-0 in the Carling Cup Final, only the second time that trophy had gone to Old Trafford. That avoided a second barren season, but any hope of catching Chelsea and landing the top domestic prize disappeared with a 3-0 defeat at Stamford Bridge on 29 April. Chelsea retained the Premiership title with two games to spare, becoming the first London side to record back-to-back Championships since Arsenal in the 1930s. They had suffered five defeats, though two of those were dead rubbers, coming after the title was secured. Only Manchester United matched Chelsea's attacking potency – both teams found the net 72 times – while John Terry once again marshalled the meanest defence in the division.

Michael Owen

A handful of cameo appearances for mid-table Stoke City in 2012-13 persuaded Michael Owen to call time on his playing career at the end of the season. It rang down the curtain for one of the deadliest strikers of the postwar era.

The star of Liverpool's Youth Cup-winning side of 1996, Owen scored on his senior debut at the end of the 1996-97 season, aged 17. He bagged 30 more in 1997-98, earning him the PFA Young Player of the Year award, and more significantly an England call-up. When, in February 1998, he lined up against Chile, Owen became the youngest England player of the century; at 18 years 59 days he took the record previously held by Duncan Edwards and soon he became the youngest player to score for England when he netted against Morocco. England manager Glenn Hoddle took him to the World Cup in France 1998, but not as first-choice striker. Owen changed that after he came off the bench to score against Romania. In the second-round clash with Argentina he won a penalty, then struck the goal of the tournament.

Owen's glittering career has presented numerous highlights, including a stunning two-goal tally to seize the FA Cup from Arsenal in 2001, and the marvellous hat-trick in the 5-1 demolition of Germany in a World Cup qualifier four months later. It was such performances which earned him the 2001 European Footballer of the Year award, the first British player to achieve that honour since Kevin Keegan in 1979. He celebrated, in true Owen style, by striking his hundredth goal for Liverpool in the same month.

His second World Cup in Japan & Korea in 2002 brought him goals against Denmark and Brazil. And the penalty he won in the game against Argentina in the "Group of Death" was instrumental in England's momentous defeat of their historic rivals.

In the summer of 2004 Owen left Anfield to join Beckham at Real Madrid. His season at the Bernebeu was a frustrating one. No one bettered his goal return in relation to minutes on the pitch, but fierce competition restricted his opportunities and Newcastle United paid a club record £17 million to bring him back to the Premiership. He recovered from an injury-hit domestic season in time for Germany 2006, but was left facing another long lay-off after suffering cruciate-ligament damage in the group decider against Sweden.

Owen made barely 70 appearances for the Magpies in his four-year spell at St James' Park, the end of his contract in 2009. A surprise move to Old Trafford followed, Sir Alex Ferguson snapping up a tried and tested goalscorer he could use as an impact player. Opportunities were limited, though Owen did get on the scoresheet in United's 2-1 win over Aston Villa in the 2010 League Cup Final. He left Old Trafford for Stoke with a one-in-three goal record, while his international strike rate of 40 goals in 89 games speaks volumes for his finishing ability. Owen hung up his boots lying fourth in the list of England sharpshooters.

United edge out Liverpool

United pipped Liverpool for the runners-up spot and automatic Champions League qualification, while Thierry Henry brought down the curtain on Highbury after 93 years with a hat-trick against Wigan, helping the Gunners clinch fourth place at Spurs' expense.

The relegation issues were settled before the final day. Sunderland set a new Premiership record in notching just 15 points, four less than when the Black Cats suffered the drop in 2002–03. Portsmouth, eight points adrift at one stage, had looked nailed on to join them. But with Harry Redknapp back at the helm, Pompey staged a remarkable revival, taking 20 points from nine games in the run-in to ensure their survival. Jubilation on the south coast, contrasted with long faces in the Midlands as Birmingham and West Brom joined the Championship-bound Mackems.

Replacing them were Reading, who suffered just two League defeats all season and broke the 100-point barrier, with Sheffield United taking the other automatic spot and Watford, tipped by many as relegation candidates, coming through via the play-offs. Hornets manager Adrian Boothroyd was a former number two to Kevin Blackwell at Leeds, and he got the better of his old boss in a match worth around £40 million, in cash terms said to be the biggest game in world football.

10-man Arsenal go down fighting

Arsene Wenger's men produced their most consistent form in the Champions League. Real Madrid and Juve were both swept aside in a sparkling run to the Final in Paris. There they faced favourites Barcelona, who had just retained their Primera Liga title. Arsenal took a first-half lead through a bullet Sol Campbell header, despite having been reduced to ten men. Jens Lehmann, the hero of the semis after his last-minute penalty save from Villareal's magician Juan Riquelme, was red-carded in the 20th minute for bringing down Eto'o. The Gunners fought bravely and had chances to put daylight between the sides, but conceded twice in the last fifteen minutes. They had set a new Champions League record of ten games without conceding, but the fans were left to reflect on what might have been if the game had been played out eleven against eleven.

It was England v Spain in the UEFA Cup Final, too. Middlesbrough pulled off two of the greatest Houdini acts of the modern era against FC Basel and Steaua Bucharest, hitting four goals against each at the Riverside to snatch victory from the jaws of defeat. There was no glorious send-off for Steve McClaren, in his last game before taking over the reins of the national team. Boro fell behind to a classy Sevilla outfit, and were picked off in the final quarter as they chased an equaliser. The better team won, though 4-0 was a harsh scoreline.

RIGHT: The Arsenal faithful trudge through the rain on the way to the towering new stand at Highbury, in December 1993.

OPPOSITE ABOVE: Steven Gerrard scores for Liverpool in their victory over West Ham United in the FA Cup Final.

OPPOSITE BELOW: The FA Cup was back in the Anfield trophy room for the seventh time, and Gerrard had turned in the kind of trademark performance, which would see him named PFA Player of the Year.

Gerrard inspires FA Cup victory

Liverpool were worthy FA Cup winners. They came back from 3-1 down to beat Luton 5-3 in the tie of the Third Round, then put out both Manchester United and Chelsea en route to a Millennium Stadium showdown with promoted West Ham. In a pulsating Final, the Hammers led 2-0, and 3-2 with seconds to go. But a year on from his inspired performance in Liverpool's dramatic Champions League victory, Steven Gerrard again led from the front. His stunning 90th-minute strike – his second of the match – took the game into extra-time, and he was also on target in the 3-1 shoot-out victory. The FA Cup was back in the Anfield trophy room for the seventh time, and Gerrard had turned in the kind of trademark performance which would see him named PFA Player of the Year.

Arsenal had a curate's egg of a season. They were beaten eleven times in the League, a far cry from the "Invincibles" of 2003–04. The Gunners came within seconds of going out to Doncaster Rovers in the last eight of the Carling Cup, surviving a shoot-out at Belle Vue before going down to Wigan in the semis. Arsenal appeared to be a club in transition, with players and pundits alike suggesting that Patrick Vieira's departure to Juventus had left a large void.

Steven Gerrard

A prime candidate for the accolade of the most complete midfielder of the modern era, Steven Gerrard has been a driving force in the Liverpool and England engine room since the turn of the millennium. A boyhood Reds fan, he was spotted by the club at the age of eight and made his first-team debut 10 years later, early in the 1998-99 season. As captain of England U-18s he was also soon part of the international set-up, winning his first senior cap under Kevin Keegan in May 2000 and scoring his first goal in the 5-1 mauling of Germany the following year. He was named PFA Young Player of the Year in 2001, the season in which Liverpool collected three trophies: League, FA and Uefa cups. In that remarkable European final against Alaves, Gerrard scored one of the goals in a 5-4 win. Even such high drama could not compare with the Champions League final in Istanbul four years later, where Gerrard, by now sporting the captain's armband, inspired one of the greatest comebacks in footballing history. His header early in the second half spurred the revival against an AC Milan side that had romped into a 3-0 lead. A year on from that famous shoot-out victory, Gerrard was at it again in the FA Cup final. With opponents West Ham holding a 2-0 advantage, he set up Cisse to pull one back, then lashed in an equaliser, only for the Hammers to retake the lead. A terrific last-minute strike from the skipper forced extra-time, and 'the Gerrard final" was complete when he also scored in the shoot-out, which Liverpool won to give him a second winners' medal. It was no surprise when he was named PFA Player of the Year for 2006, but as Liverpool slipped down the pecking order, opportunities to add to the medal collection became fewer and further between. Gerrard had to wait until 2012 and a third League Cup win for his next silverware. For pure personal glory he would have done better to consent when Chelsea wooed him. But "Stevie G" was a Red through and through, determined to succeed at Anfield.

As the exciting, new-look side took shape following the appointment of Brendan Rodgers in 2012, Gerrard remained the talisman. He assumed a deeper-lying quarterback role, where he pulled the strings as effectively as he did in his days as a rampaging box-to-box player. He weighed in with his share of goals, too, deadeye accuracy from the spot helping him overhaul Kenny Dalglish's 172-goal mark in a Liverpool shirt during the 2013-14 campaign. One of just eight England centurions, he captained the England side at Brazil 2014, and also has the distinction of being the only player to score in the final of both domestic cup competitions, the Champions League and Uefa Cup.

Arsene Wenger

The choice of this quietly spoken, cerebral polyglot raised a few eyebrows among Arsenal fans when he was named as the man to take over from Bruce Rioch in September 1996. But Wenger was a very experienced coach, well known and respected within footballing circles. In 1981 he became youth coach at Strasbourg, the club he had played for. He then had spells at Cannes and Nancy, but it was when he joined Monaco that he started to make a name for himself. He won the French League with Monaco in 1988, his attractive side including the mercurial talents of Glenn Hoddle and Chris Waddle. In 1997–98, less than two years after arriving at Highbury, Wenger masterminded a famous League and Cup Double. He repeated the feat in 2001–02, and it looked as if his outstanding team had taken Manchester United's mantle as the best in the Premiership. Arsenal looked on course for a third Double in five years in 2002–03, but the team faltered after a blistering start. The Gunners had to be content with runners-up to United, though they retained the FA Cup with a victory over Southampton. In 2003–04 Wenger's side completed its League programme unbeaten as the Gunners claimed their third Premiership crown of his reign. A year later, he brought the FA Cup to Highbury for the fourth time in eight years, Arsenal beating Manchester United on penalties in the Final. A rebuilt side packed with exciting young talent showed erratic League form in 2005–06 but reached the Champions League Final, going down to favourites Barcelona 2-1 in Paris.

It seemed only a matter of time before the "Professor" unearthed more gems and added to the trophy haul. But the barren years stacked up, and players brought in to replace the likes of Nasri, Fabregas and Van Persie concerned many Gooners. In 2014, when he passed the 1,000-game mark as Arsenal manager, the team added FA Cup victory over Hull City to an unbroken run of top-four finishes under his stewardship.

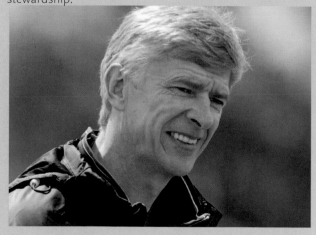

ABOVE: Sven Goran Eriksson and Steve McClaren during England's opening group match against Paraguay.

OPPOSITE BELOW: Steven Gerrard scores in England's group match against Sweden.

World Cup 2006: 40 years of hurt – and counting

England fans are hardy perennials when it comes to pre-tournament optimism, but in the run up to Germany 2006 the feeling abroad was even more hopeful than usual. The "golden generation" had cruised through the qualifying campaign, a draw in Austria and shock defeat in Northern Ireland the only blemishes in the ten-match series. England were named as one of the eight seeded countries, and the draw could scarcely have been more favourable.

The problems began as the clock ticked round to 9 June, and revolved round the first-choice strike partnership. Michael Owen had had an injury-hit season at Newcastle, and Rooney was stretchered off with a broken metatarsal in United's Championship showdown with Chelsea at Stamford Bridge. Both were included, but with only two other recognised strikers on the plane, Peter Crouch and surprise wildcard selection Theo Walcott, the firepower options looked thin.

The campaign got off to a dream start against Paraguay, David Beckham's third-minute free-kick skimming off the head of defender Carlos Gamarra for the only goal of the game. Next up were rank outsiders Trinidad and Tobago, who frustrated England until the 83rd minute, when Crouch rose to plant Beckham's cross past Shaka Hislop. Gerrard's left-foot screamer in injury-time sealed the win and confirmed England's place in the last 16 with a game to spare.

Owen limps out

The 38-year winless streak against Sweden continued in the group decider. Joe Cole volleyed into the top corner from 35 yards and then turned provider when his cross was met perfectly by Gerrard. However, defensive lapses from set pieces allowed Sweden to level twice. It was a case of job done, topping the group and thereby avoiding Germany in the last 16, but England had again failed to press home their advantage after a promising start.

David Beckham had come in for considerable criticism over his performances in the group matches but the skipper issued the perfect riposte with a trademark free-kick, which beat Ecuador in the first knockout round. Beckham became the first English player to score in three World Cups, his 30-yard curler setting up a mouthwatering clash with Portugal.

Shades of '98

The game proved to be an eerie reworking of France '98: a hotheaded moment from the young golden boy resulting in a red card; ten-man England valiantly holding out for the remainder of the match and extra-time, only to suffer an agonising shoot-out defeat. Back then it was Beckham, this time it was Rooney, red-carded just after the hour mark for a stamping incident involving Chelsea's Ricardo Carvalho. After a goalless 120 minutes, Portugal missed twice from the spot, but that open invitation to proceed to the semis was declined as Lampard, Gerrard and Carragher all fluffed their lines.

United Back on top

After ceding the Premiership title to rivals Arsenal and Chelsea for the past three seasons, Manchester United returned to the position of top dogs in 2006–07. Only Chelsea managed to hang on to United's coat-tails; Liverpool and Arsenal fought their own private battle for third place, 21 points adrift of the champions. Chelsea's faint hopes disappeared when they could manage only a 1-1 draw at the Emirates, while a Ronaldo penalty won the Manchester derby, results that left Mourinho's men with a seven-point deficit and just two games remaining. United were worthy champions, having won 28 games – four more than their nearest rivals – and found the net 83 times, 19 more than Chelsea.

BELOW: Wayne Rooney celebrates scoring Manchester United's third goal in the club's 4-2 victory over Everton at Goodison Park.

RGHT: Manchester United players celebrate with the Barclays League Trophy at the end of the 2006–07 season.

BELOW RIGHT: David Beckham, Steven Gerrard and Frank Lampard defend a Brazilian free-kick in the first international match to be staged at the new Wembley Stadium.

Sheffield United relegation controversy

The last relegation spot went down to the wire, with Sheffield United, West Ham and Wigan all fighting to preserve their top-table status on the final day of the season. The Blades and the Hammers were on 38 points, Wigan on 35. West Ham faced a daunting trip to Old Trafford, while Wigan could stay up on goal difference if they could win at Bramall Lane. Sheffield United, who had been 10 points clear of the drop zone at one stage, had the most favourable position, needing only a point at home to Wigan. They went down 2-1, the winner coming from a penalty converted by former Blade David Unsworth. News came through that a Carlos Tevez goal had beaten a United side with half an eye on the Cup Final, confirming the worst for Blades fans. It couldn't have been closer between Sheffield and Wigan: the figures in the Wins, Draws and Losses columns were identical, but, crucially, Wigan had a one-goal superior goal difference.

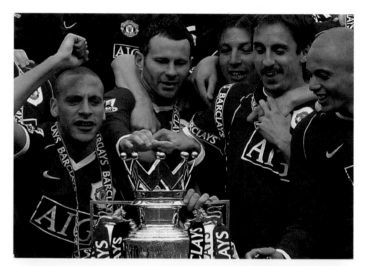

OPPOSITE ABOVE: John Terry and Frank Lampard celebrate Chelsea's 1-0 victory over Manchester United in the 2007 FA Cup.

OPPOSITE BELOW: Didier Drogba scores the winning goal in the Cup Final past Manchester United keeper Edwin van der Sar.

Drogba strikes for Mourinho's men

Chelsea missed out in the title race but had the consolation of doing the domestic cup double. They didn't have to face Manchester United in the Carling Cup, for the holders were dumped out by a Freddie Eastwood goal at Roots Hall. Southend were unlucky to go down at Spurs in the quarters, but League Two side Wycombe Wanderers went a stage further, the first time since Chester City in 1974-75 that a team from the fourth tier of English football had made it through to a League Cup semi-final. But it was two big guns who battled it out at the Millennium Stadium, Chelsea taking on an Arsenal side packed with Arsene Wenger's whiz kids. 17-year-old Theo Walcott drew first blood, his first goal for the Gunners putting him in the record books as the second youngest player to score in a domestic cup final, behind Norman Whiteside. Two goals by the Premiership's hotshot Didier Drogba meant that the trophy went to Stamford Bridge for the second time in three years.

In the FA Cup Manchester United faced top-division opposition in each round, as they had done in the victorious 1947-48 run under Matt Busby. Chelsea had an easier ride to the final, though they had to come back from 3-1 down to Spurs in the Sixth Round to force a replay, where Mourinho's men prevailed. An extra-time semi-final win over Blackburn carried Chelsea into the first final at the new Wembley Stadium. It was another extra-time goal that decided the showpiece, Drogba prodding the ball past the advancing van der Sar after playing a deft one-two with Lampard.

Didier Drogba

It is often said that a team is only as good as its strikers, and at his peak Didier Drogba was up there with the very best; a great technician who was also an intimidating physical presence. He was born in the Ivory Coast town of Abidjan, but spent large chunks of his childhood in France under the wing of an uncle who played professional football. His performances for Levallois, a club in the Parisian suburbs, attracted the attention of Paris Saint Germain, but Drogba opted instead for Le Mans. He was almost 24 when he finally tasted top-flight competition, after signing for Guingamp in January 2002 In his one full season at the club Drogba hit 17 goals, the division's third highest scorer. Marseille had finished just three points ahead of Guingamp, enough to clinch a Champions League spot, and Drogba was signed to bolster the attack for that campaign. He also helped Marseille reach the final of the Uefa Cup, where they went down to Valencia. When Mourinho moved to Stamford Bridge in summer 2004, the Ivorian was high on his shopping list. The fee was £24 million, which he began repaying before August was out by netting the first of the 157 goals he plundered in eight seasons with the Blues. His firepower was pivotal in three title-winning campaigns and four FA Cup wins, and he topped the Premier League's list of sharpshooters in 2006–07 and 2009–10 He relished the big occasion, setting a record by scoring in his fourth FA Cup final when he bagged the winner against Liverpool in the 2012 showpiece. With his last kick in a Chelsea shirt he slotted home the spot-kick that beat Bayern Munich in the 2011–12 Champions League final shoot-out, having scored a trademark bullet header in the dying seconds of normal time when his side was staring defeat in the face. Mourinho had long since departed, but the man who brought Drogba to Stamford Bridge was in no doubt that he was "one of the most important players in the history of the club".

After a spell playing in China, Drogba returned to European football with Galatasaray, with whom he picked up another championship medal. That paved the way for an emotional return to Stamford Bridge when the teams met in the knockout stage of the 2013–14 Champions League. Drogba finished on the losing end to a side helmed once again by Mourinho. The latter bemoaned the lack of world-class strikers at his disposal, and would surely have liked to have a young Drogba spearheading his attack.

Four years after making his international debut in 2002, Drogba was part of an Ivory Coast side that qualified for the World Cup finals for the first time. He is the Elephants' top goalscorer, and winner of the African Footballer of the Year award in 2006 and 2009

European domination

Chelsea and United also reached the semi-finals of the Champions League, along with Liverpool, who had put out holders Barcelona in the first knockout round. It was the first time that Premiership clubs had occupied three semi-final berths in the Champions League, and the bookies' odds suggested that the trophy was heading to England as the last of the quartet, AC Milan, were installed as outsiders.

Milan made a mockery of the betting with a crushing 5-3 aggregate victory over Manchester United. United took a narrow 3-2 lead to a rain-soaked San Siro, where they were comprehensively outplayed. Kaká added to the brace he bagged at Old Trafford after 11 minutes, and goals from Seedorf and Gilardino made it a forgettable evening for United fans. Liverpool heaped more semi-final misery on Chelsea, going through on penalties to set up a repeat of the extraordinary 2005 final, this time in Athens.

The Reds went behind on the stroke of half-time, Pippo Inzaghi deflecting a Pirlo free kick past Reina. Milan doubled their lead eight minutes from time when Inzaghi, played through by Kaká, rounded Reina to score from a narrow angle. Kuyt headed a late consolation but there was no repeat of the dramatic comeback in Istanbul.

RIGHT: Dirk Kuyt scores Liverpool's only goal as they go down 2-1 in the final to AC Milan at the Olympic Stadium in Athens.

BELOW: Joe Cole scores past José Reina in the UEFA Champions League semi-final between Chelsea and Liverpool at Stamford Bridge. Chelsea won the game 1-0

United and Chelsea contest the major honours

Manchester United and Chelsea occupied the top two spots in the Premiership for the third year running in 2007-08, and continued their battle royal in Moscow, where the teams contested a dramatic Champions League Final.

There was early-season turmoil in both camps. United dropped seven points in their first three games and found themselves at the wrong end of the table, the club's worst start to a Premiership campaign for a decade. It never looked to be anything other than a blip, however, and a run of 14 wins and a draw in their next 16 games put the reigning champions on course to defend their crown.

Mourinho exit

Chelsea's wobble – defeat at Villa, two points dropped at home to Blackburn and a tame draw against Rosenborg at the Bridge in the Champions League – had rather more significant fallout. Barely a month into the season it was announced that José Mourinho, the man who had spoken of building an all conquering dynasty at Chelsea, was leaving "by mutual consent". Despite guiding Chelsea to two championships and three domestic cups in just three years, the Special One paid the price for falling out of favour with his employers. Avram Grant, who had joined the club as director of football just two months earlier, was handed the top job and invited to follow an extremely tough act.

Chelsea's 2-1 defeat by Spurs in the Carling Cup Final was to set an unfortunate pattern for Grant; two more runners-up spots awaited him, and he would find that second place wasn't good enough for a club that had grown accustomed to amassing silverware.

Records fall to Giggs

Arsenal and Liverpool both remained unbeaten in the League until December, but it was United and Chelsea who were battling for the Premiership crown at the business end of the season. The teams met at Stamford Bridge with three games to go, United holding a three-point advantage. A Michael Ballack double gave Chelsea a 2-1 win and brought them level, though United remained top on goal difference. Both won their next games to take the race to the final game of the season. United went to Wigan knowing that victory would secure the championship; anything less could allow Chelsea, who were playing host to Bolton, to snatch the crown. In the event, it was Chelsea who faltered, conceding a late equaliser, though it hardly mattered as United ran out 2-0 winners at the JJB. Ronaldo bagged his 31st Premiership goal – he would find the net an astonishing 42 times in all competitions – while a Ryan Giggs strike ensured that the championship was on its way to Old Trafford yet again. It was Giggs's 758th outing in a United shirt, equalling Bobby Charlton's record. He would set a new mark in the Champions League Final.

LEFT: Fernando Torres slides in and beats Michael Essien to the ball to equalise for Liverpool in the Champions League Semi-final at Stamford Bridge. Chelsea won 3-2 after extra time.

217

Pompey play up

The 2008 FA Cup provided a breath of fresh air, ending a 12-year run in which the trophy had gone to one of the Big Four. Havant & Waterlooville of the Conference South encapsulated the giant-killing mood by twice taking the lead at Anfield before going down 5-2 in the Fourth Round. Championship strugglers Barnsley put the Reds out in the next round, and repeated the trick against Chelsea in the quarters. At the same stage a Sulley Muntari penalty gave Portsmouth victory over Manchester United, while Cardiff City's win at Boro meant that there was just one top-flight team in the last four, the first time that had happened in a hundred years. Not everyone put that down to the vagaries of cup football; Bobby Robson was among those who bemoaned the fact that some top teams appeared to be disrespecting the competition by fielding weakened sides.

A spectacular Joe Ledley volley settled the Cardiff-Barnsley semi, putting the Bluebirds into their first final since the historic win over Arsenal in 1927 They faced West Brom's conquerors Portsmouth, who prevailed in the showpiece courtesy of a Kanu goal. The Cup went to Fratton Park for only the second time in the club's history, the first having come 69 years earlier, on the eve of the Second World War.

England fail to qualify for Euro 2008

There was no little irony in the fact that while Premiership clubs dominated the Champions League, the national team failed to qualify for the finals of Euro 2008 Defeats in Croatia and Russia were setbacks, but being held to a goalless draw at home to Macedonia was a major body blow. Israel did England a huge favour by beating Russia in the final round of matches, which left Steve McClaren's men requiring just a point at home to a Croatia side that had already booked their place in Austria and Switzerland. England failed to grasp the lifeline. A 3-2 defeat meant that the team missed out on a major

tournament for the first time since the 1994 World Cup. There was a small crumb of comfort as Russia went on to reach the semi-finals, and Croatia came within a whisker of joining them, though it was of little consequence to McClaren, who had long since been shown the door.

FA appoint Capello

The FA again looked overseas for a replacement, appointing Fabio Capello, a coach with impeccable credentials. In 16 seasons of club management Capello had won nine championships with four different clubs in two countries. The two Serie A successes with Juventus were revoked in the wake of the corruption scandal that rocked Italian football, but Capello's CV was still first rate.

BELOW: Portsmouth's manager Harry Redknapp holds the FA Cup aloft following Portsmouth's 1-0 victory over Cardiff. It was Pompey's second FA Cup victory.

BOTTOM: The new England manager Fabio Capello watches his team against Trinidad at Port of Spain.

Europe:
big four make last eight

The Premiership's Big Four all made it through to the last eight of the Champions League, a record for the competition. Manchester United and Barcelona faced each other after comfortable wins over Roma and Schalke, respectively. Chelsea overturned a 2-1 defeat at Fenerbahce to set up yet another semi-final clash with Liverpool, who overcame Arsenal 5-3 on aggregate. It was the third time in four years the clubs had met in the last four, the Reds running out winners on the two previous occasions. Chelsea had their revenge this time, Drogba grabbing a brace in the 3-2 extra-time victory at the Bridge, after the game at Anfield had finished level. In the final they faced Manchester United, who saw off Barcelona with a 25-yard Paul Scholes drive in the home leg. Sir Alex Ferguson praised the pocket genius who had missed the 1999 final through suspension, confirming that he would be on the team-sheet for Moscow.

First all English Championship final

The first European Champions' Cup Final to be contested by two English clubs was all square after 120 minutes, Lampard's goal on the stroke of half-time cancelling out a Ronaldo header. Drogba saw red during an extra-time fracas, but United had little time to capitalise on the man advantage. Ronaldo, the Premiership's top scorer, missed from the spot, a lapse that paved the way for John Terry to shoot for cup glory. He slipped at the crucial moment and saw his effort rebound off the post. Chelsea blinked first in the sudden-death exchange, van der Sar saving from Anelka. Terry was inconsolable as United celebrated being crowned kings of Europe for the third time on the 50th anniversary of the Munich disaster.

ABOVE LEFT: United's Christiano Ronaldo scores to put his team into the lead.

ABOVE: John Terry shoots for cup glory but slips at the crucial moment and sees his effort rebound off the post. Terry was inconsolable as United went on to win after van der Sar saved Anelka's spot-kick.

LEFT: Manchester United players pictured after winning the Champions League Cup. United celebrated being crowned kings of Europe for the third time on the 50th anniversary of the Munich disaster.

United match Liverpool's league record

There was a time when talk of Doubles and Trebles was regarded as fantasy football. The elite clubs had shown that such giddy heights were indeed attainable, and the fans, with inflationary zeal, were already looking for the next target. Midway through the 2008-09 season, the buzz on the Old Trafford terraces was all about United's bid for an unprecedented Quintuple.

The reigning champions, bolstered by the arrival of £30 million striker Dimitar Berbatov, deposited one trophy in the cabinet before Christmas by winning the World Club Cup, beating LDU Quito in the final. Next up was the Carling Cup Final and a shoot-out victory over Spurs. United were in a rich vein of form, underpinned by a near-impregnable defence. When Roque Santa Cruz scored at Old Trafford on 21 February, it was the first goal United had conceded in the Premiership since the 2-1 defeat at Arsenal on 8 November. Edwin van der Sar's run of 1,334 minutes without picking the ball out of the net smashed Petr Cech's record.

Liverpool's double consolation

Liverpool ran United close, and completed a League double over their arch-rivals with a stunning 4-1 win at Old Trafford in March. United then lost at Fulham, but steadied the ship by reeling off seven straight victories. The title was secured with a game to spare, United ending the campaign four points clear of the Reds, whose record of 18 championships they had now equalled. Benitez's side had undoubtedly closed the gap, losing just twice in the League. No team had ever failed to take the League crown with such a record, but a double-digit figure in the Draws column proved costly; United's 28 wins was the key statistic. It was the 11th title of the Ferguson era – Ryan Giggs playing a part in each of those glorious campaigns – and the second time that United had completed a hat-trick of championships.

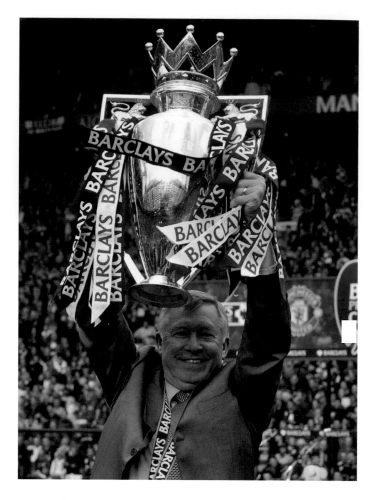

ABOVE: Sir Alex Ferguson celebrates another Premiership title following the game against Arsenal at Old Trafford.

BELOW: Liverpool's Yossi Benayoun scores against Newcastle. At the end of the season the Magpies were relegated to the Championship after 16 years in the top flight.

Wayne Rooney

After watching 16-year-old Wayne Rooney score a brilliant winner against his Arsenal team in October 2002, a goal that ended the Gunners' 30-match unbeaten run, Arsene Wenger said he was the most exciting young talent in English football. Sir Alex Ferguson went even further, describing Rooney as "the best young player this country has seen in the past 30 years" after obtaining his signature in summer 2004

Growing up in Croxteth, the young Rooney was a staunch Evertonian. He joined the club's academy after being spotted at the age of nine, and his stocky build, allied to the precocious talent, meant he was soon competing with older age groups. Manager David Moyes handed him his senior debut in August 2002, two months short of his 17th birthday, and he was soon on the record-breaking trail: Everton's youngest goalscorer, England's then-youngest international – he won his first cap against Australia in February 2003 – and the youngest player to find the net for the national team when he scored against Macedonia in September 2003 At 17 years 317 days, he took the latter record from team-mate Michael Owen. That first international goal was in a Euro 2004 qualifier, and the following summer Rooney lit up the tournament, his four goals and sparkling performances inviting comparisons with the impact made by Pelé at the 1958 World Cup. Following his move to United two months later, a deal worth around £25 million, Rooney wasted no time justifying the tag of hottest property in English football. Since striking a hat-trick on his Old Trafford debut against Fenerbahce, he has contributed hugely to United's five championship wins and picked up two League Cup winners' medals. He was also a key member of the side that brought the Champions League trophy back to Old Trafford in 2008 Individual honours include the PFA Young Player of the Year, which he won in his first two seasons at United. In 2010 he took both the senior award and the Football Writers' equivalent, the latter being the original, prestigious honour first awarded to Stanley Matthews in 1948 In 2013-14, when he turned 28, Rooney passed Jack Rowley's 211 goals for the Red Devils, moving him into third on the all-time list behind Bobby Charlton and Denis Law. Charlton's record 249 haul lay well within reach. He was also well to the fore in the Premier League sharpshooters' list, within touching distance of third-placed Thierry Henry (175) and Andrew Cole (187). Even Alan Shearer's table-topping 260 goals was within his compass.

If there was one uncertain note against Rooney's name when compared to the very best, it was in the international arena. Thirty-eight goals for England going into the 2014 World Cup put him within 11 of the record – also held by Charlton – but many felt he had yet to take a tournament by the scruff of the neck as other of the game's greats had done. He was red-carded against Portugal in the quarter-final of the 2006 World Cup, and South Africa four years later was also forgettable. That Euro 2004 quartet remains the high watermark of his international career – his only other tournament goal came at Euro 2012 – yet he remains the go-to player, the talisman most likely to end England's long wait for silverware.

ABOVE: Wayne Rooney and Dimitar Berbatov, who arrived from Spurs for £30 million at the start of the season, celebrate winning the Premier League title. The title was secured with a game to spare, United ending the campaign four points clear of Liverpool, whose record of 18 championships they had now equalled.

Saha's record strike in vain

Manchester United's bid for a clean sweep ended with an FA Cup semi-final defeat at the hands of Everton. Sir Alex Ferguson had reached that stage eight times and never tasted defeat, but came unstuck as an under-strength side went down on penalties. Everton had put already put out Liverpool and Villa, and faced yet another top-six side in the final, Chelsea. Louis Saha gave the Merseysiders a dream start with a goal after 25 seconds, the fastest in the competition's history. Chelsea equalised through a Drogba header and Lampard's left-foot drive ensured that the cup was going to Stamford Bridge for the fifth time. It was a red-letter day for Ashley Cole, who became the first player in over a century to pick up five winners' medals.

No Euro repeat for Ferguson

The Premiership's Big Four all reached the Champions League quarter-finals once again. Arsenal and United eased into the last four with wins over Villareal and Porto, but the tie of the round was a Liverpool-Chelsea clash that brought an avalanche of goals. Chelsea went through 7-5 on aggregate to book their fifth semi-final berth in six years.

United brushed Arsenal aside in the semis, and a repeat of the 2008 final looked to be on the cards when Chelsea returned from the Nou Camp with a 0-0 draw. Hiddink's men also nullified Barcelona's much-vaunted attack for 90 minutes in the home leg, and seemed to be heading for the final, thanks to Essien's thunderous volley. The game was turned on its head deep into injury time

Paul Scholes

Famously taciturn off the pitch, Paul Scholes was a player who did his talking on it, a vital cog in Manchester United's midfield for 15 years and "a beautiful player to watch", according to no less a figure than Sir Bobby Charlton. This Salford-born maestro made his first-team debut aged 19 in September 1994, the latest of "Fergie's Fledglings" to be promoted from a star-packed youth side. Diminutive in stature, he was a pocket dynamo whose range of passing, vision and eye for goal put him firmly in the world-class bracket. The only string lacking in his bow was tackling. Rash challenges often had referees reaching into their pocket, but there were always team-mates to make up any shortfall in that department; better to leave a master technician to do what he did best. When he was a fixture in the United engine room, the team were champions on 11 occasions, and he collected three FA Cup winners' medals. Though suspension forced him to miss the famous night in 1999 when United snatched Champions League victory from under Bayern Munich's noses, he was an integral part of that Treble-winning campaign. Nine years later, he was in the side that overcame Chelsea on penalties to bring United their second European crown under Ferguson, having scored a screamer to put out Barcelona in the semis.

Arguably, the national side didn't get the best from one of the undoubted jewels of the modern era. First capped in 1997, Scholes had his moments in an England shirt: his stunner against Tunisia at France '98 stands out, along with a hat-trick against Poland in a Euro 2000 qualifier and the brace against Scotland in a Hampden Park play-off that booked England's place in the finals of the tournament. Often played out wide to accommodate a glut of attacking midfielders during Sven-Goran Erikkson's reign, Scholes had had enough after Euro 2004 He quit international football at the age of 29, when many thought the team should have been built around him. Most would regard 66 caps as an injustice to his talent.

The flame-haired magician continued to weave his spells on the pitch for seven more years in a United shirt, and even when he stood down in summer 2011 to join the Old Trafford coaching staff, Ferguson had no qualms about bringing the 37-year-old back into the playing fold for an autumn flourish. Class, as the saying goes, is permanent. He retired at the end of the 2012–13 season, his 718 appearances in a United shirt putting him third behind Giggs and Charlton in the club's appearance chart. A magnificent servant to United during a golden era, the naturally reticent Scholes would of course leave it to others to assess his immense contribution to the game.

when Chelsea's rock-solid defence opened up fleetingly, enough for Iniesta to find the top corner from the edge of the box. There were unedifying scenes as Chelsea players berated the Norwegian referee, who had rejected several penalty claims.

Many thought a Barça team shorn of three first-choice defenders would struggle to contain Rooney, Ronaldo and Co., but it was La Liga's champions who played to their potential, while the United machine, for once, misfired. Xavi and Iniesta were the orchestrators-in-chief, while Eto'o and Messi struck in each half to consign United to their first defeat in a major European final. United had to settle for three trophies, and their 67-year-old manager immediately began planning for the acquisition of further silverware with a squad he regarded as the best in his 23 years at Old Trafford.

RIGHT: Didier Drogba scores Chelsea's first goal in their 2-1 victory over Everton in the 2009 FA Cup Final. Saha had put the Merseyside ahead after only 25 seconds.

BELOW: Man of the Match Lionel Messi takes on Wayne Rooney and Michael Carrick in the Champions League Final at the Stadio Olympico, Rome. Barcelona went on to win the game 2-0

OPPOSITE: Paul Scholes on the ball during in Osaka during the 2002 World Cup.

Welsh Premier League 1992–2004

1992–93

1	Cwmbran Town	87
2	Inter Cardiff	83
3	Aberystwyth Town	78
4	Ebbw Vale AFC	66
5	Bangor City	64
6	Holywell Town	59
7	Conwy United	57
8	Gap Connah's Quay	55
9	Porthmadog FC	53
10	Haverfordwest County	53
11	Caersws FC	52
12	Afan Lido	52
13	Mold Alexandra	51
14	Llanelli AFC	41
15	Maesteg Park	40
16	Flint Town United	39
17	Briton Ferry Athletic	39
18	Newtown AFC	36
19	Llanidloes Town	30
20	Abergavenny Thursdays	28

1993–94

1	Bangor City	83
2	Inter Cardiff	81
3	Ton Pentre AFC	71
4	Flint Town United	66
5	Holywell Town	64
6	Newtown AFC	63
7	Gap Connah's Quay	57
8	Cwmbran Town	57
9	Ebbw Vale AFC	57
10	Aberystwyth Town	55
11	Porthmadog FC	49
12	Llanelli AFC	46
13	Conwy United	45
14	Mold Alexandra	43
15	Afan Lido	40
16	Haverfordwest County	40
17	Caersws FC	39
18	The New Saints	34
19	Maesteg Park	33
20	Briton Ferry Athletic	33

1994–95

1	Bangor City	88
2	Afan Lido	79
3	Ton Pentre AFC	77
4	Newtown AFC	68
5	Cwmbran Town	67
6	Flint Town United	63
7	Barry Town	59
8	Holywell Town	58
9	The New Saints	55
10	Inter Cardiff	53
11	Rhyl FC	53
12	Conwy United	49
13	Ebbw Vale AFC	45
14	Caersws FC	44
15	Gap Connah's Quay	43
16	Porthmadog FC	40
17	Aberystwyth Town	39
18	Llanelli AFC	36
19	Mold Alexandra	34
20	Maesteg Park	12

1995–96

1	Barry Town	97
2	Newtown AFC	80
3	Conwy United	76
4	Bangor City	69
5	Flint Town United	66
6	Caernarfon Town	61
7	Cwmbran Town	57
8	Caersws FC	55
9	Inter Cardiff	54
10	Gap Connah's Quay	53
11	Ebbw Vale AFC	53
12	The New Saints	52
13	Porthmadog FC	50
14	Aberystwyth Town	48
15	Cemaes Bay FC	46
16	Holywell Town	43
17	Briton Ferry Athletic	42
18	Rhyl FC	42
19	Ton Pentre AFC	40
20	Afan Lido	36
21	Llanelli AFC	31

1996–97

1	Barry Town	105
2	Inter Cardiff	84
3	Ebbw Vale AFC	78
4	Caernarfon Town	78
5	Newtown AFC	71
6	The New Saints	69
7	Conwy United	68
8	Bangor City	65
9	Cwmbran Town	65
10	Porthmadog FC	62
11	Gap Connah's Quay	57
12	Cemaes Bay FC	49
13	Aberystwyth Town	47
14	Caersws FC	42
15	Flint Town United	41
16	Carmarthen Town	40
17	Technogroup Welshpool	39
18	Ton Pentre AFC	39
19	Rhyl FC	38
20	Holywell Town	29
21	Briton Ferry Athletic	16

1997–98

1	Barry Town	104
2	Newtown AFC	78
3	Ebbw Vale AFC	77
4	Inter Cardiff	74
5	Cwmbran Town	73
6	Bangor City	68
7	Gap Connah's Quay	66
8	Rhyl FC	61
9	Conwy United	53
10	Aberystwyth Town	51
11	Caersws FC	46
12	Carmarthen Town	44
13	Caernarfon Town	43
14	The New Saints	42
15	Rhayader Town	39
16	Haverfordwest County	38
17	Porthmadog FC	35
18	Flint Town United	34
19	Technogroup Welshpool	25
20	Cemaes Bay FC	9

1998–99

1	Barry Town	76
2	Inter Cardiff	63
3	Cwmbran Town	57
4	Aberystwyth Town	57
5	Caernarfon Town	50
6	Newtown AFC	49
7	Conwy United	49
8	The New Saints	47
9	Carmarthen Town	47
10	Caersws FC	44
11	Bangor City	39
12	Gap Connah's Quay	38
13	Haverfordwest County	34
14	Afan Lido	31
15	Rhayader Town	26
16	Rhyl FC	23
17	Holywell Town	18

1999–2000

1	The New Saints	76
2	Barry Town	74
3	Cwmbran Town	69
4	Carmarthen Town	69
5	Llanelli AFC	66
6	Aberystwyth Town	61
7	Gap Connah's Quay	57
8	Newtown AFC	48
9	Bangor City	48
10	Afan Lido	46
11	Rhyl FC	44
12	Caersws FC	41
13	Cefn Druids	41
14	Rhayader Town	34
15	Inter Cardiff	30
16	Haverfordwest County	29
17	Conwy United	23
18	Caernarfon Town	11

2000–01

1	Barry Town	77
2	Cwmbran Town	74
3	Carmarthen Town	58
4	Newtown AFC	58
5	Caersws FC	57
6	Aberystwyth Town	55
7	Rhyl FC	54
8	The New Saints	54
9	Gap Connah's Quay	50
10	Haverfordwest County	49
11	Afan Lido	47
12	Rhayader Town	40
13	Cefn Druids	38
14	Bangor City	37
15	Oswestry Town	36
16	Port Talbot Town	35
17	Llanelli AFC	29
18	Inter Cardiff	13

2001–02

1	Barry Town	77
2	The New Saints	70
3	Bangor City	69
4	Caersws FC	58
5	Afan Lido	58
6	Rhyl FC	56
7	Cwmbran Town	55
8	Gap Connah's Quay	51
9	Aberystwyth Town	51
10	Carmarthen Town	48
11	Caernarfon Town	44
12	Port Talbot Town	43
13	Newtown AFC	38
14	Cefn Druids	32
15	Llanelli AFC	31
16	Oswestry Town	30
17	Haverfordwest County	28
18	Rhayader Town	15

2002–03

1	Barry Town	83
2	The New Saints	80
3	Bangor City	71
4	Aberystwyth Town	60
5	Gap Connah's Quay	59
6	Rhyl FC	58
7	Afan Lido	52
8	Caersws FC	51
9	Cwmbran Town	50
10	Newtown AFC	42
11	Port Talbot Town	39
12	Cefn Druids	38
13	Haverfordwest County	35
14	Caernarfon Town	34
15	Carmarthen Town	32
16	Oswestry Town	28
17	Technogroup Welshpool	28
18	Llanelli AFC	17

2003–04

1	Rhyl FC	77
2	The New Saints	76
3	Haverfordwest County	62
4	Aberystwyth Town	59
5	Caersws FC	55
6	Bangor City	54
7	Cwmbran Town	48
8	Gap Connah's Quay	42
9	Caernarfon Town	42
10	Newtown AFC	41
11	Port Talbot Town	39
12	Porthmadog FC	36
13	Cefn Druids	35
14	Afan Lido	32
15	Technogroup Welshpool	25
16	Carmarthen Town	20
17	Barry Town	16

Welsh Premiership League 2005–2009

2004–05

1	The New Saints	78
2	Rhyl FC	74
3	Bangor City	67
4	Haverfordwest County	63
5	Caersws FC	62
6	Carmarthen Town	61
7	Cwmbran Town	53
8	Aberystwyth Town	53
9	Technogroup Welshpool	51
10	Newtown AFC	46
11	Porthmadog FC	45
12	Gap Connah's Quay	36
13	Port Talbot Town	29
14	Llanelli AFC	29
15	Caernarfon Town	28
16	Airbus UK Broughton	24
17	Cefn Druids	22
18	Afan Lido	21

2007–08

1	Llanelli AFC	85
2	The New Saints	78
3	Rhyl FC	69
4	Port Talbot Town	59
5	Bangor City	55
6	Carmarthen Town	54
7	Neath FC	54
8	Haverfordwest County	47
9	Aberystwyth Town	46
10	Technogroup Welshpool	46
11	Airbus UK Broughton	42
12	Cefn Druids	38
13	Newtown AFC	37
14	Caernarfon Town	36
15	Gap Connah's Quay	34
16	Porthmadog FC	27
17	Caersws FC	26
18	Llangefni Town	24

2005–06

1	The New Saints	86
2	Llanelli AFC	68
3	Rhyl FC	64
4	Carmarthen Town	57
5	Port Talbot Town	56
6	Technogroup Welshpool	54
7	Aberystwyth Town	52
8	Haverfordwest County	50
9	Bangor City	45
10	Caersws FC	45
11	Porthmadog FC	44
12	Gap Connah's Quay	38
13	Caernarfon Town	37
14	Cefn Druids	32
15	Airbus UK Broughton	32
16	Newtown AFC	31
17	Cwmbran Town	19
18	Cardiff Grange Quins	15

2008–09

1	Rhyl FC	90
2	Llanelli AFC	83
3	The New Saints	71
4	Carmarthen Town	62
5	Port Talbot Town	56
6	Bangor City	55
7	Haverfordwest County	55
8	Aberystwyth Town	46
9	Gap Connah's Quay	41
10	Newtown AFC	40
11	Technogroup Welshpool	40
12	Airbus UK Broughton	39
13	Cefn Druids	34
14	Neath FC	34
15	Prestatyn Town	33
16	Porthmadog FC	32
17	Caersws FC	25
18	Caernarfon Town	20

2006–07

1	The New Saints	76
2	Rhyl FC	69
3	Llanelli AFC	63
4	Technogroup Welshpool	60
5	Gap Connah's Quay	56
6	Port Talbot Town	51
7	Carmarthen Town	50
8	Aberystwyth Town	48
9	Bangor City	48
10	Haverfordwest County	39
11	Porthmadog FC	35
12	Airbus UK Broughton	29
13	Cefn Druids	28
14	Caersws FC	27
15	Caernarfon Town	26
16	Newtown AFC	24
17	Cwmbran Town	20

The Welsh Premier League was formed in October 1991 by the Football Association of Wales (FAW). The FAW, along with the other three home nations' associations (The Football Association, Irish Football Association and Scottish Football Association), had a permanent seat on the International Football Association Board. Traditionally, the strongest teams in Wales had always played in the English leagues. Aberdare Athletic, Cardiff City, Merthyr Town, Newport County, Swansea City and Wrexham have all been members of the Football League.

BELOW: Born in Cardiff to Welsh parents, Ryan Giggs (left) became one of the finest footballers of his generation. When he made his international debut in 1991, Giggs broke the record as the youngest debutant for Wales. He went on to win 64 caps.

Scottish Premier League 2000–2009

1999–2000

1	Rangers	90
2	Celtic	69
3	Hearts	54
4	Motherwell	52
5	St Johnstone	42
6	Hibernian	41
7	Dundee	41
8	Dundee United	39
9	Kilmarnock	37
10	Aberdeen	33

2000–01

1	Celtic	97
2	Rangers	82
3	Hibernian	66
4	Kilmarnock	54
5	Hearts	52
6	Dundee	47
7	Aberdeen	45
8	Motherwell	43
9	Dunfermline Athletic	42
10	St Johnstone	40
11	Dundee United	35
12	St Mirren	30

2001–02

1	Celtic	103
2	Rangers	85
3	Livingston	58
4	Aberdeen	55
5	Kilmarnock	49
6	Hearts	48
7	Dundee United	46
8	Dunfermline Athletic	45
9	Dundee	44
10	Hibernian	41
11	Motherwell	40
12	St Johnstone	21

2002–03

1	Rangers	97
2	Celtic	97
3	Hearts	63
4	Kilmarnock	57
5	Hibernian	51
6	Aberdeen	49
7	Dunfermline Athletic	46
8	Dundee	44
9	Livingston	35
10	Partick Thistle	35
11	Dundee United	32
12	Motherwell	28

2003–04

1	Celtic	98
2	Rangers	81
3	Hearts	68
4	Dunfermline Athletic	53
5	Dundee United	49
6	Motherwell	46
7	Dundee	46
8	Hibernian	44
9	Livingston	43
10	Kilmarnock	42
11	Aberdeen	34
12	Partick Thistle	26

2004–05

1	Rangers	93
2	Celtic	92
3	Hibernian	61
4	Aberdeen	61
5	Hearts	50
6	Motherwell	48
7	Kilmarnock	49
8	Inverness CT	44
9	Dundee United	36
10	Livingston	35
11	Dunfermline Athletic	34
12	Dundee	33

2005–06

1	Celtic	91
2	Hearts	74
3	Rangers	73
4	Hibernian	56
5	Kilmarnock	55
6	Aberdeen	54
7	Inverness CT	58
8	Motherwell	49
9	Dundee United	33
10	Falkirk	33
11	Dunfermline Athletic	33
12	Livingston	18

2006–07

1	Celtic	84
2	Rangers	72
3	Aberdeen	65
4	Hearts	61
5	Kilmarnock	55
6	Hibernian	49
7	Falkirk	50
8	Inverness CT	46
9	Dundee United	42
10	Motherwell	38
11	St Mirren	36
12	Dunfermline Athletic	32

2007–08

1	Celtic	89
2	Rangers	86
3	Motherwell	60
4	Aberdeen	53
5	Dundee United	52
6	Hibernian	52
7	Falkirk	49
8	Hearts	48
9	Inverness CT	43
10	St Mirren	41
11	Kilmarnock	40
12	Gretna	13

2008–09

1	Rangers	86
2	Celtic	82
3	Hearts	59
4	Aberdeen	53
5	Dundee Utd	53
6	Hibernian	47
7	Motherwell	48
8	Kilmarnock	44
9	Hamilton	41
10	Falkirk	38
11	St Mirren	37
12	Inverness CT	37

BELOW: Hartson can't contain his joy after scoring Celtic's second goal in the 2-0 victory over Liverpool in 2003

Scottish Cup Finals

2000	Rangers	v	Aberdeen	4-0
2001	Celtic	v	Hibernian	3-0
2002	Rangers	v	Celtic	3-2
2003	Rangers	v	Dundee	1-0
2004	Celtic	v	Dunfermline Athletic	3-1
2005	Celtic	v	Dundee United	1-0
2006	Heart of Midlothian	v	Gretna	4-2 (ET and Penalties)
2007	Celtic	v	Dunfermline Athletic	1-0
2008	Rangers	v	Queen of the South	3-2
2009	Rangers	v	Falkirk	1-0

Hearts separate Old Firm

Between 1980 and 1999 Rangers and Celtic occupied the top two League places on five occasions. In the other 15 seasons either the champions or runners-up spot went to a team outside the Big Two. In the 2000s the SPL took on a more regular pattern; only Hearts in 2005-06 managed to separate the Old Firm. Celtic won six championships, Rangers four, and between them the Glasgow giants appropriated the cup silverware 17 of the 20 times it was fought for. Predictability was laced with romance in the shape of some notable giant-killing acts in the cup competitions, proving that hope springs eternal on a football pitch.

One of those slayings came in the 1999-2000 Scottish Cup, when Celtic were humbled by Division One part-timers Inverness Caledonian Thistle, prompting the famous headline "Super Caley Go Ballistic Celtic Are Atrocious". Celtic finished the season a country mile behind Rangers, and a League Cup win was never going to be enough to save John Barnes. Aberdeen, defeated in both Cup Finals that year, propped up the SPL and should have faced a play-off as the top division was expanded to 12 clubs. The fact that Falkirk's ground wasn't up to scratch meant Division One's top two, St Mirren and Dunfermline, were promoted and Aberdeen's status was preserved.

Martin O'Neill arrived at Celtic Park in summer 2000 and landed the treble in his first season. Henrik Larsson was on unstoppable form, hitting 53 goals in all competitions. Rangers, by contrast, didn't get the expected return for the £12 million expended on Tore André Flo, a record deal for the SPL.

Cup glory for Livingston

Livingston won promotion to the SPL that term, and the team that operated as Meadowbank Thistle until the mid-1990s enjoyed a fine couple of seasons. They finished third in 2001-02 and won the League Cup two years later. Hibs, the team they vanquished in that 2004 final, must have thought they'd done the hard work knocking out Celtic and Rangers.

Alex McLeish succeeded Dick Advocaat in December 2001, and within six months he had both domestic cups in the cabinet. Celtic had the last word in the League, though, finishing 18 points clear of their rivals. While the Big Two continued the carve-up, Division One runners-up Airdrieonians went out of business, the first club to go under since Third Lanark in 1967. Airdrie United rose from the ashes, and with fresh backing entered the League after buying out another crisis-hit outfit, Clydebank.

Above: John Hartson on the attack for Celtic in the UEFA Cup quarter-final, Second Leg match against Liverpool at Anfield on 20 March 2003

Right: Marvin Andrews playing for Rangers, when he won the double of the League Cup and the Scottish Premier League title in 2005. His career included a spell at Livingston, with whom he won the Scottish League Cup in 2004

O'Neill steps down

Rangers completed a seventh treble in 2002-03 The League finale was a nail-biter, Gers taking it with a one-goal superior goal difference. Celtic were again beaten by Caley Thistle in the Cup, lost the League Cup Final to Rangers and also went down to Porto in the UEFA Cup Final. The Hoops clinched the 2003-04 Championship with room to spare, and Barcelona-bound Larsson signed off with a brace in the 3-1 win over Dunfermline in the Cup Final. Celtic were rocked by two late Motherwell goals on the final day of the following season, defeat at Fir Park allowing Rangers – 1-0 winners at Easter Road – to snatch the title by a point. Celtic suffered a further blow as O'Neill stepped down for personal reasons. His successor, Gordon Strachan, won the League at the first attempt, with Hearts providing the main threat. Neither George Burley nor Graham Rix lasted long at Tynecastle; it

seemed that owner Vladimir Romanov fancied himself as manager too. Celtic suffered another shock defeat to Division One Clyde in the Cup, but overcame Dunfermline in the League Cup Final. All the players wore a No.7 shirt to mark the passing of "Jinky" Johnstone. Hearts lifted the Scottish Cup, beating Gretna on penalties in the final. Gretna had been admitted to the League just four years earlier, and after three successive promotions had a brief taste of the top flight before the pack of cards collapsed. The club went into administration and resigned from the League in 2008, but had the memory of becoming the first third-tier side to reach the Cup Final.

LEFT: Ronald Waterreus playing for for Glasgow Rangers during a Premier League match against Livingston. He joined Rangers in 2005 and quickly established himself as first choice goalkeeper. He was also involved in Rangers' historic 2005-06 Champions League run where they reached the knockout stage for the first time.

ABOVE: Nacho Novo in action for Rangers in 2005 It was Novo's superb strike that brought victory over Falkirk in the 2009 Cup Final.

OPPOSITE LEFT: Celtic's goalkeeper Artur Boruc watches the ball as Arsenal's Eduardo attempts to round him during the Champions League second leg match at Arsenal's Emirates Stadium in 2009 A penalty was awarded to Arsenal as Boruc was judged to have made contact with the Arsenal forward.

OPPOSITE RIGHT: Neil Lennon in action for Celtic against Motherwell. Lennon was made manager on a temporary basis following the departure of Tony Mowbray in March 2010, an appointment that was later made permanent as results improved.

Smith returns to Ibrox

Alex McLeish left Ibrox in 2006, having taken Rangers to the last 16 of the Champions League, the first Scottish club to do so. After Paul Le Guen's brief, unhappy stay, Rangers turned to Walter Smith, revered for his triumphs in the 1990s. The team's form picked up dramatically, though not enough to prevent Celtic from winning the League. The Hoops emulated Rangers by reaching the Champions League knockout stage, beaten narrowly by AC Milan. In 2007-08, Strachan matched Jock Stein's achievement of winning the League title in his first three years. Rangers, who had been on for a quadruple, lost the League on the final day and went down to Zenit St Petersburg in the Uefa Cup Final. Consolation came with a domestic cup double.

2008-09 was another final-day decider, Rangers getting the win they needed at Tannadice to take top honours, while a Nacho Novo screamer brought victory over Falkirk in the Cup Final. Gordon Strachan added a League Cup win over Rangers to his tally before leaving Parkhead. Ex-player Tony Mowbray didn't last a season, Neil Lennon promoted from within to steady the ship. Results improved – apart from a shock Cup defeat to Division One side Ross County – and Lennon was given the job on a permanent basis. Ross County couldn't repeat the magic in the Cup Final against Dundee United, the latest fairytale that didn't quite have a romantic ending.

Failed to Qualify

The 2000s was a barren decade for the national team, which failed to qualify for any of the major championships. The closest Scotland came was a play-off against England for a place at Euro 2000 A Don Hutchinson goal gave the Scots victory at Wembley, but two Paul Scholes goals at Hampden put England through on aggregate. Craig Brown left in 2001 after failing to get the team to the World Cup, ushering in a disastrous run of results under Berti Vogts. Walter Smith, Alex McLeish and George Burley all came and went between 2004 and 2009 Burley had a particularly torrid time, winning just three of 14 games in his 22-month tenure, and having to deal with considerable internal strife. The SFA turned to Dundee United boss Craig Levein to halt the slide and lead Scotland to their first championship since France '98.

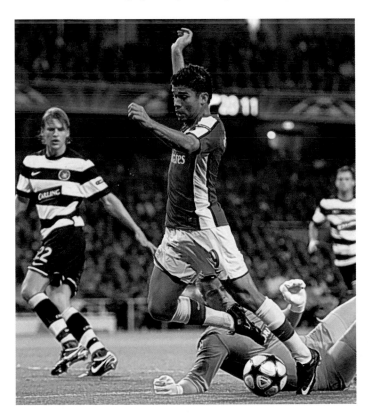

2010–present day
A Global Game

The new decade saw the arrival of a new Mancunian powerhouse in the English game. Backed by Abu Dhabi money, City showed they were more than mere "noisy neighbours" with two championships in three years. Sir Alex bowed out, United faltered. Financial Fair Play sought to force clubs to live within their means. Wealth and league position dovetailed, but romance was alive and well as Wigan Athletic lifted the Cup. If Spain and Germany had the edge in European competition, the Premier League remained untouchable as a spectacle, attracting massive global audiences.

2010 At the World Cup in South Africa England lose to Germany 4-1 in the second round

2010 Atletico Madrid beat Fulham 2-1 in the inaugural Europa League Final

2010 Chelsea complete League and FA Cup Double

2010 Portsmouth become the first English top-flight club to go into administration

2011 The Nations Cup, a revived home International Championship minus England, is contested

2012 Roy Hodgson replaces Fabio Capello as England coach

2012 Rangers enter administration

2012 Manchester City win the Premier League for the first time in 44 years

2012 Chelsea win the Champions League

2013 Sir Alex Ferguson steps down as Manchester United manager after winning his 13th championship in 26 years

2013 Wigan Athletic become the first FA Cup winners to be relegated

2013 Chelsea win the Europa League

2013 Gareth Bale joins Real Madrid for a world record £85 million

2013 Goal-line technology introduced in the Premier League

2014 David Moyes sacked after less than a season in charge at Old Trafford. Louis van Gaal replaces him

2014 Celtic secure their 45th championship in March, the earliest title winners for 85 years

2014 St Johnstone win the Scottish Cup, their first major honour

Chelsea double up

Manchester United went into the 2009-10 season seeking a record fourth straight championship, the all-important 19th that would put them clear of Liverpool in the all-time list. They would have to do it without the firepower of Ronaldo and Tévez, who headed to the Bernabéu and Eastlands, respectively. Free transfer Michael Owen was handed Ronaldo's No. 7 shirt, with Antonio Valencia joining from Wigan.

The League developed into a two-horse race, United vying with Carlo Ancelotti's Chelsea. Arsenal were secure in third, while Liverpool's decline – seventh place, with double figures in the losses column – meant the top four would have a new entrant for the first time in five years. Chelsea held a one-point lead over United on the final day, and an 8-0 demolition of Wigan rendered their rivals' 4-0 win over Stoke academic. Drogba's hat-trick meant he pipped Rooney for the Golden Boot, and Chelsea's 103 goals set a new Premier League mark. Rooney, who came off the bench to hit the winner in United's 2-1 win over Villa in the League Cup Final, won the Player of the Year award. Spurs beat Manchester City in the battle for fourth, the Lilywhites' best League showing for 20 years. Portsmouth, Hull and Burnley were all relegated before the last day, but Pompey shrugged off the cares of administration to reach the FA Cup Final, going down to a Drogba free-kick at Wembley.

Ancelotti eclipsed Mourinho in winning the Double at the first attempt, but the Portuguese came out on top when Inter Milan met Chelsea in the last 16 of the Champions League. Arsenal were given a lesson by Barcelona in the quarters, and United went out to Bayern Munich at the same stage. Arjen Robben's spectacular volley at Old Trafford made it 4-4, with Bayern through on away goals. It meant there was no Premiership representation in the semis for the first time since 2002-03 Fulham went furthest in Europe, eliminating Juventus en route to the inaugural Europa League Final. A brace from Diego Forlán gave opponents Atlético Madrid a 2-1 victory in the Hamburg showpiece, Fulham's 19th match in the competition.

BELOW: Chelsea celebrate winning the 2009-10 Premier League title following a resounding 8-0 victory over Wigan.

OPPOSITE: The England players line-up before their final World Cup Qualifier match against Moldova on 6 September 2013

Frank Lampard

In May 2013 Frank Lampard notched his 203rd goal for Chelsea, taking him past Bobby Tambling's all-time scoring record that had stood for over 40 years. A year later, he struck his 250th career goal, a record befitting a top striker. Midfielders who can regularly find the net are a priceless commodity, and in the Premier League era none has done so with such regularity as Lampard, making him one of the bargain buys of the last two decades.

Football was in Lampard's genes, for his namesake father was a West Ham stalwart full-back who won a couple of caps. Frank Snr was a tough taskmaster who instilled a sense of discipline and dedication in his son, qualities that would ensure he made the most of his natural ability. Frank signed for the Hammers after leaving school, and needed broad shoulders when criticism came his way at a club where his uncle – Harry Redknapp – and father were manager and assistant, respectively. He made his league debut in 1995 during a loan spell with Swansea City, and a year later ran out in the famous claret-and-blue shirt for the first time, quickly establishing himself as a first-team regular. There was also a call-up to the England U-21 side, which he went on to captain.

The move to Stamford Bridge came in summer 2001 during Claudio Ranieri's reign, the £11 million fee looking a tad expensive as he made a steady but unspectacular start, notching 15 goals in his first two seasons. Then he found his feet, hitting that same number or better in nine out of 10 seasons from 2003–04 It included a run of five consecutive campaigns when his tally reached the 20-goal mark, including a prolific return of 27 in 2009–10 He scored both goals in the win at Bolton that sealed the 2004–05 Premier League title, ending Chelsea's 50-year wait for championship success. That was in Jose Mourinho's first season at the club, a period when big money was splashed on high-profile signings. Lampard's contribution was as vital as that made by any of the imports, a level of performance recognized in his Football Writers' Player of the Year award and runner-up placing to Ronaldinho in both the World and European Footballer of the Year polls. He has been pivotal in Chelsea's rise over the past decade, instrumental in the steady stream of silverware that has been delivered to the Stamford Bridge trophy room. The haul includes two further championships and four FA Cup wins. In the 2009 Wembley final it was his goal that beat Everton, and a year later, when Lamps could barely stop scoring, there followed the coveted Double. But the high point must surely have been captaining the side that beat Bayern Munich in the 2012 Champions League final, a game that went some way to erasing the disappointment to defeat by Manchester United four years earlier. When the match went to a shoot-out, a successful Lampard spot-kick was almost a given, so reliable has he been from 12 yards during his career. A year on from that victorious night in Munich, Lampard also held the Europa League trophy aloft following Chelsea's victory over Benfica.

On the international stage, he won his first cap in 1999, though it wasn't until Euro 2004 that he became a certain starter for England. He scored three times in that tournament, showing that his eye for goal was no less keen at the highest level. Nine years later, in a World Cup qualifier against Ukraine in September 2013, Frank joined the select 100-cap club, his 29 goals for England putting him just one shy of Alan Shearer's tally. The two would have been on a par had his strike against Germany at the 2010 World Cup, clearly over the line, not been ruled out. With over 600 games for the Blues – only Ron Harris and Peter Bonnetti have made more appearances – he ranks as one of the great servants for club and country.

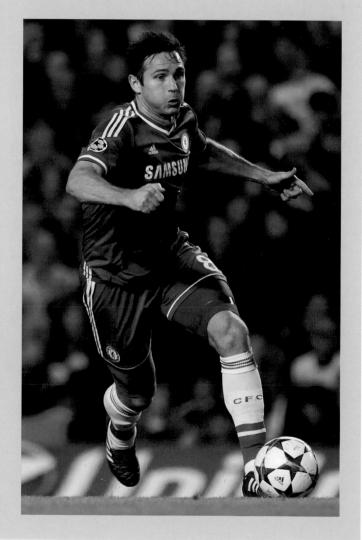

History boys

Manchester United wrested back the title in 2010-11, the 12th championship under Alex Ferguson's stewardship and an historic 19th for the club. It put United clear of Liverpool in the all-time list in the season when Ferguson took over from Sir Matt Busby as the club's longest-serving manager.

Many commentators said this wasn't a vintage United side: functional rather than exhilarating on many occasions. But the team fizzed often enough – bargain signing Javier Hernandez was particularly effervescent – and eked out priceless points from some muted performances. Success was built on home impregnability; by the time the title was secured, only West Bromwich Albion had left Old Trafford with a share of the spoils. United's away form was moderate, 25 points from 57, but the team remained unbeaten until February and took the crown with a game to spare.

Of the other contenders, reigning champions Chelsea had got out of the blocks the fastest, but a mid-season slump left Carlo Ancelotti's side 15 points off the pace at the beginning of March. Thanks to a terrific late run, Chelsea went to Old Trafford with three games to go knowing that victory would put them ahead of United on goal difference. Hernandez and Vidic scored in a 2-1 win that restored a six-point advantage, and a draw at Ewood Park in United's next outing put the issue beyond doubt.

Arsenal again flattered to deceive, battling on four fronts in February, only to finish the season empty-handed once again. A defensive howler allowed Birmingham City's Obafemi Martins to score the winner in the League Cup Final, the Blues' first major silverware since winning the same trophy in 1963. Arsenal's season fizzled out amid the usual mutterings from Gunners' fans: matchless when on song but vulnerable, no Plan B and too often trying to walk the ball into the net. Their frailty was best exposed at St James' Park, where Wenger's men capitulated after taking a 4-0 lead.

City end barren spell

Manchester City also broke a long barren spell, their FA Cup Final win over Stoke City ending 35 years of hurt. Yaya Touré was City's hero, scoring the goal that beat their city rivals in the semis, then ramming home the winner in the Final. Cup glory and a Champions League spot represented a solid return for City, with the prospect of more big-money signings to further strengthen their challenge. Liverpool, too, hit their stride after Kenny Dalglish replaced a beleaguered Roy Hodgson, who lasted just half a season at Anfield. The Reds' squad boasted Britain's most expensive footballer when Andy Carroll signed from Newcastle for £35 million, a deal funded by Fernando Torres's £50 million move to Chelsea.

Hodgson took over at West Brom and steered the Baggies clear of a tense relegation dogfight. West Ham were down before the last day, but the next five clubs in the firing line were separated by just one point. There were 14 goals in the three critical fixtures, the picture changing with each strike. Blackburn and Wigan won and survived, Birmingham and Blackpool lost and were relegated. Wolves stayed up despite a 3-2 defeat. The Seasiders made many friends in their single-season stay, scoring 55 goals, the same as fifth-placed Spurs.

On the European front, British interest in the Europa League had ended by the quarter-final stage, but United, Chelsea and Spurs all reached the last eight of the Champions League. Spurs crashed out to Real Madrid, while United won both legs against Chelsea, then eased past surprise package Schalke in the semis to set up a Wembley encounter with Barcelona. It was a repeat of the 2009 final, and England's finest were once again a distant second best. United started brightly, as they had in Rome, and Rooney delightfully cancelled out Pedro's opener. But once Barcelona's "passing carousel", as Ferguson called it, got into full swing, there was only one winner, Messi and Villa scoring without reply in the second half.

Walter Smith bows out

In Scotland the final day of the 2010-11 season witnessed another "helicopter Sunday", and it was soon clear that the chopper had to set a course for Rugby Park. Rangers, holding a one-point advantage, went three goals up at Kilmarnock inside eight minutes and ran out 5-1 winners, rendering Celtic's victory academic. Walter Smith bowed out with a third successive SPL title and 400 wins from 618 games in his two spells at Ibrox, a hard act for new boss Ally McCoist to follow.

There had been some unedifying incidents during the season's Old Firm matches, heightened volatility that provoked government-level debate. Neil Lennon took so much abuse, including death threats, that Celtic fans put aside their final-day disappointment to cheer their manager when he signalled his intention to stay on.

LEFT: Javier Hernandez scores Manchester United's first goal in the 2-1 win over Chelsea that restored his team's six-point advantage over their closest rivals.

OPPOSITE TOP: Manchester City celebrate their first trophy for 35 years after winning the FA Cup in May 2011 with a 1-0 victory over Stoke at Wembley.

Title race goes to the wire

The 2011-12 Premier League season was full of twists and turns, the last of which occurred deep into injury time on the final day. Manchester City began the season in prime form and remained unbeaten until the December trip to Stamford Bridge. Their free-flowing football yielded an avalanche of goals, the standout result a 6-1 win at Old Trafford. It was United's heaviest home defeat since losing 5-0 to the same opponents in February 1955, and you had to trawl the record books back to 1930 to find the last time that the team shipped six in their own back yard.

City suffered a mid-term wobble – the loss of Yaya Touré to Africa Cup of Nations duty particularly damaging – and the chasing pack scented a weakness in its leader. United were always the main challengers, though for a time Harry Redknapp's Spurs side looked like making it a three-way fight. Tottenham fell away in the last third of the campaign, Redknapp refusing to link his team's slide with speculation that he was about to take over from Fabio Capello as England's supremo.

Two-horse race

And so the championship became a two-horse race. City's 1-0 defeat at Swansea on 1 March, combined with United's home win over West Brom, knocked Mancini's men off top spot for the first time in five months. When United went eight points clear with six games to go,

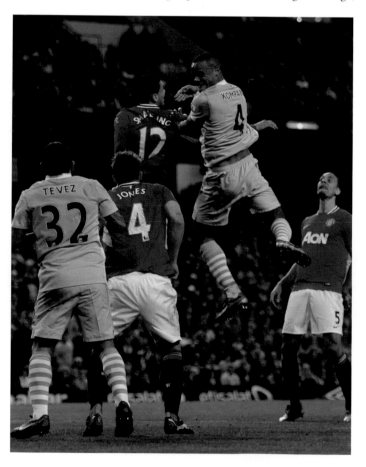

it looked all over. Everyone had been focusing on the derby clash at the Etihad as a potential title decider, yet United now had it in their hands to lift the crown regardless of that result. Not so after Ferguson's men let a two-goal lead slip at home to Everton. The game ended 4-4, the latest in a string of remarkable scorelines during the campaign. City drew level on points with their neighbours after a towering header from skipper Vincent Kompany completed the league double. That remained the case going into the final round of matches, City's goal difference eight to the good. United did all they could, Rooney's 27th goal of the season giving them all three points at Sunderland. It left City with the seemingly simple task of beating relegation-threatened QPR at home. The job appeared even easier when they took a 1-0 lead and the visitors were reduced to ten men. But City found themselves 2-1 down after 90 minutes, and even Dzeko's injury-time header still wasn't enough. Amazingly, there was enough stoppage time remaining for Sergio Agüero to dance his way through the Rangers' defence and fire the goal that gave City their first championship since 1968

United had won many a title with 89 points; this time it was good enough only for the runner-up spot. The 10-goal swing from that extraordinary Old Trafford derby did come back to haunt United in the first Premier League-era title race to be settled on goal difference

Third place crucial

Arsenal recovered from a woeful start to the season – hammered 8-2 at Old Trafford – to finish third, albeit 19 points adrift of the top two. That the Gunners preserved their 15-season run of Champions League qualification was in no small part down to the form of Robin van Persie, who headed the scoring chart with 30 goals and took both player-of-the-year garlands.

Third spot was crucial this term as fourth-placed Spurs were left sweating on Chelsea's progress in the Champions League to determine which competition they would enter in 2012–13 Chelsea were well off the pace in the league, 13 wins in 27 league games costing manager André Villas-Boas his job after just eight months in charge. Roman Abramovich had paid a reported £13 million to prise the 33-year-old Mourinho protégé away from Porto. A win record below 50 per cent was worse than not only his former mentor but any of the six coaches of the Abramovich era. AVB's replacement, former Blues' favourite Roberto Di Matteo, could do no more than guide Chelsea to sixth place. It meant their only route into Europe's premier competition would be as defending champions.

Newcastle surprised many by finishing fifth. They'd entertained royally, earning Alan Pardew the Manager of the Year award. Two other contenders for that honour were Brendan Rodgers and Paul Lambert, whose Swansea and Norwich sides served up some quality football in securing comfortable mid-table positions on their return to the top flight. Inevitably, they were on many clubs' shopping list in the usual post-season round of axe-wielding. Lambert was appointed Villa boss, while Rodgers took over at Liverpool after Kenny Dalglish's second spell in charge ended with an eighth-place finish, the Reds' worst showing since 1993–94 A Carling Cup shoot-out victory over Championship side Cardiff City – the club's first silverware for six years – proved inadequate compensation for a league campaign in which the team lost as many games as they won.

Agony turns to joy

The basement battle saw Wolves and Blackburn disappear through the trapdoor before the last day of the season. The other relegation spot was between QPR, the other promoted club, and Bolton. Rangers fans ran the full gamut of emotions as they saw three points evaporate in the blinking of an eye at Manchester City, only to discover they were safe anyway: Bolton could only draw at Stoke when they needed a win to overtake the London club. It was the first time in ten years that all three promoted teams had survived the drop.

Liverpool came close to making it a domestic cup double. The Reds prevailed in a Merseyside-derby semi-final to set up a Wembley clash with Chelsea, who came through the other semi at Spurs' expense. The latter game added further fuel to the technology debate as Chelsea were awarded a goal that replays showed didn't cross the line. They did go on to win 5-1, but the "ghost" goal put them 2-0 up early in the second half, leaving Spurs chasing the game. Bale pulled one back before the Lilywhites were undone by three late strikes.

The first Chelsea-Liverpool Cup Final saw Didier Drogba further enhance his status as a Stamford Bridge legend before departing for pastures new. His strike early in the second half, which put Chelsea 2-0 up, was his fourth in the showpiece final, a competition record. It also turned out to be the winner. Substitute Andy Carroll pulled one back and galvanised a lacklustre Liverpool side, but Chelsea were well worth their fourth victory in six years. Ashley Cole added a seventh

ABOVE: West Ham celebrate an immediate return to the Premier League after beating Blackpool 2-1 in the Championship play-off final. The Hammers had looked on course for automatic promotion, but Reading's blistering post-Christmas run took them up as champions, and pacesetters Southampton secured second place on the last day of the season. Ricardo Vaz Tê, a £500,000 January signing, scored the decisive Wembley goal in the game billed as the biggest cash prize in sport, worth up to £100 million.

OPPOSITE: Manchester City skipper Vincent Kompany powers home the header that completes the derby double over United and puts his team back in control of the title race with two games left in the 2011–12 season. The result put City ahead of United on goal difference, an edge they maintained as both clubs took maximum points from their remaining fixtures.

winners' medal to his collection, while interim manager Di Matteo did his chances of landing the job permanently no harm. The big prize still lay ahead, however: a Champions League final and the opportunity of fulfilling the owner's long cherished dream.

Neither of the Manchester clubs made it out of the group stage in Europe's premier club competition, only the third time in 17 years that United hadn't been in the mix post-Christmas. Nor did they fare much better in the second-string tournament, both clubs eliminated before the quarter-final stage against opposition they were expected to overcome. United lost both legs of their last 16 tie with Athletic Bilbao – who were a country mile behind the big two in La Liga. City went out on away goals to Sporting Lisbon, ending British interest in the Europa League for another year.

Chelsea fly the flag in Europe

Arsenal fell in the Champions League round of 16, not quite able to overturn the 4–0 thumping dished out by AC Milan at the San Siro in the first leg. Chelsea, who would finish 25 points behind Manchester City in the league, dispatched Napoli and Benfica to set up a semi-final clash with holders Barcelona, favourites to become the first team to retain the trophy. A Drogba goal gave Chelsea a slender advantage to take to the Camp Nou, where Barça had racked up over 100 goals during the season. Chelsea looked doomed as they went 2–0 down, their chances dented further as Terry saw red for a rash moment of ill discipline. A deft Ramires chip just before the break gave the Blues the away-goal advantage and something to cling on to. Messi hit the woodwork twice, once from the spot, and Chelsea's staunch rearguard action was capped by a Torres breakaway in the last minute. In the final, Di Matteo had to face Bayern Munich – conquerors of Real Madrid – on their home turf and without Ramires, Ivanovic and Meireles, as well as Terry. The talismanic Drogba was there, though, and he signed off in some style in a game where Chelsea were often second best. His bullet header on 88 minutes cancelled out Thomas Müller's aerial strike and took the game into extra-time. Petr Cech, the other hero of the hour, saved former teammate Arjen Robben's spot-kick to keep the score tied at 1–1 after 120 minutes. He repeated the feat twice in the shoot-out, more than making up for Juan Mata's miss. Cue that man Drogba again, who slotted home to deliver the coveted trophy with his final kick for the club, wiping away the memory of Moscow. It also gained Chelsea entry into the 2012–13 competition, consigning fourth-placed Spurs to Thursday night Europa-League action. It was a bitter pill for the White Hart Lane faithful to swallow, the team having looked title contenders at the season's midpoint. As the fans were coming to terms with that disappointment, they learned that Harry Redknapp was on his way. A few short months after looking a shoo-in for the England job, Redknapp was looking for a new club. As his fortunes nosedived, so Di Matteo's soared. Having achieved the goal that eluded even the : "Special One", he gave his job application form the boost that Abramovich couldn't ignore and became the billionaire-owner's eighth manager in nine years.

BELOW: The Chelsea squad celebrates a dramatic penalty shoot-out victory over Bayern Munich in the 2012 Champions League final. The Blues finished a distant sixth in the Premier League, saving their best for the cup competitions.

Footballing family rocked

BELOW: Rangers fans pledge their unswerving loyalty to the club as it becomes mired in a financial scandal. By the end of the season The Rangers Football Club Ltd is formed from the ashes of the liquidated concern.

In both Wales and Scotland, football took second place to off-field concerns. The entire footballing family was rocked by the death of Gary Speed in November 2011 He had barely closed the book on an illustrious playing career, opening a new managerial chapter, briefly with his last club, Sheffield United, then the national side for whom he played with such distinction. During his brief stewardship, Wales was the most improved side in the world, climbing the Fifa rankings from 116 into the top 50

The story dominating the headlines north of the border was the plight of Rangers, whose parlous financial situation became public knowledge when the 140-year-old club signalled its intention to go into administration in February 2012 It was the latest instalment of a familiar tale: clubs overreaching themselves, rational business planning going out of the window in the quest for sporting glory. In Rangers' case, it soon became clear that triggering an automatic 10-point deduction was the least of the club's worries; its very survival was at stake.

HMRC was seeking settlement of unpaid tax dating back over a decade, when the club sought to pay players via offshore Employee Benefit Trusts. That was under Sir David Murray's chairmanship, the man who pledged to spend ten pounds for every five expended by Rangers' Old Firm rival. The club's liability, pending the outcome of a tribunal, was somewhere north of £50 million if the ruling went the wrong way, a portion of that accrued in the nine months since Craig Whyte bought Murray's controlling share for the price of a loaf of bread. Whyte's failure to meet a £9 million PAYE and VAT bill — despite raising £24 million in advance season-ticket sales — triggered the descent into administration. Belatedly, he failed the fit and proper

person test and was handed a life ban by the SFA. Of more immediate concern to Rangers was an embargo on player acquisitions, while stars such as Steven Whittaker and Steven Naismith were reported to be taking a 75 per cent wage cut to help slash the bills.

While Rangers courted potential buyers, Celtic eyed a domestic treble. The league title was never in doubt, but the Hoops suffered a shock League Cup final defeat to mid table Kilmarnock, their first success in the competition. Hearts accounted for Celtic in the Scottish Cup semis, then put five past Hibs in the first Edinburgh-derby final since 1896

Rangers liquidated

After the prizes were handed out, Rangers went into liquidation, while Whyte's takeover and running of the club became subject of a criminal investigation. Former Sheffield United chief executive Charles Green headed a consortium that purchased the club's assets for £5 5 million and set about attempting to keep The Rangers Football Club Ltd in the elite division. The other main agenda item was transferring the players' contracts to the newco club. On neither issue did the new owners fare well. Several players, including Whittaker, Naismith and Kyle Lafferty, opted to terminate their contracts and become free agents. The new Rangers also failed to secure the backing of eight SPL clubs, the two-thirds majority needed to ratify their top-table place. It appeared that the club with a world-record 54 domestic championships would not be competing for a 55th title in 2012–13, battling instead in one of the lower divisions.

Capello walks

England was the only home-nation representative at Euro 2012, remaining unbeaten in the qualifiers. Fabio Capello, already due to step down after the tournament, jumped ship early when he clashed with his employers over who should lead the team on the pitch. The FA decided John Terry had to be stripped of the captaincy with a court case regarding an alleged racial slur hanging over his head. Capello walked.

The clamour went up for Redknapp, whose Spurs side were flying. Not for the first time the FA overlooked the popular choice, turning instead to Roy Hodgson, who had recovered from a bruising experience at Anfield by doing a fine job at West

Brom. His CV included Inter Milan and the Switzerland and Finland national sides, and he opened his account with victories over Norway and Belgium in the warm-up games to the main event in Poland and Ukraine. For once expectations were modest. Lampard, Barry and Cahill were late withdrawals, Jack Wilshere a long-term absentee and Rooney unavailable for the opening two games. Add in a new manager with his feet barely under the table and the tournament got under way without the usual hype.

More shoot-out woe

England surprised many by topping a group comprising France, Sweden and co-hosts Ukraine. After a low-key 1-1 draw against the French – Joleon Lescott's towering set-piece header cancelled out by a Samir Nasri strike – Hodgson's men came from behind to beat Sweden 3-2, England's first victory in a competitive fixture over that country. Rooney marked his entry into the tournament with a close-range header that was enough to beat Ukraine. Two years on from the injustice of Lampard's goal-that-never-was, it was England's turn to have a slice of luck as John Terry cleared a Devic shot when it was already over the line.

Heading the group meant England avoided European and world champions Spain in the quarters, but an unheralded Italy side dominated the match. With Andrea Pirlo pulling the strings, Italy deserved to win in 90 minutes, yet the game had to wait for a penalty shoot-out to see the net bulge for the first time. Montolivo's miss made it advantage England, but Ashleys Young and Cole both failed with their spot-kicks and England exited a major tournament on penalties for the sixth time in 22 years.

England were dogged, unbeaten in regular time in their four games. But Gary Lineker spoke for many when he said the national side was "behind technically and tactically", playing in straight lines and surrendering possession too cheaply. That left the players chasing the ball for long periods and inviting the opposition onto them.

England had just 32 per cent possession against Italy, and the most successful pass completion was between Joe Hart and substitute Andy Carroll. Hodgson countered that he set little store by such figures. Possession in areas that didn't hurt a side counted for little; ball retention in the final third translating to efforts on goal was what counted. He conceded England could have kept the ball better and posed a greater attacking threat, but praised a resilient defensive unit. Captain Steven Gerrard said that compared with South Africa 2010 it was a happier camp and a better team performance. The bottom line was that England yet again showed itself to be a quarter-final team, and yet again unable to break the shoot-out jinx.

LEFT: The football world was shocked and saddened at the death of Gary Speed, who had made a promising start to his managerial career with Sheffield United and the Wales national team. England also lost its manager mid-season, Fabio Capello quitting after clashing with the FA over who should lead the team.

Sir Alex bows out after 13th title

In the Premier League era Manchester United had invariably responded swiftly after ceding the crown. Blackburn '95, Arsenal '98 and 2002, Chelsea 2010: all had seen the title revert to Old Trafford in the year following those successes. The Gunners-Chelsea three-year lockout between 2004 and 2006 was the longest United had been kept from the league trophy. The incentive to reclaim top domestic honours could not have been greater, given the way it had been snatched from their grasp by their city rivals in "Fergie time" of the 2011-12 campaign. Sir Alex used that final-day hurt to inspire his squad. He also added significant firepower to it in the shape of Robin van Persie, the latest Arsenal player to head up the M6. City had also been in the hunt for the Dutch master, who made his choice after listening to "the little boy inside him". Roberto Mancini went on a bigger spending spree, Jack Rodwell, Scott Sinclair and Javi Garcia among the additions to the champions' ranks. Serbian defender Matija Nastasic was the pick in terms of enhancing the first team, but there was no marquee name to match van Persie. The latter's decision to choose red over blue went a long way towards determining the destination of the championship, before a ball was kicked.

The Manchester clubs again took up the front-running role, but this time City were always playing catch-up. After 29 games United had accrued 74 points – one shy of the title-winning haul in 1996-97 They were 15 clear with eight to play as the big two geared up for an Old Trafford clash. City won for the second year running, but this time it made no difference to the title race. United clinched the 13th title of the Ferguson era – the 20th overall – with four games to spare. A 3-0 win over Aston Villa, courtesy of a hat-trick from his "unbelievable" summer acquisition put the matter beyond issue. Van Persie again took top marksman honours, with 26 goals, but his first championship was the last for Sir Alex, who decided it was time to abdicate after a glittering 26-year Old Trafford reign. The fact that almost £100 million was wiped off United's share value as the news broke – more than the club banked from the sale of Cristiano Ronaldo – was an indication that this sporting and financial giant was losing its greatest asset. The anointed successor, David Moyes, had done a "miraculous" job – Ferguson's epithet - in his 11 years at Goodison, overachieving in a period where budget and league position tended to dovetail. The glaring omission on the resumé was silverware, and Moyes was heading for pastures where the trophy cabinet groaned like no other.

BELOW: Sir Alex Ferguson takes the applause at his 1,500th and final game in charge, a 5–5 draw at the Hawthorns. It was not a record, but no manager held sway over a club of United's size for so long or with such success.

Manchester United's rivals fail to impress

While Ferguson praised the quality of the squad he was bequeathing, others thought the First XI well short of the best he had assembled, and the stroll to the title had as much to do with shortcomings among the other contenders. Mancini put City's stuttering defence down to the transfer targets he failed to land in the summer, including Eden Hazard – snapped up by Chelsea – as well as van Persie. Mario Balotelli returned to Italy in the transfer window, having shown all too rare glimpses of his undoubted talent. Several of City's stars impressed less as defenders of the crown than in pursuit of it. As for the other potential challengers and traditional rivals, Arsenal, Chelsea and Liverpool were in a state of flux. Roberto di Matteo found the halo of Champions League victory faded before the Christmas lights were switched on. Rafael Benitez was appointed "The Interim One", struggling to win over the Stamford Bridge faithful with memories of titanic Liverpool-Chelsea battles and some spiky comments. Spurs also had a new name on the manager's door as André Villas-Boas filled Harry's boots at the Lane.

North London battle for Champions League spot

On the last day of term the only unresolved issue was the final Champions League spot, yet another north London scrap with Arsenal holding a point advantage over Spurs but with a tougher fixture on paper: away to a Newcastle side that was a shadow of the one that had qualified for Europe the previous season. Any slip by the Gunners would let in Spurs, who entertained a Sunderland side breathing a sigh of relief at having evaded the drop. Spurs did all they could, taking three points with the latest wonder goal from Gareth Bale, only to hear that Arsenal had matched that result to preserve their unbroken top-four run in the Wenger era. The key was a brilliant late-season flourish from the Gunners, who had limped out of both domestic cups to lower league opposition. Trailing Spurs by seven points in early March, they were the division's form side during the run-in, taking 26 points from 30 Spurs had to content themselves with Europe's second-string competition and their best ever points total of the Premier League era.

Speculation inevitably arose as to how long Spurs could hold on to Bale, who swept the board in the player of the year polls. He followed Andy Gray and Cristiano Ronaldo into the record books in collecting both PFA awards. At 23 he was one of the hottest properties in world football, a description that might once have been applied to Michael Owen, David Beckham and Paul Scholes, who all decided it was time to leave the stage. Another bidding farewell was Jamie Carragher, who might not have acquired superstar status but was a model of consistency in notching over 700 games for Liverpool, second only to Ian Callaghan on the Reds' honours board.

At the foot of the table, QPR and Reading's fates were sealed when they fought out a goalless draw with three games to go. Rangers had appointed Harry Redknapp after a dire autumn run under Mark Hughes. Six months after steering Spurs to fourth spot and being touted as the new England supremo, Harry found himself firefighting once again, and this time failed to work his usual magic.

The final place for the drop was extremely tight, eight clubs separated by just six points with half a dozen games to go. With the next TV deal on the near horizon, clubs were more desperate than ever to stay with the moneyed elite. The pressure showed in some itchy trigger fingers, the bosses of Southampton, Sunderland and Reading all in the firing line mid-term, as well as Hughes. Nigel Adkins lost his job after steering Saints into a decent position, only to be invited to perform another escapology act as Brian McDermott's successor at Reading. Of the new men in the respective hotseats, the surprise pick was Paolo di Canio, who led Swindon to the Division Two championship and was in contention for a second successive promotion when he left the club. In only his second game after taking over from Martin O'Neill he went a long way to winning over Sunderland fans with a stunning 3-0 away victory in the Tyne-Wear derby.

Gareth Bale

Gareth Bale in full flight, ball at his feet, is one of the most exhilarating sights in the modern game. The combination of power and scorching pace has left many a top-class defender with shredded nerves. Cardiff-born Bale was a product of Southampton's much vaunted academy. He made his debut aged 16, and in his two years with the south-coast club developed into one of the most highly-rated young full-backs in the country. Spurs swooped in summer 2007, the £7 million fee one of the shrewdest pieces of business ever done in the game. Over the next six years Bale blossomed into one of the Premier League's most exciting talents. He also moved further up the pitch, for it was clear that his offensive capabilities could not be fully harvested when there were defensive duties to be carried out. On the European stage, he came of age in Spurs' 2010–11 Champions League campaign. He was unstoppable against Inter Milan at the San Siro, hitting a hat-trick against the holders in a pulsating 4–3 group-stage defeat. Brazilian defender Maicon was run ragged that night, and there was another Bale masterclass in the return fixture. His sparkling form that season earned him the first of two PFA Player of the Year awards. The second came in 2012-13, when he plundered 21 league goals. Bale completed the set of individual honours by adding the PFA Young Player of the Year and the Football Writers' Association award in his final season before decamping to the Bernabeu in a record £85 million deal. There he linked up with Cristiano Ronaldo and Karim Benzema in a potent attack dubbed the "BBC" in the Spanish press. Despite a few injury niggles, he still passed the 30 mark for goals and assists in his first La Liga campaign scoring the winning goal in the Copa del Rey and the second of Real's four goals in the Champions League Final.

Like his boyhood hero Ryan Giggs, Bale was fast-tracked into the Wales senior side, winning his first cap aged 16 in May 2006 He had only just broken into the Saints first team when he took the field against Trinidad and Tobago, becoming the youngest international in Wales' history. Five months later, 17-year-old Bale broke another record when he got on the scoresheet in a Euro 2008 qualifier against Slovakia. A glorious free-kick made him the national team's youngest ever scorer. Even if Gareth Bale does not grace the finals of a major international tournament, his impact at club level has already been immense. Many more honours will surely follow for the player described by his former manager Harry Redknapp as "the full package".

Wigan combine Cup run with relegation battle

Unusually, Wigan Athletic were battling on two fronts in the last month of the season. Trying to avoid the drop was nothing new, but Roberto Martinez's side enjoyed a terrific run to the FA Cup final, the stand-out result a 3-0 quarter-final win at Everton. The tie of the round was at Old Trafford, where United squandered a 2-0 lead against Chelsea and paid heavily as they went down to a brilliant Demba Ba strike in the replay. The Senegalese star repeated the feat in the heavyweight semi-final clash with Manchester City, but it came when Chelsea were trailing to goals from Nasri and Aguero. City held out and were red-hot favourites to beat a Wigan side that overcame Championship flag-wavers Millwall in the other semi. The reigning champions were comfortably ensconced in the runners-up spot and in the Wembley showpiece faced an injury-hit Latics side that arguably had two even more important "cup finals" to come in the fight to preserve their Premier League status.

The battle of the Robertos – Mancini v Martinez – went the way of the underdog, a game that would be mentioned in the same breath as Sunderland '73 and Wimbledon '88. A thumping Ben Watson header as the clock ticked into injury time was the only score in a contest where form and reputation went out of the window. Wigan were good value for their victory, which delivered

the first silverware to a club that didn't gain league status until 1978. It was the kind of day dreams are made of for Watson, whose season had been blighted by a broken leg. He had only just come off the bench when he planted a near-post header beyond a flailing Joe Hart. City's Pablo Zabaleta became only the third man to be dismissed in the final, ordered off after picking up a second yellow for bringing down man-of-the-match Callum McManaman late in the game. There was no prouder man at Wembley than Wigan chairman Dave Whelan, who had suffered a broken leg playing for Blackburn in the 1960 final, one of the "hoodoo" victims of the early postwar period.

Mancini was sacked 48 hours after City's tepid Wembley display, mere Champions League qualification clearly not good enough for the ambitious paymasters. It meant the country's top three sides would all go into 2013-14 under new management. Wigan, meanwhile, could not combine Wembley glory with another miraculous escape. A 4-1 defeat at the Emirates in their penultimate game ended an eight-season run in the top flight, the first club to win the FA Cup and be relegated in the same season.

Champions League disappointment for England's finest

The Champions League was a disappointment for English football's big guns. The Premier League had supplied eight finalists in as many years, but this season all fell by the wayside before the quarters, the first time since 1996 that there was no representation in the last eight. The Premier League winners and holders of the Champions League trophy both failed to get out of their group. City faced strong opposition, including Real Madrid and Borussia Dortmund, but the failure to register a single victory was another black mark that would return to haunt Mancini. For Chelsea it was Europa League consolation, the first holders to fail to reach the knockout stage.

Manchester United and Arsenal went just one round further. The Gunners faced runaway Bundesliga leaders Bayern Munich and scored a terrific 2-0 win in the Allianz Arena, but the damage had already been done at the Emirates, where they were comprehensively outplayed. Wenger's men went out on away goals. United's defeat to Real Madrid left Ferguson fuming. Holding a 2-1 aggregate lead at Old Trafford, with a valuable away goal from the Bernabeu, United lost Nani, given his marching orders for planting his studs in Arbeloa's midriff as he tried to control a dropping ball. José Mourinho's side took full advantage with a quickfire double.

Three home representatives made it through to the last eight of the Europa League. Newcastle and Spurs went out to Benfica and Basel respectively, Tottenham on penalties after the tie ended 4-4 Chelsea squeezed through against Rubin Kazan despite losing the away leg, and beat Spurs' Swiss conquerors to set up an Amsterdam final against Benfica. Fernando Torres's surging run and deft finish put the Blues ahead, his ninth goal on the European trail. Cardozo levelled from the spot, and with impeccable timing – in both senses, for the whistle was seconds away – Branislav Ivanovic rose to power home Mata's corner. It was the 11th trophy of the Abramovich era, further evidence that the revolving-door managerial model of Stamford Bridge was no impediment to success. With the all-German Champions League final still 10 days away, it meant that Chelsea briefly held both European trophies.

Welsh success

It was a good year for Welsh football. As well as claiming the best individual performer in Bale, Wales boasted a Swansea side that continued to impress under Michael Laudrup. The Swans collected their first major trophy with a 5-0 demolition of Bradford City in the Capital One final. Michu, surely the season's bargain buy at £2 million, was among the scorers. It was a game too far for Bradford, who had taken three Premier League scalps en route to becoming the first fourth-tier side to reach a domestic final since 1962. Cardiff City, who had been knocking on the door of top-flight football for so long, clinched promotion to the elite division for the first time in over half a century. It meant the south Wales derby would take place at the top level for the first time, and no doubt helped assuage Bluebirds fans whose team now played in red, a case of the Malaysian-ownership piper calling the tune. Hull City pipped Watford for the other automatic promotion spot, back at the top table after three years' absence. It was double disappointment for the Hornets, beaten by Crystal Palace in the play off final. The game was settled by a penalty, won by Old Trafford-bound Wilfried Zaha and converted by 39-year-old Kevin Phillips.

ABOVE: Three-time Ballon d'Or winner Lionel Messi is well marshalled by Charlie Mulgrew and Mikael Lustig during the Celtic-Barcelona Champions League group stage encounter. With goals from Victor Wanyama and teenage substitute Tony Watt, the Hoops took three points on their way to qualification for the knockout stage.

OPPOSITE: David Moyes, Sir Alex Ferguson's anointed successor, talks with Wayne Rooney during the Barclays Premier League match between Manchester United and Stoke City.

Plans to restructure Scottish league

In Scotland Celtic strolled to the SPL title and enjoyed a Champions League run to the Last 16, the highlight of which was a group-stage victory over Barcelona's maestros. A 3-0 Scottish Cup final win over Hibernian completed the double. Having come from 3-0 down to beat Falkirk in the semis, Hibs might have thought their name was finally on the trophy, but the long wait goes on. St Mirren came from behind to beat Hearts 3-2 in the League Cup final, the Buddies' first success in that competition. As Rangers began the long haul back to the top by winning the Third Division, Hearts became the latest club to peer over the precipice of financial meltdown. Only uncertainty over the exact position of the club's Lithuanian backers saved the Jambos from an 18-point penalty and automatic relegation. Scottish football was, in the words of Aberdeen chairman Stuart Milne, "on its knees financially". There was general agreement on the need to restructure, but the devil was in the detail when it came to settling upon a model to increase competition and create a thriving pyramid system.

Scottish fans had little to cheer on the international front, either. Gordon Strachan replaced Craig Levein after a poor start to the 2014 World Cup campaign, but two points from 18 meant the Tartan Army were assured another summer off. Wales' double over Scotland gave Chris Coleman's side cause for celebration, though they too were well off the pace. Northern Ireland, like Scotland, were winless halfway through the programme, leaving England once again as the only home nation with a realistic chance of qualifying for Brazil. Not that it was all plain sailing. England needed a late goal to salvage a draw at home to Ukraine, and had to settle for a point in Poland and Montenegro after taking the lead. But with three home games in their final four fixtures, Roy Hodgson was confident that his team could finish the job without recourse to the play-offs.

The last word on the 2012-13 season has to be about the man who held the fort for Scotland in the wake of Jock Stein's death in 1985, a brief period on the international stage sandwiched between phenomenally successful spells in club management either side of the border. With Aberdeen and Manchester United he broke the established order, reinventing teams time and again in his unquenchable desire to play attacking football, to win with style. In his final game, at the Hawthorns with nothing but pride at stake, he watched his side take a 5-2 lead before being pegged back to 5-5 As the man himself famously said after the dramatic Champions League finale of 1999: "Football – bloody hell!"

All change at the top

With new managerial regimes at the top three clubs, the 2013–14 season promised much – and delivered in spades. José Mourinho reclaimed his old station at Stamford Bridge, where the mutual love-in between Special One and fans was assured. Manchester City supporters, many of them Mancini loyalists, were less convinced that their La Liga recruit, ex-Malaga boss Manuel Pellegrini, was the man for the job at the Etihad. But inevitably, the central spotlight was on the man following the biggest managerial act in football. Things could scarcely have gone worse for David Moyes. He brought in Marouane Fellaini from his old Goodison stable, adding Chelsea playmaker Juan Mata in the winter window. A £65 million transfusion of new blood couldn't prevent United from sliding to their worst league finish since 1990. A team that had been a fixture in the top three since 1991-2 slumped to seventh, the poorest title defence since Blackburn Rovers in the mid-90s. Most accepted that a rebuilding job needed to be done, but the fall from grace was too steep for the owners, who dismissed Moyes when Champions League qualification was confirmed beyond reach.

Four teams took up cudgels in the battle for United's crown. City and Chelsea were well backed before a ball was kicked, but Arsenal, bolstered by the arrival of midfield maestro Mesut Özil for a club record £42 million, laid down a marker that they were prepared to compete with the plutocrats. Making up the quartet was Liverpool, whose resurgence under Brendan Rodgers was one of the stories of the season.

City win three-way fight

Arsenal made the early running. The Gunners' four-month occupation of top spot far exceeded that of the other contenders in a season where the lead changed hands 25 times. Wenger's side was also first to drop off the pace, leaving a three-way fight for the title in a dramatic final month. Chelsea comfortably won the mini-league between the top clubs but faltered against teams in the lower reaches. Among the costly defeats was a home loss to Sunderland, Mourinho's first league reverse at Stamford Bridge in 78 games. Liverpool had the momentum, on a nine-match winning run when they faced Manchester City at Anfield in mid-April. Both teams had their destiny in their own hands, and the advantage swung the Reds' way as they prevailed in a 3-2 thriller. Liverpool then edged Norwich to make it 11 victories on the spin; three more and the title was theirs for the first time in 24 years. The wheels came off when Liverpool met Chelsea, the final clash between the title rivals. Chelsea's 2-0 victory was down to a Mourinho tactical masterclass or parking a fleet of double-deckers, according to viewpoint. With two games to go, City and Liverpool looked on course to finish on level points, with City's superior goal difference coming into play. The final turning point in a tortuous, wonderfully entertaining season came when Liverpool squandered a 3-0 lead in a calamitous dozen minutes at Selhurst Park in their penultimate fixture. It left City needing only a point against West Ham at the Etihad to don the crown for the second time in three years. A routine victory maintained the two-point gap over Liverpool and avoided the anxieties of the 2012 late show.

A Premier League first

The top two both broke the 100-goal barrier, a Premier League first. In Luis Suarez Liverpool boasted the division's top marksman, his 31 goals and exemplary work ethic earning him both the PFA and Football Writers' awards, admirable rehabilitation for a player who began the season fulfilling the remains of a 10-match ban. Strike partner Daniel Sturridge, cast off by both City and Chelsea, also found the net 21 times, the first time since the days of the St John-Hunt partnership that two Liverpool strikers had hit 20 goals. Rodgers would have been less pleased with the half century in the Goals Against column. Chelsea, by contrast, had the most miserly defence, but Mourinho bemoaned the impotence of his strike force as he suffered his first trophyless campaign. City had the best balance between firepower and defensive solidity, and the fans were quick to sing the praises of "The Engineer" who taken the team back to the top. Pellegrini provided more flamboyance on the pitch than in press conferences, his calm authority winning over the terrace doubters. If there was a cloud over the Blue Moon, it was the breach of Financial Fair Play rules that attracted Uefa sanctions. City were hit with a £49 million fine, a cap on transfer spending and the wage bill, plus a restriction on their Champions League squad to 21 players.

Tottenham's £100 million spree did not cause a major book-balancing headache as it was largely financed by the world-record sale of Gareth Bale to Real Madrid. The bigger problem was that the goods in André Villas-Boas' shopping basket failed to live up to expectations, with the honourable exception of Danish midfielder Christian Eriksen. Spurs found themselves at the back of the top-seven mini-league before Christmas, and a 5-0 home defeat to a rampant Liverpool, following hard on the heels of shipping six at the Etihad, saw AVB axed. Spurs promoted Tim Sherwood, who steered the team to a top-six finish and the Round of 16 in the Europa League. That meant another tilt at Europe's second-string competition – not good enough for Sherwood to be given a second season. Joining Spurs on the Thursday night trail were Everton, whose crowd-pleasing football under Moyes' successor Roberto Martinez briefly put Arsenal's Champions League spot in jeopardy. Seventy-two points was a best return of the Premier League era for the Toffees.

Poyet's "miracle" escape

The basement battle was as enthralling as the race for the top, precious few points covering the bottom half of the table for most of the season. Seven relegation-threatened clubs wielded the axe – Fulham did so twice – in a bid to avoid the drop. The big winners in the managerial merry-go-round were Crystal Palace and Sunderland. Palace, on seven points when Tony Pulis took over in November, were a side transformed as they eased well clear of the danger zone. Gus Poyet brought fresh hope to the Stadium of Light after di Canio's brief, turbulent reign. The ex-Brighton boss steered Sunderland to the Capitol One cup final as well as delivering a "miracle" escape. Thirteen points from five games – a run that included away trips to the two Manchester clubs and Chelsea - made the Black Cats only the second club to survive having propped up the table at Christmas. Cardiff and Fulham fared less

well from their managerial moves. Both were down before the last game, the Bluebirds relegated after one season, Fulham after 13 years. Norwich, who sacked Chris Hughton with five games to go, were also Championship-bound.

The Capital One Cup saw an unusual sight: four of the big boys on course for semi-final battle. The two Manchester giants made it through, but Spurs and Chelsea slipped up against lower Premier League opposition. Spurs suffered a 2-1 home defeat to West Ham, while Chelsea fell to an extra-time goal by Sunderland's Ki Sung-yeung at the Stadium of Light, putting the division's bottom side through. The draw kept the neighbours apart. City thrashed the Hammers 9-0 on aggregate, but Gus Poyet's Sunderland caused another shock in beating United in a shoot-out where only three spot-kicks were converted. Sunderland's attempt to take a third major scalp looked on when they took the lead at Wembley through a deft Fabio Borini strike, but City's class told in the end and they ran out 3-1 winners, goals from Touré, Nasri and Navas.

BELOW: Brendan Rodgers talks to Luis Suarez and Daniel Sturridge, Liverpool's top marksmen, during the match between Liverpool and Manchester City at Anfield in April 2014.

OPPOSITE: A delighted Arsène Wenger celebrates Arsenal's victory in the FA Cup Final in May 2014.

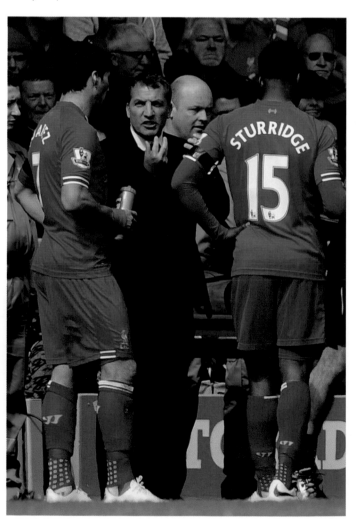

Premiership 2010—2014

2009—10

1	Chelsea	86
2	Manchester United	75
3	Arsenal	75
4	Tottenham Hotspur	70
5	Manchester City	67
6	Aston Villa	64
7	Liverpool	63
8	Everton	61
9	Birmingham City	50
10	Blackburn Rovers	50
11	Stoke City	47
12	Fulham	46
13	Sunderland	44
14	Bolton Wanderers	39
15	Wolverhampton W.	38
16	Wigan Athletic	36
17	West Ham United	35
18	Burnley	30
19	Hull City	30
20	Portsmouth	19

2010—11

1	Manchester United	80
2	Chelsea	71
3	Manchester City	71
4	Arsenal	68
5	Tottenham Hotspur	62
6	Liverpool	58
7	Everton	54
8	Fulham	49
9	Aston Villa	48
10	Sunderland	47
11	West Bromwich Albion	47
12	Newcastle United	46
13	Stoke City	46
14	Bolton Wanderers	46
15	Blackburn Rovers	43
16	Wigan Athletic	42
17	Wolverhampton W.	40
18	Birmingham City	39
19	Blackpool	39
20	West Ham United	33

2011—12

1	Manchester City	89
2	Manchester United	89
3	Arsenal	70
4	Tottenham Hotspur	69
5	Newcastle United	65
6	Chelsea	64
7	Everton	56
8	Liverpool	52
9	Fulham	52
10	West Bromwich Albion	47
11	Swansea City	47
12	Norwich City	47
13	Sunderland	45
14	Stoke City	45
15	Wigan Athletic	43
16	Aston Villa	38
17	Queen's Park Rangers	37
18	Bolton Wanderers	36
19	Blackburn Rovers	31
20	Wolverhampton W.	25

2012—13

1	Manchester United	89
2	Manchester City	78
3	Chelsea	75
4	Arsenal	73
5	Tottenham Hotspur	72
6	Everton	63
7	Liverpool	61
8	West Bromwich Albion	49
9	Swansea City	46
10	West Ham United	46
11	Norwich City	44
12	Fulham	43
13	Stoke City	42
14	Southampton	41
15	Aston Villa	41
16	Newcastle United	41
17	Sunderland	39
18	Wigan Athletic	36
19	Reading	28
20	Queen's Park Rangers	25

2013—14

1	Manchester City	86
2	Liverpool	84
3	Chelsea	82
4	Arsenal	79
5	Everton	72
6	Tottenham	69
7	Manchester United	64
8	Southampton	56
9	Stoke City	50
10	Newcastle United	49
11	Crystal Palace	45
12	Swansea City	42
13	West Ham United	40
14	Sunderland	38
15	Aston Villa	38
16	Hull City	37
17	West Bromwich Albion	36
18	Norwich City	33
19	Fulham	32
20	Cardiff City	30

FA Cup Finals

2010	Chelsea	v	Portsmouth	1-0
2011	Manchester City	v	Stoke City	1-0
2012	Chelsea	v	Liverpool	2-1
2013	Wigan Athletic	v	Manchester City	1-0
2014	Arsenal	v	Hull City	3-2 (aet)

ABOVE: Arsene Wenger celebrates Arsenal's FA Cup victory over Hull.

José Mourinho

The line between arrogance and confidence can sometimes be clouded. José Mourinho, the self-styled "Special One", has been labelled with both attributes, but whatever view is taken regarding the personal qualities of this darling of the media, no one can dispute that he delivers in a results business.

Born in Setubal, this son of a pro goalkeeper soon realised that he would not make it as a top player. Thus he embarked on his coaching apprenticeship at an early age, beginning with a part-time job with local side Vitória Setúbal. He mixed theory with practice, studying sports science at university, and benefited from working under Bobby Robson following the latter's appointment as Sporting Lisbon boss in 1992. It was nominally a translating role initially, but during an association that also took in spells at Porto and Barcelona, Mourinho became more a right-hand man. The former England manager said Mourinho's reports from scouting missions were second to none; his assistant was a meticulous, astute student of the game. When Robson vacated the manager's chair at the Nou Camp, Mourinho worked under successor Louis van Gaal. His days as a No. 2 ended in 2000 when he was appointed Benfica coach, a relationship that quickly turned sour after a presidential election ousted the man who recruited him. His next port of call was unsung Portuguese outfit Uniao Leiria, whom he took to third in the division before joining Porto early in 2002 In his first full season Mourinho completed the domestic double and lifted the Uefa Cup with a 3-2 win over Celtic. Porto retained the championship in 2003–04, and were also crowned kings of Europe. Many will recall Mourinho's jubilant touchline celebration at Old Trafford as Porto put out Manchester United en route to the final, where Monaco were comfortably dispatched. It was while basking in that victory that Mourinho took the reins at Chelsea. He moulded a side that had not won the title for half a century into the dominant force in English football. Chelsea broke the 90-point mark in 2004–05 and 2005–06, loosening Manchester United and Arsenal's decade-long grip on the Premier League. He added the FA Cup to the trophy cabinet in 2007 but missed out on his ambition to steer the Blues to Champions League glory. He left Stamford Bridge in September 2007, and there was no shortage of suitors. First port of call was Inter Milan, whom he guided to the Scudetto in his first season and an historic treble in 2010 After wrapping up the domestic double, Inter beat Bayern Munich in the final of Europe's premier club competition, their first victory since 1965. No Italian side had ever completed such a hat-trick. Typically, he departed while at the top, arriving at Real Madrid with the aim of unseating Pep Guardiola's mighty Barcelona. In 2011–12 he did just that, becoming the first manager to win championships in England, Italy and Spain, with those Portuguese titles fleshing out one of the most impressive coaching records of the modern era. Only Ernst Happel and Giovanni Trapattoni had masterminded title wins in four different countries, and Mourinho joined them in style: 100 points and 121 goals both set new benchmarks for La Liga.

Even while managing on the Continent, Mourinho said he would one day return to English football, a prediction realised in summer 2013 when he returned to the Bridge. Chelsea had been crowned European champions in the intervening years, and the charismatic, entertaining, always quotable José Mourinho had his sights fixed on repeating that success under his watch, correcting an omission that rankled from his first spell at the club.

Silverware for Arsenal

Manchester United's nightmare run continued in the FA Cup, first-hurdle fallers as Swansea became the latest team to leave Old Trafford with the spoils. Conference side Kidderminster Harriers went further than United, the best showing among the non-leaguers as they put out Peterborough before falling to Sunderland in the next round. Aston Villa's home defeat by League One Sheffield United attracted much media attention, an upset coming in the wake of Paul Lambert's comments that the competition was a distraction to clubs whose main focus was Premier League survival. Other managers, he said, would agree – and team selection over recent years provided supporting evidence for Lambert's point – but there was a backlash by those who believed the game was poorer for the suggestion that the premier cup competition should be cast aside so lightly.

The Fifth Round threw up two heavyweight clashes: Arsenal-Liverpool and Manchester City-Chelsea, the country's top four sides. The home team prevailed in both cases. Holders Wigan, now led by former Manchester City cult hero Uwe Rösler, also reached the quarters, causing the shock of the round by dumping City out of the competition in their own back yard. In the semis they drew Arsenal, who put four past Everton in the last eight. The other semi pitted Hull against Sheffield United, guaranteeing the presence of an unsung side in the showpiece. Nigel Clough's League One Blades became only the ninth third-tier representative in the last four. Hull had made only one previous appearance in the semis, losing to Chapman-era Arsenal in 1930. In both games the underdogs got their noses in front but failed to press home the advantage. Steve Bruce's Hull fired four second-half goals to reach their first final, while Arsenal squeezed past the holders on penalties.

The draw had been kind to Hull, Premier League strugglers Sunderland their only top-flight opposition en route to Wembley. They were also guaranteed Europa Cup football as Arsenal preserved their top-four status and Champions League qualification. The Gunners, who had faced Spurs as well as both Merseyside clubs, trod a much more difficult path to the final and were hot favourites to end their silverware drought as Wenger passed the 1,000-game mark in charge. At 2-0 down inside 10 minutes, Arsenal were rocking. A Cazorla free kick brought them back into it, and from a 71st-minute corner Koscielny scored from close range to force extra time. Aaron Ramsey's neat finish from a Giroud backheel won the game, removing the monkey that had rested on the club's back since 2005.

Four English sides reach Champions League group stage

All four Premier League representatives made it through the group stage of the Champions League, new territory for Manchester City. They matched holders Bayern Munich stride for stride but were edged into second place on head-to-head record. Arsenal also had to settle for the runners-up spot after finishing on level points with the 2012-13 runners-up Borussia Dortmund and Napoli. Chelsea and Manchester United reaped the fruits of their table-topping qualifying campaign by drawing lesser lights, Galatasaray and Olympiakos respectively. Both progressed, though United had to overturn a two-goal deficit from the away leg. City and Arsenal's hopes were all but dashed following Last-16 home legs that bore an eerie similarity. Drawn against Barcelona and Bayern respectively, both went down to 10 men, lost a goal, then conceded a crucial second in the dying minutes. Neither could turn it round in the away leg.

BELOW: David Meyler of Hull City scores their fifth goal in the FA Cup semi-final against Sheffield United at Wembley Stadium on 13 April 2014.

Scottish Premier League
2010–2014

2009–10

1	Rangers	87
2	Celtic	81
3	Dundee Utd	63
4	Hibernian	54
5	Motherwell	53
6	Hearts	48
7	Hamilton	49
8	St Johnstone	47
9	Aberdeen	41
10	St Mirren	34
11	Kilmarnock	33
12	Falkirk	31

2010–11

1	Rangers	93
2	Celtic	92
3	Hearts	63
4	Dundee United	61
5	Kilmarnock	49
6	Motherwell	46
7	Inverness CT	53
8	St Johnstone	44
9	Aberdeen	38
10	Hibernian	37
11	St Mirren	33
12	Hamilton	26

2011–12

1	Celtic	93
2	Rangers	73
3	Motherwell	62
4	Dundee Utd	59
5	Hearts	52
6	St Johnstone	50
7	Kilmarnock	47
8	St Mirren	43
9	Aberdeen	41
10	Inverness CT	39
11	Hibernian	33
12	Dunfermline	25

2012–13

1	Celtic	79
2	Motherwell	63
3	St Johnstone	56
4	Inverness CT	54
5	Ross County	53
6	Dundee Utd	47
7	Hibernian	51
8	Aberdeen	48
9	Kilmarnock	45
10	Hearts	44
11	St Mirren	41
12	Dundee	30

2013–14

1	Celtic	99
2	Motherwell	70
3	Aberdeen	68
4	Dundee Utd	58
5	Inverness CT	57
6	St Johnstone	53
7	Ross County	40
8	St Mirren	39
9	Kilmarnock	39
10	Partick Thistle	38
11	Hibernian	35
12	Hearts	23

Scottish Cup Finals

2010	Dundee United	v	Ross County	3-0
2011	Celtic	v	Motherwell	3-0
2012	Heart of Midlothian	v	Hibernian	5-1
2013	Celtic	v	Hibernian	3-0
2014	St Johnstone	v	Dundee Utd	2-0

Welsh Premier League
2010–2014

2009–10

1	The New Saints	82
2	Llanelli AFC	80
3	Port Talbot Town	65
4	Aberystwyth Town	64
5	Bangor City	63
6	Rhyl FC	62
7	Airbus UK Broughton	49
8	Prestatyn Town	48
9	Neath FC	47
10	Carmarthen Town	45
11	Bala Town	45
12	Haverfordwest County	44
13	Newtown AFC	41
14	Gap Connah's Quay	41
15	Porthmadog FC	24
16	Technogroup Welshpool	23
17	Caersws FC	13
18	Cefn Druids	9

2010–11

1	Bangor City	70
2	The New Saints	68
3	Neath FC	58
4	Llanelli AFC	53
5	Aberystwyth Town	42
6	Airbus UK Broughton	41
7	Prestatyn Town	40
8	Port Talbot Town	36
9	Newtown AFC	35
10	Carmarthen Town	35
11	Bala Town	33
12	Haverfordwest County	19

2011–12

1	The New Saints	74
2	Bangor City	69
3	Neath FC	62
4	Llanelli AFC	59
5	Bala Town	49
6	Prestatyn Town	28
7	Airbus UK Broughton	39
8	Aberystwyth Town	33
9	Port Talbot Town	33
10	Afan Lido	32
11	Carmarthen Town	32
12	Newtown AFC	23

2012–13

1	The New Saints	76
2	Airbus UK	54
3	Bangor City	51
4	Port Talbot	47
5	Prestatyn Town	40
6	Carmarthen	37
7	Bala Town	56
8	Connah's Quay	40
9	Newtown	37
10	Aberystwyth	37
11	Llanelli	36
12	Afan Lido	27

2012–13

1	The New Saints	73
2	Airbus UK Broughton	59
3	Carmarthen Town	48
4	Bangor City	48
5	Newtown	42
6	Rhyl	38
7	Aberystwyth Town	51
8	Bala Town	45
9	Port Talbot Town	38
10	Gap Connah's Quay	38
11	Prestatyn Town	35
12	Afan Lido	15

RIGHT: Ryan Giggs announced his retirement from football in 2014 and was appointed No. 2 to new Manchester United manager Louis van Gaal with many expecting him to assume the top job after serving an apprenticeship.

Chelsea stumble in Champions League semis

In the quarters United drew Arsenal's conquerors, favourites to retain the trophy. Many thought Pep Guardiola's Bayern would be out of sight after the Old Trafford leg, but a game of few chances ended a goal apiece. United were briefly ahead in the tie after taking the lead at the Allianz Arena through a Patrice Evra screamer, but conceded immediately and lost two more goals to go out 4-2. Chelsea were matched against a Paris Saint Germain side dominating French football on the back of deep-pocketed Qatari owners. At 2-1 down going into stoppage time in Paris, Chelsea were reasonably placed in the tie, but concession of a late third goal left Mourinho furious and his team needing a big performance at the Bridge. There were shades of the famous night against Napoli in 2012 as Demba Ba came off the bench to sweep home a late second goal, a 2-0 scoreline that put Chelsea through on away goals.

Chelsea faced an Atletico Madrid side that had eliminated Barcelona and was on course for the Spanish title. Mourinho had had much the better of meetings with Diego Simeone's side when he was in charge at Real Madrid, and after a goalless away leg the chance for the Portuguese to win the Champions League with a third different club was on the cards; even more so when Fernando Torres drew first blood against his old club. The night turned sour as the Blues shipped three goals, while at the other end Atletico's on-loan Chelsea 'keeper Thibaut Courtois was on top form.

BELOW: The St Johnstone team celebrate their victory over Dundee United at Celtic Park on 17 May.

Title stroll for Celtic and Rangers

Celtic's Champions League race was run before Christmas, but a third successive domestic title was in the bag with seven games to spare. Not since 1929 had the championship been settled so early. Hearts anchored the division in a campaign all but doomed from the outset by a 15-point deduction for entering administration. Terry Butcher's Hibs finished one place above, needing to survive the play-offs if the Edinburgh derby was not to take place in the Championship. Rangers cruised into the second tier, undefeated in League One as their journey back to the top continued in emphatic style. Ally McCoist's side had designs on a promotion-Scottish Cup double but were undone by Jackie McNamara's Dundee United in the semis, Premiership quality negating home advantage in a game played at Ibrox. Their opponents in the final were St Johnstone, who bucked league form by overcoming Aberdeen – Celtic's conquerors – in the last four. The Perth club came from behind to reach the final for the first time in their 130-year history. Disappointment for Dons fans was tempered by the fact that their team had already ended a 19-year trophyless spell by lifting the Scottish League Cup, edging Inverness Caley Thistle on penalties after a goalless 120 minutes. Two places and five points separated the Tayside finalists, but Saints went into the Celtic Park showdown with three successive league wins to draw on. The run continued with a 2-0 victory, a well merited triumph for Tommy Wright's side and a first major honour for the McDiarmid Park club.

Mixed fortunes for home nations on World Cup trail

England completed their World Cup qualifying programme unbeaten to book a place at the Brazil 2014 jamboree. For the other home nations the long wait for an appearance at the finals went on. Wales and Scotland trailed Croatia and Serbia as well as runaway leaders Belgium, while Northern Ireland recorded but a single win in finishing a point ahead of Luxembourg, who propped up their group. The highlight for Gordon Strachan's men was undoubtedly a double over Croatia, Robert Snodgrass on target in both matches. An "incredibly proud" Scotland boss sang the praises of his team after the win in Zagreb against a side ranked fourth in the world. It meant they ended the campaign with three wins in four, putting the Tartan Army in good cheer for the battles ahead. Having got the better of Scotland in both group encounters, Chris Coleman's Wales also ended their campaign with a flourish, taking a well-earned point against a star-studded Belgium side on their own turf. Aaron Ramsey, who scored a late equaliser, and Craig Bellamy, making his 78th and final appearance for the national team, led from the front as Coleman wrestled with the age-old problem of high-profile absentees, notably Gareth Bale. As Bellamy signed off, a youngster 18 years his junior made his entrance. Liverpool academy's Harry Wilson collected his first cap with a cameo off the bench, at 16 years 207 days the youngest player to pull on the famous jersey. In taking Bale's record, Wilson also netted £125,000 for his grandfather, who placed a £50 bet on his turning out for Wales when he was a babe in arms.

Hodgson's new-look squad

If claiming one of the 13 Uefa-zone World Cup spots looked a tough assignment for the home nations, hopes of tournament football were boosted by the expansion of the 2016 European Championship from 16 to 24 teams. Qualification was less of an issue for England. Brazil made it nine tournaments out of 10 since missing out on USA '94, but how would Roy Hodgson's new-look squad fare? The emergence of Raheem Sterling, Daniel Sturridge and Ross Barkley – and in particular the selection of Luke Shaw as left-back cover for Leighton Baines at Ashley Cole's expense – suggested youth would be given a

BELOW: Steven Naismith harries Luka Modric during Scotland's World Cup qualifier against Croatia at Hampden Park, October 2013. Naismith scored in a 2-0 win that completed the double over the team that finished group runners-up. A campaign that began dismally under Craig Levein thus ended on a high note – nine points from the last four games – with Gordon Strachan in charge.

OPPOSITE: Roy Hodgson and Steven Gerrard appear downcast and chastened as they face the media in the wake of England 's World Cup exit following defeats to Italy and Uruguay. Hodgson was backed by the FA to see the team through to Euro 2016, while his captain, who won his 114th cap in the dead rubber against Costa Rica – one shy of David Beckham's record for an outfield player – was left pondering his international future.

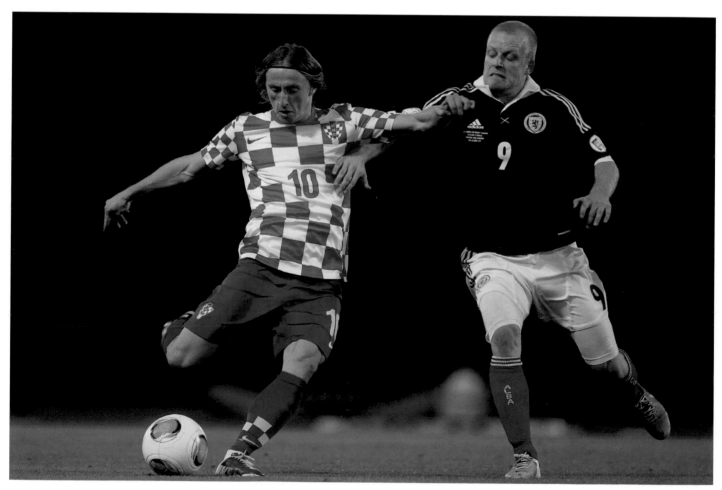

Roy Hodgson

A distinguished playing career is no guarantor of coaching success, a footballing truism for which Roy Hodgson's path to the top of the game provides clear evidence. Hodgson was on Crystal Palace's books and a non-league journeyman before taking his first step in management in his late 20s. That was with Swedish side Halmstads BK, whom he steered from relegation favourites to title winners in a matter of months. Fresh tactics and training methods underpinned the turnaround and other Swedish teams adopted Hodgson's ideas: a flat back four instead of a sweeper, high defensive line, pressing high up the pitch and zonal marking. Ball retention was vital. One man who didn't need convincing was Bob Houghton, with whom Hodgson had worked at Maidstone United. Both were converts to the same new philosophy, and became managerial rivals when Houghton took over at Malmö. Sven-Goran Erikkson, who won the Uefa Cup with IFK Gothenburg, was a disciple, and there are those who trace Sweden's run to the semi-final of the 1994 World Cup back to Hodgson's influence on the national game.

Save for a spell at Bristol City, Hodgson remained in Sweden until 1990, adding two more championships with Malmo to the two he won with Halmstads BK. After a couple of seasons with Swiss club side Neuchâtel Xamax, he was appointed national team boss, taking Switzerland to the second round at the 1994 World Cup and through a successful qualifying campaign for Euro '96. He lasted barely a season at Blackburn Rovers, a period separating two stints with Inter Milan, whom he led to the Uefa Cup final in 1997. There were further club appointments in Switzerland and Italy, plus a Danish title with FC Copenhagen in 2001, before Hodgson returned to the international sphere with the United Arab Emirates. Having also coached a Finland side that came close to qualifying for Euro 2008, he returned to English football. His three-year tenure at Fulham peaked with a Europa Cup final appearance in 2010, where the Cottagers went down 2-1 to Atlético Madrid. Hodgson was rewarded with the Manager of the Year award for taking a side that was struggling when he took over in late 2007 to the brink of a major European trophy. Liverpool came calling, but patchy results saw him sacked mid-season, and he ended the 2010–11 campaign guiding West Brom to a comfortable mid-table position. Appointed England coach in May 2012, Hodgson led the team that had qualified for the European Championships under Fabio Capello to the tournament, staged in Poland and Ukraine. After topping a group that pitted them against France, Sweden and Ukraine, Hodgson's men suffered defeat in a shoot-out, this time at the hands of Italy in the quarters. Brazil 2014 offered the chance to put his own stamp on the team, but it came up short, eliminated after 180 minutes of group-stage football. He had blooded new young talent, however, and received immediate FA backing as the man to lead the side through to Euro 2016.

ABOVE: Wayne Rooney fires home from close range to draw England level with Uruguay in their second group match at Brazil 2014. His 40th international goal put him equal fourth with Michael Owen on the all-time list, a personal milestone overshadowed by another 2-1 defeat for the team and exit from the tournament with a game to spare.

OPPOSITE: Ross Barkley takes on Yeltsin Tejeda of Costa Rica during their final Group D game in Belo Horizonte.

chance. Spurs' Andros Townsend, who made an electrifying debut against Montenegro in the qualifiers, might also have been on the plane, but both he and Theo Walcott were ruled out through injury. Hodgson also belatedly lost another exciting young gun in Alex Oxlade-Chamberlain. Twelve of the squad had no previous tournament experience, just six having tasted a World Cup adventure. That included Joe Hart, who went to South Africa but got no game time. Eleven players had 10 caps or fewer, an average age of 26 seen as an advantage in Brazil, where young legs would be needed in energy-sapping conditions. Perhaps as importantly, the majority were unscarred by past defeats.

Rooney sparks debate

Skipper Steven Gerrard and Frank Lampard, whose 13-year stay at Stamford Bridge had come to an end, provided an ever-diminishing link with the "golden generation". Wayne Rooney was also in that camp, and one of the main talking points during the build-up was whether the United star's place in the starting XI was assured. With just one tournament goal to his name – at Euro 2012 – since lighting up the same competition in 2004, there were those ready to contemplate an England side with a fit Rooney warming the bench. Ex-team-mate Paul Scholes fanned the flames by suggesting the 28-year-old might have passed his peak, but there was no shortage of insiders quick to assert that Rooney remained England's go-to player, his form and fitness vital to the team's chances.

Unseeded England stood 13th in the Fifa ranking when the groups were drawn, behind opponents Italy – England's nemesis at Euro 2012 – and a Uruguay side spearheaded by Suarez and Cavani that had reached the semis in South Africa. The South American side had

needed to beat Jordan in a play-off, however, suggesting opposition from the tournament's home continent might have been stronger. Rounded out by Costa Rica, dark horses who qualified as runners-up to USA in the Concacaf zone, the group was daunting enough for FA chairman Greg Dyke to be caught on camera making a cutthroat gesture when the draw was made.

There were five Liverpool players in Hodgson's starting XI for the opener against Italy in the steamy heat of Manaus. It was one of the Anfield brigade, in-form striker Daniel Sturridge, who got England's campaign up and running, sweeping home Rooney's inch-perfect cross to cancel out Marchisio's first-half strike within three minutes. The game was settled by a Balotelli far-post header after England were undone on their left flank early in the second half. There was little despondency in defeat. The team looked a threat going forward, Sterling in particular catching the eye. Hodgson said the performance, if not the result, was the most positive of his two-year reign, though the match did little to dispel the widely held view that England's Achilles' heel was the defence. A 2-1 reverse in a game that always looked a close call was no surprise. The same couldn't be said of Uruguay's 3-1 defeat at the hands of Costa Rica, a result that blew Group D wide open. It piled even more pressure on the two beaten sides' clash in São Paulo. The Italy match also added more fuel to the Rooney debate. Much of it centred on the waste of England's 39-goal man out wide; that he needed to be in the thick of the action, up front or at No. 10, where he could do most damage. The heat map showed he had just two touches inside the box against the Azzurri, something the England coach said would be addressed.

England's hopes fade after two defeats

Hopes of reaching the knockout stage were left dangling by a thread after England went down by the same score to Uruguay. Rooney was restored to a more central role, with Sterling out wide in an unchanged side. It worked inasmuch as the United man ended his World Cup finals drought, prodding home Johnson's cross on 75 minutes to put him level with Michael Owen in the all-time list, only the fifth England player to reach the 40-goal mark. But that merely cancelled out Luis Suarez's deft first-half header, planted past Joe Hart after the Liverpool man got on the blind side of Jagielka. Suarez also had the last word, lashing the ball home six minutes from time after the defence failed to deal with a hopeful punt down the middle. Uruguay thus converted their only two attempts on target, Suarez clinical even when clearly less than fully fit. Where the Italy game offered promise and pride in defeat, this was a more dispiriting loss, and Italy's subsequent defeat by surprise package Costa Rica extinguished any faint hope that England might squeeze through with three points. It meant a dead rubber against a Costa Rica side assured of their place in the last 16, and the first group-stage exit since 1958. England had no direct interest in the crunch Uruguay-Italy match to decide who would take the other spot in the knockout stage; that is, until Suarez was found culpable in a biting incident involving Giorgio Chiellini. Barely a year after having a 10-match penalty imposed for a similar indiscretion, with Chelsea's Branislav Ivanovic on the receiving end, Suarez was hit with a four-month Fifa ban, making him unavailable to Liverpool for a quarter of the new domestic season. Speculation was rife as to whether this flawed genius might have tried his Anfield employers' patience once too often.

Meanwhile, the inquest on England's performance began with a game still to be played. The FA moved swiftly to endorse Hodgson as the man to lead England through to Euro 2016 even before the squad decamped to Belo Horizonte for the final fixture. The coach shuffled the pack for the first ever meeting with Los Ticos. Only Cahill and Sturridge kept their places for a game taking place at the scene of England's greatest humiliation; where Finney, Wright, Mortensen et al were humbled by the part-timers of USA in 1950. Lampard was given the armband, his 106th cap putting him level with Sir Bobby Charlton in the appearance hall of fame. He led the side in a goalless draw, ensuring England didn't depart empty handed. On another day Sturridge might have had a hat-trick, as could Rooney in the Uruguay match. It underlined that international football, more so than the hurly-burly of the Premier League, hinged on snapping up chances created or presented.

Expectations had been modest, though anchoring a group containing non-vintage Italian and Uruguayan sides, plus a country ranked 28 with a population of less than five million, was indisputably sub-par. But there were glimmers in the gloom. Hodgson spoke of a six-year project and a team full of potential. The FA backed him as the man to develop the tyros who had featured, and rising stars such as Everton centre-back John Stones and Liverpool defender Jon Flanagan, stand-bys this time round. All would be better equipped to make their mark at France 2016 and beyond. The FA chairman targeted the 2022 World Cup – scheduled to take place under a scorching Qatar sun – which if nothing else reaffirmed that football is built on hopes and dreams.

Acknowledgements

The photographs in this book are from the archives of the *Daily Mail*.
Particular thanks to:
Steve Torrington, Dave Sheppard, Brian Jackson, Alan Pinnock, and all the staff.

The following photographs are © Topham Picturepoint:
Pages: 9; 11(T&B); 13; 14; 15; 22; 36 Pages 208, 222, 230, 231, 232, 233, 234, 235,
236, 237, 238, 239, 240, 241, 242, 243, 244, 245, 246, 247, 248, 249, 250, 251, 252,
253, 254 and 255 © Getty Images

Design by John Dunne.